Residential Location and Urban Housing Markets

NATIONAL BUREAU OF ECONOMIC RESEARCH
Conference on Research in Income and Wealth

GREGORY K.
INGRAM,
Editor

Residential Location and Urban Housing Markets

Studies in Income and Wealth
Volume 43
by the Conference on Research
in Income and Wealth

Published for the
NATIONAL BUREAU OF
ECONOMIC RESEARCH, INC.
by
BALLINGER PUBLISHING COMPANY
A Subsidiary of J. B. Lippincott Company
Cambridge, Mass.
1977

This book is printed on recycled paper.

International Standard Book Number: 0-88410-479-6

Library of Congress Catalog Card Number: 77-10831

Printed in the United States of America

Library of Congress Cataloging in Publication Data
Main entry under title:
Residential location and urban housing markets.

    (Studies in income wealth; 43)
    Includes bibliographical references.
    1. Housing—United States—Addresses, essays, lectures.
I.   Ingram, Gregory K.   II.   Series: Conference on Research in Income and Wealth. Studies in Income and Wealth; 43.
HC106.3.C714   vol. 43 [HD7293]   330′.08s
ISBN 0-88410-479-6   [301.5′4′0973]   77-10831

Relation of the National Bureau Directors to Publications Reporting Conference Proceedings

Since the present volume is a record of conference proceedings, it has been exempted from the rules governing submission of manuscripts to, and critical review by, the Board of Directors of the National Bureau.

(Resolution adopted July 6, 1948, as revised November 21, 1949, and April 20, 1968)

PREFATORY NOTE

This volume contains the papers presented at the Conference on the Economics of Residential Location and Urban Housing Markets held in Cambridge, Massachusetts, on May 15 and 16, 1975. We are indebted to the National Science Foundation for its support and to the members of the Program Committee—Gregory K. Ingram, chairman, Frank de Leeuw, and Eugene Smolensky—for their guidance. We wish to thank Ester Moskowitz, who prepared the manuscript for press, and Felix Cooper, who drew the charts. Finally, we thank Anna Tremblay and Madeleine Lane for their help with preparations for the conference.

Funds for the economic research conference
program of the National Bureau of Economic
Research are supplied by the National Science
Foundation.

Contents

List of Figures

List of Tables

Introduction

Gregory K. Ingram

Before the 1960s most studies of housing by economists emphasized the macroeconomic aspects of housing markets, such as the role of residential construction in the business cycle and the aggregate value of residential real estate. In addition, economists interested in financial markets became involved in the analysis of housing markets through their studies of real estate mortgage markets. Both approaches are evident in early NBER publications.[1] Although work on the macroeconomic side of housing markets has continued, in the early 1960s many economists began to study microeconomic and spatial aspects of housing markets in urban areas, including topics such as the household's choice of residential location and type of dwelling unit; the structure of housing prices within urban areas; the behavior of housing producers; and the provision of public services by local governments. This volume focuses upon this relatively new area of the economics of residential location and urban housing markets.

Although analyses carried out over the last fifteen years have taught us a great deal about how urban housing markets work, the problems in this field abound. At the risk of oversimplification, I have categorized the major problems in the economics of residential location and urban housing markets into those of theory, measurement, and policy analysis. The studies in this volume each address one or more of these categories, and they have been grouped roughly according to their major emphasis.

PROBLEMS OF THEORY

The theoretical underpinnings of residential location within urban areas were developed in the early 1960s with the work of Alonso, Wingo, and others.[2] These theories of residential location are essentially adaptations of a model proposed by von Thunen to explain the pattern of agricultural land uses surrounding a market town. The simplest residential location theories assume that economic activity in an urban area occurs at a single center and that travel costs are similar in all directions; the theories produce equilibrium household locations and distributions of lot size that are radially symmetric about the single center.

It has become apparent, however, that many of the simplifying assumptions of these theories do not agree with reality, and we have had mixed success in modifying these underlying theories to incorporate more realistic assumptions. First, it is obvious that the monocentric assumption does not apply to modern metropolitan areas where workplaces and other centers of activity are not concentrated in the central business district or even in the central city. In Boston, for example, roughly a third of the metropolitan area's total 1970 employment was in the city of Boston, and less than a fifth in the central business district. Multiple centers or continuous distributions of employment and other activities more closely approximate reality than does the monocentric representation.

A second problem with the simple residential-location theories is that they ignore the existence of long-lived capital stocks. Households participating in the housing market are concerned with characteristics of residential structures beyond simply location and lot size; they value such qualities as structure type, number of bedrooms and bathrooms, unit layout and size, and the unit's state of repair. Furthermore, residential structures are durable, heterogeneous, and often difficult to modify; so structure characteristics may change slowly. If structure durability has a significant impact on market outcomes or prolongs the time of adjustment to equilibrium, residential-location theories must incorporate stock adjustment on the supply side of the housing market.

A third problem for residential location theories might be termed locational interdependence; that is, a household's location decision may depend directly or indirectly upon the location choices of other classes of households. Examples of interdependencies include racial discrimination, the public goods or externalities that may be produced by the agglomeration of household-location choices, and possibly the service levels (such as education or safety) produced by local governments. Interdependencies in location can easily produce multiple solutions to location problems or make static equilibrium solutions unattainable. Relatively few theories of residential location have incorporated interdependencies or even an endogenous local public sector.

In addition to multiple activity centers, durable stocks, and locational interdependencies, other complications might be introduced into theories of residential location and housing markets. Examples of potentially important considerations include tenure choice, the role of housing as an investment as opposed to a consumption good, zoning requirements, and income tax regulations.

PROBLEMS OF MEASUREMENT

Although lack of suitable data for housing market studies continues to handicap some empirical work, many specialized data sources are available for housing market research. Moreover, the content and form of decennial census data has steadily improved, and housing analysts have become more adept in its use. When suitable data are available, two major choices must be made in order to measure housing: measures can be made of either stocks of housing capital or flows of housing services; and the stocks or flows can be assumed to be either homogeneous or heterogeneous.

For example, stocks can be measured as homogeneous housing capital, and the procedure used to report housing starts measures housing stocks simply in terms of numbers of dwelling units. This is a crude measurement technique because new dwelling units embody different amounts of housing capital. In this case, data are also available on the value of new residential construction, but these suffer many of the classic problems of aggregation. Many housing market analysts attempt to measure flows of homogeneous housing services in terms of a quantity index of housing services, but developing an overall quantity index has proven difficult because of the same aggregation problems.

More recently, much attention has been devoted to measures that assume that the stocks or flows are heterogeneous, i.e., a dwelling unit is defined as a bundle of attributes obtained in a single purchase. Numerous studies based on this approach have used hedonic indexes to value housing attributes. Even with this approach, however, the housing attributes dealing with quality have not been well measured. Indeed, our lack of success in quantifying attributes such as dwelling unit quality, neighborhood quality, and the quality of local public services is probably the major problem facing empirical work on urban housing markets at this time. Finally, the hedonic index approach often incorporates so many attributes (twenty to thirty are typical) that subsequent analysis such as the estimation of demand equations can be unwieldy.

PROBLEMS OF POLICY ANALYSIS

In many respects, the quality of policy analysis in economics is directly related to the appropriateness of the theory at hand and the accuracy of the available data and parameter estimates. It is apparent from the preceding paragraphs, therefore, that our ability to analyze policies in urban housing markets is limited. As our observations of housing market activity lead us to extend theories and to develop more disaggregated techniques of measurement, we are confronted by an awkward choice between two alternatives for policy analysis. The first approach, termed the "grand simplification," employs representations of residential location and housing markets based on the monocentric model of long-run equilibrium. These representations are relatively transparent, understandable, and easy to check for errors; yet they almost certainly exclude many aspects of housing markets that may have important consequences for policy evaluation. The second approach, termed the "grand incorporation," employs representations of housing markets with more realistic assumptions and produces complex, numerically solved, computer-based models that are not easily intelligible. These representations, ironically because they include more complexities, are often difficult to believe when used for policy analysis because they are so difficult to understand and to check for errors.

SUMMARY OF STUDIES

The studies presented in this volume focus on many of the difficulties just outlined. They have been grouped into four parts, with the first three parts corresponding roughly to the problem areas of theory (Chapters 1-3), measurement (Chapters 4-6), and policy analysis (Chapters 7-8).

In Part I, which concerns the theoretical aspects of residential location and housing choice, Richard Muth discusses empirical work motivated by his vintage model of housing services, which incorporates aspects of housing stock durability. Using census data to relate age of dwelling units, distance from the central business district, and income of resident households, the author finds that household income increases with distance from the CBD, and that age of dwelling units does not appear to be an important determinant of household location by income level. He reports comparable results for 1950, 1960, and 1970 census data, although the strength of the association between household income and distance from the CBD has tended to increase over this period. These results lead Muth to suggest that dwelling unit age may not be a good indicator of dwelling unit quality, and that filtering models based on dwelling unit age may be invalid.

In Chapter 2 Mahlon Straszheim outlines what might be described as a model of decision making in the local public sector. Noting that households jointly purchase a location, a level of local public services, and a housing unit, he believes it may be possible to predict household preferences for public services within a local jurisdiction, given data on the jurisdiction's housing stock and household preferences for dwelling units. Straszheim lays the theoretical groundwork for this approach using the change-of-variable technique. His goal is to integrate decisions about the supply of local public services into a model of the housing market.

Chapter 3 by Katherine Bradbury and others, reports preliminary empirical estimates of a household-location model based on Boston data. One of the major components of a spatially disaggregated regional growth model being developed at MIT, this model allows for the durability of housing stocks and includes structure conversion or rehabilitation as well as new construction in its supply-side activities. Furthermore, the model treats housing as a bundle of attributes that are valued differently by different classes of households. This is perhaps the first simultaneous equation model of a housing market that has incorporated durability and heterogeneity as characteristics of housing stocks.

Ann Schnare and Raymond J. Struyk (Chapter 4), investigate the extent to which and the reasons why blacks pay more than whites for housing in urban areas. The authors first measure price differentials paid by blacks at two different times, 1960 and 1970, and in two different cities, Boston and Pittsburgh. They then analyze data on changes in the population of blacks and whites in these two cities, contending that the decrease in price differentials blacks experienced from 1960 to 1970 is due primarily to the rapid loosening of the urban housing market and the increased availability of units.

Chapter 5, by William Apgar, describes a technique for using Census Bureau data more efficiently to estimate linear regression equations. He demonstrates that the two-way cross tabulations of data found in the fourth and later counts of the 1970 Census can be used to estimate ordinary least squares regression coefficients. Although this technique can be used in any application involving Census data, Apgar illustrates it with several housing market examples. He also suggests a number of revisions in Census Bureau practices that would make Census data more useful without compromising the confidentiality of individual questionnaire responses.

Chapter 6, by Werner Hirsch and Stephen Margolis, describes an attempt to estimate the impact that a variety of habitability laws may have on the cost of housing occupied by low-income households. After describing a theoretical model, the authors report parameter estimates based on an interstate sample of households compiled by the University of Michigan Income Dynamics Panel Study. They find that rent receivership, the most severe form of habitability law, may increase rents paid by low-income households by as much as 16 percent.

The third section, involving policy analysis, includes two studies that use models to simulate the response of the housing market to particular policy interventions. Chapter 7, by Frank de Leeuw and Raymond J. Struyk, briefly describes the Urban Institute housing model and its use in examining several housing policies. Although the Urban Institute model is dimensionally small—it typically includes five or six zones and thirty to forty households—it incorporates several important housing market characteristics such as the durability of existing units and neighborhood effects. Using two representative sets of parameters for the model, the authors examine the impacts of housing allowances and new-construction subsidies on the structure of prices in urban housing markets. They find that housing allowances may increase the housing prices paid by recipient households, and that construction subsidies produce benefits for households living in existing units as well as for those who buy new housing.

In Chapter 8, Gregory K. Ingram and Yitzhak Oron present a housing market model that focuses on the production of dwelling quality by owners of existing units. In this model, a housing supplier produces quality by combining a dwelling unit's capital with operating inputs, and he alters the unit's stock of capital by incremental investment or disinvestment. After calibrating production functions for the model, the authors explore two issues: First, using just the supply model, they determine the likely magnitude and duration of rent increases for housing units if the demand for dwelling quality is increased by a housing allowance or similar program. They find that a typical housing allowance program is likely to increase rents in the short run by less than 10 percent and that this increase is likely to dissipate in less than six years. Second, when the supply model is combined with a demand model, the market-clearing simulations suggest housing allowances will increase the average level of housing quality, but that some households may substitute other housing attributes for quality.

During the past few meetings of the Conference on Income and Wealth, it has been customary to have a session composed of student papers selected by a review committee. The first selection included here (Chapter 9) is a study by Susan Nelson of Princeton which sets forth a theoretical model that relates reduced labor market opportunities for blacks to their spatial segregation in the housing market. The author uses a search model over space in the labor market to determine how housing market segregation could produce higher unemployment rates or lower wage rates for blacks. Nelson's study is virtually the first theoretical analysis of this topic, which is the subject of controversy in the empirical literature.

The other paper (Chapter 10), by Marcy Avrin of Stanford, is an empirical study of the effect that zoning and zoning changes have had on residential property values in San Francisco since the city's zoning regulations were changed in 1960. By compiling data on property sales Avrin is able to investigate the effect of zoning regulations over time (before and after the change) as well as at one point in time (across zoning districts). The author's empirical findings support the conclusion that zoning restrictions increase the value of all residential property but that increases vary by allowed density levels.

The studies presented in this volume cover many topics and convey a sense of the range of issues in the economics of residential location and urban housing markets. At the same time, the studies do not cover all topics in this field, nor do they integrate neatly as a progress report or survey. Taken together, however, they reflect the approaches and subjects that housing market analysts are focusing on now, and they are a good sampling of current work in the field.

NOTES TO INTRODUCTION

1. For example, see David L. Wickens, *Residential Real Estate* (1941) and the six volumes in the NBER series, *Studies in Urban Mortgage Financing,* published in the early 1950s.

2. For example, see William Alonso, *Location and Land Use* (Cambridge, Mass.: Harvard University Press, 1964); Lowden Wingo, Jr., *Transportation and Urban Land* (Washington, D.C.: Resources for the Future, 1961); John F. Kain, "The Journey-to-Work as a Determinant of Residential Location," *Papers and Proceedings of the Regional Science Association*, IX (1962); Edwin S. Mills, "An Aggregative Model of Resource Allocation in a Metropolitan Area," *American*

Economic Review (May 1967); and Richard Muth, *Cities and Housing* (Chicago: University of Chicago Press, 1969).

�֎ *Part I*

Residential Location and Housing Choice

 *Chapter One*

The Influence of Age of Dwellings on Housing Expenditures and on the Location of Households

Richard F. Muth

In this study I describe the results of an empirical investigation into the determinants of expenditures on housing and of the location of households by income. My principal goal is to explain the intracity variation in such magnitudes. The specific empirical work presented here, though, is concerned with certain implications of a theory of durability of residential structures I advanced in a recent paper (Muth 1973).

MOTIVATION

Most work on economic aspects of urban residential location has been concentrated on the effects of accessibility of a site to the downtown area or central business district (CBD) of a city (especially see Alonso 1964, Mills 1967, Muth 1969, and Wingo 1961). The further CBD workers live from their jobs, the greater their total transport costs, and, hence, the lower the unit prices they pay for housing. Lower housing prices, in turn, mean lower prices for land. Consequently, population density and intensity of use of residential land declines with distance from the CBD. Empirical evidence tends to agree relatively well with the implications of these models (Mills 1969 and Muth 1969).

Models of urban residential land use also have implications for the location of households by income (Alonso 1964 and Muth 1969). A

Note: The research reported on here was supported initially by National Science Foundation Grant GS-39005 and later by the Domestic Studies Program of the Hoover Institution.

3

condition for the optimal location of a household containing a CBD worker is that the change in the expenditure necessary to acquire the quantity of housing consumed at this location be exactly offset by the change in transport expenditure associated with any change in location. The effect of income differences on household location, then, depends on the relative strengths of income differences on housing consumption and on the marginal costs of transport, including the opportunity costs of time spent in travel. On empirical grounds, it seems reasonable that the effect of increased income on housing expenditures exceeds that on marginal transport costs (see Muth 1969, pp. 29-34). One would thus expect both that higher-income CBD-worker households would live farther from their jobs than others and that the dispersion of population in cities would tend to vary directly with the average income of CBD workers.

My previous empirical work provides some weak support for the proposition that population dispersion in cities increases with average income (Muth 1969, pp. 153-155 and 163-164). I also found strong positive, simple associations between both income and housing expenditure with distance from the CBD. However, these simple positive associations tended to result from the negative intercorrelation between distance from the CBD and age of dwelling units, for when a variable for age of dwelling unit was included in the analysis, the partial effects of distance were negligible. Both average income and expenditures on housing at a given income level in 1950 (1960) tended to vary inversely with the fraction of dwellings built prior to 1920 (1940). (Muth 1969, especially pp. 196-202.) The empirical research begun with this paper was initially aimed at testing alternative explanations for the findings just described.

There are at least two alternative explanations for the finding that distance from the CBD has no apparent effect on average income. The first, suggested by the discussion above, is simply that the effects of increased incomes on housing consumption and marginal transport costs are about the same. If so, the tendency for higher-income households to live farther from the CBD would have to be explained wholly by factors other than accessibility to workplaces. The other explanation is that not every household has a member employed in the CBD, and the income level of a census tract is a weighted average of the incomes of CBD workers and other households. As suggested by Moses (1962) and Muth (1969) if housing prices decline with distance from the CBD, so also must the wage incomes of locally employed workers of given skill. The decline in the incomes of non-CBD-worker households would then tend to offset any tendency for the incomes of CBD-worker households to increase with distance from the CBD. If this second explanation were the correct one, income changes would exert an effect on the rate of housing price decline with distance from the CBD and, thus, population dispersal within urban areas.

Regardless of the reason for the apparent lack of a partial association between income and distance, my earlier work implied that the major reason why higher-income families live farther from the CBD is associated with the age of dwellings. In the literature on real estate and urban economics, the decline in income level of the occupants of a structure as it ages is generally explained by the notion of filtering. (For a typical discussion of filtering see Ratcliffe 1949.) As dwellings age they deteriorate, or grow obsolete, or both. Furthermore, over time incomes rise and more housing is demanded by families at all income levels. Thus, when a family moves from any particular dwelling, its place is taken by one of relatively lower income. On the filtering hypothesis one would expect a more or less steady decline over time in the relative income level of families as dwellings grow older.

Casual observation as well as a recent study of the St. Louis area (Nourse and Phares), however, suggests many instances of older neighborhoods within central cities and whole suburbs that have remained in higher relative income occupancy for long periods of time. At the same time, occupancy of older neighborhoods frequently passes to lower relative income occupancy in a single, rather brief episode. Lower-income immigrants into American urban areas have long tended to concentrate in the older, more centrally located parts of U.S. cities. The immigration into northern and western cities, much of it from the rural South, during and following World War II was no exception. As the size of this group increases, the residential area it occupies spreads outward from the center of the city. This process has been characterized as residential succession (Duncan and Duncan 1957).

In more recent work (Muth 1973), I proposed an explicit theory of how age of dwellings affects the relative income levels of their occupants and rental expenditures at given income levels. In this analysis, housing markets consist of consumers with a given relative income level and preference for housing and producers who sell housing services to them. The relative rental value of dwellings of different sizes is determined by the condition that all such consumers must be on the same indifference curve. If the elasticity of real-income compensated demand is constant and equal to -1.0, the expression for relative rental level is a particularly simple one. Dwelling units may be built to any size, but once built the rate of flow of housing services they provide per unit of time declines at a constant relative rate over time. It is further assumed that real incomes and real construction costs grow at constant relative rates over time. Producers of housing select the size of new dwellings and the length of time to hold them in the housing stock so as to maximize the present value of newly built dwellings. Entry and exit of producers is assumed to equate this present value to zero.

The model implies that the demand function for the size of new dwellings is of the same form as the conventional demand curve for housing services. The appropriate price variable is the rate of return on new dwellings multiplied by construction costs per unit of size. Under the assumptions made in the model, the size of new dwellings, the size of dwelling for which the maximum rental per unit of housing is paid, and the maximum rental all grow at constant relative rates over time. The length of time units are held in the housing stock (T) is a function of the income elasticity of housing demand (β) and the rates of depreciation (δ), interest (i), income growth (ρ), and growth in construction costs (λ); T is constant provided the factors just noted are. Rental expenditures, $R_t(u)$, on dwellings of different age (u) at a given moment in time (t) are proportional to the remaining life of the dwellings, namely:

$$R_t(u) = \alpha y(t)^\beta (\delta + \beta\rho - \lambda)(T - u) \tag{1-1}$$

where α is a constant.

With unanticipated immigration by a lower relative income group, the rental offers of the latter for older, smaller dwellings, which are closer to the optimum size for the lower-income group, will be higher than offers of the native population. Provided the immigrant group is small enough, the maximum rental per unit of size paid for housing by this group is less than the maximum paid by the native group. Under these conditions, the immigrant group is wholly housed in older dwellings built for the higher-income native group. The ratio of maximum per-unit rentals depends principally upon the size of the immigrant group, the relative income levels of the two groups, and the age of the newest dwellings occupied by the immigrant group. Given the size of the immigrant group, the last will be smaller the greater the population growth rate of the city. The larger the size of the lower-income group the newer the dwellings it inhabits and the higher the maximum rental per unit of housing service it pays.

The relation of rentals paid by the lower-income group to age of dwelling is similar to that for the higher-income group:

$$R_2(u) = \alpha y_2^\beta \left[(\delta + \beta\rho - \lambda)(T - u) + (\hat{q}_1/\hat{q}_2) \right] \qquad (1\text{-}2)$$

where $\hat{q}_i$ is the size of dwelling yielding the maximum rental per unit of housing service for group i; subscript 1 designates the higher-income group; subscript 2, the lower. The second term in the bracket in (1-2), however, implies that rental expenditures of the lower-income immigrant group tend to be larger, given income and age of dwelling, than for the higher-income group, even though the maximum rental per unit of housing service paid may be smaller because dwellings of a given age that were built originally for the higher-income group are larger than if they had been constructed for the lower-income group.

With residential succession, the average income level in older dwellings is lower than if succession had not taken place. The larger the immigrant group, the lower their relative income level; and the greater the population growth rate, the lower the average income level in dwellings, say, twenty years old or older relative to that in newer dwellings. At the same time, members of the higher-income group who remain in dwellings older than, say, twenty years live in newer, larger dwellings on the average than would have been the case had succession not occurred. By Equation (1-1), then, average rental expenditures in dwellings more than twenty years old are greater than those made on newer dwellings when both kinds are occupied by members of the higher-income group.

INITIAL FINDINGS BASED ON 1970 INCOME DATA

My initial intention was to use only 1970 census income, age, and other data for my investigation. The 1970 census presents both mean and median income data by census tract, a more complete break-down of dwellings by age than earlier censuses, and data on place of work by census tract. Since in defining residential succession I wished to have income data for comparable areal units for 1950, 1960, and 1970, in selecting cities for analysis I began with the list of all census-tract cities of 1950. My model of residential succession suggests that rate of population growth and size of the immigrant group are important factors in determining the effects of age of dwelling on household income and rental expenditures. Thus, I wanted to examine data for cities differing in those characteristics.

Though the measurement of population growth is straightforward enough, there are many ways of giving empirical content to the notion of a twentieth-century urban immigrant group. The two I selected were the poverty population and immigrants from outside any SMSA. The former was measured by the fraction of families in the urbanized area with incomes below $3,000 per year in 1959 from the 1960 census; the latter, by the ratio of central-city families in 1960 who resided outside any SMSA in 1955 to all families in the particular SMSA (Census 1963, Table 4). The thirty-two urbanized areas for which there are at least thirty quasi-tracts—central city census tracts which were comparable for 1950, 1960, and 1970 or which could be formed into comparable combinations for the three census years—were then divided into eight groups. These groups were defined by the eight possible combinations of above- and below-median values for each of three characteristics: population growth rate, size of poverty population, and size of rural immigrant population. One city was selected at random from each of the eight classes for analysis. (Miami was the only city in its cell in the three-way classification. The specific cities employed are identified in Table 1-2.) Using the eight cities so selected, four comparisons per year can be made on the effects of any of the three characteristics, with the other two held constant.

For each of the eight cities, regressions of mean income on various measures of age of dwelling and accessibility were run. The 1970 census reports a much fuller breakdown of dwellings by year built than previous censuses. The following are available by census tract: 1969-March 1970, 1965-1968, 1960-1964, 1950-1959, 1940-1949, and 1939 or earlier. The 1950 census data, however, are reported mainly for 1919 or earlier; the 1960 data, for 1939 or earlier. Because little housing was constructed during either the depression years of the 1930s or the war years of the early 1940s, about the only comparisons that could be made with earlier census data were between housing less than or more than thirty years old. Using the 1970 census data, however, I calculated a much more detailed distribution of dwellings by age: less than 5 years, 5-10, 10-20, 20-30, and more than 30 years old.

All but one of these fractions were first entered into a regression analysis as explanatory variables. If the regression coefficients for the various age classes were to show a fairly regular decline as average age of dwelling increases, support would be provided for what I take to be the filtering hypothesis. My analysis of residential succession suggests a quite different pattern, however. Up to a certain age, average income would be constant, then a sharp break would occur, followed by a lower constant income level with increasing age in dwellings inhabited by the immigrant group.

If the filtering hypothesis were correct, the appropriate variable to employ would be a measure of the average age of dwellings. Two age measures were used. For $AVAGE1$ it was assumed that dwellings built prior to 1940 averaged forty-five years in age in 1970. For $AVAGE2$, average age for those more than thirty years old was calculated from the negative exponential distribution implied by the city's average population growth rate from 1900 to 1960 (see Muth 1973, p. 147). On the residential succession hypothesis, however, a single age class would be sufficient to describe the effects of age of dwelling on income. The analysis described in the first section suggests that for sensible parameters, the newest dwellings occupied by the immigrant group would be between twenty and thirty years old (Muth 1973, Table 4). Measures of the fractions of the immigrant group occupying dwellings no more than twenty and thirty years old were employed in turn to test the succession hypothesis and to compare it with that of filtering.

This same regression analysis also permitted a test of the two explanations for the apparent lack of a partial association between income and distance from the CBD once age of dwelling is controlled. For the first time, the 1970 census reports place of work by census tract, although income is not shown separately for families whose heads work in the CBD. In what follows the latter are designated by subscript 1; all others, by subscript 2; the fraction of families whose heads work somewhere other than in the CBD, by f; income, by y; and distance in miles from the CBD, by k. Then, let $y_1 = a + bk$; $y_2 = c + dk$; and therefore, $y = (1 - f)y_1 + fy_2$, or

$$y = a + bk - (a - c)f - (b - d)fk \qquad (1\text{-}3)$$

With the fraction of non-CBD-worker households and its interaction with distance held constant, the coefficient of distance reflects the increase in income of households whose heads work in the CBD. Since it is anticipated that $b > 0$ and $d < 0$, as described in the first section, the coefficient of the interaction term fk is expected to be negative. However, if there were no locational advantages to higher-income CBD-worker households in living farther from the CBD, b would be zero.

The 1970 regression results were full of surprises. In the first runs, the signs of the b and d coefficients in (1-3) were generally as anticipated, but their numerical values were absurdly large. A little checking quickly revealed the reason: simple correlation coefficients between k and fk of about 0.99 in all cities. Checking further, I found that there was little variation among quasi-tracts in the fraction of workers employed outside the CBD and virtually no correlation of the latter with distance. (The simple correlation was positive in four cities and negative in four, but never greater than 0.2 numerically.) This lack of any correlation bears out what I have long suspected from casual observation—that the residences of workers employed in the CBD are uniformly scattered throughout the city. The virtual constancy of f, however, prevents estimation of separate income versus distance effects for households with and without a CBD worker.

Once fk was deleted, the collinearity problem cleared up, but I was presented with two more surprises. The first was that the coefficients of age of dwelling were quite small and erratic. The numbers that were positive and significant at the one-tailed, 5 percent level are shown in Table 1-1. Of the entries shown there, only two coefficients for 5-10 and 10-20-year-old dwellings give any statistical grounds for rejecting the null hypothesis that age of dwellings had no effect on the income level of their inhabitants. The age coefficients exhibit virtually no pattern from one age class to the next or from one city to the next. Likewise, the form in which age effects were entered into the regression made virtually no difference to the results.

On the other hand, the coefficients of distance from the CBD were remarkably strong in all cities and quite uniform among them (Table 1-2). (To facilitate comparisons among years primarily, the coefficients and standard errors shown in the table are expressed relative to average income for all quasi-tracts in the particular city and year.)

Table 1-1. Sign and Significance of Age-of-Dwelling Coefficients, 1970 Regressions[a]

	Coefficient (no. of cities)	
Dwelling Variable	*No. Positive*	*No. Significant (1-tail, 5% level)*
Age (years)		
Less than 5	3	0
5-10	5	2
11-20	5	2
21-30	0	0
20 years or older	6	1
30 years or older	3	1
$-AVAGE1$	4	1
$-AVAGE2$	3	1

[a]Separate regressions are marked off by rulings.

Table 1-2.   Summary of Partial Coefficients[a] of Income on Distance for Full[b] Regressions

Year	Migrants[c] High		Migrants[c] Low	
	Poverty High	*Poverty Low*	*Poverty High*	*Poverty Low*
	Population Growth Rate High			
	Kansas City	*Indianapolis*	*Miami*	*Akron*
1950	.11	.23	−.0145	−.0136
	(.066)	(.050)	(.061)	(.070)
1960	.17	.24	.055	−.000
	(.024)	(.027)	(.062)	(.062)
1970	.20	.14	.16	.034
	(.028)	(.025)	(.068)	(.031)
	Population Growth Rate Low			
	Omaha	*Milwaukee*	*Baltimore*	*Buffalo*
1950	−.007	.070	.11	.039
	(.061)	(.021)	(.031)	(.049)
1960	.19	.11	.17	.096
	(.074)	(.018)	(.021)	(.037)
1970	.15	.13	.14	.11
	(.048)	(.021)	(.030)	(.034)

[a]Increase in income per mile divided by average income for all quasi-tracts in the particular city and year.

[b]All variables for age of dwelling included.

[c]From outside SMSAs.

When four age-class variables were used, the coefficient of distance was positive and statistically significant in seven of the eight cities. (In six of the eight, income increased from roughly $1,100 to $1,500 per mile.) In the eighth, Akron, the distance coefficient was roughly twice its standard error when only one age variable was used in the regression. Also, Akron was the only one of the eight for which the age effects were at all robust.

FURTHER FINDINGS ON INTRACITY INCOME VARIATION

Because the 1970 findings were so different from what I had anticipated, I decided to make as nearly the same comparisons as census data permitted for 1950 and 1960. From tract income distributions for the earlier years, mean income was calculated using a Pareto approximation to the upper open-end class. (In a few cases this approximation broke down; so the regressions for 1950 and 1960 are based upon somewhat fewer observations.) For 1950 it was possible to calculate separate age effects for dwellings no more than ten years old, ten to twenty years old, and twenty to thirty years old. For 1960, however, only dwellings no more than ten and ten to twenty years old could be distinguished in the published data on age of dwelling.

Age effects were stronger and distance effects weaker for the 1950 comparisons than for the 1970 ones. Neither was as much so, however, as my earlier published results for 1950 (Muth 1969, pp. 200-202). Except for dwellings no more than ten years old, each age variable was generally positive in six of the eight cities, significantly so in three. Though the probability of three or more significantly positive coefficients in eight observations is less than one in a hundred if no true relation exists, these effects varied considerably from city to city. The distance coefficients were positive in only five cases, but were significantly so in four. These findings thus suggest that, contrary to my earlier conclusion, distance effects on income existed in 1950.

For my 1960 regressions, age effects were even weaker than in 1970. More than half of each of the age-of-dwelling coefficients were negative, and only one out of the eight was positive and significant statistically. Distance effects were somewhat stronger in 1960 than in 1950 but somewhat weaker than in 1970. Seven of the coefficients were positive, and six of these were significant. Taken together, the findings suggest distance effects have become progressively stronger over time but that only for 1950 were age effects of any appreciable importance.

The pattern of simple correlation coefficients provides some insight into the statistical reasons for these findings. Between 1950 and 1970, the distributions of the eight simple correlation coefficients of income on distance were remarkably similar. Indeed, the median of the eight fell slightly, from 0.53 to 0.47. However, the simple correlation of income on age became much weaker. For 1950, seven of the eight coefficients of income on proportion of dwellings no more than thirty years old were 0.48 or greater, the median also being 0.53. In 1970, though, only one of the coefficients of income on the fraction of dwellings twenty years old or less was as large as 0.48, and the median was only 0.20.

The intercorrelation of distance and age of dwelling also became much weaker. For 1950, seven of the eight coefficients for distance and proportion thirty years old or less were 0.7 or greater. In 1970, in contrast, only one of the coefficients of distance on proportion twenty years old or less was as large as 0.7. From all this I would conclude that the true effect of age on income did indeed become weaker, that of distance stronger. Distance effects, however, became increasingly less masked by the intercorrelation of distance and age.

Though my experimental design was originally chosen to compare various factors affecting the size of age effects, the contrasts of distance effects revealed by Table 1-2 is suggestive of a substantive explanation for my findings. In only eight of twelve possible comparisons is the poverty effect relatively strong, and in only six does high population growth produce a relatively large distance coefficient. (For such sign comparisons, at least ten or more out of twelve agreements are needed for significance at the two-tailed, 5 percent level.) For eleven of the twelve paired comparisons, however, the city with the above-median rate of immigration from outside SMSAs had the largest distance coefficient. A closely related finding is that in thirteen out of sixteen cases, the later year has the larger distance coefficient relative to the city's mean income level.

One explanation for the finding that income increases more rapidly with distance where immigration of poor families is above average might run as follows. Initially, low-income immigrants into urban areas settle in parts close to the city center, possibly because the oldest dwellings are there. The effect of boundary externalities on housing prices of the kind discussed by Bailey (1959) are sufficiently strong relative to the differential advantages of dwellings of different ages that expansion of the area occupied by this immigrant group is made into locations immediately adjacent to group's previous location. The observed increase in household income with distance is thus due primarily to the difference in average incomes between the immigrant group in an inner annulus and a native group in an outer one. The larger the immigrant group the greater its average distance from the center; hence the greater the average increase in household income per mile. This explanation is consistent with findings that the larger the migrant population, the stronger the effects of distance upon income in cities at a given time and the stronger those distance effects over time.

Though it is relatively easy conceptually to think in terms of two different income groups and expansion of the lower of the two into the area previously occupied by the higher, it is much harder to give empirical content to such a notion. There were principally two ways by which I tried to do so. One was to define dummy variables for lower-income occupancy in 1950 and for shifts from higher- to lower-income occupancy during the 1950s and 1960s, respectively. This was done in an admittedly quite subjective way based upon an examination of mean income, percent black, and percent five years (one year) old or more residing in the same dwelling five years (one year) earlier in 1970 and 1960 (in 1950). Whether or not a given tract was spatially contiguous to another lower-income tract in the same year also influenced my classification of doubtful cases, since most of the obvious instances of lower-income occupancy were spatially contiguous to another such tract.

Another variable used (SNY, below) was the ratio of mean tract income for an earlier to a later census year if tract income for the later year was below the mean for all central-city combinations of tracts used, and SNY was zero otherwise. The larger the value of this variable, presumably, the greater the degree or likelihood of succession. In analyzing the 1970 income data and expenditure-income ratios (the latter are described more fully in the following section), four different measures of succession were tried: the sum of my three subjective dummies; the sum of the dummies for succession during the 1950s and during the 1960s; and SNY, using both 1950 and 1960 as the earlier year. All four yielded very much the same results. In what follows I discuss results obtained using SNY, since it is more objective and thus reproducible; on a-priori grounds, 1950 seems more appropriate for the earlier year.

In addition to SNY, I also included two measures of the race characteristics of a tract's population: $NG1$, which equaled 1 if the percent black was at least 70; and $NG2$, which equaled 1 if the percent black was at least 5 but less than 70; and zero otherwise. The variables were included in the income comparisons to remove the effect on the increase in average income with distance that arises because blacks not only have lower incomes than whites but are concentrated closer to the city center. Inclusion of SNY and the two racial dummies generally had little effect on the age variable I used: the fraction of dwellings in 1970 built since 1949. Without these three, only two of eight age coefficients were positive and significant at the one-tailed, 5 percent level; with them only 1 was. The effect of including the succession and race variables was, generally, to reduce the size of the distance coefficients by about half. The median of the distance coefficients was about $1,100 per mile without them and $570 per mile with them included. With these three included, though, the distance coefficient was significantly positive in five of the eight cities; in only two of the cities did the distance coefficient become insignificant statistically when succession and race were held constant. Quite similar results were found using 1960 income data. I would conclude, therefore, that the increase in income that is observed as one moves farther from the city center reflects something in addition to the concentration of low-income groups toward the center.

EXPENDITURE-INCOME RATIOS

Equations (1-1) and (1-2) imply that housing expenditures (R) in relation to income (y) and average age of dwellings are of the form

$$R/y = y^{\beta - 1}(a - bu + cs) \tag{1-4}$$

where s is a variable indicating the presence of succession. Form (1-4) was chosen for estimation in order more nearly to equalize the residual variance of housing expenditure at different income levels. Form (1-4), or any other form of (1-1) and (1-2), presents problems of nonlinearity of the equation in the coefficients to be estimated. To get around these problems I decided to fix β, the income elasticity of housing demand, at various values in what I believed was a plausible range: $1 \leqslant \beta \leqslant 1.5$. With $\beta = 1$, of course, the expenditure-income ratio is a straightforward linear regression on u and s, and for fixed $\beta > 1$ it is a linear regression on $y^{\beta - 1}$, $y^{\beta - 1}u$, and $y^{\beta - 1}s$ without a constant term. Furthermore, taking $\beta = 1.25$ and $\beta = 1.5$ for 1970 data essentially divided the coefficients for $\beta = 1$ by 10 and by 100 (y averaged about $10,000 per year), making them implausibly small but not appreciably affecting the fit of the equation. Therefore, I decided to take $\beta = 1$.

I did a considerable amount of other experimenting with the data for 1970. It was indicated earlier that four different measures of residential succession were tried, and SNY using 1950 for the earlier year was selected. Two measures of average age of dwelling were tried, differing in the value assumed for the open-end age class. For $AVAGE1$ it was assumed that buildings built prior to 1940 were on average built in 1925; hence they averaged 45 years of age in 1970 and 35 in 1960. For 1950 it was also assumed, as for 1970, that dwellings more than thirty years old averaged 45 years of age. $AVAGE2$ was estimated for each year as described earlier. I used $AVAGE1$ as my age measure because it gave numerically larger and more plausible coefficients than $AVAGE2$.

In calculating housing expenditure from census data, a rental-to-value ratio must be applied to census data on average value of single-family, owner-occupied dwellings. Here I experimented with various values in the range 0.08 to 0.16, and even attempted to estimate this ratio by regressing the product of the renter fraction and the ratio of average contract rent to income on the product of the owner fraction and the ratio of average value to income and other variables. I used a rent-to-value ratio of 0.10 in my final runs because it yielded somewhat stronger coefficients for *SNY* than any larger values, although somewhat weaker ones for *AVAGE*1.

The results obtained for my succession measure were not particularly strong for 1970. Three of the *SNY* coefficients were negative, although in the five cities with positive coefficients three were significant at the one-tailed, 5 percent level. The three significant coefficients were of some quantitative importance; multiplying them by the mean of *SNY* where its value was positive increased the estimated expenditure-income ratio for a 35-year-old structure from about 0.12 to 0.13. In only one of eight cities, though, did inclusion of *SNY* appreciably reduce the coefficient of *NG*1, the dummy variable indicating predominantly black occupancy.

When I repeated the regressions using 1960 data, however, the *SNY* coefficient was negative for six cities, and only one of the two positive coefficients was significant at the 5 percent level. Since the final form of the equation was chosen in part to make the succession coefficients as strong as possible, I would reject the hypothesis that housing expenditures are larger than otherwise where residential succession has occurred. The further results described below thus refer to regressions with *SNY* omitted.

The coefficients of *AVAGE*1 were considerably stronger than those of *SNY* and rather more consistent from year to year. These are shown in Table 1-3 for the three census years. For each of the three years seven of the eight age coefficients were negative, and at least four were significantly so at the 5 percent level (five in 1960). The coefficients were reasonably stable numerically, their medians being —0.82 in 1950 and 1970 and —1.2 in 1960. Likewise, the coefficients indicate a fairly strong quantitative importance. For 1970, a coefficient of —0.8 converts an expenditure-income ratio of 0.15 for a new dwelling to 0.12 for a 35-year-old one. One fact literally jumps out of the table: The coefficients are much larger numerically and a higher proportion are significant for cities with low population growth rates than for those with high growth rates. Ten of the twelve coefficients for the former groups are significant, but only three of the latter.

Also shown in Table 1-3 are the constant terms in the regressions. For each of the three years there is some variability from city to city, but much less than for the other coefficients estimated. Clearly, though, there is a strong tendency for expenditure-income ratios to

Table 1-3.   Coefficients of Variables in Regressions[a] for Expenditure-Income Ratios (figures in parentheses are estimated standard errors)

City	Constant			$AVAGE1 \times 10^3$			$NG1 \times 10^2$		
	1950	1960	1970	1950	1960	1970	1950	1960	1970
Population growth rate high									
Kansas City	.186 (.016)	.172 (.019)	.141 (.015)	-0.028 (0.464)	-0.812 (0.609)	-0.484 (0.385)	0.62 (1.31)	1.80* (0.54)	-1.45 (0.41)
Indianapolis	.193 (.015)	.140 (.016)	.117 (.017)	-1.08* (0.41)	-0.442 (0.467)	-0.366 (0.412)	1.28 (0.97)	2.17* (0.55)	1.59* (0.60)
Miami	.221 (.020)	.179 (.015)	.154 (.017)	2.25 (1.18)	1.09 (0.70)	0.687 (0.683)	4.40* (2.34)	4.51* (1.14)	0.60 (1.03)
Akron	.209 (.016)	.200 (.010)	.176 (.007)	-0.557 (0.516)	-1.52* (0.35)	-1.23* (0.19)	b	1.89* (0.93)	0.232 (0.369)
Population growth rate low									
Omaha	.196 (.025)	.189 (.013)	.155 (.022)	-0.161 (0.733)	-1.42* (0.45)	-0.908 (0.602)	-2.44 (2.37)	-0.729 (0.768)	1.95* (0.81)
Milwaukee	.270 (.013)	.236 (.015)	.151 (.010)	-2.52* (0.34)	-2.69* (0.45)	-0.725* (0.242)	b	1.57* (0.48)	0.090 (0.341)
Baltimore	.231 (.011)	.150 (.008)	.132 (.008)	-1.74* (0.33)	-1.06* (0.27)	-1.03* (0.21)	5.97* (1.27)	5.12* (0.45)	3.44* (0.44)
Buffalo	.243 (.023)	.249 (.031)	.197 (.029)	-2.33* (0.65)	-3.51* (0.94)	-2.13* (0.71)	b	b	0.685 (0.728)

*Significantly less than zero at the one-tailed, 5 percent level.

[a] NY excluded, $NG1$ and $NG2$ included whenever more than one observation equaled unity.

b Omitted from regression where at most one combined tract had a value of unity.

decline over time. In all cases but one, the ratio is smaller in a later than in an earlier year for the same city. One interpretation of this decline is that the income elasticity of housing demand is less than 1.0, with the result that with rising incomes a smaller proportion is spent on housing. I am reluctant, though, to accept this explanation, in view of the substantial body of other evidence that suggests housing expenditures increase at least in proportion to income (see de Leeuw 1971). Another explanation is that as central-city taxes have risen relative to those in suburban areas, central-city housing prices have fallen relative to those in suburban areas, thus eliminating the net advantages of one location over the other.

Finally, the coefficients of $NG2$, which stands for mixed neighborhoods, was negative about as often as positive. The one or two cases a year that were significant at the two-tailed, 5 percent level, though, were positive. The coefficients of the black neighborhood variable, $NG1$, are shown in Table 1-3. Virtually all are positive, many significantly so at the one-tailed, 5 percent level. Both their magnitude and significance tend to increase from 1950 to 1960 and then to decline in 1970. A coefficient of 2.0, more or less typical of the significant ones in 1970, indicates the expenditure-income ratio for 35-year-old dwellings would be 0.14 in black neighborhoods as compared with 0.12 in white ones.

CONCLUSIONS AND TENTATIVE IMPLICATIONS

Any inferences based upon empirical work are necessarily tentative. Because the findings discussed above differ so strikingly from some of my earlier ones, I have been made all the more aware of this often-forgotten methodological point. If anything can be concluded from these results, though, it would seem to be that age of dwelling no longer has any appreciable effect upon the pattern of location of households by income level in urban areas. These findings cast considerable doubt upon the empirical validity of the filtering hypothesis in urban housing markets. Equally, they suggest to me that the pattern of neighborhood succession which takes place as an immigrant population grows is not very much affected by the age of dwellings.

While I am not yet prepared to abandon the notion of an immigrant population, the results suggest the poverty population does not correspond particularly well to this notion. Migrants from rural areas, rather, would seem to produce stronger effects upon the locational patterns of households classified by income level. Neither am I yet willing to abandon the belief that as the incomes of

CBD-worker households rise, their housing expenditures rise relative to their marginal costs of transport. The major explanation for the observed rise in household income with distance from the city center is to be found elsewhere, however. For in the cities studied, only about 10 percent of employment was located in the CBD; the CBD-worker-household effect is simply not a very important one in the income data. And, indeed, as the relative rate of decline in housing prices becomes smaller over time as average income and the speed of urban automobile travel has increased, the locational advantage to higher-income CBD-worker households in living farther from the center would have declined. Yet my findings suggest that the relative increase in household income per mile has risen over time.

Not only is neighborhood succession not very closely associated with age of dwelling, but there is little tendency for housing expenditures to be high in relation to income in parts of cities that have succeeded to lower-income occupancy. My vintage model thus appears to be of little help in understanding neighborhood succession, but predictions regarding the effects of age of dwelling on housing expenditure seem more successful. Qualitatively, seven of the eight cities exhibited negative coefficients in each of the three census years I examined, and four or five each year were significant. The age coefficients are moderately stable from year to year, but my theory did not lead me to expect these coefficients to vary inversely with a city's population growth rate.

Are the a and b coefficients of (1-4) quantitatively consistent with Equation (1-1)? Some calculations relating to this question are shown in Table 1-4. While I have a fairly good idea of the other parameters necessary to calculate the coefficients, it was necessary to estimate α from the data. Since

$$R = \alpha y^\beta \left[1 + 1n \frac{q(u)}{\hat{q}} \right]$$

α can be calculated from the rental of dwellings $\hat{u}$ years old, whose size, q, is equal to the optimal current size, $\hat{q}$. The vintage model as formulated in my earlier paper (Muth 1973) implies $\hat{u} = T - (\delta + \beta\rho - \lambda)^{-1}$. (The calculation of T, the age at which units are retired from the housing stock, is discussed in Muth 1973.) From median values of my a and b coefficients I then calculated $\alpha = (R/y)(\hat{u}) = 0.152 - 0.00082\hat{u}$, which, together with other values shown in Table 1-4, permits calculation of expected values of a and

Table 1-4.   Effects of Alternative Depreciation Rates on Dwelling Characteristics[a]

	$\delta = 0.02$	$\delta = 0$
T	43.7	87.1
$\hat{u}$	15.1	20.4
α^b	0.140	0.135
a	0.214	0.176
b	0.0049	0.0020
$-\ln W'(20)$	0.061	0.019

[a]Assuming $\beta\rho = 0.025$, $\lambda = 0.01$, $i = 0.07$.

[b]Estimated from $\alpha = R/y(\hat{u}) = 0.152 - 0.00082\,\hat{u}$.

b. For $\delta = 0.02$ these are much larger than my estimates; for $\delta = 0$ they are only somewhat larger than my estimates, especially the calculated b for cities with high rates of growth of population.

Some additional insight into this question is provided by examining the relative rate of decline of the market value of dwellings over time. The latter, of course, is the integral of discounted future quasi-rents. My vintage model implies that the market value (W) as a function of age is

$$W(u) = \frac{\alpha y^\beta (\delta + \beta\rho - \lambda)}{(i - \beta\rho)^2}\ (i - \beta\rho)(T - u)$$

$$- 1 - \exp\left[-(i - \beta\rho)(T - u)\right]$$

As such the relative rate of decline of market value varies with age, increasing rapidly as a dwelling nears replacement age. As shown in Table 1-4 for twenty-year-old dwellings, $\delta = 0.02$ implies a relative decline in value of about 6 percent per year; $\delta = 0$, about 2 percent. The latter agrees closely with the annual relative rate of decline estimated by Grebler, Blank, and Winnick (1956, pp. 377-382). If the implication is previously mentioned spatial patterns of income emerges. To "validate" this over time, then my vintage model is reasonably consistent with the decline both in observed rentals and market values of dwellings over time. The vintage model explanation for these declines and the ultimate replacement of dwellings is that, being fixed, the flow of housing services given off by dwellings declines relative to the market demand for housing, not absolutely.

Though I feel it reasonable to claim some modest empirical success for my vintage model, the model would appear to provide little help in understanding the locational pattern of households by income level in urban areas. It seems clear, however, that average incomes increase with distance from the city center and that this rate of increase has grown relatively greater over the postwar years. Work done by some of my students suggests that the average income of a census tract both affects and is affected by the rental value of its dwelling units. Breuckner (1975), in particular, has found that succession as measured by the variable I call *SNY*, tends to occur principally in parts of the city where dwellings are smaller than average. The age of dwellings, however, is not a very good surrogate for size of dwelling, as is assumed in the vintage model. To explain the location of households by income and the pattern of neighborhood succession would seem to require a theory of the distribution of dwelling units by size in urban areas.

REFERENCES

Alonso, William. 1964. *Location and Land Use*. Cambridge, Mass.: Harvard University Press.

Bailey, Martin J. 1959. "Note on the Economics of Residential Zoning and Urban Renewal." *Land Economics*, August.

Brueckner, Jan. 1975. "The Determinants of Residential Succession." Processed.

Census. 1963. U.S. Bureau of the Census, *U.S. Census of Population: 1960*, Final Report PC(2)-2C, Mobility for Metropolitan Areas. Washington, D.C.: Government Printing Office.

de Leeuw, Frank. 1971. "The Demand for Housing: A Review of Cross-Section Evidence." *Review of Economics and Statistics*, February.

Duncan, Otis Dudley, and Beverly Duncan. 1957. *The Negro Population of Chicago*. Chicago: University of Chicago Press.

Grebler, Leo; David M. Blank; and Louis Winnick. 1956. *Capital Formation in Residential Real Estate: Trends and Prospects*, Princeton, N.J.: Princeton University Press for NBER.

Mills, Edwin S. 1967. "An Aggregative Model of Resource Allocation in a Metropolitan Area." *American Economic Review*, May.

_____. 1969. "The Value of Urban Land." In Harvey S. Perloff, ed. *The Quality of the Urban Environment*. Washington, D.C.: Resources for the Future.

Moses, Leon N. 1962. "Toward a Theory of Intra-Urban Wage Differentials and Their Influence on Travel Patterns." *Papers and Proceedings of the Regional Science Association*.

Muth, Richard F. 1969. *Cities and Housing*. Chicago: University of Chicago Press.

_____. 1973. "A Vintage Model of the Housing Stock." *Papers and Proceedings of the Regional Science Association*.

Nourse, Hugh O. and Donald Phares. 1974. "The Filtering Process: Aging or Arbitrage." In Solomon Suther and Sara Suther, eds. *Racial Transition in the Inner Suburb*. New York: Praeger.

Ratcliff, Richard V. 1949. *Urban Land Economics.* New York: McGraw-Hill.
Wingo, Lowden, Jr. 1961. *Transportation and Urban Land.* Washington, D.C.: Resources for the Future.

Comments on Chapter One

William C. Wheaton

In this study Muth tries to analyze the underlying reason for a pervasive locational pattern in America: the higher the income of a household, the further it is likely to be living from the urban center. The explanation Muth offers is derived from his earlier development (Muth 1973) of a vintage model of the urban housing stock. In that model, housing built in one period deteriorates in relative terms as time passes. New housing is built in response to increases in aggregate demand and, hence, an age distribution of the stock emerges. The market allocates older units to low-income households because of their inability to bid high enough to capture new housing. Since older housing is more centrally located, the previously mentioned spatial pattern of income emerges. To "validate" this theory, Muth proposes to see if the simple correlation (positive) between income and commuting distance vanishes as age of unit is introduced. If it does the model is purported to be verified; if not, other explanations must be sought.

My first reaction to this study involves its general methodology. Given the proposition Muth wishes to test, I cannot see how the accompanying empirical work serves as validation. It is a well-known problem in causal inference (Blaylock 1971) that a vanishing partial correlation coefficient cannot distinguish between the following two cases at hand:

1. Because of the gradual evolution of the stock, location determines the age of unit which in turn determines the income of occupant.

2. Location determines income and age separately, but the latter has no causal connection with the former.

Thus Muth's "test" is ill-designed in the first place. Interestingly, the results of the empirical work show that the introduction of age does not appreciably weaken the income-location linkage, but rather that the age-income partial is weak. Here again, however, Muth's use of a single-equation model does not allow even a rejection of the hypothesis that age has a separate effect. At a minimum there should be a recursive system of equations in which the indirect effect of location on income (by determining age) can be compared with its direct impact.

Even this, however, might not be sufficient, for there is the serious question of simultaneity. Throughout Muth's work, there is the assumption that unit "age" is not desired by consumers. Ceteris paribus, I find this a highly questionable assumption. Many and perhaps even a majority of the older houses in today's stock are large, spacious, well-constructed units. If age had not brought with it deterioration and changing neighborhoods, these units might be the most sought after. My own work on hedonic indexes with Boston data indicates that many households prefer older units—ceteris paribus with respect to other attributes. If, however, condition is not controlled for (which is the case here) some of its effect is picked up by unit age and accounts for the slight negative effect of the latter on income. The problem then is that "age" (including the condition effect) is determined by income in addition to being its determinant. Since the location by income pattern affects unit maintenance, and hence "age," we have substantial simultaneity—an issue Muth never mentions. In short, Muth's empirical work is not an appropriate test of his hypothesis. This leads me to a second issue—whether the hypothesis itself can shed much light on the evolution of the spatial distribution of income in the United States.

The income location pattern in any city is the evolving outcome of a competitive process between households of vastly different wealth and tastes. In this context, I doubt that any aggregate statistical analysis can "explain" the emerging market outcome. Even if all variables besides age were controlled, what would a negative partial between the latter and local income tell us? Only that ceteris paribus, wealthy people live in newer units, not necessarily that they *prefer* these units or that this relationship is at all important in explaining *why* they live there. It is only with a disaggregated analysis of consumer preferences and supply behavior that we will gain an appreciation of how and why the market produced its observed outcome. Within such a framework there has been some recent research that approaches the same question Muth raises—that of explaining the locational pattern by household income in American cities.

As Muth mentions, both some of his earlier work and that of Mills (1972) suggest that location in the long run, when capital is mobile, occurs as the result of a tradeoff between travel costs and housing expenditure. A problem with this approach is the use of a one-dimensional measure of housing services. If in fact housing has many attributes (and it does) and consumers have different orderings over this commodity space (and they do), then the theory of aggregation tells us that no single measure of housing services exists. This raises some question as to whether empirical estimates of parameters in the model mean very much. Alonso (1965) avoids this problem by viewing location as a tradeoff between travel and land expenditure. With capital mobile in the long run, housing is implicitly treated as an "other" good that can be freely supplied in any quantity at any location. The supply parameter of some nonexistent commodity called housing "services" does not affect location—it is consumer preferences for low-density living and minimal travel time that do—and both of these can be estimated for different households.

Within Alonso's framework, the characteristics of the existing housing stock do not influence the long-run locational pattern. Since existing units can in principal be modified to any density or size, the pattern of income by location must be caused by differences in the preference for land and travel. If, as income increases, land demand rises more rapidly than the disutility of travel, wealthier households will have relatively flat "bid price surfaces" and will outbid lower-income groups for more distant sites. If greater income has little effect on land demand, but significantly increases the disutility of travel, the reverse holds and the market solution will be for income to decrease with distance.

Using an extensive home-interview survey for San Francisco, I recently estimated utility parameters for several socioeconomic classes of households for a series of housing attributes including size, condition, age, travel time, land, and neighborhood quality (Wheaton 1973a). Comparing the results across income groups I found that both the demand for land and the disutility of travel increased with wealth, and at about the same rate. Using these results to simulate a long-run market equilibrium, I generated a locational pattern in which income increased ever so slightly with distance to the CBD (Wheaton 1973b). At first glance then, this might seem to indicate that differences in consumer preferences for land and travel are sufficient, on their own, to explain the U.S. spatial pattern. A closer examination, however, revealed that the equilibrium locations in the simulation resulted from exceedingly small differences in the bids between income classes. The rich lived on the periphery of urban areas because they outbid the poor, but by less than 10 percent! This verifies that while income does result in greater concern both for land and travel, the two effects almost cancel each other out. Differences in demand for these commodities (at least by income), then, are probably *not* an important determinant of U.S. land use.

Where does this leave us, in our search for an explanation of American locational patterns? The deteriorating housing stock is ruled out because, first, it can always be rehabilitated and, second, the housing problem is caused by low-income occupancy. Differences in the preference for land and travel have now also been ruled out, and so we are left with one remaining consideration—externalities, both those resulting from the city itself (noise, pollution) and those arising from the presence of low-income residents (crime), and pecuniary externalities that result from urban fiscal fragmentation. These factors have been well-elaborated elsewhere, and the builders of urban models should begin to incorporate them explicitly.

REFERENCES

Alonso, William. 1965. *Location and Land Use.* Cambridge, Mass.: Harvard University Press.

Blaylock, Herbert. 1971. *Causal Models in the Social Sciences.* Chicago: Aldine-Atherton.

Mills, Edwin S. 1972. *Studies in the Structure of the Urban Economy.* Washington, D.C.: Resources for the Future.

Muth, Richard, 1973. "A Vintage Model of the Housing Stock." *Papers and Proceedings of the Regional Science Association.*

Wheaton, William. 1973a. "A Bid Rent Approach to Housing Demand." Processed. Cambridge, Mass.: Massachusetts Institute of Technology.

_____. 1973b. "Income and Urban Residence: An Analysis of the Consumer Demand for Location." Processed. Cambridge, Mass.: Massachusetts Institute of Technology.

Chapter Two

Interdependence between Public-Sector Decisions and the Urban Housing Market

Mahlon R. Straszheim

INTRODUCTION

In the typical urban area, decisions by local governments, households, and housing suppliers are highly interrelated.

The reason for much of this interdependence is that space is the principal basis for defining local public-sector jurisdictions. Most metropolitan areas are composed of many jurisdictions, each of which provides services and levies taxes on its own inhabitants. Local jurisdictions also typically control zoning and the issuance of building permits. These public-sector decisions affect the prices of land and housing and are a factor in determining who will choose to move into the zone. Housing and land prices together with zoning rules influence the nature of new development. At the same time, the price and quality of housing available in a jurisdiction will be factors in determining who will choose to reside there and, hence, the vote on public-sector decisions. Housing market outcomes and local public-sector decisions are thus highly interdependent.

In any model of public-sector decisions, housing stocks must play a prominent role. Housing stocks differ substantially across jurisdictions, and the time lags involved in changing the existing stock are relatively long. In jurisdictions with little vacant land for development, an area's housing stock may undergo relatively little change over time as long as prices remain above the level required to encourage normal maintenance. Even relative to other areas, the age and quality of a zone's housing may change only very slowly. Given the preferences of certain types of households for particular kinds of housing, variations in housing stocks among zones can be a useful predictor of the income and life cycle of the neighborhood's residents (Straszheim 1975). The limited empirical evidence on consumer preferences for public-sector outputs indicates that preferences are related to incomes and life cycle as well (Hirsch 1970; Borcherding and Deacon 1972). This suggests that differences in public sector actions from zone to zone and over time are likely closely related to the types of housing stocks available and their changes.

The theoretical literature has stressed the advantages of a system of multiple jurisdictions with different tax and service levels in each. To the extent that there are differences among households in income or tastes which affect the demand for government services, there is an obvious incentive for households to stratify into "homogeneous" jurisdictions according to their preferences for a smaller or greater role for the public sector. It has been shown that an efficient outcome will require that there be such differences (Tiebout 1956; McGuire 1974). Specifying voting procedures, zoning rules, and taxing instruments that will secure an efficient solution is more complex; it seems likely that customary voting and taxing instruments will not produce such a result (Buchanan and Goetz 1972).

In the typical metropolitan area there will not likely be sufficient jurisdictional fragmentation so that all residents in a zone will be in common agreement on the public sector budget and associated taxes. First, the number of jurisdictions is typically limited. In some urban areas there may exist only a few large jurisdictions, while in others the number may be substantially larger. Scale economies limit the extent to which jurisdictions can be reduced in size. In addition, externalities increase with reduction in size, much complicating the determination of efficient public-sector actions and limiting the opportunity to decentralize decision making. Certain income redistribution objectives can also be achieved by limiting the number of jurisdictions. (And state legislatures may consider other objectives as well.)

Housing stocks also typically vary within jurisdictions because housing units are often constructed over an extended period of time during which prices for housing, land, and construction vary. Thus, while variation in tastes for public services and housing can likely best be described by a continuous probability distribution with a positive covariance between housing and public-service preferences, the latter must be matched against a finite set of residential zones, each of which contains a fixed and heterogeneous housing stock. Under these conditions, it becomes increasingly unlikely that there is a spatial configuration of households matching the existing set of housing stocks which will yield unanimity on public-sector voting in each jurisdiction.

There may also be variation in preferences for public services within a zone that cannot be traced to differences in housing consumption. Households may have moved into a zone on the basis of faulty expectations about public-sector outputs or tax burdens. Also, because of relocation costs and other factors—for example, job location—that restrict residential mobility, some households may find themselves in a jurisdiction in which their preferences for public-sector outputs differ from those of their neighbors, though they all have identical housing units.

Relatively little attention has been devoted in the literature to the specification of difference among voters. In this study I discuss procedures for explicitly modeling the relationships between fixed housing stocks, variations in income and preferences across households, and local-government decisions. The principal issue addressed is the decision-making process of jurisdictions with heterogeneous interests, in large part arising from a fixed stock of housing which itself is hetereogeneous.

The general procedure outlined below is to represent differences in preferences parametrically, relating differences in how households in any jurisdiction vote on public-sector decisions to differences in housing stocks or underlying utility functions. This uses the technique of change of variable, in which probability density functions on housing stocks or tastes are translated into a density function describing voting preferences. The housing stock is regarded as fixed at a point in time. Decisions on current-period services and taxes and on zoning are analyzed; the latter affect future votes, tax burdens, and housing prices, all of which are important to the welfare of existing residents.

The analytic procedure using change of variable is quite general. For a variety of assumptions regarding initial probability distributions and change of variable, the resultant density function describing voting outcomes will be continuous. However, as in most change-of-variable problems, the class of problems that can be solved analytically is relatively small. Further development of these models is likely to involve numerical evaluation. The discussion in this chapter is focused primarily on the issues involved in the specification of the models rather than in their numerical solution and is intended to highlight the advantages and disadvantages of this general approach. Illustrative examples are presented.

In several important respects the models are partial equilibrium ones. The analysis focuses only on how decisions are made in one zone, taking all events "outside" the zone as given. "Competitive" behavior or the perceived "mutual dependence" between jurisdictions and its effects on decisions by each jurisdiction are not addressed.

Household locations are exogenous to the models. The models describing preferences of existing residents imply a variety of different assumptions regarding how the household's locational decision might be formulated. These are spelled out below. Neither the relocation decision nor the problem of matching households to available housing stocks in particular jurisdictions is addressed in this study.

I also describe the basic change-of-variable approach. Applications of the model are based on particular assumptions regarding the factors that generate the underlying distribution of residents' preferences for public-sector decisions. In conclusion I review the insights derived from the models in this study as they relate to the more general problem of modeling public-sector-housing market interactions.

REPRESENTING VARIATIONS IN VOTER PREFERENCES BY CHANGE OF VARIABLE

In most general terms, variation in housing consumed and utility functions might be represented by a probability density function, $f(h, \lambda)$, where h denotes housing; and λ, a vector of parameters describing preferences. For example, λ might include the number and age of children in the household, the age of head of household, etc. Let λ have $n-1$ elements. Assume that households' preferences for public-sector outputs, g_i, are related to h and λ as follows:

$$g_i = d_i(h, \lambda); i = 1, \ldots, n \qquad (2\text{-}1)$$

The elements g_i are themselves random variables, a transformation of h and λ, whose density function is given by change of variable. Assume the inverse functions $c_1, \ldots, c_n$ exist:

$$h = c_1(g_1, g_2, \ldots, g_n) \qquad (2\text{-}2)$$
$$\lambda_1 = c_2(g_1, g_2, \ldots, g_n)$$
$$\vdots \qquad \vdots$$
$$\lambda_{n-1} = c_n(g_1, g_2, \ldots, g_n)$$

and that the transformation is one to one. (This is guaranteed locally if the partial derivatives are continuous at the point of interest and if the Jacobian $|\partial c/\partial g|$ does not change sign.) The density function describing households' preferences for g is given by:

$$G(g_1, \ldots, g_n) = f[c_1(h, \lambda), c_2(h, \lambda), \ldots, c_n(h, \lambda)] \cdot \quad (2\text{-}3)$$

$$\frac{\partial(c_1, \ldots, c_n)}{\partial(g_1, \ldots, g_n)}$$

In the models analyzed below, the public-sector decisions being voted upon are assumed to be one-dimensional. To derive the density function for g (where g is now assumed to be one-dimensional) on the basis of the transformation from (h, λ) to g, $n - 1$ "dummy" variables must be defined; the latter are then integrated out to get the marginal density function on g. Let z_i denote $n - 1$ dummy variables, related to h and λ as follows:

$$z_i = d_i(h, \lambda); i = 2, \ldots n \quad (2\text{-}4)$$

The specification of z_i is dictated solely by analytic convenience. Integrating out the z_i yields the density function for g:

$$G(g) = \int \ldots \int f[c_1(h, \lambda), c_2(h, \lambda), \ldots, c_n(h, \lambda)] \quad (2\text{-}5)$$

$$\cdot \frac{\partial(c_1, \ldots, c_n)}{\partial(g,z)} \, dz_2, \ldots, dz_n$$

This provides a flexible analytic procedure for representing variation in tastes.

The density function $G(g)$ describes the degree of heterogeneity among voters. A variety of assumptions might be employed to determine how these differences in opinion over g are reconciled. For example, the probability that anyone votes might be related to preferences for g and could be readily incorporated once the density function is known. In most of the models below it is assumed that voting outcomes reflect preferences of the "median" vote. This simple rule has considerable appeal when a simple issue is being voted on, or preferences are single-peaked (Barr and Davis 1966; Bowen 1943; Comanor 1974). (The complexities of multi-dimensional public-sector decisions would be treated by a straightforward extension of the change-in-variable model describing preferences. However, the interpretation of voting results is much more complex when several issues are being voted on in a single election.)

The nature of available housing in any jurisdiction can be easily determined (e.g., from census data or household interview surveys taken in transportation planning studies). Specifying models that describe the variation in tastes of residents at any point in time and the relationships between h, λ, and voter preferences for g is more complex.

The simplest approach would be based on customary demand functions, and would assume a direct relationship for g in terms of housing consumed, tastes, and the price of public services, without tracing the relationship between g and those parameters to underlying utility functions or to the way households form expectations when they chose to reside in any zone. This has the advantage that existing empirical studies may be useful in specifying the relevant parameters.

In the models below it is assumed that the public-sector budget must be balanced in each jurisdiction. While there are many possible taxing policies, two important special cases are a head tax (a constant charge per household) and a property tax. The latter is assumed to be assessed on housing values in nondiscriminatory fashion, with each household's tax bill directly related to the size of h. Assume housing prices are proportional to h and that public services are provided by a linear cost function:

$$C(g, N) = N\beta g \qquad (2\text{-}6)$$

where $C(g, N)$ = cost of providing public sector output g to the N citizens in the jurisdiction, and β = cost per unit of g per person.

Balancing the public-sector budget implies that the tax bill for public services will vary with house size:

$$\beta g N = t P_h \int_0^\infty h f(h)dh \qquad (2\text{-}7)$$

where t = tax rate, and P_h = price of housing. Thus

$$\beta g N = t P_h \, \mu N, \text{ or } t\frac{\beta g}{\mu P_h} \qquad (2\text{-}8)$$

where μ = mean house size in jurisdiction. Hence, the unit price of public services is a linear function of house size: $P_g(h) = h\beta/\mu$.

The simplest demand model is based on the assumption of a linear relationship between housing, public service prices, and households' preferred choice of public-sector output. Assume the demand equation as follows:

$$g^0 = a_0 + a_1 h + a_2 P_g(h) \tag{2-9}$$

where $a_1 > 0$, $a_2 < 0$. If $P_g(h)$ is based on a property tax, Equation (2-9) will be linear in g and h:

$$g^0 = a_0 + h(a_1 + a_2 \frac{\beta}{\mu}) \tag{2-10}$$

Depending on the form of $f(h)$, a linear transformation from h to g may much simplify the determination of $G(g^0)$. If $f(h)$ is normal, $G(g^0)$ will also be normal, the mean and median will coincide, and the voting outcome can be easily solved analytically. [Since h cannot be negative, the assumption that h is normal is only an approximation; however, normality would provide a good approximation to the shape of $f(h)$ for most jurisdictions.]

This simple demand model formulation implies a common utility function with variation in preferences for g traceable only to variations in housing. Introduction of variation in tastes complicates the specifications. The simplest way is to assume that a_0 is a random variable described by a probability distribution, $f(a_0)$. If a_0 and h are normally and independently distributed, the density function for g will be normal, and can be readily described. In the more general case in which a_0 and h are independent (continuous) random variables, the density of their sum can also be relatively easily determined. In the case above, let $f_1(a_0)$ and $f_2(h)$ be the density functions. Define a dummy variable $z = [a_1 + a_2(\beta/\mu)]h$. The Jacobian (J) of the transformation from (a_0, h) to (g_1, Z) is given by:

$$J = \begin{vmatrix} \dfrac{\partial a_0}{\partial g} & \dfrac{\partial a_0}{\partial z} \\[2mm] \dfrac{\partial h}{\partial g} & \dfrac{\partial h}{\partial z} \end{vmatrix} = \begin{vmatrix} 1 & -1 \\[2mm] 0 & \dfrac{1}{a_1 + a_2 \dfrac{\beta}{\mu}} \end{vmatrix} = \dfrac{1}{a_1 + a_2 \dfrac{\beta}{\mu}} \tag{2-11}$$

and hence the density of g_0 is given by integrating out the dummy variable z.

$$G(g^0) = \int_{\infty}^{\infty} f(g - z) \frac{1}{a_1 + (a_2 \frac{\beta}{\mu})} f_2 [z/a_1 + a_2 \frac{\beta}{2\mu})] dz \tag{2-12}$$

In the case where other terms in the formula for g are random variables, e.g., a_1 or a_2, obtaining the density function for g is slightly more complex. For example, suppose a_1, the coefficient on h, is also a random variable, and the joint distribution of (h, a_1) can be described by the density function $f(h, a_1)$. In this case let the dummy variable z be defined equal to a_1. The Jacobian of the transformation from (h, a_1) to (g, z) is therefore:

$$J = \begin{vmatrix} 1 & 0 \\ -\dfrac{(g - a_0)}{z + a_2 \dfrac{\beta}{\mu}} & \dfrac{1}{z + a_2 \dfrac{\beta}{\mu}} \end{vmatrix} = \dfrac{1}{z + a_2 \dfrac{\beta}{\mu}}$$

and the density function for g_0 is given by integrating out z:

$$G(g^0) = \int_{\infty}^{\infty} f[(g - a_0)/(z + a_2 \frac{\beta}{\mu}), z] \, (z + a_2 \frac{\beta}{\mu})^{-1} dz \qquad (2\text{-}13)$$

This will likely require numerical evaluation for virtually any specification of $f(h, a_1)$ that is not a uniform distribution.

These voting models based on customary demand functions are flexible and may approach the limits of our knowledge about preferences for public-sector outputs. The more challenging specification is to relate current residents' preferences to underlying utility functions, and to the reasons why households chose any given zone (and have chosen to remain). This approach implicitly introduces a host of questions as to how households form expectations regarding the level of public services and taxes in the chosen zone relative to other options at the time of their move. In the next section, several classes of models are developed in which voter preferences for g are related to underlying utility functions and different assumptions regarding expectations.

SPECIFICATION OF THE SOURCES OF VARIATION IN PREFERENCES FOR PUBLIC SERVICES

Perfect Foresight: Variation in Utility Functions

In one class of models it is assumed that households have perfect foresight, correctly anticipating the level of g voted in the zone. If it is further assumed that there is continuous variation in g across zones, so that all households can pick a zone with just the g they prefer, all residents in a zone will be in unanimous support of the prevailing *g*. (This also assumes costless relocation.) This model yields unanimity in a vote on *g* in any jurisdiction. Since households in a given zone all receive the same *g*, the variation in utility functions among residents (necessary to yield unanimity on *g*) can be derived from the observed variation in the existing housing stock.

Describing this variation in preferences is most easily handled by assuming a common utility function, with certain parameters allowed to vary across households. Let the utility function for households be denoted by $U(h, g, x, \lambda)$, where *g* = public-sector output, *h* = housing, *x* = all other goods, and λ = parameter denoting household tastes, which vary across households according to a known probability distribution (λ is assumed to be one-dimensional, for ease of exposition). Utility maximization yields three equations for *h*, *g*, and *x* in income, *Y* a vector of prices, *p*, and λ.

$$h = f_1(Y, p, \lambda) \qquad (2\text{-}14)$$

$$g = f_2(Y, p, \lambda)$$

$$x = f_3(Y, p, \lambda)$$

The solution of the demand equation for housing in terms of income is $Y = d(h, p, \lambda)$; substituting the latter into the demand equation for *g* yields an expression for *g* in terms of *h*, *p*, and λ:

$$g^0 = f_2[d(h, p, \lambda), p, \lambda] \qquad (2\text{-}15)$$

Since all households locating in a zone correctly anticipate the prevailing *g* and face the same prices, expression (2-15) amounts to a one-to-one transformation from *h* into λ. This transformation is the basis for deriving the variation in utility functions for the density function for *h*. The usefulness of this class of models is in describing how the vote on *g* varies among jurisdictions with different housing stocks.

Differing Expectations: A Common Utility Function

An alternative class of models that do not yield unanimity on the level of *g* is based on the assumption that tastes are identical across households, but that households formed differing expectations on *g* when they chose to buy *h* in the zone. Assuming *h* and *g* are complements, those households that purchased large houses expected a large *g* to be voted. Observed differences in housing are therefore a proxy for differences in ex-ante expectations. The vote on *g* reveals the differences of opinion. In this case some households will be disappointed (and the question of whether this will encourage exit is raised—an issue not dealt with in this study). For present purposes it will be assumed that current residents are momentarily captive.

A special case of this approach is the assumption that households enter the zone expecting to get precisely the g they prefer when confronted with the prevailing prices for g and h. Under this assumption, demands for g and h can be represented by the standard first-order utility maximization conditions with respect to g, h, and x. In this case the only source of variation in preferences for g as a function of h, λ, and p (Equation (2-15)) in any jurisdiction can be related to differences among residents of a zone in their consumption of h. Variation in preferences for g depends only on the density function for h, $f(h)$, and the form of the utility function.

The following illustrates this class of models, assuming public services are financed by a "head" tax, defined as a constant charge on each dwelling unit regardless of its size. The budget constraint is linear with a head tax. The tractability of the results depends on the choice of a utility function and the nature of $f(h)$.

To illustrate, assume households have a Stone-Geary utility function:

$$U = a_1 \ln (g - b_1) + a_2 \ln (h - b_2) + a_3 \ln (x - b_3)$$

which is maximized subject to a budget constraint:

$$Y = P_x X + P_h h + P_g g$$

where P_g is the tax levied on each household, and is invariant to h. The first-order conditions are familiar and lead to linear expenditure relations:

$$g = b_1 + \frac{d_1}{P_g} (Y - b_1 P_x - b_2 P_h - b_3 P_g) \qquad (2\text{-}16)$$

$$h = b_2 + \frac{d_2}{P_h} (Y - b_1 P_x - b_2 P_h - b_3 P_g)$$

$$x = b_3 + \frac{d_3}{P_x} (Y - b_1 P_x - b_2 P_h - b_3 P_g)$$

where $d_i = a_i / \Sigma_j a_j$. As noted earlier, it is assumed that households correctly anticipate the price of g, but choose an h in the expectation that the g they prefer will also result. Using the demand relationship between h and Y, a solution for Y in terms of h can be substituted into the demand equation for g, yielding an equation in h and prices. This indicates how households with different housing would vote for g:

$$g^0 = b_1 - \frac{d_1 P_h}{d_2 P_g} b_2 + \frac{d_1 P_h}{d_2 P_g} h \qquad (2\text{-}17)$$

Since $h \geqslant b_2$, (2-17) is always positive. Since it is a linear expression in g and h, the density function for g^0, $G(g^0)$, is

$$G(g^0) = \frac{d_2 P_g}{d_1 P_h} f(h) \qquad (2\text{-}18)$$

In the case where $f(h)$ is normal, g^0 will also be normal. The mean (and median) of g^0 is $b_1 - (d_1 P_h/d_2 P_g) b_2 + (d_1 P_h/d_2 P_g) \mu$. The variance of g^0 (as one possible measure of the variation in voter preferences) is $(d_1 P_h/d_2 P_g) \sigma_h^2$. (Again, this is only an approximation, since h can assume negative values if it is normal but is constrained to be $\geqslant b_2$ by the utility maximization model.) The voting outcome for g^0 is thus linear in μ. The elasticity of the g^0 chosen with respect to μ is $(d_1 P_h/d_2 P_g)(\mu/g^0)$, which exceeds 1.0 for small μ and tends toward 1.0 in the limit as μ rises. Interpretation of this elasticity is relatively straightforward: d_1 and d_2 are the marginal propensities to consume g and h respectively. As d_1/d_2 is increased, the elasticity is increased at each level of h. Comparisons across zones are straightforward, since the relationship between the median of g^0 and μ is linear.

Under the assumptions of a nondiscriminatory property tax, the results of a voting equilibrium with this type of model are much less tractable. Assume households maximize a utility function $U(g, h, x)$, subject to the budget constraint:

$$Y - P_x X - P_h h - \frac{h\beta}{\mu} g = 0$$

The first-order conditions are as follows, where subscripts on U denote partial derivatives:

$$\frac{U_g}{U_h} = \frac{\beta h}{P_h \mu + \beta g} \tag{2-19}$$

$$\frac{U_h}{U_x} = \frac{P_h h + \beta g}{\mu P_x}$$

$$Y - P_x X - P_h h - \frac{h}{\mu} \beta g = 0$$

The nonlinearity in the budget contraint arising from introduction of a property tax results in far more complicated expressions for voting equilibrium.

To illustrate the simplest case, consider the utility function $U = ag + bh + c \ln x$. (A linear function in all arguments is unsatisfactory since this results in corner solutions, with the household consuming all its income on one good.) In this case the expression for U_h/U_x becomes:

$$\frac{bx}{C} = \frac{P_h h + \beta g}{\mu P_x} \tag{2-20}$$

Substituting for x yields an expression with the product term hg:

$$Y \mu - P_h h \mu_h - \beta h g = \frac{c}{b} (P_h h + \beta g) \tag{2-21}$$

Since g is linear in h in this case, i.e., $g = (b/a)h - (P\mu/\beta)$, quadratic demand equations for h or g in terms of Y and prices result, as follows:

$$Y \mu - \frac{\beta b}{a} h^2 - (\frac{c}{b} P_h + \frac{c\beta}{a})h + \frac{c}{b} P_h \mu = 0 \tag{2-22}$$

$$Y \mu - (P_h \mu + \beta g - c P_h) (\frac{a}{b} g + \frac{a}{b} \frac{P_h \mu}{\beta} - c\beta g) = 0 \tag{2-23}$$

In each case the positive root gives the appropriate solution for h and g.

To determine how households with different housing stocks will vote, expression (2-22) for h is substituted for Y in the demand equation (2-23) for g. This yields an expression showing how voting preferences for g are related to housing stocks. Y appears in only one term in the expression for g^0.

$$g^0 = \frac{cb}{2a} + \frac{P_h \mu}{\beta} - \frac{cP_h}{\beta} \pm \left\{ (c\beta + 2P_h \frac{a}{b} \mu - cP_h \frac{a}{b})^2 \right. \tag{2-24}$$

$$\left. + 4\beta \frac{a}{b} [Y\mu - (1 - c\mu) \frac{a}{b} P_h^2 \frac{\mu}{\beta}] \right\}^{1/2}$$

Solving for Y in terms of h yields

$$Y = \frac{1}{\mu} [\beta \frac{b}{a} h^2 + (\frac{c}{b} P_h + \beta \frac{c}{a})h - \frac{cP_h \mu}{b}] \tag{2-25}$$

Substituting in (2-24) yields g^0 as a function of h in the following form:

$$g^0 = D_1 + (D_2 h^2 + D_3 h + D_4)^{1/2} \tag{2-26}$$

where $D_1, D_2, D_3,$ and D_4 are constants. Equation (2-26) may involve multiple solutions for g in terms of h, or negative solutions. The latter must be excluded; of the positive solutions, only the largest value is relevant to the household utility maximization problem. The appropriate transformation therefore must include only the positive value of the square root term defining g^0. This transformation is complex, as is the Jacobian appearing in $G(g^0)$, eliminating any hope of ready interpretation of the probability density function $G(g^0)$.

$$G(g^0) = \frac{8(g^0 - D_1)}{[D_3^2 + 4D_2(g^0 - D_1)]^2} \text{-}1/2 \; f(h) \tag{2-27}$$

Since $G(g^0)$ is not a recognizable density function, its properties can only be examined numerically. However, it is possible to make certain inferences about the voting equilibrium. If the transformation from h to g^0 is unique and monotonic over the range of $f(h)$, the transformation is order preserving, and hence the median of $G(g^0)$ will be defined by the g^0 preferred by the household with median h. The voting equilibrium can therefore be determined by solving (2-14) for h equal to median h. Examination of (2-14) and (2-15) reveals that dg^0/dY and $dY/dh > 0$; hence dg^0/dh will be positive through-out the range of h, and the transformation will be order preserving. For the household with median $h = \mu$, the expression for Y in terms of h becomes:

$$Y = \beta\frac{b}{a}\mu + (\frac{c}{b}P_h + \beta\frac{c}{a}) - \frac{cP_h}{b}\,\frac{\beta}{} = \frac{\beta}{a}(c + b\mu) \tag{2-28}$$

Substituting into (2-24) yields:

$$\text{Med}(g^0) = (\frac{cb}{2a} + \frac{P_h\mu}{\beta} - \frac{cP_h}{\beta}) + \frac{b}{\beta a}\left\{(\beta + 2P_h\mu\frac{a}{b} - cP_h\frac{a}{b})^2\right.$$
$$\left. + 4\beta\frac{a}{b}[\frac{\beta}{a}(c + b\mu) - (1 - c\mu)\frac{a}{b}P_h^2\frac{\mu}{\beta}]\right\}^{1/2} \tag{2-29}$$

which can be solved.

The example above is the simplest case I have found. For example, the Stone-Geary utility function yields equations in higher powers of g when a property tax is employed. In general, models relating votes on g to housing stocks tend to involve rather complex transforma-tions when utility functions are employed. These more complex density functions in g^0 will require numerical evaluation.

Other Sources of Variation in Tastes

In both of the above models, variation in preferences for g could be fully described by the marginal distributions for either h or λ. One broad class of models contains variation in residents' preferences independent of variation in available housing stocks. The discussion below indicates some of the issues in specifying such models. Often they implicitly involve the household location decision and why the reasons for the household's choice of zone.

Although preferences for g are likely to vary continuously over a wide range, only a relatively small number of jurisdictions are ordinarily available to choose from, and this restriction is an important source of variation in tastes independent of the amount of housing consumed. Under these circumstances, preferences in any one zone will not be completely homogeneous, even though house-holds stratify according to their preferences for g, as Tiebout and McGuire outline. Under their assumption, differences in preferences for g would exist within each zone even if all housing in every zone were the same. As the number of available jurisdictions is increased (or the underlying variation in utility functions is reduced), heterogeneity of tastes in each jurisdiction will be reduced.

A second source of variation in tastes arises from relocation costs. As relocation costs increase, households are more likely to find themselves in a jurisdiction in which public-sector decisions are not those they prefer. As residential composition, incomes, and tastes change over time, voting outcomes will vary as well. At any point in time, higher relocation costs imply greater variation in tastes among residents.

A third case arises from differences among households in their expectations regarding g prior to their move into a zone. The model described in which variation in housing consumed, h, represents variation in preferences, was a special case. Clearly, there may be many different bases for households' formation of expectations regarding g.

ZONING DECISIONS

In addition to determining government services and tax levels in a jurisdiction, its members make important decisions that affect the type of development of the zone. Zoning rules on minimum sizes for lots and structures, permissible amounts of rental property, and the nature of nonresidential development all may have important effects on the type of new construction undertaken, and hence, on the socioeconomic characteristics of incoming residents.

To describe how residents make decisions about zoning, several components of the housing development process must be described. Zoning rules affect the financial returns to various types of developments; with some time lag, development will occur in response to profit opportunities. The type of new housing in turn will influence the preferences of future residents for public services, and will affect tax burdens for all residents.

In the model below, the relationship between particular zoning rules and the rate or type of new construction is assumed to be exogenous. It is assumed that current residents can predict how any zoning rule will alter the course of new development. Only two time periods are considered, the present and the future. Current residents choose a zoning strategy that maximizes their welfare by majority vote, and with no influence exerted by developers or other interested parties.

The utility maximization decision for current residents is to choose that z which leads to a future g and an associated tax bill which maximizes current residents' welfare. Formulation of the voting outcome on a zoning policy is again a problem in change of variable. However, in this case two transformations must be considered. Let $f_z(h')$ denote the future housing stock, conditional on zoning policy z; $g'(z)$ is the outcome of the vote on g in the future; and $g'P_g(h) = g'\beta h/\mu'(z)$ is the tax bill for future government service g' to a future resident household with housing h. (The primes on g and h denote future outcomes.) To describe current residents' preferences for zoning strategies, z, requires that current voters predict future votes on g. Those predicted future votes, conditional on the current zoning decision, determine the level of g and tax burdens in the future. Thus, describing the outcome of the vote of current residents on zoning requires that future voting outcomes be predicted for each possible zoning decision, each of which involves a change-of-variable problem.

Two financing alternatives were considered in the previous section: a head tax and a housing property tax. The former is uninteresting for present purposes since its use removes all considerations of differential tax burdens; the objective of current residents would be to select that zoning strategy which results in entry by households who will vote for a level of g in the future identical with the preferences of current residents. The median voter today would in essence control the zoning outcome, and entry over time would therefore result in increasingly greater neighborhood homogeneity.

The case of property tax financing is more interesting. Here, a zoning policy that alters the distribution of housing stocks has two consequences: If mean house size, μ, is reduced, tax bills for existing residents per unit of g must rise. In addition, if preferences for g and h are positively correlated, the effect of lowering μ is a vote for a lower g. A zoning rule that lowered μ could not receive support. Conversely, an increase in μ through zoning increases the tax base, but also increases the amount of g voters will support. The "income effect" of lower tax bills may offset the loss in utility that residents (preferring a lower g) will sustain if a higher level of g is voted. Current residents who fall below the median μ before the zoning change may accept a higher level of g in the future because of the tax benefits of having neighbors with larger h.

These consequences can be described formally. Assume each zoning choice, z, yields a unique mean housing size in the future, μ'. Current residents therefore maximize utility with respect to μ'.

$$\max U(g, h, x, \lambda)$$

$$\text{Subject to: } Y = P_h h + P_x x + g(\mu') \frac{h\beta}{P_h \mu'}$$

For existing resident households, with given h and λ, utility maximization with respect to μ' requires:

$$\frac{dU}{d\mu} = \frac{\partial U}{\partial g'} \frac{\partial g'}{\partial \mu'} + \frac{\partial U}{\partial x'} \frac{\partial x'}{\partial \mu'} = 0 \qquad (2\text{-}30)$$

(This requires that $\partial g'/\partial \mu'$ and $\partial x'/\partial \mu'$ exist and are continuous and that the future vote on g varies continuously with the mean level of housing.) Since

$$x' = \frac{1}{P_x}[Y - P_h h - g'(\mu')\frac{h\beta}{P_h \mu'}]$$

(2-30) becomes:

$$\frac{\partial U}{\partial g'} \frac{\partial g'}{\partial \mu'} + \frac{\partial U}{\partial x'} \left\{ \frac{h\beta}{P_h P_x \mu'} \frac{\partial g}{\partial \mu'} - \frac{g'(\mu')}{\mu'}] \right\} = 0$$

$$\frac{\partial U}{\partial g'} / \frac{\partial U}{\partial x'} = -\frac{\partial x'}{\partial g'} = -\frac{h\beta}{P_h P_x \mu'} (1 - \frac{1}{\eta}) \qquad (2\text{-}31)$$

where η is the elasticity of g' with respect to μ'. The sign of the righthand side may be positive or negative, depending on whether η is less than or greater than unity. This result has a simple interpretation. If $\eta < 1$, an increase in μ' will allow current residents to acquire more x and more g. If both g and x have positive marginal utility, there would be unanimous support to increase μ as much as possible. (The amount by which μ could be increased would be determined by the amount of vacant land available and the willingness of those wanting large h to build in this jurisdiction.) Alternatively, if $\eta > 1$, the tax bill of current residents for any level of g will rise as μ rises, and less x can be purchased; current residents can enjoy more g only by giving up x. (It is possible that an increase in μ' actually leaves all current residents within their current budget opportunity locus. New residents contribute less to the tax bill facing current residents than they cost by voting a high g.)

While empirical results are far from conclusive on the nature of the relationship between μ and g, it is likely that at both extremes of the income distribution, the elasticity is less than one. In a neighborhood of low-income households, the entry of somewhat wealthier ones would not be likely to result in a vote for large increases in g. At the high end of the income distribution, private services are often a substitute for public services, and hence the elasticity of g with respect to μ is likely less than one for higher-income neighborhoods.

Figure 2-1 portrays the choices open to current residents before and after the zoning change. Several budget lines denoting choices between x and g for different households with different incomes are portrayed. The x intercepts depend on utility functions, incomes, and expectations, which together determine how large an h was initially purchased by each household. Property tax financing implies increasing tax burdens on households with larger h. The original problem of determining the vote on g amounts to analyzing the transformation from $f(h)$ to $G(g)$. For each zoning decision that increases μ, a higher g will be voted in the future. Each current resident therefore confronts a set of points above his current budget line. The locus of possible future voting outcomes on g, conditional on the zoning policy, are denoted by the BC curves. Each point on the BC curve for any current resident is derived from a prediction of the future vote under an alternative zoning policy. (It is assumed here that all can predict future votes.)

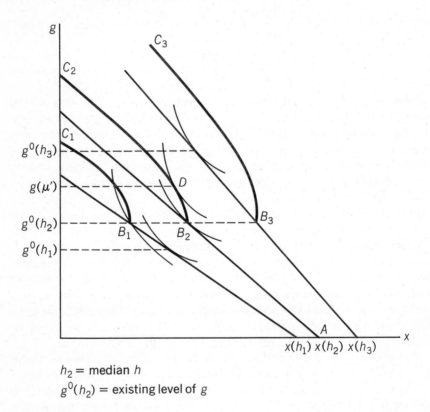

$h_2 =$ median h

$g^0(h_2) =$ existing level of g

Figure 2-1. Variation in Voter Preferences for Zoning Alternatives.

The zoning strategy adopted will be given by finding the median of current residents' preferences for μ', where each resident is choosing a point along his *BC* locus. It will be shown below that under certain assumptions the vote by current residents on g and their vote on μ' for the future can be represented by two distributions, one of which is a monotonic transformation of the other. Since this implies no change in order, the zoning vote is therefore given by the outcome preferred by the median voter from the existing distribution of h. In this case, it is the tangent point D of the indifference curve of the household, with h = median of the existing distribution $f(h)$, to the locus AB_2C_2. It should be noted that there are some residents with h below that of the median voter who are better off after the zoning change than at present, though they would have preferred a different zoning strategy than that selected. The household with h_1 is just indifferent to the outcomes before and after the zoning change.

There are two steps in the analytic development of such a model of zoning decisions. The first is to predict future votes on g (and hence tax burdens) conditional on each $f_z(h)$. This is in essence what was done in the preceding two sections. The second is to determine how current residents, who control the zoning decision, rank these possible outcomes. This involves specifying a utility function (or functions if variation in tastes is to be included).

The principal difficulty in predicting future voting outcomes conditional on any z is that the density function describing housing stocks is altered by the zoning action. Thus, even if the original $f(h)$ has a simple analytic shape—for example, normal—the new density function will differ. Likewise, if the density function describing voter preferences for g before the zoning change was normal, or had some other known form, making determination of the median of $G(g)$ simple, it will not be so after the zoning change.

There is one special case in which the determination of g^0 conditional on z is relatively simple, namely, when all new entrants have h *above* the new median. In this instance the new median g is determined solely by the *number* of new entrants (but not the size of h they occupy), and the shape of the original probability density function $g(g^0)$. If N is the original community size and there are to be N' new entrants, the new median is given by g', where

$$\int_0^{g'} g(g^0)\, dg = 0.5\left(1 + \frac{N'}{N}\right) \tag{2-32}$$

In this circumstance, current residents' preferences determine g'.

The more general case is that in which some new entrants prefer a level of *g* *below* that which is ultimately voted. In this case preferences of entrants help determine the voting outcome, and there is no substitute for calculating the new density function describing preferences for *g* and finding its median. For virtually any interesting specification of $f(h)$ for current residents, and preferences for *g* by incoming residents as related to h, the density function density $G(g')$ conditional on any z must be examined numerically. If future votes on *g* can only be described numerically (or if g' and μ' are complex functions in z), the transformation from h to z involved in describing current residents' preferences for z will itself be complex and require numerical examination.

One way in which the determination of z can be simplified is in the specification of how existing voters form expectations regarding future voting outcomes. Instead of deriving a solution for g' for every μ' based on utility maximization voting behavior for all households who will occupy the zone in the future, existing households' expectations might be represented in a more ad hoc fashion. In essence this simplifies the specification of the transformation from z to g', i.e., the description of the BC loci in Figure 2-1. If the BC loci can be described analytically, it may be possible to get a reasonable tractable statement of the transformation from h to z. One way to achieve this type of simplification is to base expectations regarding the future vote on *g* on the mean rather than the median of the distribution describing preferences. Future tax burdens will also be related to mean h in the future. If, further, preferences for *g* are linearly related to h and $P_g(h)$, and it is assumed that the household with $h = \mu'$ determines the future vote on *g*, g' is a linear function in μ'.

$$g^0 = a_0 + a_1 h + a_2 (\frac{\beta h}{\mu})$$

$$= a_1 + \mu' \quad a_1 + \frac{a_2 \beta}{\mu'} \quad = (a_0 + a_2\beta) + a_1\mu' \qquad (2\text{-}33)$$

$$= A_1 + A_2\mu'$$

Existing households (with fixed h and λ) would maximize $U[g'(\mu'),$ $x'(\mu'), h, \lambda]$ subject to μ', which would determine g and x in the future. Utility maximization would require:

$$\frac{U_g}{U_x} = -\frac{\partial x}{\partial \mu'} / \frac{\partial g}{\partial \mu'} = \frac{A_1 h\beta/P_x(\mu')^2}{A_2} = -\frac{A_1 h\beta}{A_2 P_x(\mu')^2} \qquad (2\text{-}34)$$

Depending on the choice of a utility function, Equation (2-34) may be complex, at least a quadratic in μ'. The simplest case is $U = a \ln g + bx$. In this case (2-34) becomes:

$$\frac{aA_2}{A_1 + A_2\mu'} = -\frac{bA_1h\beta}{A_2P_x(\mu')^2} \tag{2-35}$$

or

$$\mu' = \frac{A_1}{2aA_2P_x}[bh\beta + bh(g)^2 + 4ab\beta P_xh]^{1/2}$$

While this transformation from h to μ' yields a complex density function, it is monotonic since $d\mu'/dh > 0$ for all positive h. The solution to the zoning strategy is therefore given by solving (2-35) for the case where $h = \mu$.

CONCLUDING OBSERVATIONS: MODELING THE INTERACTIONS

In this study, I have taken up only one small part of the problem of the interactions between the housing market and the public sector, namely, ways of modeling the link from existing housing stocks in a jurisdiction to voting on public-sector decisions. The principal motivation for taking this partial-equilibrium approach is to abstract from the very many complexities of modeling all the interdependencies in the evolving process of housing market adjustments and household relocation over time. Large-scale simulation models are probably required to address many of the important general-equilibrium aspects of urban development processes.

Implicit in the approach of this paper is an endorsement of the importance of relatively fixed housing stocks and jurisdictional boundaries. The NBER urban simulation model (Ingram, Kain, Ginn 1972) is one large-scale model organized around the housing stock adaptation process. That model focuses on two sets of decisions over time; household relocation choices and incremental housing stock adaptations. In this study I suggest a third process to be modeled, again in incremental fashion: public-sector decision making in jurisdictions with essentially fixed boundaries and fixed stocks. Public-sector outcomes would in turn be one argument in the household relocation models, as well as affecting housing development processes via the zoning process.

Since the models above consider only how one jurisdiction behaves independent of events in all other jurisdictions, they are not well suited to addressing problems of tax capitalization. While there is a theoretical argument for public-sector decisions to be capitalized into property values, the nature of tax capitalization in any jurisdiction depends on outcomes in all other jurisdictions and on the distribution of household preferences. Depending on the degree of heterogeneity in tastes and households' willingness to move, housing and public-sector opportunities in one jurisdiction may or may not be regarded as a close substitute by residents of other jurisdictions. The extent to which alternative sites are regarded as substitutes will influence the extent to which particular decisions on public service and tax levels in any one area are capitalized into housing values there and in all other jurisdictions. An analytic solution of how public-sector decisions affect property values is, in short, a general-equilibrium problem as complex as that of determining how all households might arrange themselves among diverse housing units in different jurisdictions.

While the models in this chapter as an application of a standard change-of-variable problem are formally quite simple, unfortunately the transformation from a probability distribution describing housing stocks and tastes to one describing voter preferences generally proves to be quite complex analytically. Use of a property tax as a financing device results in a nonlinear budget constraint that virtually eliminates any hope of finding simple analytic results. The evaluation of density functions as a basis for predicting voting outcomes must be done numerically. However, if numerical evaluation is necessary, virtually any utility function and density functions can be employed.

There are other ingredients to a descriptive model of local-government decision making which should also be considered in extending these models. There will be other interested parties besides local residents who will affect outcomes. These include public-sector employees, merchants, developers, landholders, and (possibly) the outside sector. Objectives of these groups will differ. Public employees are likely to be concerned principally about employee compensation; for some, this will be wages, while those in a management role may be concerned about the size and growth of the public budget. Some merchants may favor a strategy that maximizes total community income, since this is likely to be a good proxy for retail sales. Other retailers may prefer a strategy that maximizes per capita income. Developers will prefer a strategy that maximizes the rate of growth and, probably, one (at least in most metropolitan areas) that allows more rather than fewer rental units, and high- rather than low-density single-family development.

The dynamics of the adjustment process of changing g are also important. Existing capital facilities, public budgets, and employee numbers are important constraints in the short run. For example, tenure and attrition rates in the labor force may be important constraints. Existing sewer and other public facilities may be long-lived capital stocks and a significant constraint on the types of additional capital that can be put in place in the future. A fully satisfactory model of local-government decisions must include these complexities.

REFERENCES

Barr, James L., and Otto A. Davis. 1966. "An Elementary Political and Economic Theory of the Expenditures of Local Government." *Southern Economic Journal*, October.

Borcherding, Thomas E., and Robert T. Deacon. 1972. "The Demand for Services of Non-Federal Governments." *American Economic Review*, December.

Bowen, Howard. 1943. "The Interpretation of Voting in the Allocation of Economic Resources." *Quarterly Journal of Economics*.

Buchanan, James, and Charles L. Goetz. 1972. "Efficiency Limits of Fiscal Mobility: An Assessment of the Tiebout Model." *Journal of Public Economics*.

Comanor, William S. 1974. "The Median Voter Rule and the Theory of Political Choice." Discussion Paper 346. Harvard Institute of Economic Research.

Hirsch, Werner. 1970. *The Economics of State and Local Government.* New York: McGraw-Hill.

Ingram, Gregory; John F. Kain; and J. Royce Ginn. 1972. *The Detroit Prototype of the NBER Urban Simulation Model.* New York: National Bureau of Economic Research.

McGuire, Martin. 1974. "Group Segregation and Optimal Jurisdictions." *Journal of Political Economy*, January-February.

Straszheim, Mahlon. 1975. *An Econometric Analysis of the Urban Housing Market.* New York: National Bureau of Economic Research.

Tiebout, Charles. 1956. "A Pure Theory of Public Expenditures." *Journal of Political Economy*, October.

✳ *Chapter Three*

Simultaneous Estimation of the Supply and Demand for Housing Location in a Multizoned Metropolitan Area

Katharine Bradbury, Robert Engle,
Owen Irvine, and Jerome Rothenberg

INTRODUCTION

In this chapter we report on work-in-progress of a research project designed to model the growth and internal composition of the Boston metropolitan area, and the location of household and business activities there. The overall model is an interlocking system of three submodels: (1) a "macro" model, determining the level and composition of economic activities in the area; (2) a household allocation model, determining the spatial distribution of the household population and housing unit supply over the area; (3) a business allocation model, determining the spatial distribution of business activity over the area.

This model was designed for use in policy analysis. Changes in the many policy variables in the model will lead to redistributions of economic activity within the metropolitan area and changes in growth patterns of the region. Comparison of alternative scenarios provides the information upon which policy judgments can be made. In order to satisfy this objective, it is important to formulate a behavioral model that incorporates a rich choice of meaningful policy alternatives.

Each of the three submodels incorporates its own set of policy

Note: This work has been supported by National Science Foundation Grant GS37010X, and previously by funds from the Ford Foundation. The authors express thanks to their colleagues on the project, John Harris, William Wheaton, and Frank Fisher for helpful suggestions at various stages of the research and to many previous graduate students who assisted in preliminary phases.

issues, which can be examined in isolation. In this study we present preliminary results only for the housing location submodel, but results from other submodels are described in Engle (1974a, 1974b, 1974c) and Engle et al. (1972). Because this is only a first stage in our efforts to formulate and estimate the complex relationships determining household location, we do not focus on the policy implications of our estimates. Instead, we report the present findings to give an indication of the promise that our special approach seems to hold and to suggest how policy variables will influence the spatial character of the metropolitan area.

The formulation of our behavioral model is based on three propositions about special characteristics of urban housing markets.

1. Urban housing is an extremely durable good that is spatially fixed. Therefore, the distribution of accommodations at a point in time will extend its influence into a distant future, and public policy can only gradually affect the spatial distribution of the stock of housing. A corollary to this proposition is that supply responses take two distinct forms: construction of new units and conversion (comprising physical modification, retirement, and demolition) of existing ones. Since conversion responses can occur at any time, and since they influence the profitability or desirability of the units, they are likely to be decided upon by owners on a continuing basis. Substantial modifications are therefore possible to the entire housing stock, making this conversion mode of supply response potentially very important in describing neighborhood evolution.

2. Housing is a package of elements, comprising not only structural features, but also land, neighborhood characteristics, local public services, and accessibility to desirable destinations within and outside the urban area. Decisions by economic agents, whether owners, landlords, neighbors, developers, or local government, only affect components of the overall housing package.

3. Differences within each type of component and among components matter significantly to households, and households differ in their tastes for various configurations of these components. Changes in the attributes of the housing package will therefore differ in their effect in attracting the spectrum of household types.

THE APPROACH

Many approaches have been used to model metropolitan household location. Early models based on gravity concepts of attraction between economic units proved unable to characterize the important behavioral balance between attraction and increasing costs as more agents desire the same location. More recently, large simulation models have been formulated (de Leeuw, Struyk, Marshall 1973; Ingram, Kain, Ginn 1972), which estimate some parameters of the model econometrically and then impose rather arbitrary market adjustment, supply response, or locational choice algorithms to close the system for simulation. Somewhat simpler models (Wheaton 1974; Harris, Nathanson, Rosenberg 1966), based on the equilibrium assumptions underlying the bid rent model, estimate closed systems for demand behavior but do not integrate this with supply and have some unattractive features; for example, vacancy rates are not included.

Our approach is to formulate a model that can be estimated econometrically from observed aggregate data. The model is based on appropriate and often testable behavioral assumptions concerning economic agents. In order to gain the luxury of estimates of all the parameters of demand functions, supply responses, and market adjustment functions, some simplifications must be made. We feel the latter do not impair the validity of the approach, and we present our preliminary estimates as evidence of its promise.

We model a demand for housing accommodation and its supply. Our critical focus is on the spatial distribution of housing; so the chief dimension of both demand and supply is the location of each accommodation. We divided the Boston metropolitan area into 89 zones: Boston itself is divided into 14 Boston Redevelopment Authority districts, and to this we added 75 surrounding cities and towns.

The location of any particular accommodation specifies many components of the housing package. For demanders the important dimensions of a location include the average types of structural units available, the physical environment of the zone, the demographic character of the neighborhood, the character of local shopping facilities, the variety, quality, and cost of available public services (parks, schools, health and sanitation services, streets, tax rates), and the accessibility to desirable destinations in the rest of the SMSA. For suppliers the location suggests prospects for revenues and costs associated with the provision of additional units of different types, since each location is characterized at a given time by specific prices and vacancy rates, on the one hand, and vacant land availability, zoning constraints, sewer systems, and stocks available for conversion, on the other.

The selection of political jurisdictions to represent locations is important. We aggregate to, but not beyond, the level of the political jurisdiction both because of data availability and because we believe the public service-tax component of the locational dimension is especially important to both the demand and supply sides. In addition, code and zoning regulations stem from the local governments and constitute significant constraints on housing supply options. The descriptive and theoretical literature suggests that fiscal federalism operates by self-selection of common-minded land users and their control of government instruments to cater to their common interests while excluding disparate groups. This self-selection process should impart a greater degree of homogeneity to land-use patterns within each political jurisdiction than would be expected on the basis of nonpolitical factors alone. Thus, the jurisdiction may furnish a tolerable degree of situational homogeneity to serve as the observational unit. Clearly, large cities and towns will be less homogeneous, and our segmentation of Boston is a recognition of this.

The demand for housing over zones is traced in terms of occupancy by low-, middle-, and high-income-family households. These three categories of demand serve to allocate the urban population over space in a partition that is not only interesting in itself because of its relevance to many socioeconomic problems and public policy issues, but is in a form that can be determined within our macro submodel. That submodel determines a household income distribution for the metropolitan area as a whole and thus provides a direct input into our household allocation submodel.

The three household groups are seen as competitors for the scarce resource of housing accommodations. Presumably all groups would prefer to locate in attractive zones with good public services and high accessibility. However, because of the heavy competition for the limited number of accommodations in such zones, prices of units there tend to rise high enough to restrict demand to be no greater than the number of units available (while allowing for a vacancy rate that reflects normal turnover of households among units). The aggregate demand curve is the sum of the different household-group demand curves.

If the price in a zone rises to ration relatively heavy demand, there will be incentives to suppliers to produce new units there either by new construction or by conversion of old units to new functions. The supply response is articulated both by mode—conversion or new construction—and by structural type—single-family units, units in multiunit structures (two to four units per structure), and units in apartment structures (more than five per structure). This breakdown is useful because new-construction technology differs along these lines, and the relative ease or difficulty of structural conversion of existing units is most probably linked to the structural type.

The geographic partition of demand and supply in effect treats the market for housing accommodations in each zone as a separate housing submarket. Various households demand units based in part upon the structural characteristics of the zone's average housing package and in part on a host of other zonal attributes, and the suppliers produce different quantities of units of differing structural types depending on the revenues and costs of supply in that zone both in absolute terms and relative to others. The difference between aggregate demand and aggregate supply for accommodations in a zone is the number of vacant units.

Each zone "clears" its housing market by a combination of price adjustment and quantity adjustment. We employ a vacancy rate to supplement price as a reflection of the market's current state. In a market characterized by durability, moving costs, and lumpy consumption (one unit per household), price does not adjust rapidly enough or far enough to clear the market in a reasonably short time. The market's immediate and moderate-term responses to excess demand are registered partly by movements in the vacancy rate. For example, in a tight market, prices may not rise far enough to choke off sufficient demand to clear the market (inclusive of a "normal" vacancy rate), so vacancy rate falls below the normal level. Alternatively, in periods of slack demand prices may not fall far enough to clear the market; then vacancy rates will rise above normal levels.

Vacancy rates supplement prices in influencing the behavior of demanders and suppliers. The higher the vacancy rate in a zone, the less search is necessary for a demander to find a suitable unit. High search costs discourage demand as do high zonal prices. For suppliers vacancy rates play two roles in defining expected revenues from additional units in different zones. First, the figure obtained by subtracting the vacancy rate from unity reflects the probability that an additional unit in the zone will be sold or rented; second, the rate points to future adjustments of price within that zonal market.

HOUSING DEMAND

Theoretical Foundations

We perceive the household choice to be the selection of a housing package designated by its zonal location. The package consists of a vector of housing structure and land characteristics, social environmental components, public-sector characteristics of the zone, and potential[1] accessibility from the zone to other desirable destinations in the SMSA. It is important to note that households do not deal directly in the land market; they demand housing accommodations, not land.

The structural and land characteristics of a zone's housing package are described in terms of average or representative units. Variables such as the percent of the units in a zone that are large, old, with luxury plumbing, or in apartment buildings describe the distribution of units. Similarly, the population density suggests the typical amount of land input per unit. These summary measures of course fail to capture the entire distribution of actual occupancies; for example, small houses exist in neighborhoods that have mostly large units, leading to some demand in a zone by household types that prefer small units. Although these observations should average out for large groups of individuals, they may of course be responsible for some noise in the estimates. However, in general, it will be true, for example, that high-income families will demand accommodation in zones that contain a relatively high proportion of luxury units, because the zonal average indicates both their probable own accommodation choice and the probable character of their neighbors.

A second class of components refers to the social environment of the zone, i.e., the nature of the residents and of their zonal occupancy. We characterize the former by the percent of the zonal population that is nonwhite and the percent on welfare; the latter, by the residential population density (population per acre). Another variable, the crime rate, refers partly to the social environment and partly to local public-sector activity.

The third class of components, local public-sector activity, is reflected by the pupil-teacher ratio in the school systems and the effective real estate tax rate. It is through variables such as these that local public policy has its primary effect on the demand for housing.

The fourth class of components of the housing package refers to accessibility. We define accessibility of a zone to be inversely related to the anticipated real cost of travel by residents of that zone. For each zone the expected real cost to a destination depends upon the location of the latter and the nature of the transportation network. Different household types have different destinations and different modal choices. The measurement of accessibility is complicated by the facts that the identity of each zone's inhabitants is not determined until *after* the locational choice has been made and that some systematic forms of self-selection occur. So the pattern and real cost of trips is a probabilistic matter. Accordingly, in order to capture some sense of this complexity we have constructed a number of accessibility indexes: a general job accessibility index by income class in which destinations and their probable importance in measures of the relative frequency of trips, distance, and economic cost per trip are integrated in weighted form; an index of highway availability;

and an index of transit availability (not shown in the present results).

This vector of average structural, social environmental, public-sector, and accessibility components constitutes the zonal housing package. Housing choices are influenced, but not exclusively so, by the nature of the package available in each zone. The choices depend as well on the income level of the household which simultaneously determines the preferences for different housing package configurations and the desirable tradeoffs between housing and nonhousing commodities. Finally, the choices depend on the prices of the different housing packages available, including the cost of finding a suitable unit. In summary, an array of different zonal housing packages is available to any household. The packages differ in their attractiveness, which depends partly on the income class of the household. They differ also in prices, the sensitivity to which also depends partly on income class. The household balances off relative attractiveness with relative price and selects the best compromise.

Income level is handled in our model in a way that illuminates our prime interest in the spatial distribution of the population. Each demand function is formulated as the determination of the share of each SMSA family income class that is located in each zone. We have a separate zonal location demand function for each of the three income classes—high, middle, and low—into which we partition family households. An observation involves use of the set of attributes and relative prices of a given zone as explanatory variables to predict the percent of each SMSA family income class that will reside in that zone.

Price has a special role to play in this formulation. Only because prices differ from one zone to another can we understand the location of the low-income families in the most unattractive zones. A simple correlation between the location of low-income households and zonal attributes would suggest that low-income households love dilapidated housing. This conclusion is however a "reduced form" result. It indicates that once the demand and supply equations are solved—and that is what takes place in the real world process of competition for scarce attractive housing packages—low-income groups get what is left over because groups with more market power have already taken their pick.

In our structural model, the tradeoff between price, zonal search costs, and the attributes of the zonal housing package determine which income group finally locates in a particular zone. Coefficients on zonal attributes for the different household groups reflect relative group preferences for the attribute combined with the group's relative willingness to exchange money for preferred housing accommodations. It is these differences in the pattern of coefficients among income classes which lead to that critical characteristic of U.S. metropolitan areas, the sharp socioeconomic segmentation of residential neighborhoods and even political jurisdictions.

The specification of the demand for housing determines the number of occupants as a function of market price and vacancy rate as well as attributes, as in many conventional Walrasian demand functions. The attributes serve essentially to define the commodity and its quality, and the vacancy rate serves as an aspect of the real price of the commodity to the user.

To make clear the connection between our approach and a variety of others, which we shall characterize as perfect market models, let us denote the bid by group i for housing in a particular zone j as P_j^i. This bid may differ from the market price. It will depend on the attributes, X, of the zone through an implicit bid rent function specific to the particular group:

$$P_j^i = g^i(X_j) \tag{3-1}$$

This formulation makes it possible for different user groups to evaluate the same attributes differently according to their own utility functions and budget constraints.

Since each user will buy one and only one location, unlike the conventional demand theory with multiple commodities, that single locational choice will be based on the competitive bidding of the different users for the finite set of locations—the existing set of accommodations available in the several zones at any time.

In a perfect market the highest-bidding group will win the accommodations in each zone, and the winning bid will become the zone's market price. If the actual number of accommodations in the zone exceeds the number wanted by the highest-bidding group, the remainder will go to the group offering the next highest bid, and the market price will be that lower price of the group of second highest bidders that actually occupies some of the zone's accommodations. If the actual number of units falls short of the number desired by the highest-bidding group, the excess of users will settle in other zones where they are either highest or second highest in zones that have excess accommodation. Shortages in the first zone will force the group to raise its whole set of bid prices in its competition to allocate first and second choices among its members. Each set of bid prices implies a different utility level for the group: the higher the bid, the lower the utility. All users are allocated to one zone or another in this way. In any zone where they reside the zone's market price will either equal or be less than their bid price.

From the above, the market price in a zone (supposing all accommodations to be homogeneous) depends on the number of accommodations available relative to demands for them. The former depends on past and near-present supply decisions. A zone that would have been the first choice of a given group if it had had enough units available to keep the price down, may drop to second or lower choice if it has a smaller number of units permitting the price to be considerably higher.

Thus, the demand function for a given group i can be given as a function of both the group's bid and the zone's market price:

Number of occupants in zone j from group $i = f(P_j, P_j^i)$ $\qquad$ (3-2)

Then $P_j = P_j^i$ for the occupying group in each zone. For that same group $P_k > P_k^i$ in every other zone. Thus, a perfect market would imply that function f (in Equation (3-2)) should be a step function: for $P_j = P_j^i$, the whole group locates in j; for $P_j > P_j^i$, no member of the group locates there.[2] In a perfect market, the long-run supply response to different zones equalizes rates of return to suppliers, setting relative numbers of units that influence household choices. Under certain conditions (as when additional housing packages, which include density and other nonstructural zonal attributes, can be supplied at constant costs) each zone will be homogeneous with respect to users.

Our treatment diverges somewhat from this procedure. First, in our model, supply is taken as jointly determined with prices and demand, but we do not assume that our observations reflect long-run supply equilibrium. Relative numbers of units available in the different zones do not establish perfect user homogeneity. Thus, for any zone, competition results in $P_j \leqslant P_j^i$ for user groups. Second, we do not assume that all users are in their long-run equilibrium. The high cost of changing occupancy prevents users from being in perfect adjustment to relative prices in the different zones at every moment.

Third, we introduce vacancy rates as a market adjustment variable. At any time a market-clearing identity is fulfilled:

Number of units available in zone j = $\sum\limits_{i}$ (number of households of group i) + vacant units $\qquad$ (3-3)

As noted earlier, we assume that price does not adjust rapidly to market changes; so vacancy rates represent a residual adjustment and, together with price, act therefore as a pair of indicators of the current state of the market; furthermore, they reflect the cost of search for appropriate housing units in a zone and so are a genuine part of the real price of housing there.

Finally, our model deals with accommodations that are not uniform in each zone, but are varied. Members of different groups can find different kinds of accommodation in the same zone.

For all these reasons we estimate each group's demand function as a continuous function of market price, vacancy rate, and implicit bid price, i.e., the g^i function of zonal attributes is

Number of occupants in zone j from group $i = f*(P_j, VR_j, P_j^i)$ (3-4)
$= f*[P_j, VR_j, g^i(X_j)]$

Empirical Results

The demand by a particular household group for housing in a particular zone depends upon the zonal housing package attributes, the cost of the search necessary to find a suitable unit in the zone, and the price level prevailing there. It also depends, however, upon the prices, search costs, and attributes of other zones that are close substitutes for the given zone. In general, the demand in any zone must depend upon all the prices, costs of search, and housing package attributes in all other zones. Unfortunately, the strength of the cross elasticities varies endogenously. As a simple first solution, the price, search costs, and attributes of each zone were taken relative to the SMSA average for each variable.[3]

The price variable is designed to be the price per unit of a standard accommodation in a zone. Using actual sales data, price indexes for each zone were constructed by a regression method described in Bailey, Muth, Nourse (1963) and illustrated with the same data in Engle (1977). This method eliminates the need to identify the standard unit, but hinges on the assumption that different types of units in a zone experience similar rates of price change. Tests of this hypothesis were generally accepted. Because this price series is an index, it is only possible to determine the rates of change of prices in different zones. The model is therefore estimated in rate-of-change form.[4]

The model as described above can be formalized by a series of demand functions for each family income group:

$$D_z^y/\overline{D}^y = D^y (A_z^1/\overline{A}^1, A_z^2/\overline{A}^2, A_z^3/\overline{A}^3, A_z^4/\overline{A}^4, P_z/\overline{P}, V_z/\overline{V}) \qquad (3\text{-}5)$$

where D_z^y is the number of households of income y who demand location in zone z, and D represents the SMSA average. A^1, A^2, A^3, A^4 are the vectors of components of the zonal housing package corresponding to structural and land attributes, social environment, public service tax, and accessibility, as described earlier; P_z is the zonal price; and V_z, the initial zonal housing unit vacancy rate, which is a measure of search costs; and A^{-1}, A^{-2}, ..., V are the SMSA means. Because the available price variable is an index of price changes, the model was estimated in terms of decadal differences. A linear form was chosen as a trial specification. Two-stage least squares (TSLS) was used to estimate the coefficients of the equations because of the simultaneous nature of a number of the right-hand variables. The change in price, the change in all the structural attributes, the change in population density ($\Delta POPDEN$), the change in the percent nonwhite ($\Delta BLACK$), and the change in the percent of households on welfare ($\Delta WELFARE$), were all treated as endogenous.

The estimated coefficients for the *LOW-*, *MIDDLE-*, and *HIGH-* income family household groups are shown in Table 3-1, with all the variables defined in detail in Appendix 3A. As noted earlier, the sample consists of the 89 zones of the Boston SMSA. Asymptotic standard errors and other diagnostic information are presented for each equation.

These preliminary results display an encouraging degree of consistency with theoretical expectations. The a priori expectations for the signs of the coefficients are displayed in Table 3-1. In 80 percent of the cases, these are satisfied and in only two cases are the expectations rejected at the 95 percent level for a one-tailed asymptotic test. The coefficients themselves are elasticities: a coefficient of 0.5 in Table 3-1 means that if the zone were to increase its relative supply of the attribute by 1.0 percent, the zone's share of that income group would increase by 0.5 percent.

All three estimated coefficients in the price change variable, $\Delta PRICE$, are negative—as economic theory would lead us to believe a priori. The standard errors of this variable, however, are large, making the confidence intervals wide. It is interesting to note that low-income families are much more sensitive to the price of the housing package than either of the two other income groups. This is reasonable, considering that many households in this group are living in poverty. Another complicating factor contributing to these results is that many members of the two upper-income groups are homeowners rather than renters. A homeowner, viewing his house as an investment as well as a consumption good, may desire to purchase a unit in a zone where prices are rising rapidly, with a view to capturing future capital gains.

Each zonal housing market is viewed as adjusting itself through both price and quantity variations in all but the very long run. Excess zonal demands or supplies are registered by movements in both the

Table 3-1.   Estimates of Household Demand Equations by Two-Stage Least Squares[a] (figures in parentheses are asymptotic standard errors)

Symbol	Type	A Priori Expected Sign			Estimated Coefficients		
		Low	Middle	High	Low	Middle	High
$\Delta PRICE$	Endog.	–	–	–	–.49 (.35)	–.20 (.26)	–.19 (.58)
$VACRATE_{60}$	Exog.	+	+	+	–.06 (.06)	.11* (.04)	.24* (.09)
$\Delta BATHROOMS$	Endog.	+	+	+	–.01 (.10)	.26* (.08)	.74* (.17)
$\Delta LARGE$	Endog.	+	+	+	.02 (.19)	–.30* (.15)	–.41 (.32)
OLD_{60}	Exog.	–	–	–	–.09 (.14)	–.20* (.11)	–.62* (.23)
$\Delta POPDEN$	Endog.	–	–	–	–.02 (.03)	–.02 (.03)	–.08 (.06)
$BLACK_{60}$	Exog.	?	–	–	.05* (.03)	–.05* (.02)	–.09* (.04)
$\Delta BLACK$	Endog.	?	–	–	.08* (.03)	–.06* (.03)	–.14* (.06)
$\Delta WELFARE$	Endog.	+	–	–	.05 (.06)	–.07* (.04)	.04 (.09)
$CRIME_{70}$[b]	Exog.	–	–	–	–.04 (.04)	–.03 (.03)	–.17* (.07)
$\Delta EFFTAX$	Exog.	–	–	–	–.08 (.12)	–.02 (.09)	–.21 (.20)
$\Delta PTRATIO$	Exog.	–	–	–	–.31* (.12)	–.01 (.09)	–.07 (.20)
$\Delta JOBACC$	Exog.	–	–	–	–.47* (.22)	.37* (.16)	.27 (.38)
$\Delta HIGHWAY$	Exog.	–	–	–	–.002 (.07)	–.05 (.05)	–.23* (.12)
Constant					.63 (.33)	.37 (.25)	.83 (.55)
R^2					0.39	0.50	0.52
SSR					2.13	1.24	5.87
SE					0.17	0.13	0.28

Notes

R^2 = coefficient of multiple determination.
SSR = sum of squared residuals.

SE = standard error of the regression.
*Significant at 5 percent level in one-tailed asymptotic test.

[a]The instruments used with the endogenous variables were the exogenous variables of the supply equations and the 1960 predetermined values of the endogenous variables. Except as noted, all variables are 1960-1970 changes in ratios to the SMSA means.

[b]The 1970 level relative to the SMSA was used because 1960 data were lacking.

zonal price and the zonal vacancy rate. The zonal vacancy rate for the beginning of the decade, $VAC\ RATE_{60}$, is included in the demand equations. The $VAC\ RATE_{60}$ coefficients increase in size from the LOW equation, in which the coefficient is insignificant and negative, through the $HIGH$ one. This is consistent with the higher opportunity costs of search for high-income households. In the equations for $HIGH$- and $MIDDLE$-income families, the estimated coefficients on $VAC\ RATE_{60}$ are positive, as we expected on the basis of a priori economic theory concerning the costs of search, and they are statistically quite significant.

Four structural attributes were utilized in these preliminary regressions: the percent of a zone's units that are large (7 rooms or more), $\triangle LARGE$; the percent of a zone's units that are over thirty years old, OLD_{60} the percent of a zone's units that have more than one bathroom, $\triangle BATHROOMS$; and the population density $\triangle POPDEN$. The coefficients on $\triangle BATHROOMS$ increase in size from the LOW to the $HIGH$ equation, supporting the a priori expectation of a much stronger preference for more luxurious and larger units by higher-income families. The coefficients in $MIDDLE$ and $HIGH$ are not only large in absolute size, but are also statistically very significant; the one in $HIGH$ (0.74) is, in addition, the most economically and statistically significant coefficient in the $HIGH$-income equation.

The coefficients on OLD_{60} are all negative, consistent with our a priori assumption that households prefer newer units, ceteris paribus; and the values increase from LOW to $HIGH$, again as expected. The coefficients in $MIDDLE$ and $HIGH$ are statistically fairly significant and are, in addition, among the largest in absolute size. Indeed, the variables characterizing the structural components of the zonal housing package plays a very important role in our estimated demand equations.

Population density, $\triangle POPDEN$, also proved to be an important variable: all the signs are negative, as expected, and increase in absolute size from the LOW to the $HIGH$ equation, supporting our hypothesis that the higher the family's income, the stronger its preference for low density. This observed preference of high-income families for space partially explains the presence of the high-income suburban ring so common in U.S. metropolitan areas.

All four of the social environmental attributes were found to be significant in one or more of the equations. The percent of nonwhite households in a zone was included to capture the preference of whites to live segregated from nonwhites. Both the percent nonwhite at the beginning of the decade, $BLACK_{60}$, and the change in the percent nonwhite, $\triangle BLACK$ (treated as endogenous), were included, and their estimated coefficients turned out to be statistically significant in all three equations. The signs on both variables were positive in the equation for *LOW*-income families, reflecting the high proportion of nonwhites in this group: the majority of nonwhite households in the Boston SMSA are of low income.[5] The coefficients of both variables are negative in the *MIDDLE* and *HIGH* equations, strongly confirming the preference for segregation by Boston SMSA whites; and the larger negative coefficients on both variables in the *HIGH* equation imply that this preference is more intense among higher-income whites. It is noteworthy that the preference appears quite strongly even when we control for the higher welfare population, higher tax rates, poorer schools, and higher crime rates of the central city—conditions often cited as reasons for the flight by whites to the segregated suburban communities.

Approximately 65.6 percent of the low-income households were on welfare in 1970. Therefore, it was expected that the coefficient on the percent of a zone's households on welfare, $\triangle WELFARE$, would be positive in the *LOW* equation. The results partially support the hypothesis that the existence of a large welfare population in a zone constitutes a "negative externality" to middle- and high-income families independent of the fiscal burden caused by their presence and independent of the crime rate to which a large welfare population may contribute disproportionately. A priori, all family households were expected to prefer low relative crime rates. This was supported by the negatively signed coefficients on $CRIME_{70}$ obtained in all the estimated equations.

The local public service variables also proved significant. The importance of the quality of the local public schools to the zonal housing package is supported by our results. All three estimated coefficients on $\triangle PTRATIO$ were negative, as expected, as were those for local effective tax rates. High-income families seem to be the most sensitive to (or most adept at avoiding) high relative tax rates.

A priori, we expected that households at all income levels would prefer more accessibility to less. The higher the relative value of the general job accessibility index, $\triangle JOBACC$, the lower is the zone's accessibility. Therefore, a negatively signed coefficient was expected. Some urban economists have argued that the poor have the strongest preferences for accessibility. However, the rich would seem to incur the highest opportunity cost for their time spent in commuting. Therefore, the expected pattern of the size of the coefficients on $\triangle JOBACC$ was uncertain. As can be seen from Table 3-1, low-income families do prefer locations that are highly accessible to their jobs. The positive coefficients in the *MIDDLE* and *HIGH* equations suggest that these households are less averse to job travel than we expected. We are investigating this further with improved accessibility measures.

The negatively signed estimated coefficients on the highway index in all three equations suggest that the negative externalities generated by highways crossing a zone are important. The absolute size of the coefficients increases with the income level of the household, as expected, i.e., high-income families are the most sensitive to the negative externalities generated by highways. The automobile is the major source of pollution and congestion in the Boston SMSA; these results suggest that all households are sensitive to the externalities it generates. To evaluate this interpretation, more recent work is designed to disclose whether the highway variable reflects negative externalities mostly, or some composite of such externalities and facets of accessibility.

THE SUPPLY OF HOUSING

Our model of housing supply focuses on the number of housing units made available to households in a zone and their structural type (in terms of units per structure). In effect, we are modeling the behavior of two basic types of housing supplier: builders of new units and owners of existing ones. Conversion supply is given parity with new construction, but with expectations that the determinants of the two will differ to some extent.

Suppliers of housing presumably compare the present values of revenues and costs when deciding upon a housing investment just as would an investor in any other enterprise. The quantity and type of housing forthcoming in any zone in a particular period will be related to the costs and revenues of producing these units at the particular location. A careful analysis of these costs and revenues for different structural types and modes of supply provides the structural model behind the supply equations.

The decision to supply a unit of housing is a decision to combine factors of production, such as capital, labor, land, and possibly an existing structure which can be converted, to produce a "new" unit. The amount of housing produced in a zone will therefore depend on the price and possibly the quantity of the factors available in the zone, and on the final selling price of housing. Because capital and labor are equally available at all zones in an SMSA and approximately at the same price (except perhaps for the availability of credit to the ghetto), the major differences across zones will be in output prices and in factors relating to land and to conversion of existing structures.

We begin our exposition of the housing supply model with a discussion of new construction and of how the land market interacts with new-supply decisions. Then the determination of the structural type of new units is analyzed. Finally, a model of conversion supply is proposed and estimated. This separate treatment should not obliterate the fact that these sources and types of housing supply interact and compete in and across all zones, both in the input markets and in the housing market as a whole, where consumers are faced with the full array of sources and types of units.

New Construction

The most important input price variation for producers of new housing units in a metropolitan area is the price of land. The locational variation in the price of land is the central focus of much of the literature on urban land use and is important in our housing supply model as well. Alonso (1960, 1965) and others (Richard Muth, Edwin Mills, Lowdon Wingo) have developed models in which competition among different kinds of users for scarce urban land determines the price of land in each location and the allocation of land among user types. The starting assumption of the models is that the only differences in the marginal revenue productivity of different locations in an urban area are due to distance to a central market, whose proximity is valued differently by different users. The models then predict concentric rings of land devoted to different urban uses, and declining densities of any use as distance from the center increases.

But metropolitan development does not take place literally as these land use models depict, with all land in a given annulus used up (at varying densities) before the next annulus is bid away from the (given base-price) agricultural use. In fact, we observe parcels of undeveloped vacant land at all distances from the "center," and the percent vacant varies in a systematic way, increasing with distance from the center. The price of this vacant land, other than at the very edge of the urban area, is certainly not zero (or some constant agricultural price). The price reflects the price of comparable (in a locational sense) developed land, and hence relates to alternative uses to which a lot could be put.

To understand the existence of vacant parcels in any annulus within the urban area, we must assume that some of the demand (for the fixed amount of land in the annulus) is by demanders who choose not to develop the land to whatever its most profitable current use is. Vacant land yields no revenue in the present, and in fact is liable to taxes; yet buyers hold it vacant. These buyers are willing to pay as much as producers who turn it to revenue-yielding purposes (or if they already hold it vacant, they are willing to resist such bids by producers). It must be that they expect other returns. Specifically, holders of vacant land speculate on rising land values. When these speculators choose to "cash in" their capital gains, they can be seen as suppliers of vacant land to producers of housing or nonresidential services. If speculators' reservation prices (below which they wish to hold land vacant) are distributed randomly (perhaps because of risk preferences and expectations), then the land supply curve has its usual upward slope: the lower the market price, the larger the number of speculators whose reservation price is not exceeded, hence, who hold land. Taxes on land value will reinforce this slope, since they increase carrying costs of holding land vacant as its price rises.

As demand by other land users in the annulus grows, the opportunity cost of holding land vacant is higher, and hence less of it is held. "Other" demand for land is derived from business use, use by the public sector and other institutions, and residential land use. We expect this derived demand for land in any one location (or annulus) to be quite price-elastic, since close substitutes (nearby parcels) exist. Therefore, demanders arbitrage across land markets to keep prices in line with marginal revenue productivity (which depends on "accessibility" in the eyes of the highest bidder). As a result, we observe that the curves of land prices and land use densities predicted by land use models decline as we move away from the center and the shares of vacant land increase. As population or income in an urban area grows over time, the derived demand for land in all uses increases. As a result, more and more land is absorbed into the urban fringe, *and* vacant land within the developed urban area declines. The metropolitan area develops simultaneously out *and* up, extensively and intensively.

In the context of this housing supply model, each "location" to which the analysis is applied is a city, town, district with fixed total land area. In each zone, speculators are assumed to behave in the same way, "supplying" increasing fractions of the total land to other uses as demand (hence price) increases. Thus a relation in which the price of land is a decreasing function of share of land vacant is assumed to hold across towns. This assumption does not imply that holders of vacant land control the price of land, for in fact the price is the outcome of interaction among all land users who are in the market for land. Rather, this speculation model is chosen as a useful way to look at "land supply" to housing producers and others. Similar stories can be told for subdivision of occupied lots, reclamation of marginal acreage, and many other forms of land supply. The outcome of this approach is that the percent of vacant land is a good indicator of the price of land.

Other inputs into new housing production may be limited for the whole urban area, but each zone is a small part of that area and hence suppliers can be considered to perceive these inputs as perfectly elastically supplied.

We model new housing as produced by a competitive industry with a production function having constant returns to scale:

$$Q = Q(L, N) \tag{3-6}$$

where Q is total housing units produced and L and N are the amount of land and nonland inputs, respectively. This production function implies a relationship between output price and factor prices:

$$p = p(r, n) \tag{3-7}$$

where r and n are the price of land and nonland inputs, respectively, and p is the price of a unit of housing.

If the elasticity of substitution between land and nonland inputs in the production of housing is not zero, producers will use less land and more nonland inputs to produce a unit of housing where land price is higher. Consequently, the land input per housing unit is a function of the price of land (or really the factor price ratio):

$$L/Q \equiv m = m(r/n) \text{ or } L = m(r/n)Q \tag{3-8}$$

where L is total land used by housing suppliers and, hence, m is the land per unit, or lot size.

In the previous section we developed the proposition that the price of land can be expressed as a function of the fraction "developed," i.e.,

$$r = r(V/T) = r(\text{v}) = r[(T - L - J)/T] \tag{3-9}$$

where T is total land area in a town; J, land area previously developed; V, the amount vacant; $v \equiv V/T$. For simplicity this function is often assumed to have a constant elasticity.

If all these functions are well-behaved, then from (3-7), (3-8), and (3-9) we can derive a "supply function" for housing in each town which relates quantity produced to output price, incorporating the effect of land development on the factor input price:

$$p = f(Q/T) \quad \text{or} \quad Q/T = s(p) = f^{-1}(p) \tag{3-10}$$

Q/T can be thought of as gross residential density or, more simply, as a quantity of output along a supply curve that has been standardized for the size of city or town. The price of land rises as more land in a town is developed. For the housing new construction industry, this rising factor supply schedule causes supply to be an increasing function of price, in spite of constant returns to scale in production.

The shape of this supply curve depends crucially upon two of the underlying relationships: the responsiveness of lot size (and hence total derived demand for land at any output level) to changes in the price of land and the responsiveness of the price of land to changes in the quantity developed (or demanded) by housing producers.

Taking percent derivatives of supply equation (3-10) at a point, we obtain the relationship between output prices and quantities given by Muth (1974, p. 228):

$$\frac{dQ}{Q} = \frac{k_N \sigma + e_L}{k_L} \frac{dp}{p} \tag{3-11}$$

where k_N and k_L are the factor shares, e_L is the price elasticity of land supply, σ is the elasticity of substitution between the factors of production, and the prices of nonland inputs are held constant. If $\sigma = 1$, the factor shares are constant, and the price elasticity of housing supply varies with the price elasticity of the supply of land for new construction. The speculation model of vacant land release suggests that the price elasticity of the residential land supply varies directly with the supply of vacant land. Thus we would expect housing to be more elastically supplied in the suburbs than in dense central-city areas. Our econometric specification must recognize this variation in elasticity across the metropolitan area.

If $\sigma < 1$ (Muth 1969, pp. 82-83 and 315, offers support for this hypothesis) the factor shares are a function of factor prices, and share of land in housing will be greater in the city center than in the suburban fringe of a metropolitan area, where land is less expensive. Thus, in the non-Cobb-Douglas case, the implication of Equation (3-11) is that there is a second factor contributing to the higher price elasticity of housing supply in the less-developed areas of the metropolitan region: The effect of the lower price elasticity of land supply is augmented by the greater sensitivity of output price to land price (higher land share) in producing a lower price elasticity of housing supply in more central parts of the urban area.

An additional element that varies among zones and directly affects the new housing production function is the amount of land in other uses. It has the same effects on the price and elasticity of the supply of land as does the amount of land consumed by housing producers. Housing producers in a town with increasing "other land use" face higher land prices, ceteris paribus, according to (3-9). Thus we need to include in (3-11) a term reflecting any shifts in the land supply curve during the decade. (Differing initial conditions are captured by the initial supply elasticity of land.) The appropriate form for this equation has also been derived by Muth (1974) and is

$$\frac{dQ}{Q} = \frac{k_N \sigma + e_L}{k_L} \frac{dp}{p} + e_{L,J} \frac{dJ}{J} \tag{3-12}$$

where $e_{L,J}$ is the elasticity of supply of L with respect to J (other land use), and dJ/J is the percent change in J. The greater the increase in other land use, the less land there is available to housing producers, hence the less housing production, ceteris paribus. When we assume a constant elasticity in (3-9) the second term in (3-12) simplifies to dJ/L.

The foregoing are not the only factors that impinge on the supply of new housing in a metropolitan area. Because of the lags that characterize adjustments in housing market price and quantity and the unitary character of purchases or leases (one household to one housing unit), vacancy rates are an important adjustment mechanism in equating housing supply and demand. Thus builders of new units can be expected to use vacancy rate changes as indicators of the direction of future price movements. Since occupancy rates are almost never 100 percent, they also indicate the probability of actually selling or leasing a unit when it is made available on the market. Both of these points suggest that when vacancy rates are high or rising, producers will be discouraged from adding to the housing stock.

Within the separate jurisdictions of a metropolitan area, there are also important government interventions into the operations of the housing market. Cities and towns in a metropolitan area have various zoning policy tools at their disposal to try to control or direct the residential and nonresidential development of the jurisdiction. Municipalities can zone limited areas for business and commercial use, set up residential subareas with differing maximum density limits (height, frontage, lot size), and grant or withhold variances to the rules they establish. Such regulations may simply cause producers to put units they would have built anyway into spatially contiguous homogeneous subareas, or the effect may actually be to restrict some kinds of housing production in the zone. If producers are prevented from using the land-per-unit ratio of their choice, their profits may be reduced, and one would expect less housing production. Zoning regulations on minimum lot size, for example, when binding, reduce the amount of effective land available to producers.

From (3-11) and the additional factors discussed above, we derive a supply equation for new construction to be estimated econometrically:

$$\frac{dQ}{Q} = a_0 + a_1 \left[f(v) \frac{dp}{p} \right] + a_2 \frac{dJ}{L} + a_3 \frac{d\ VAC\ RATE}{VAC\ RATE} + a_4\ OPEN + \epsilon$$

$$(3\text{-}13)$$

where Q, v, p, J, and L are defined as above, $d\ VAC\ RATE/VAC\ RATE$ is the percent change in the housing unit vacancy rate, and $OPEN$ is the fraction of land in the town which is both vacant and not restricted to minimum lot sizes greater than 25,000 square feet. The function f represents the relationship between percent land vacant and the parameters discussed earlier that enter the price elasticity term: the elasticity of substitution, the factor shares, and the elasticity of land supply. Although we know that $f(v)$ is an increasing function we do not know its exact functional form. For simplicity we assume that f depends on the ratio of vacant land to residential land at the beginning of the period. Therefore, we expect a_1 and a_4 to be positive and a_2 and a_3 to be negative.

The supply relation was estimated using decadal percent changes in the number of housing units in a cross section of 89 Boston metropolitan area subregions. The equation is estimated by TSLS, with prices and vacancy rates treated as endogenous. The instruments are taken from the demand equation. Because the equation is nonlinear in the variables, nonlinear functions of the exogenous variables are also valid instruments, and several of these are used.

The estimated equation with asymptotic standard errors is given below; complete definitions of the variables are given in the appendix:

$$\frac{NEW\ TOTAL}{TOTAL_{60}} = \frac{.116}{(.0278)} + \frac{.0713}{(.0116)}$$

$$* \frac{VACANT\ ACRES_{60}}{RESIDENTIAL\ ACRES_{60}} \frac{\Delta PRICE}{PRICE_{60}}$$

$$- \frac{.172}{(.118)} * \frac{\Delta \; OTHER \; ACRES}{RESIDENTIAL \; ACRES_{60}} - \frac{.125}{(.0384)}$$

$$* \frac{\Delta(VAC \; RATE)}{VAC \; RATE_{60}} + \frac{.199}{(.106)} OPEN + e$$

The standard error of the regression = 0.13; R^2 = 0.4358. The overall fit of the equation is reasonable, the individual coefficients have small standard errors, and the signs are as expected. In particular, the t ratios on the price elasticity and vacancy rate are quite large.

The estimates imply price elasticities of new housing supply that range from 0.87 in the open suburbs to almost zero (0.0007) in the dense center city. In addition, new housing will be forthcoming as vacancy rates are decreased; so the net response due to changing demand conditions will be felt through both price and quantity measures. Alternative land uses do appear to compete strongly for land and will act to discourage new supply. The availability of vacant land that does not face zoning restrictions will lead to new construction.

Structural Types of New Construction

Having proposed and estimated a model of new-construction supply of housing units for geographic zones in a metropolitan area, we turn now to a careful examination of structural types in new housing. Where the price of land is higher (across zones or over time within a zone), a housing unit will be produced with less land relative to other inputs to economize on the more expensive factor. This factor substitution is expected whether we think there are different technologies for different structural types (and each structural type is built where its technology is most profitable), or one technology for all types, as long as that one has a nonzero elasticity of substitution. If there are different technologies, but one output in the eyes of the consumers, then one technology will be most profitable with given input prices, and the situation is much the same as under the assumption of one technology, except that there may be kinks or discontinuities in the supply function. Equation (3-8) implies that for any given land price, the land per unit (lot size) of new construction is uniquely determined, decreasing as land price increases. If we could define structural types in terms of a range of land-to-nonland input ratios, given any input price ratio, we would know the structural type of all new construction. This is illustrated in Figure 3-1.

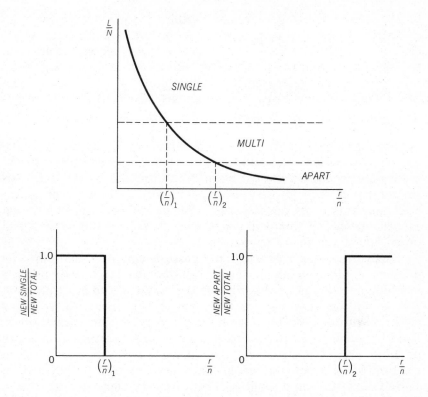

Note: r = price of land input; n = price of nonland input; L = amount of land input; N = amount of nonland input. Other variables are defined in the appendix.

Figure 3-1.

However, when we actually observe the structural types of new construction in different zones in the metropolitan area, we do not see such unanimity as to the appropriate type for each zone. Within the theoretical context of this model, there are several reasons for this lack of uniformity.

First of all, our "observations" are for an entire decade of new-construction responses. The model suggests that over that time span, it might well be that residential and other development could cause the price of land to cross a threshold between types, thus making appropriate at least two types of structural response within a town when the decade is taken as a whole.

Second, cities, towns, and districts are not completely homogeneous areas, although we treat them as such in the model. We argue that the degree of homogeneity within a town is greater than similarities between towns. However, neighborhood attributes affect land prices within towns as well, but at a lower degree of variation. In using these zones as our unit of observation, we have abstracted from this internal heterogeneity. Furthermore, we may expect some "smearing" near the edges of jurisdictions. If one town's "appropriate" structural type is single-family and its neighbor's is multifamily units, we may see some overlap at the border.

Third, historical and institutional restrictions interfere with the deterministic effect of land price on structural type. Zoning, neighborhood effects, and the timing of release of land parcels and their size (whether through demolition, lot splitting, or sales of vacant land) may make only one structural type possible on a given lot, even though, given full flexibility, a producer would combine land and other inputs in different proportions.

Finally, there is a problem of measurement or definition. The production function implies that the land-nonland ratio responds as a continuous function of the price of land (as depicted in Figure 3-1), that is, lot size decreases as the price of land increases. What we measure with our census data on structural type (single, multifamily defined as composed of two to four units, and apartments with five or more units per structure) only corresponds very crudely to a measure of land per unit or an input ratio of land to nonland. A single-family unit on a small lot might have less land per unit than a large-lot duplex or even a low-rise "garden apartment" complex. Thus we may classify units in the wrong segment of the continuum.

Taking all these effects into account, we still expect the price of land to be a good predictor of structural type. However, rather than being an on-off switch between types, the relationship between land price and the distribution of structural types in new construction is expected to be smoother, since all the factors discussed above contribute to heterogeneity of types, given land price.

Local-government actions such as zoning and provision of sewers can also affect the choice of structural type built by the producer. The availability of sewer lines has been used explicitly by local governments to control development in some areas around Washington, D.C. It may or may not be cheaper to build a particular housing unit where sewers are available, because the cost of internal sewage treatment systems (septic tank) need not be included by the builder, but connections to the sewer system must be built. However, high-rise structures cannot be serviced by septic tanks. Thus, sewer availability plays a role in determining the technological feasibility of different structural types.

Zoning, cited above as one of the interferences between land price and structural type, is a local-government policy tool whose impact can be modeled more explicitly. Zoning regulations generally restrict housing producers' choices asymmetrically, that is, they set a maximum (e.g., unit per land area density or height) and allow any uses which do not exceed the maximum. We want to model two such types of zoning regulations. One variable is a zero-one dummy for the case in which the town zoning code prohibits apartment structures; the apartment share of new construction is then expected to be zero, and the variable is included by multiplying it ($A = 0$ when apartments are banned) by all the right-hand variables in the apartment share equation. The second type of zoning is the establishment of lot size minima for part or all of the residential (and vacant) area of a town. The variable is a measure of the percent of the town that is restricted to lot sizes greater than 25,000 square feet. Where this minimum lot size applies, any units built must be single-unit structures surrounded by over half an acre of land. Thus, if a town's residential and vacant land is all so zoned, all units built will be singles. If a town has no zoning, the price of land and sewer availability will determine the shares of each structural type in total new construction. If minima apply in part of a town, singles will be built in that part and land price and sewer availability will determine what is built in the unzoned areas.

$$\frac{NEW\ SINGLE}{NEW\ TOTAL} = f(r) + h(SEWER) + \epsilon$$

$$\frac{NEW\ APART}{NEW\ TOTAL} = A * g(r + A * k(SEWER) + \epsilon$$

where r is the price of land, A is the apartment-banned dummy variable, and f, g, h, and k are functions. Then the model including zoning is

$$\frac{NEW\ SINGLE}{NEW\ TOTAL} = PZ + UZ*f(r) + UZ*h(SEWER) + \epsilon$$

$$\frac{NEW\ APART}{NEW\ TOTAL} = UZ*A*g(r) + UZ*A*k(SEWER) + \epsilon$$

where PZ is the fraction of land zoned for lot sizes greater than 25,000 square feet, and UZ is 1.0 minus PZ, the share unzoned.

The fraction of decadal new construction that is single family and the fraction for apartment units (five or more units in the structure) are therefore modeled as functions of the price of land, zoning, and sewer availability. The share of new construction that is multifamily (two to four units in the structure) is the residual, that is, total new construction less singles and apartment units.

Land price is represented, as before, by percent of land vacant at the beginning of the period. The 1960 percent vacant land is entered into the equations as a set of seven dummy variables ($V1$ through $V7$), each of a range of values of the variable. It is discrete rather than continuous, because, as postulated earlier, land price is not a linear function of percent vacant, and even if it were, we would not expect the shares of new construction that are single or apartment units to be linear functions of land price.

Our regressions were run using ordinary least squares. The results were as follows (standard errors are shown in parentheses below coefficients):

$$\frac{NEW\ SINGLE}{NEW\ TOTAL} = \underset{(.0425)}{.958\ PZ} - \underset{(.00111)}{.00278\ UZ*SEWER}$$

$$+ \underset{(.119)}{.392\ UZ*V1} + \underset{(.123)}{.618\ UZ*V2} + \underset{(.109)}{.700\ UZ*V3}$$

$$+ \underset{(.110)}{.799\ UZ*V4} + \underset{(.0854)}{.828\ UZ*V5} + \underset{(.0881)}{.907\ UZ*V6}$$

$$+ \underset{(.0878)}{.768\ UZ*V7} + e$$

$R^2 = 0.7921$; standard error of the regression = 0.157.

$$\frac{NEW\ APART}{NEW\ TOTAL} = \underset{(.00105)}{.00276\ A*UZ*SEWER} + \underset{(.112)}{.518\ A*UZ*V1}$$

$$+ \underset{(.117)}{.298\ A*UZ*V2} + \underset{(.103)}{.145\ A*UZ*V3}$$

$$+ \underset{(.104)}{.130\ A*UZ*V4} + \underset{(.0803)}{.0936\ A*UZ*V5}$$

$$+ \underset{(.0815)}{.0644\ A*UZ*V6} + \underset{(.0779)}{.192\ A*UZ*V7} + e$$

$R^2 = 0.7770$; standard error of the regression = 0.149.

The progression of coefficients across the categories is in the expected directions (increasing for singles, decreasing for apartments) except for the last category. In each case, the coefficient on $V7$ (= 1 if fraction vacant $\geqslant 0.5$) is not significantly different in a statistical sense from that on $V6$. These coefficients are displayed graphically in Figure 3-2.

SEWER enters both equations as expected, implying that for each ten percentage points of sewer availability in a zone, an additional three percentage points of new construction are apartments, not singles, ceteris paribus. A t test of the coefficient on PZ in the *SINGLE* equation shows it is not statistically significantly different from unity, which is what the model predicted. The use of the zoning variables multiplicatively (both UZ and A) surpasses either their exclusion or their inclusion as a separate linear continuous variable by improving both the overall fit (higher R^2, lower sum of squared residuals) and the individual coefficients.

Conversion Supply

The second major means of housing stock adjustment is by changing existing housing units to provide a different quality or quantity of services. By 1970, over 10 percent of the 1960 Boston SMSA housing stock (and almost 20 percent of the 1960 City of Boston stock) had been demolished, lost through other means, or changed by conversion or merger. Considering the size of the housing stock in comparison with new construction, these data indicate that such processes have an important impact on aggregate housing supply. Our focus in this model for both new construction and

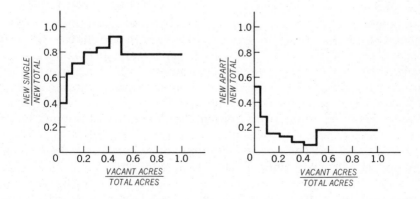

Note: See appendix for definition of variables.

Figure 3-2.

conversion-demolition is on changes in the number of housing units and their structural type (units in structure). What we call the conversion-demolition process includes a number of distinct activities by property owners: converting a structure by increasing or decreasing the number of housing units it encloses; and withdrawing the units in a structure from the housing stock through conversion to nonresidential use or through demolition. Demolition may take place because a structure is worn out or because other uses for the site are more profitable; it may be done in order to create open space or to make possible the construction of a new (residential or nonresidential) structure on the site. In the latter case, only half the process (the demolition) is considered as conversion-demolition; the replacement structure (if residential) is a part of new construction.

In the discussion of residential new construction, the point was emphasized that as an area develops and the price of land rises, the lot size (or the factor input ratio of land to nonland) of newly built units declines. Since units are durable, as development occurs, units of different densities may be found side by side. The older units display factor proportions which no longer reflect the least-cost technology, once factor prices have changed (generally with higher relative prices of land), that is, these units are not of the type that would be built in that location if all the development had occurred in the present; or, looking at the issue from the other side, replacement units would economize more on land.

Conversion supply is accomplished, as is new construction, by the combination of land, labor, capital, and materials inputs. Conversion supply differs from new construction in that certain of the inputs—land and some of the capital—are already in place in a given quantity and form. Converters do not deal in the market for land; thus, they respond to a set of signals different from those faced by new suppliers. Owners (or potential purchasers of existing property) compare the operating costs and revenues of the current use with the incremental capital costs (and demolition costs) and operating costs and revenues of uses to which the structure could be converted (or by which it could be replaced). Because incremental costs are smaller for conversion than for demolition-new construction, less disequilibrium is required to elicit the former than the latter supply response.

In the aggregate (that is, adding up the decisions of the individual suppliers) the most important determinant of conversion-demolition supply activity in a zone is the stock and type of housing units available. The extent to which demand for housing in the area has risen since the units were put in place, i.e., the degree to which the stock is out of equilibrium, is also a factor. Increased demand, expressed per unit of area, encourages more intensive uses of the area, that is, the production of more housing units on the given land. (Conversion will occur when output price times the new number of units in the structure minus annual incremental capital and operating costs is greater than output price times the old number of units.) Thus, in a rough sense, we would expect more conversion activity (whether addition or subtraction of units) in old units than in new, because the former are less well-adapted to current demand conditions. In addition, worn-out units, whether old or not, are most likely to be demolished, since their current returns are not as high as they would be on potential replacements. Demolition activity thus reflects the need for normal replacement as well as radical conversion. The latter, demolition for replacement with a very different kind of structure, is more costly than building the structure on vacant land, and hence is undertaken only when the current structure is very far out of equilibrium and when there is very little vacant land (these two conditions occur together not coincidentally but rather because of the way the land market operates).[6]

In addition to the existing stock and its current appropriateness, many of the same local conditions that affect new construction also affect conversion-demolition activity. High housing unit vacancy rates are a signal of excess supply in the market. To an individual supplier, the significance of a vacant unit is that there is no current return to be foregone by changing the property use. Price changes act in much the same way, except that since they reflect the rate of price change for both the original and resultant structures, they may not indicate the direction of conversion. Government programs such as urban renewal and public housing have direct impacts through land-clearing demolition and various kinds of subsidies to rehabilitation or alteration activity, and through these direct impacts may also affect decisions made by competing private suppliers in the same zone. Zoning, where it takes the form of minimum lot sizes, presumably inhibits the conversion of single-unit structures into multi-unit types, although often such zoning is enacted to control future development of open land rather than to impose restrictions on existing units.

The results of estimating conversion-demolition equations are shown in Table 3-2. In each case, the dependent variable is the net decadal change in units of that structural type per acre not due to new construction. The dependent variable and independent variables relating to housing stock (old stocks, deteriorating stocks, public housing) are divided by total acreage to control for the effects of arbitrary differences in area on the amount of housing supply

Table 3-2. Conversion-Demolition Supply Equations (figures in parentheses are asymptotic standard errors; $N = 89$)

	CONV SINGLE	CONV MULTI	CONV APART
Constant	0.0444 (0.0685)	0.0596 (0.0785)	0.0122 (0.112)
$\Delta PRICE/PRICE_{60}$ (endogenous)	0.146 (0.0977)	−0.139 (0.106)	−0.200 (0.151)
$VAC\,RATE_{60}$	−2.33 (1.71)	−1.90 (1.87)	2.99 (2.40)
$\Delta VAC\,RATE$ (endogenous)	−0.560 (2.17)	−5.30 (2.46)	3.13 (3.10)
$OLD\,SINGLE_{60}$	−0.199 (0.0430)	0.148 (0.0353)	0.0598 (0.0447)
$OLD\,MULTI_{60}$	0.0151 (0.0131)	0.0742 (0.0183)	0.0190 (0.0184)
$OLD\,APART_{60}$			0.310 (0.00926)
$DETER\,SINGLE_{60}$	−1.23 (0.149)		
$DETER\,MULTI_{60}$		−0.941 (0.120)	
$DETER\,APART_{60}$			−1.94 (0.0547)
$MLS\,ZONING$	−0.000791 (0.00543)	−0.0000612 (0.000577)	0.000664 (0.000722)
$PUBLIC\,HOUSING$ (endogenous)		0.0236 (0.179)	1.02 (0.154)
$LEASED\,PUB\,HOU$ (endogenous)		−0.954 (0.499)	−3.93 (0.582)
$NEW\,TIGHT$ (endogenous)	−0.000500 (0.0000909)	−0.000733 (0.000132)	
R^2	.9186	.9540	.9874
SE	.112	.117	.147

activity taking place. The very strong importance of existing stocks is well documented in the table. In each equation, the deteriorating stock is highly associated with demolitions. Old stock accounts for much of the conversion activity, the general direction being to increase densities, although a small share of multifamily units may be changing into singles. New construction of housing in areas without much vacant land (measured by *NEW TIGHT* ≡ *NEW TOTAL/ VACANT ACRES*, treated as endogenous) contributes significantly to demolitions of singles and multis. *NEW TIGHT* is not included in the apartment equation because apartments are less often torn down to make room for new units. This is since apartments already represent a more intensive use of land, and demolition costs are higher, than is the case for singles or multis.

The aggregate data we have suggest that most (three-quarters) of the changes in the singles stock, measured by *CONV SINGLE*, are demolitions (*CONV SINGLE* is negative for every city, town, and district in the sample). Thus, the significantly positive sign on price in the *CONV SINGLE* equation is not surprising. Where returns are rising, existing uses are not abandoned. Similarly, where vacancy rates are high, more demolitions occur. In the other equations, *CONV* is a mixture of conversions (in and out) and demolitions, and the price change coefficients are not significantly different from zero.

Zoning appears insignificant in all the equations, suggesting that it is more effective with regard to new construction. The other government policy tool, public housing, has a strong impact on conversion-demolition, especially of apartments. It appears that the more conventional forms of public housing, in which subsidies are provided for construction or rehabilitation, have a positive effect on the number of apartment (and multifamily) units, but that the leased public housing program discourages augmentation of the stock through conversion, or encourages demolitions. However, it should be noted that simply treating these public housing variables as endogenous does not enable us to distinguish between the effects of the public housing programs and the housing conditions that cause a jurisdiction to adopt the public housing approach for solving its housing problems.

SUMMARY

In concluding, we wish merely to note the special features of our approach and the chief thrust of our findings. Demand and supply relations for housing units have been derived and estimated using simultaneous equation econometric methods. The supply functions determine changes in different numbers and types of housing structure in the different zones; the demand functions determine the zonal distribution of the population partitioned into three income groups. Through price and vacancy rate change, supply and demand jointly determine the location of households and housing structures.

The demand relations model the decadal change in the proportion of each income group locating in each zone as a function of accommodation prices, vacancy rates, and zonal attributes. This last can be broadly described as including public service and tax rate variables and structural, socio-environmental, and accessibility attributes. Our results suggest that different income groups have different relative tastes for these attributes. Two supply modes are treated separately—new construction and conversion-demolition. Decadal changes in new units in any zone are a function of expected revenue changes (as reflected in price changes and vacancy rates) and expected costs, largely differential availability and land costs, as reflected in initial vacant acres and minimum lot zoning. The composition of new construction in terms of structural types is determined largely by land prices that indicate differing land-capital ratios. Decadal changes in zonal units through conversion-demolition are largely a function of the same expected revenue and cost measures that reflect the number of existing structures of different type, age, and condition in the zone that are available for inexpensive conversion or ripe for demolition.

Our econometric estimations, by TSLS, generally gave encouraging results. The overall fits were reasonable and the signs and patterns of relative magnitude of coefficients across structural type and supply mode on the supply side, and household type on the demand side are generally consistent with a priori expectations. Several variables do show puzzling results, and in our ongoing work we are attempting to deal with problems exposed in the first stage of our study reported here.

Appendix 3A: List of Variables

Except as indicated, all data pertain to individual zones.

Symbol	Description
LOW	Number of family households earning less than $7,000 in 1970 dollars
MIDDLE	Number of family households earning between $7,000 and $15,000 in 1970 dollars
HIGH	Number of family households earning over $15,000 in 1970 dollars
SINGLE	Number of single-family housing units divided by total acreage
MULTI	Number of multifamily housing units divided by total acreage
APART	Number of apartment units divided by total acreage
TOTAL	Total number of housing units

Symbol	Description
NEW SINGLE	Number of single units in 1970 built since 1960
NEW MULTI	Number of multifamily units in 1970 built since 1960
NEW APART	Number of apartment units in 1970 built since 1960
NEW TOTAL	Total number of units in 1970 built since 1960
CONV SINGLE	1960-to-1970 change per acre in stock of single-family units due to conversions, retirements, and demolitions
CONV MULTI	1960-to-1970 change per acre in stock of multifamily units due to conversions, retirements, and demolitions
CONV APART	1960-to-1970 change per acre in stock of apartment units due to conversions, retirements, and demolitions
CONV TOTAL	1960-to-1970 change per acre in total number of housing units not due to new construction
OLD	Percent of 1960 units built before 1930
LARGE	Percent of all units with 7 or more rooms
BATHROOMS	Percentage of all units with more than one bathroom
DETERIORATE	Percentage of all units that are deteriorating
POP DEN	Population per acre of land: residential, vacant, and recreational
BLACK	Percent of population that is nonwhite
CRIME	Comprehensive crime rate of Federal Bureau of Investigation
WELFARE	Percent of households on welfare
VACANT ACRES[a]	Number of acres of vacant land
MLS ZONING	Percent of residential and vacant land zoned for lot sizes larger than 25,000 square feet
SEWER	Sewer availability: percent of population served by public sewers
PT RATIO	Pupils-teacher ratio in high schools
EFF TAX	Effective property tax rate
JOB ACC	General road accessibility to employment defined as

$$JOB\ ACC^j = \sum_{K=1}^{89} X_K C_{jK}$$

where C_{jK} = travel time from zone j to zone K and X_K = employment of income type (HIGH, MIDDLE, or LOW) in zone K relative to SMSA total employment of that income type

Symbol	Description
RESIDENTIAL ACRES[a]	Number of acres in residential use
TOTAL ACRES[a]	Total acreage minus acres under open water
HIGHWAY	Highway availability index: [3 (number of limited access super-highways) + 2 (number of four-lane highways) + number of two-lane highways] ÷ total acreage
VAC RATE	Overall housing unit vacancy rate: (units vacant for rent + vacant for sale) ÷ occupied and vacant units
ΔPRICE	Housing price 1970 ÷ housing price 1960
PZ	Fraction of area zoned for minimum lot sizes greater than 25,000 square feet: MLS ZONING ÷ 100
UZ	Fraction of area not zoned for minimum lot sizes greater than 25,000 square feet: $1 - PZ$

Symbol	Description
OTHER ACRES[a]	Acres of land devoted to manufacturing
OPEN	Estimate of fraction of area vacant and not subject to minimum lot size zoning: *UZ * VACP*
A	Zero-one dummy: $A = 0$ when town's zoning code prohibits apartments
OLD SINGLE	Estimate of number of single units per acre more than 30 years old: *SINGLE * OLD*
OLD MULTI	Estimate of number of multifamily units per acre in structures more than 30 years old: *MULTI * OLD*
OLD APART	Estimate of number of apartment units per acre in structures more than 30 years old: *APART * OLD*
DETER SINGLE	Estimate of number of single-family units per acre which are deteriorating: *SINGLE * DETERIORATE*
DETER MULTI	Estimate of number of multifamily units per acre which are deteriorating: *MULTI * DETERIORATE*
DETER APART	Estimate of number of apartment units per acre which are deteriorating: *APART * DETERIORATE*
PUBLIC HOUSING	Number of "conventional" and "turnkey" (federal) public housing units per acre in 1974
LEASED PUB HOU	Number of units of federally sponsored leased public housing per acre in 1974
NEW TIGHT	Number of new housing units built during 1960-1970 per acre of vacant land initially available: *NEW TOTAL ÷ VACANT ACRES;* measures likelihood of demolition activity as means of making land available for new construction
VACP	*VACANT ACRES ÷ TOTAL ACRES*

The seven dummy variables for vacant land are defined as follows:

$V1 = 1$ if $VACP < 0.05$; 0 otherwise
$V2 = 1$ if $0.05 \leqslant VACP < 0.10$; 0 otherwise
$V3 = 1$ if $0.10 \leqslant VACP < 0.20$; 0 otherwise
$V4 = 1$ if $0.20 \leqslant VACP < 0.30$; 0 otherwise
$V5 = 1$ if $0.30 \leqslant VACP < 0.40$; 0 otherwise
$V6 = 1$ if $0.40 \leqslant VACP < 0.50$; 0 otherwise
$V7 = 1$ if $0.50 \leqslant VACP$; 0 otherwise

[a]The 1960 acreage data is derived from a 1963 land-use survey; the 1970 data, from a 1972 survey.

NOTES TO CHAPTER THREE

1. "Potential" rather than "actual" because different households work at different locations in the SMSA and thus have different actual accessibilities from a common origin.

2. There will be a few zones with multiple occupancy. As shown above, in these zones the market price will be below the bid of the highest bidder so f will not strictly be a step function.

3. Our more recent econometric work improves on the treatment of price by substituting two different price variables for the simple one used here. One measures a given zone's price relative to the average for zones closely substitutable to it; the other measures the average for the zone and that closely substitutable group relative to the SMSA average.

4. Indexes could not be constructed for some zones. Therefore, the rates of change over the decade 1960-1970 were projected upon the census rates of change of value and composition to obtain an approximation for the other zones.

5. The dependent variables of these estimated equations contain households of all races. Currently we are separating out the nonwhite households so as to estimate separate income class demand equations for them, and determine whether low-income whites have similar preferences to whites in the high- and middle-income groups or are closer to the present mixed low-income group.

6. In a more recent treatment than is reported here we attempt to elaborate relative conversion costs further by separately determining conversions to the different structural types, and by using as explanatory variables in the separate equations the number of existing units of each structural type.

REFERENCES

Alonso, W. 1960. "A Theory of the Urban Land Market." *Papers and Proceedings of the Regional Science Association.*

_____. 1965. *Location and Land Use: Toward a General Theory of Land Rent.* Cambridge: Harvard University Press.

Bailey, M.; R. Muth; and H. Nourse. 1963. "A Regression Method for Real Estate Price Index Constructions." *Journal of the American Statistical Association.*

de Leeuw, F.; R. Struyk; and S.A. Marshall. 1973. *Urban Institute Housing Model: Second Year Report.* Washington, D.C.: The Urban Institute.

Engle, R.F. 1974a. "A Disequilibrium Model of Regional Investment." *Journal of Regional Science*, December.

_____. 1974b. "Issues in the Specification of an Econometric Model of Metropolitan Growth." *Journal of Urban Economics.*

_____. 1974c. "The Supply and Demand for Metropolitan Manufacturing Employment and Output." Paper presented at the North American meeting of the Regional Science Association, November. See *Papers and Proceedings of the Regional Science Association* (1975).

_____. 1977. "De Facto Discrimination in Residential Assessments." *National Tax Journal* (forthcoming).

Engle, R.F.; F.M. Fisher; J.R. Harris; and J. Rothenberg. 1972. "An Econometric Simulation Model of Intra-Metropolitan Housing Location: Housing, Business, Transportation and Local Government." *American Economic Review*, May.

Harris, B.; J. Nathanson; and L. Rosenburg. 1966. "Research on an Equilibrium Model of Metropolitan Housing and Locational Choice." Interim Report, Planning Services Group, Institute for Environmental Studies, Graduate School of Fine Arts, University of Pennsylvania, March.

Ingram, G.K.; J.F. Kain; and J.R. Ginn. 1972. *The Detroit Prototype of the NBER Urban Simulation Model.* New York: National Bureau of Economic Research.

Muth, Richard. 1969. *Cities and Housing.* Chicago: University of Chicago Press.

_____. 1974. "The Derived Demand Curve for a Productive Factor and the Industry Supply Curve." *Oxford Economic Papers,* July.

Wheaton, W. 1974. "A Bid Rent Approach to Housing Demand." MIT Working Paper 135. July.

Comments on Chapter Three

John M. Quigley

Few economists would quarrel with an econometric analysis of housing market behavior designed to pay careful attention to the three characteristics of the market for residential services—durability, fixity, and heterogeneity—that distinguish it from most other economic markets.

In reacting to this "preliminary analysis" or progress report on model building, I wish to emphasize two points in particular. First, to my knowledge, this analysis represents the first attempt to sketch out and estimate empirically a model of housing supply behavior which differentiates housing by type over urban space. Secondly, the class of models represented by this work-in-progress is directed toward a quite demanding standard. Until quite recently, there were practically no analyses of the housing market that were not based on the convenient, but rather unsatisfactory, assumptions that housing services are homogeneous, that vacancy rates are zero, that markets are in long-run equilibrium, and that locations are along a line. A research design intended to deal in a serious way with the complexity of the durable, heterogeneous, and locationally fixed housing commodity has a potentially high payoff.

A serious investigation of the supply and demand for housing services within a single metropolitan area faces formidable difficulties. What we call the housing market is really an interrelated market for two kinds of goods. One of these is a market for the services of residential capital—those services provided by a structure type, a

Note: In preparing these remarks, I benefited from discussion with Eric A. Hanushek.

configuration of living space, and so forth. However, since the consumption of these services is site specific, the economic actors must also compete in a market for locations—which provide such services as accessibility, public goods, and "neighborhoods."

This complementarity suggests several possible strategies in developing econometric models of these markets for subsequent testing. Strategy A, the most desirable but the most complex approach, would involve specifying the complete set of interrelated supply and demand relationships, to include both housing attributes and location simultaneously. The objective of this strategy would be to untangle the choices really being made by economic actors:

1. Households, which substitute among alternative housing units or "types" and among alternative locations or "zones" in response to relative prices, that is, the market price of each type of housing available in each zone.
2. Entrepreneurs, who produce, through new construction or through conversion, changes in the number of units of various types at alternative locations in response to these same market prices.

The key point is that market prices, which vary jointly by type and location, make some types of residential capital more desirable to certain kinds of households at one location and to other kinds of households at other locations. This same set of prices causes the profitability of supply transformations to vary by type and location. An equilibrating process adjusts prices and vacancy rates to reduce suppliers' profit differentials and households' incentives to move. Something tolerably approaching a short-run equilibrium may well result.

The mere outline of the intricacy implicit in this line of inquiry for modeling housing market interactions may help us understand why little progress has been made in implementing such a complex strategy. Since there are many possibilities for substitution in consumption and in production, there are a host of potentially important cross-price effects that affect the behavior of consumers and suppliers. In addition, there are unresolved measurement problems inhibiting econometric applications; we have only a crude understanding of the appropriate way to measure those housing bundles whose prices vary and those significant characteristics of locations over which they vary.

Two more limited research strategies would focus serious attention on either housing services or locational attributes and would treat the other half of this market somewhat superficially.

For example, abstratcing from locational considerations, strategy B would specify a behavioral model for exploring the supply and demand relationships for housing bundles or types of dwellings. Such a strategy would explore the interrelationships among the segmented submarkets for types of dwellings that are only imperfectly linked through substitutions in production and consumption. In its pure form, this strategy would assume that locational attributes were ubiquitous or would "hold them constant" in a crude way to focus attention on the market for housing services. Alternatively, strategy C would focus attention on the supplies of and the demands for locational characteristics by different kinds of households and would neglect or "hold constant" in some plausible way the stocks of residential capital and their spatial distribution. Either of these lines of inquiry would lead to an econometric model which would provide only limited, but potentially useful, insight into the complex inter-dependencies of the urban housing market; either would improve our understanding of how the market process works.

Bradbury et al. claim to "model a demand for housing accommo-dation and its supply" and present "preliminary estimates as evi-dence of its promise." Since the study is largely empirically oriented, its success must be judged, not by the revelation of theoretical insight, but on other important grounds—the choice of research strategy, the attention to issues of measurement, and the interest and importance of the empirical results.

The authors choose a curious mixed strategy for analyzing be-havior in the housing market. They discuss their strategy as if they had estimated supply and demand relationships using strategy A, but in fact they have chosen the strategy "one from column B and one from column C."

The analysis presents little justification for the formulation of the particular supply and demand relationships the authors choose to estimate. They rely mainly on Marshallian insight that a standard supply and demand curve characterize a market. Indeed, we do not discover until later that the analysis has been formulated so that there is no prior sign on the slope of the supply curve and that the demand curve could have a positive slope for high-income house-holds!

The verbal analysis includes an excellent discussion of the role of prices and vacancy rates in equilibrating the supply and demand sides of the market, but it appears that in empirical application the supplies and demands are for different goods in separate but related markets.

The demand side of the market is characterized by several equations that focus on locational attributes and virtually ignore housing availability; the strategy comes from column C. Regressions are reported that relate changes in population distributions across eighty-nine locations or zones to nine variables measuring the locational attributes of the zones, three measures of the housing stock, a price change term, and the vacancy rate.

This formulation implicitly assumes that housing attributes are homogeneous within zones (which are defined as seventy-five suburban towns and fourteen zones in the city of Boston) and that they are virtually ubiquitous across the metropolitan area. The formulation assumes away virtually any spatial differentiation among housing stocks that would cause households to substitute among different locations, i.e., it disregards characteristics of the housing stock that are available in suburban Lincoln but not the South End of Boston and which would affect consumer choice.

Of particular importance in the analysis is the price measure because it is the key variable in motivating housing demanders to substitute among housing types and locations. The price change term is computed from an index based on repeat sales in each of the eighty-nine zones. The only thing that matters in the derivation of this index is the sale price of a given property in two calendar years. Thus the measure implicitly assumes that the prices of all dwelling units in each town changed proportionately throughout the decade. To the extent that there is more turnover in single-family housing than in multifamily or apartment units, the price term does not measure price variations in the latter two very well. In any case, the construction of the index assumes that the rate of price change of all properties within each of the towns is identical. But if the rates of price appreciation of different types of residential housing varied for the metropolitan area as a whole, the index could well be measuring the distribution of the types of housing across towns. (Indeed, if the rates of price appreciation were *constant* for each housing type in the metropolitan area, but varied among housing types, the price index would *only* be related to the distribution of housing across towns, or at least, the distribution of repeat sales.)

In summary, the estimated demand equation relates changes in proportions of income classes in each zone to a somewhat ad hoc set of measures of changes in zonal characteristics and price, and practically ignores changes in housing characteristics.[1]

The strategy behind the supply analysis, in contrast, comes from column B. The authors present several equations relating changes in housing accommodations in each zone to vacancy rates, their changes, the preexisting stock, and available vacant land, but otherwise the locational and demographic characteristics of the towns, which are so important in the demand analysis, are virtually ignored. The same ambiguous price variable is used to investigate the supply response, and it is noted that "the price variable has a critical importance in leading the market's adjustment process out of disequilibrium."[2]

Note that the demand analysis measures the demand for location, with little effort to "hold constant" the spatial distribution of residential capital, with no effort to "hold constant" the locational differences among zones. Is the price term to be interpreted as a capitalized location rent (in the demand equation) or is it interpreted as the output price of housing (in the supply equation)? If so, what is the slope of the supply curve? What is the anticipated behavior of demanders for owner-occupied units, who are 54 percent of the Boston housing market?

This is, of course, an empirical question, and the proof of an econometric analysis is in the estimates. There are rigorous statistical standards, and there are looser interpretations of patterns or coefficients—their signs, magnitudes, and significance levels. I would submit, however, that it takes unusually strong and sometimes puzzling a priori notions to analyze the results displayed in this study and conclude that the "results display encouraging consistency with theoretical expectation for both demand and supply." When the authors examine the price variable in the demand equations, they conclude it is "one of the economically most significant variables." When others look at the price coefficients they may see t ratios of 1.40, 0.76, and 0.33.

In the supply equations, the effect of higher prices is to stimulate conversions of existing dwelling units from higher density to lower density structure types. Higher prices do stimulate new-construction activity in the aggregate, but are not considered to influence its distribution among structure types.

Since the price term used throughout the supply and demand analysis is called upon to perform two functions—to measure the price of sites when housing is not distinguished and the price of housing when sites are not distinguished—it is possible that it measures neither very adequately. The results of the empirical analysis also "display encouraging consistency with [this] theoretical expectation."

NOTES TO COMMENTS ON CHAPTER THREE

1. It is difficult to understand the reasoning which leads to the regression model with an endogenous price change and an exogenous tax change. Why are

1960 values used for the vacancy rate, the proportion of "old" houses, and the proportion black, and 1960-1970 relative changes used for the other variables reported in Table 3-1. What is even more curious is that the latter two variables are measured as 1960 levels in this version of the study and were measured as 1960-1970 relative changes in the original version.

2. Why was the price term included in the regression for estimating the distribution of new units across towns and excluded from the regressions for estimating the distribution of new single-family and apartment units?

It is even more difficult to understand why the analysts chose such a peculiar functional form for estimating the latter regression, in effect including a vector of zeros as observations on all variables in towns where apartments are banned.

Finally, there is no obvious reason why the dependent variables in the new-construction regressions should be measured as ratios to the number of existing dwelling units in 1960 while the dependent variables in the conversion regressions should be measured as ratios to the land area of the town.

Part II

**Measuring Prices and Quantities
in the Housing Market**

Chapter Four

An Analysis of Ghetto Housing Prices over Time

Ann B. Schnare and
Raymond J. Struyk

INTRODUCTION

Less than twenty years ago, an inverse relationship between the unit price of housing in an area and the concentration of blacks there was a generally accepted principle that was frequently offered as a justification for the discriminatory practices of realtors, financial institutions, and innumerable lobbies of concerned citizens. In recent years, however, this hypothesis has been viewed with increasing skepticism, especially by members of the professional research community, who often argue that a chronic shortage of quality housing in established black neighborhoods normally results in ghetto premiums, rather than discounts.

Unfortunately, most empirical evidence regarding the relationship between race and rent pertains to market conditions in the 1950s and early 1960s. In the overwhelming majority of these studies it was found that units located in predominately black neighborhoods were more expensive than otherwise similar dwellings in neighborhoods that were mainly white (Becker 1957, Gillingham 1973, Haugen and Heins 1964, Muth 1969, Rapkin 1966, Ridker and Henning 1967, Wihry 1971). These results were by no means universal (Lapham

Note: The authors wish to thank Frank de Leeuw for important comments at the formative stages of this work and Jack Goodman, Larry Ozanne, and Jo Culbertson for comments on an earlier draft. Financial support by the Urban Institute is also gratefully acknowledged.

1971, Bailey 1966); and indeed, since the factors that contribute to the price of ghetto housing vary over space and time, there was no reason to expect them to be. Nevertheless, the preponderant finding of ghetto markups during the early 1960s does seem to indicate a certain similarity between a fairly large number of metropolitan areas.

In Tables 4-1 and 4-2, we summarize two such studies, each designed to apply the same methodology to a variety of housing markets. Gillingham, who based his analysis on a relatively rich body of data drawn from the 1960 Bureau of Labor Statistics Comprehensive Housing Survey, found markups ranging from 10 to 23 percent in each of five metropolitan areas; Wihry found similar premiums in nine out of eighteen cities. While the reliability of the latter's estimates are plagued by his reliance on relatively poor aggregate data, his results combined with those of the others cited above suggest that in the past ghetto markups were a relatively common market phenomenon.

Considerably less is known about more recent relationships between housing prices and race. Studies of New Haven in 1968 and 1969 (King and Mieszkowski 1973) and of St. Louis in 1967 (Kain and Quigley 1970) showed racial markups of about 8 percent for

Table 4-1. Wihry's Analysis of Median Census Tract Rents and Values in Eighteen Central Cities in 1960[a] (dollar premium associated with a 1 percent increase in the proportion of households that are nonwhite)

Central City	Median Value	Median Rent	Central City	Median Value	Median Rent
Charlotte, N.C.	40.4*	.03	Milwaukee	15.6	.21*
Cincinnati	11.6	.04	Montgomery	6.6	−.06
Cleveland	19.5*	.21*	Norfolk	46.7	−.06
Dayton	0.5	−.02	Paterson-Clifton-Passaic	63.7	57*
El Paso	−130.1	−.62	Pittsburgh	19.4*	.34*
Flint	21.4	.11*	Rochester	54.1*	.29*
Grand Rapids	15.9	.13	St. Louis	33.4*	.06*
Lansing	−34.6	−.18	Syracuse	118.9	.55*
Louisville	−8.2	−.06	Topeka	−41.8	.03

*Underlying regression coefficient is significant at 5 percent level or better.

[a]Unit of observation is census tract; model is linear. For all dwelling units, other independent variables included in the regression model are distance from CBD, proportion of dwellings with more than one person per room, proportion of dwellings built during 1940-1960, proportion of dwellings with shared or no bath, proportion of dwellings dilapidated or lacking some or all plumbing facilities, and the median number of rooms per unit. For details, see Wihry (1974).

Table 4-2. Gillingham's Analysis of BLS Survey Data on Dwellings in Multiunit Structures in Five SMSAs, 1960-1961[a]

	Rent of Black Households in Stated Block as Percent of Rent of White Households in All-White Blocks		
	Block Less than 20% Black	*Block 20-80% Black*	*Block Over 80% Black*
Chicago	12.8*	17.6*	22.9*
Detroit	6.4	9.3*	10.3*
Washington	16.1*	2.2	2.1
Baltimore	13.1	18.8*	17.2*
St. Louis	5.8	4.7	11.4*

*Underlying regression coefficient is significant at 5 percent level or better.

[a]Unit of observation is the individual dwelling unit in multiunit structures; model is semilog in form. Other independent variables are a set of dummy variables for unit age; set of number-of-room dummies; dummies for more than one bathroom and less than full bath; dummy for furniture and appliance included in rent; dummy for substandard condition; dummies for lack of hot or cold water, central heat, any installed heat, number of persons per room; dummy for garage included in rent; dummy for central air conditioning included in rent; proportions of units on block lacking some plumbing, crowded, and/or in structures with five or more units; and median income of tract. Basic data are from BLS Comprehensive Housing Survey, which are described in U.S. Bureau of Labor Statistics, *The Consumer Price Index: History and Techniques* (Bull. 1517). Results are from Gillingham (1973, Table V-2).

rental units, while Berry and Bednarz (1975) in a study of Chicago from 1970 to 1972 found a small, but statistically significant, discount for owner-occupied homes. Since it is impossible to generalize from these few scattered observations, it is likewise impossible to ascertain the current nature of housing prices in predominantly black neighborhoods.

Additional empirical research based on more recent housing samples is needed now because areal analyses conducted more than fifteen years ago may no longer be applicable to the housing markets of today. While this potential for obsolescence is inherent in most statistical research, it poses a particular problem in the case of racially related rent differentials.

In the late 1960s, an era of legislative and executive reforms began, designed to end overt discrimination in the housing market and the mortgage insurance industry. Government attempts to promote equal opportunity in housing, coupled with a rapid rate of white suburbanization and a decline in the growth of the urban black population, may have increased the black sector's ability to expand in response to housing shortages, making excess demand in black neighborhoods a less frequent market occurrence. If this hypothesis is correct, it would make earlier econometric estimates inappropriate, and indeed, would lead one to expect that the large ghetto markups of the early 1960s are a less common phenomenon today.

In this study, we examine the changes that have occurred in the relative prices of ghetto housing in two cities—Boston and Pittsburgh—and attempt to relate those changes to observable population and housing trends. The analysis is based on data that was obtained primarily from the 1960 and the 1970 censuses of Population and Housing. By applying the same two-tiered econometric technique to each of our four separate samples (Boston, 1960; Boston, 1970; Pittsburgh, 1960; Pittsburgh, 1970), we obtained price estimates that are reasonably comparable over cities and over time.

Boston and Pittsburgh were selected in order to test the overall importance of demand in sustaining housing premiums for blacks. The two cities began the decade with roughly similar characteristics: each was about the same size; each had a relatively small black population; and each registered a significant ghetto markup. However, between 1960 and 1970, the number of blacks in Boston grew by about 62 percent, compared to a 5 percent rise in Pittsburgh. If the supply response was sluggish, this divergence could have an important impact on the relative price of ghetto housing. Yet in spite of the differential growth of the black population in the two cities, estimated ghetto markups fell significantly in both.

The remainder of the study is divided as follows: (1) a summary of the various factors that might contribute to the overall relationship between housing prices and race; and (2) estimates of racially related price differentials and the econometric procedure by which they were obtained. Our hypothesis is that the premiums observed in the 1960 samples were primarily the result of an initial shortage of quality housing in predominantly black neighborhoods, and that their subsequent disappearance signaled an alleviation of that shortage. (3) We examine aggregate trends within the black sectors of the two markets in an attempt to determine whether or not actual market developments are consistent with our basic supply hypotheses, and offer some tentative reasons for the hypothesized supply response. (4) We summarize the major findings of the analysis.

HOUSING PRICES AND RACE

A variety of factors act to determine the overall relationship between housing prices and race. A primary distinction can be made between neighborhood and household markups. The former refers to differentials that are borne by all households at a given locale, irrespective of the individual's race; the latter—known as "discriminatory mark-ups"—reflect systematic differences in the prices households pay for similar dwellings in the same neighborhood, and presumably arise from the discriminatory behavior of landlords, realtors, and financial intermediaries.

Neighborhood differentials have caused perhaps the greatest confusion in the debate over the relationship between housing prices and race. In any given market, the relative price of housing in racially segregated neighborhoods reflects a complicated interplay of long-run and short-run forces which can conceivably work in opposing directions. If it is assumed that the market is in long-run equilibrium or that households are perfectly mobile, rent differentials will necessarily reflect the neighborhood racial preferences of households.[1] If blacks are effectively color blind and if whites prefer living near whites, prices will fall with increases in an area's concentration of blacks; if blacks, like whites, dislike racially mixed neighborhoods, the relationship between racial mix and rents will be U-shaped, with the relative price in the segregated zones determined by the incomes and the tastes of the two groups.

Once the assumption of long-run equilibrium is abandoned, the one-to-one correspondence between household tastes and housing prices disappears. At any given point in time, prices will reflect temporary or chronic disturbances in the housing market, as well as the more fundamental influences of racial externalities. If these disturbances are large enough or persistent enough, rent differentials may arise that are inconsistent with household tastes. Over time, the market will act to eliminate these temporary differentials, as households change their zone of residence and as the stock of housing expands in areas of excess demand. But given the many barriers that may limit the black sector's ability to expand, this adjustment process may be painfully slow.

Several factors operate to reduce the overall mobility of black households, rendering them particularly vulnerable to disturbances of this sort. In many areas, a fairly large fraction of blacks are recent migrants to the city and, accordingly, may have an inadequate knowledge of the housing opportunities throughout the metropolitan area. Mobility may also be restricted by factors such as poverty and overt market discrimination. Combined with an inelastic supply of housing, these factors may greatly reduce the ability of the black sector of the market to adjust to conditions of excess demand, and can produce short-run differentials with or without market externalities (Becker 1957; Haugen and Heins 1964). Supply restrictions need not be general for market premiums to appear; if the stock of housing available to blacks does not suit their needs, desired units may rent or sell at significant markups even with a relatively loose market for other types of dwellings (Kain 1969).

An additional factor that might produce racially related neighborhood price differentials stems from the possibility of discriminatory behavior on the part of financial intermediaries. If race is viewed as synonymous with vandalism, decay, and abandonment, credit terms in the ghetto may be relatively poor and insurance relatively expensive when compared to the rates that are charged in otherwise similar white neighborhoods. The effect of such behavior on the price of housing should vary by tenure, in general reducing the value of owner-occupied dwellings while increasing the level of rents. With restricted household mobility and with an inelastic supply of housing, differentials of this sort could persist over relatively long periods of time.

In contrast to these neighborhood price differentials, which by definition are borne by all households regardless of their race, "discriminatory markups" refer to differential rents or values within a particular area. Becker's basic model of discrimination can be used to predict rental markups in white and in border neighborhoods where landlords either have an aversion toward blacks or believe that such households will decrease the rental value of their property (Becker 1957). Potential black buyers in these same areas may be subject to similar markups because of their own inability to bargain with potential white sellers or the reluctance of brokers to disturb established racial patterns or because more stringent mortgage conditions are imposed on blacks than on whites by financial intermediaries who associate integration with declining property values (Kain and Quigley 1974, especially Chap. 3). However, since the economic rationale for such discriminatory behavior will disappear in neighborhoods that are predominantly black, and since the bargaining position of blacks within these areas will be relatively strong, differential rents within the ghetto seem somewhat improbable. What little evidence there is tends to support the basic premise that discriminatory markups are essentially a border phenomenon (Bailey 1966; King and Mieszkowski 1973).

It should be noted that not all household markups need be discriminatory. Certain characteristics of the family—such as number of children or of persons per room—may be associated with an above-average amount of wear and tear and may result in increased maintenance expenditures or a more rapid depreciation of the unit. These additional costs will not affect the value of an owner-occupied unit, holding dwelling quality constant; however, they may induce market rent differentials, given that landlords can pass on part if not all of these costs to their tenants. Differentials of this sort are not discriminatory in nature and should not be confused with markups arising from racial differences alone. Accordingly, empirical analyses of market discrimination should control for systematic variations in those characteristics of rental households that are correlated with race and cause above-average wear and tear on the unit.

This fairly long list of contributing factors should illustrate some of the basic difficulties involved in determining a causal relationship between housing prices and race. Since any of the elements mentioned above can vary across cities and over time, the pattern of prices can also be expected to vary. However, the prevalence of ghetto markups during the early 1960s indicates a certain similarity between a fairly large number of metropolitan areas. By examining ghetto markups in 1960 and their change over time in two cities, we attempt to discover whether the basic factors producing the observed differentials are likely to be operative in the housing markets of today.

ECONOMETRIC ESTIMATES OF HOUSING PREMIUMS ASSOCIATED WITH RACE

Methodology

To estimate the price of ghetto housing in each of our four samples, we regressed rents and housing values on the characteristics of the unit and its neighborhood. The primary focus of our analysis is on the coefficient of one of these neighborhood variables—the concentration of blacks in a neighborhood—which measures the marginal effect of race on rent.

Our underlying model assumes a linear and additive relationship between the logarithm of housing prices and housing attributes:

$$1n\ R_{it} = \sum_j \alpha_j\ X_{jit} + \sum_k \beta_k\ N_{kit} + \epsilon_{it} \tag{4-1}$$

where R_{it} is the rent or value of the ith unit in neighborhood t; $\{X_j\}$ and $\{N_k\}$ are sets of variables describing the j structural and k neighborhood attributes of the dwelling; and ϵ_{it} is a random error which is normally distributed with zero mean and constant variance.[2] In our analysis we assume that units in the same census tracts are in the same neighborhood; so $N_{kit} = N_{k1t}$ for all units i or 1 in tract t.

The coefficients in Equation (4-1) are estimated in two steps, using two distinct data sets, a procedure necessitated by the lack of a single data source containing all the requisite information. In Stage I, rents and housing values are regressed on the structural characteristics of the unit, using micro data obtained from the One-in-a-Hundred Public Use Sample. In Stage II, the α's in Equation (4-1) are replaced by the estimated Stage I parameters and the structural variables are brought over to the left-hand side of the equation. Averaging observations within census tracts yields an equation which is easily estimated from tract statistics:

$$\ln R_t - \sum_j \hat{\alpha}_j \overline{X}_{jt} = \sum_k \beta_k N_{kt} + \overline{f}_t \qquad (4\text{-}2)$$

where bars indicate tract averages and $\overline{f}_t$ is the tract average of $f_{it} = \epsilon_{it} + \sum_j (\alpha_j - \hat{\alpha}_j) X_{jit}$. To reduce the heteroscedasticity associated with averaged data, observations in the Stage II regressions were weighted by the square root of the number of dwellings in the tract.

Since the tract data from the 1960 census do not differentiate dwellings by tenure, owner-occupied and rental units had to be merged in the second stage of the analysis. To do this, we used the tenure-specific Stage I equations to calculate a rent-value ratio for each tract within the sample on the basis of the structural characteristics of the dwelling units contained in that tract. Using this ratio, we converted market values into market rents, and then combined these imputed rents with the actual gross rents of the tract's rental units. Thus, the dependent variable in the Stage II equations is the difference between the composite tract rent just described and the tract rent that is predicted from the Stage I regression for renters.

This general econometric technique gives rise to two types of possible parameter bias. The first is produced when tenure groups are merged in the Stage II equations. Given that at least one of the β's varies by tenure, it is difficult to predict the precise relationship between the actual tenure-specific parameters and the coefficients derived from the unstratified sample. However, with the 1970 data it was possible to distinguish owners from renters at the tract level and to run separate Stage II equations. When the coefficients from these regressions were compared to the coefficients from our basic "combined" equation, the bias associated with merging was found to be small. Most of the combined parameters were bracketed by the corresponding coefficients from the owners' and renters' equations, and when they fell beyond this range, the discrepancies were generally minor.

The second source of parameter bias stems from the two-tiered nature of the regression analysis. If $\{X\}$ and $\{N\}$ are correlated, the

Stage II estimates of β will be biased toward zero. To reduce this error, the two neighborhood proxies that appear in the Public Use Sample were included in the Stage I regressions: one signified a white household head; the other, a central-city location. Although these proxies are admittedly crude, they probably capture most of the correlation between $\{X\}$ and $\{N\}$, thereby reducing parameter bias. These two neighborhood variables are included in the Stage I equations to improve our estimates of α. Since their coefficients are undoubtedly biased, they are not used to calculate predicted tract rents in the Stage II analysis, but instead are set at their mean SMSA values.

Fortunately, the general efficacy of this procedure could be tested by using an expanded version of the 1970 Public Use Sample, available for Boston but not for Pittsburgh. This alternative file describes the unit's neighborhood, as well as its basic structural attributes, and makes it possible to include a fairly large number of neighborhood variables in the underlying Stage I equations. This modification should produce reasonably unbiased estimates of the Stage II neighborhood parameters. When these revised estimates of β were compared to the coefficients derived from our basic estimation procedure, the bias in the latter parameter set was found to be small.[3]

Estimated Racial Differentials
In the tabulation below, we show the estimated racially induced rent differentials for each of the two cities in each of the two sample years (the figures in parentheses are t ratios; the square of the proportion black was not used in the final regressions for Boston 1970 and Pittsburgh):[4]

	Boston		Pittsburgh	
	1960	*1970*	*1960*	*1970*
Proportion black	−0.1166	−0.0488	0.219	−0.344
	(1.490)	(1.471)	(4.02)	(4.16)
Proportion black squared	0.2392			0.416
	(2.280)			(4.57)

In each question, we experimented with linear and quadratic variants of the racial variable; the coefficients presented in the table are those that provided the best overall fit. Since the regressions use the semilog form, the estimated racial parameters depict the proportional price effects of variations in the concentration of blacks in a neighborhood.

The large number of neighborhood and structural attributes that were included in the underlying regression equations should make the coefficients in the table fairly reliable indicators of the net relationship between housing prices and race. The set of Stage I structural attributes is somewhat incomplete in that census statistics do not contain explicit measures of size or quality. However, this omission need not bias β, since the influence of the excluded structural attributes will probably be captured by variables that measure the number of rooms and baths, and the presence of central heat and central air conditioning. The set of Stage II neighborhood attributes is more comprehensive; while the variables differ by city and to a certain extent by year, in each regression they describe the tract's general socioeconomic status, its accessibility to employment, the quality of its public services, its general physical attractiveness, its ethnicity, and the racial composition of its residents.[5]

The coefficients in the foregoing table reveal a common trend: between 1960 and 1970, both cities experienced a net decline in the relative price of ghetto housing. This changing relationship between race and rent is depicted in Figure 4-1, where the estimated rent differentials are plotted against the percent black in the neighborhood. In Boston, the 1960 differentials were U-shaped, with minimum rents found in neighborhoods that were 25 percent black and rents in the ghetto some 12 percent higher than rents in otherwise identical all-white zones. In 1970, these premiums disappeared, and prices declined steadily as the concentration of blacks in a tract increased, with ghetto rents at least 5 percent lower than rents in all-white neighborhoods. Since in 1960 over half of Boston's black population lived in areas displaying premiums, the observed decline in relative prices affected a fairly large fraction of the area's black population.

Declines in the relative price of housing were also evident in Pittsburgh. In 1960, the relationship was linear, with rents rising steadily with the degree of concentration of blacks in a tract, reaching a maximum of about 20 percent in essentially all-black tracts. In 1970, the relationship was U-shaped, with tracts that were 40 percent black having rents some 7 percent lower than in otherwise identical all-white tracts. While rents in all-black tracts continued to be high, the differential between white and black tracts was reduced from 20 to 7 percent.

Alternative functional forms depicting the relationship between race and rent are consistent with the general relationships described

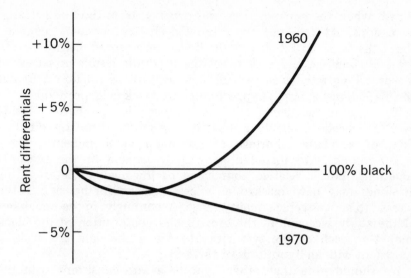

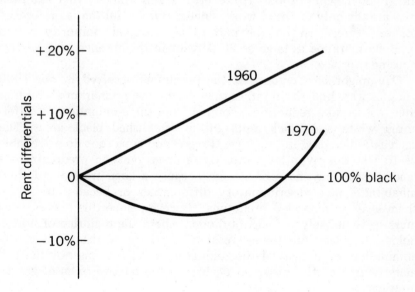

Figure 4-1.   Estimated Rent Differentials in Boston and Pittsburgh.

above. When the squared term was dropped from the 1960 Boston regressions, R^2 fell, but the estimated ghetto premiums remained about the same. In Pittsburgh the linear form proved insignificant in the 1970 sample, and as a result the quadratic results presented in the preceding tabulation provide a conservative estimate of the net decline in housing prices in predominantly black neighborhoods.

These estimated declines in the relative price of ghetto housing over the decade probably reflect the alleviation, if not the elimination, of a relative shortage of housing in predominantly black neighborhoods. We included a vacancy variable in the Stage II equations, but a relative abundance of low-quality, deteriorating dwellings may have masked an excess demand for housing in the average to above-average quality range. Accordingly, in the remainder of the study we explore the growth and composition of the black market in each of the two cities to see if the data are at least consistent with an hypothesis of this sort.

We should note that other hypotheses are consistent with the trends detected in our sample. The decline in relative prices may reflect an increased willingness on the part of blacks to live in racially integrated neighborhoods. However, it seems unlikely that externalities are the only factor at work, since it is doubtful that a preference for self-segregation on the part of an economic minority would produce markups as large as 20 percent in the absence of a relative housing shortage.

One might also argue that the premiums observed in our 1960 samples were household rather than neighborhood markups, and that their subsequent reduction stemmed from the elimination of differential white and black rents within established black areas. The aggregate data used in the Stage II regression equations do not enable us to test this hypothesis directly; average rents in predominantly black tracts may have been high because a large fraction of their inhabitants paid discriminatory differentials or because the areas themselves commanded premiums. However, since this first type of markup is unlikely in neighborhoods where the majority of households are black, it seems reasonably safe to assume that the elimination of individual discriminatory markups was not the primary source of the observed decline in the relative price of ghetto housing.

Finally, the observed price declines may simply be a statistical aberration reflecting biases induced by the omission of quality variables in the underlying Stage I equations. As noted earlier, census data do not provide much information on the overall condition of a housing unit. This omission could induce a decline in the estimated ghetto markups if (1) quality was inversely related to the neighborhood's concentration of blacks and if (2) the price of the omitted quality attributes tended to increase over time. Increases in the real incomes of blacks might produce a price response that is consistent with condition 2 and could account for part of the observed change in the relative price of ghetto housing. Although we suspect that the resulting bias would be relatively small, in the absence of additional empirical evidence it is impossible to dismiss this hypothesis.

AN ANALYSIS OF THE BLACK HOUSING SUBMARKETS IN BOSTON AND PITTSBURGH

If the 1960 ghetto premiums were the result of excess demand for quality housing in predominantly black neighborhoods and if their subsequent reduction stemmed from an alleviation of those shortages, these developments should be reflected in the net movements of demand and supply in the black sectors of the two housing markets. Accordingly, we now test whether changes in the growth and composition of the black submarkets in Boston and Pittsburgh are at least consistent with our basic supply hypothesis. We precede our analysis with a brief summary of market-wide trends in each of the two SMSAs.

Table 4-3 is a summary of twenty-year trends in population, housing, and income in the Boston and Pittsburgh SMSAs. Between 1950 and 1960, the two areas were remarkably similar: each grew by about 200,000 people, underwent suburbanization at a fairly rapid rate, and gained about 26,000 blacks. Since the latter increases occurred almost entirely within the central city, they undoubtedly placed severe strains on the stock of housing in established black neighborhoods, and could easily account for the large ghetto markups we detected in our two 1960 samples.

The experience of the 1960s is more puzzling. Although the two cities began to diverge in ways that could directly affect the fundamental relationship between housing prices and race, their price behavior was similar. The observed decline in the relative price of ghetto housing in Pittsburgh is not surprising in light of the data in Table 4-3, which indicate a situation of overall stagnation, with an increasingly slack central-city market—the home of most of the area's blacks—and a relatively stable black population.

In contrast, the aggregate trends in Boston seem to oppose the notion that falling relative ghetto prices are the direct result of an alleviation of an initial shortage of housing. During the 1960s, Boston continued to register a rapid increase in its black population,

Table 4-3. Selected Characteristics of Boston and Pittsburgh, 1950-1970
(figures in parentheses are proportional rates of growth)

	Pittsburgh			Boston		
	1950	1960	1970	1950	1960	1970
SMSA characteristics						
Population (000 omitted)						
Total	2,213	2,405	2,401	2,370	2,589	2,754
		(+8.7)	(−0.2)		(+7.4)	(+6.1)
White	2,077	2,244	2,231	2,318	2,512	2,627
		(+8.0)	(−0.6)		(+8.3)	(+4.6)
Black	136	162	170	52	78	127
		(+18.0)	(+5.2)		(+50.8)	(+62.3)
Proportion black	0.062	0.067	0.071	0.022	0.030	0.046
Median real family income (1967 = 100)						
Total	4,632	6,579	8,365	5,059	7,731	9,811
		(+42.0)	(27.1)		(+52.8)	(+26.9)
White[a]	NA	6,724	8,560	NA	7,812	9,990
			(+27.3)			(+27.9)
Black	NA	4,269	5,448	NA	5,141	5,777
			(+27.0)			(+12.4)
Relative black income	NA	0.63	0.64	NA	0.66	0.58
Vacancy rate	0.009	0.023	0.023	0.010	0.024	0.023
Proportion of population in central city						
Total	0.31	0.25	0.22	0.34	0.27	0.23
White	0.29	0.22	0.19	0.33	0.25	0.20
Black	0.61	0.62	0.62	0.78	0.81	0.82
Central-city characteristics						
Population (000 omitted)						
Total	677	604	520	801	697	641
		(−10.7)	(−13.9)		(−13.0)	(−8.0)
White	594	504	415	761	634	536
		(−15.3)	(−17.6)		(−16.7)	(−15.4)
Black	83	101	105	40	63	105
		(+22.1)	(4.2)		(+58.0)	(+65.7)
Proportion black	0.122	0.167	0.202	0.050	0.091	0.163
Median real family income						
Total	4,590	6,193	7,560	4,675	6,644	7,826
		(+34.9)	(+22.0)		(+42.1)	(+17.8)
White	NA	6,550	8,110	NA	6,826	8,299
			(+23.8)			(+21.6)
Black	NA	4,235	5,238	NA	4,896	5,434
			(23.6)			(+11.0)
Relative black income	NA	0.65	0.65	NA	0.72	0.65
Vacancy rate	0.008	0.026	0.038	0.009	0.039	0.046

Table 4-3 (cont.)

	Pittsburgh			Boston		
	1950	1960	1970	1950	1960	1970
Suburban characteristics						
Population (000 omitted)						
Total	1,536	1,801	1,881	1,569	1,892	2,113
		(+17.2)	(+4.4)		(+20.6)	(+11.7)
White	1,483	1,740	1,816	1,557	1,878	2,090
		(+17.4)	(+4.4)		(+20.6)	(+11.3)
Black	54	61	65	12	15	22
		(+13.0)	(+6.9)		(+25.3)	(+46.7)
Proportion black	0.035	0.034	0.035	0.007	0.008	0.011
Vacancy rate	0.009	0.021	0.018	0.010	0.018	0.015

[a]Median income for whites is estimated by taking a weighted average of the median income of black families and of all families.

and at the same time experienced a deceleration in the rate of white migration from the central city. These macro developments seem to imply increased pressures on the black housing market, and make the observed decline in prices somewhat unexpected.

To achieve a fuller understanding of these trends, we undertook a detailed analysis of movements within the black and white sectors of the central cities of each of two sample areas. Through this disaggregated approach we were able to relate changes in the housing stock and population of those areas to the observed declines in the relative price of ghetto housing and to establish the overall plausibility of our basic supply hypothesis. Although our analysis remains conjectural, we were able to isolate several key factors that could conceivably explain the trends we observed in our samples.

Boston

In Boston the majority of black households live in one centrally located cluster of physically contiguous tracts. This general pattern has remained essentially constant over the last twenty years. Between 1950 and 1970, the proportion of blacks in the city increased from 78 to 82 percent, even though the number of suburban blacks grew from about 12,000 to 22,000. This extreme concentration of blacks within the central city enables us to restrict our analysis primarily to demand and supply developments that occurred within its bounds.

The aggregate census data presented in Table 4-3 provide some clue to the overall growth in black housing demands between 1950 and 1970. The number of central-city blacks increased by 58 percent in the ·1950s and by 65 percent in the 1960s, a roughly similar pattern of growth that was maintained by a relatively high rate of immigration to the metropolis. During the 1960s, at least, this growth was accompanied by a rise of about 11 percent in the real income of central-city blacks, a relatively modest gain when compared to the 22 percent rise for whites. Thus, in each decade, there appears to have been a significant increase in the number of units demanded by blacks as well as a moderate increase in their average quality demands. Although there probably was a slight acceleration in the overall growth of demand in the 1960s, the experience of the two decades was not remarkably different.

Census data also provide clues to the overall change in supply, although the various patterns are often difficult to decipher. Some general trends can be discovered by dividing central-city tracts into three mutually exclusive groups: established black neighborhoods (type 3); border neighborhoods (type 2); and predominantly white neighborhoods (type 1). Type 3 areas are tracts with a population at least 20 percent black,[6] type 2 neighborhoods include all tracts immediately adjacent to such areas, and type 1 areas include the remainder of the central city. In Table 4-4, we display some pertinent characteristics of the housing stock and population of each neighborhood type in each of three census years.

Two general trends are immediately evident from that table. The first is the distinct increase in both the size and overall quality of housing in the established black areas of the city (type 3 tracts). Size increases are indicated by the rise in the fraction of units in single-family structures, from 6 percent in 1950 to 19 percent in 1970. Although these improvements occurred in each decade, during the 1960s they were offset by an accompanying rise in the size of the average black household, and as a result, there was a slight increase in the fraction of crowded units.

Census indicators of quality also increased. Between 1950 and 1970, the fraction of units with complete plumbing facilities rose from 66 to 85 percent; with central heat, from 61 to 78 percent; and with more than one bath, from about 3 (in 1960) to 7 percent. Again, with the exception of the heating variable, these increases occurred in both decades, implying a continual improvement in housing quality in type 3 neighborhoods throughout the twenty-year period. While housing quality also rose in other areas of the city, the gap between type 3 and type 1 areas decreased, even though the ratio of incomes in these two neighborhood types fell from about 0.70 in 1950 and 1960 to about 0.63 in 1970.

This apparent improvement in the stock of housing in pre-

Table 4-4. Housing and Demographic Trends in Boston, by Tract Type, 1950-1970

	1950			1960			1970		
	Type 1	Type 2	Type 3	Type 1	Type 2	Type 3	Type 1	Type 2	Type 3
Population (thous.)	617.0	130.1	54.3	483.0	118.9	97.2	365.8	148.0	137.6
No. of units (thous.)	170.5	36.0	15.6	155.3	50.2	34.5	130.0	58.8	48.3
Mean rent[a] (dol.)	40	39	32	78	73	66	130	133	106
Mean value (thous. dol.)	9.7	6.7	6.1	13.0	11.6	7.4	18.6	16.0	13.0
Percent owner-occupied	29	12	12	36	16	16	33	19	18
Percent single family	15	05	06	22	09	10	16	14	19
Percent duplex	22	11	10	21	07	10	23	12	12
Percent complete plumbing	88	80	66	91	86	79	93	89	85
Percent central heat	74	74	61	82	88	81	83	86	78
Age (years)									
0-10	5	8	3	7	4	3	10	7	6
11-20	5	1	2	4	3	4	6	3	5
Over 21	91	91	95	89	93	93	84	90	89
Percent more than one bath	NA	NA	NA	7	5	3	13	9	7
Percent black	1	.7	55	1	5	55	1	5	68
Mean real family income[b] (thous. dol.)	4.0	3.2	2.9	8.1	7.3	5.7	9.9	9.3	6.3
Percent vacant and available for rent or sale	1	1	1	3	5	6	3	4	9
Crowding (percent)									
Under 0.5 persons per room	NA	NA	NA	45	46	46	52	47	44
Over 1.0 persons per room	NA	NA	NA	8	7	11	6	7	9

[a]Contract rent in 1950; gross rent in 1960 and 1970.
[b]Data for 1950 include unrelated individuals.

dominantly black neighborhoods occurred both through the peripheral expansion of the ghetto into neighborhoods with superior
housing units and through a net upgrading of the stock in established
type 3 areas. In Table 4-5, we depict the ten-year changes for two
kinds of neighborhoods: incorporated tracts, which went from types
1 and 2 to type 3 during the decade; and established tracts, which
were type 3 at both the beginning and end of the period. In each
decade net increases were registered in the overall quality of units in
established ghetto areas, a development that could reflect either an
upgrading of existing units or an abandonment of the poorest-quality
dwellings. Peripheral expansion into higher-quality areas also contrib-
uted to the improved stock of housing, although a comparison of this
stock between 1960 and 1970 offers some evidence that incorporation was accompanied by a net decline in the level of housing
services.

The second major trend that is evident from Table 4-4 is the
dramatic increase in the vacancy rates in predominantly black
neighborhoods, from less than 1 percent in 1950 to more than 9
percent in 1970. This trend reflects net shifts in the population
between the central city and the suburbs and within and between the
three types of central-city tract. The precise nature of these shifts is
revealed in Table 4-6, in which border and established black tracts
are divided into four groups on the basis of their initial concentration
of blacks and developments in the latter tracts are distinguished from
developments in tracts that were type 1 at the beginning of the
period. Several type 1 tracts that became type 3 during the 1960s are
also distinguished from those that were still predominantly white in
1970.

In both decades, integrating and established black tracts accounted
for a large fraction of the net decline in the city population—about
53 percent during the 1950s and 78 percent during the 1960s. This
rapid rate of white out-migration from racially mixed areas led to
population declines in both border and established black areas in
spite of the concurrent growth in the city's black population. Since
black growth was for the most part directed toward border tracts,
neighborhoods with the highest initial concentrations of blacks
experienced the largest proportional population declines. As whites
fled from the path of ghetto expansion and as blacks moved from the
most heavily black tracts, the ghetto market grew increasingly slack,
despite frequent declines in the net housing stock in both incorporated and established areas.

Together, these two trends depict a general process of ghetto
upgrading and expansion that could presumably work to alleviate an

Table 4-5.   Net Changes in the Stock of Housing in Boston, 1950-1960 and 1960-1970 (figures in parentheses are growth rates)

| | 1950-1960 | | | | 1960-1970 | | | |
| | Incorporated Tracts | | Established Tracts | | Incorporated Tracts[a] | | Established Tracts | |
	1950	1960	1950	1960	1960	1970	1960	1970
Population (thous.)	77.9	63.7	54.3	33.5	78.2	71.4	97.2	61.4
Whites	71.7	36.9 (−48%)	24.4	6.4 (−74%)	74.3	31.4 (−58%)	43.7	11.1 (−74%)
Blacks	6.2	26.8 (+332%)	29.9	27.1 (−9%)	3.9	40.0 (+926%)	53.5	50.3 (−6%)
No. of units (thous.)	21.3	23.1	15.6	14.4	24.8	23.9	34.5	23.5
Mean rent (dol.)	39	68	32	62	72	108	66	104
Mean value (thous. dol.)	6.6	8.0	6.1	6.3	10.0	13.5	7.4	12.7
Percent owner-occupied	15	16	12	15	22	21	16	18
Percent single-family	6	8	6	14	9	17	10	19
Percent complete plumbing	84	83	66	72	95	89	79	89
Percent central heat	74	84	61	77	88	79	81	84
Percent more than one bath	NA	3	NA	4	3	6	3	8
Percent black	8	42	55	81	5	56	55	82
Mean real family income (thous. dol.)	3.5[b]	5.9	2.9[b]	5.3	6.5	6.3	5.7	6.4
Percent vacant and available for rent or sale	1	5	1	6	3	9	6	10
Crowding (percent)								
Under 0.5 persons per room	NA	NA	NA	NA	43	43	46	49
Over 1.0 persons per room	NA	NA	NA	NA	9	11	11	8

NA = not available.

[a]Excludes some tracts whose boundaries changed during the decade.

[b]Data include unrelated individuals.

Table 4-6. Net Population Movements in Boston, 1950-1970 (percent)

	1950-1960					1960-1970[a]						
	Border			Established	Rest of City	Border			Established		Rest of City	
	Initial Percent Black					Initial Percent Black					Incorporated	
	0-10	10-20	20-50	50+	Rest of City	0-10	10-20	20-50	50+	Total	porated	Other
Population												
Initial	93.6	36.5	15.0	39.3	617.0	84.5	19.4	30.2	57.7	483.0	33.7	449.3
Final	75.5	25.6	9.5	24.4	564.1	79.9	15.9	23.9	37.6	466.4	31.7	434.6
Net change	-18.1	-10.9	-5.5	-14.9	-52.9	-4.6	-3.5	-6.3	-20.1	-16.6	-2.0	-14.7
Proportionate change	-0.19	-0.30	-0.37	-0.38	-0.08	-0.05	-0.18	-0.21	-0.35	-0.03	-0.06	-0.03
Whites												
Initial	90.0	31.3	10.9	14.1	615.5	82.9	16.6	21.4	15.7	480.0	32.7	447.3
Final	56.1	15.8	2.2	4.5	556.3	62.4	7.0	6.9	4.0	442.7	15.7	427.0
Net change	-33.9	-15.5	-8.7	-9.6	-59.2	-20.5	-9.6	-14.5	-11.7	-37.3	-17.0	-20.3
Proportionate change	-0.38	-0.50	-0.80	-0.68	-0.10	-0.25	-0.58	-0.68	-0.75	-0.08	-0.52	-0.05
Blacks												
Initial	3.6	5.2	4.5	25.2	1.5	1.6	2.8	8.8	42.0	3.0	1.0	2.0
Final	19.4	9.8	7.3	19.9	7.8	17.5	8.9	17.0	33.6	23.7	16.0	7.6
Net change	+15.8	+4.6	+2.8	-5.3	+6.3	+15.9	+6.1	+8.2	-8.4	+20.7	+15.0	+5.6
Proportionate change	+4.39	+0.88	+0.62	-0.21	+4.20	+9.94	+2.18	+0.93	-0.20	+6.90	+15.0	+2.80
Proportion black												
Initial	0.04	0.14	0.30	0.64	0	0.02	0.14	0.29	0.73	0.01	0.03	0
Final	0.26	0.38	0.77	0.82	0.01	0.22	0.56	0.71	0.89	0.05	0.51	0.02
Change	+0.22	+0.24	+0.47	+0.18	+0.01	+0.20	+0.42	+0.42	+0.16	+0.04	+0.48	+0.02
Number of units												
Initial	26.4	9.6	4.3	11.3	170.5	34.2	6.2	11.9	22.5	155.3	10.4	144.9
Final	32.2	10.3	2.9	10.8	186.8	33.8	5.6	8.4	15.2	162.8	10.5	152.3

Proportion vacant												
Initial	0.01	0.01	0.02	0.00	0.01	0.04	0.06	0.06	0.06	0.03	0.02	0.03
Final	0.07	0.07	0.05	0.07	0.03	0.05	0.10	0.08	0.11	0.03	0.08	0.03
Crowding												
Proportion under 0.5 person per room												
Initial	NA	NA	NA	NA	NA	0.48	0.39	0.41	0.48	0.45	0.42	0.45
Final	NA	NA	NA	NA	NA	0.48	0.46	0.45	0.52	0.51	0.38	0.52
Proportion over 1.0 person per room												
Initial	NA	NA	NA	NA	NA	0.06	0.13	0.11	0.10	0.08	0.08	0.08
Final	NA	NA	NA	NA	NA	0.07	0.14	0.09	0.07	0.06	0.08	0.06

NA = not available.

[a]Excludes some tracts whose boundaries were redrawn between 1960 and 1970.

excess demand for quality housing within the predominantly black sectors of the city. Nevertheless, the similarities between the experiences of the two decades seem somewhat inconsistent with the observed decline in the relative price of ghetto housing. Since black demand rose at roughly the same rate in each of the two periods, one would expect a roughly similar pattern of prices at the end of each decade.

Of course, it is possible that the relative price of ghetto housing was even higher at the beginning of the twenty-year period and that the decline that occurred between 1950 and 1960 was similar in magnitude to the one we detected in our samples. However, if this basic premise is unacceptable—and unfortunately, we do not have the means either to refute or support it—one must determine why a roughly similar increase in black demand produced a premium in 1960 and a discount in 1970.

A reexamination of some of the variables described in Tables 4-3, 4-4, and 4-5 does point to two differences between the decades that could conceivably account for the differential pattern of prices. The first reflects developments in the white rather than black sector of the market. Although vacancy rates in predominantly black type 3 tracts rose by about the same amount in each decade, rates in predominantly white type 1 tracts increased between 1950 and 1960, and then remained stable throughout the 1960s. Presumably, this stability in the white sectors of the city stems from the decline in the rate of white out-migration from areas not adjacent to the ghetto—from 10 percent in the 1950s to 5 percent in the 1960s—and may reflect changes in the birth rate, in the rate of family formation, or in a variety of other demographic and socioeconomic factors that affect the locational decisions of households. Whatever its source, it may have created a situation whereby housing in the white sectors of the city became scarce, and thus more expensive relative to housing in black and in integrated areas. This seemingly exogenous development in the white submarket could conceivably account for part, if not all, of the observed decline in the relative price of ghetto housing, even without a fundamental change in the way in which housing was supplied to blacks.

A second trend, however, points to possible shifts within the black sectors of the market, and in particular, indicates a change in the speed at which housing was made available to blacks. Although quality improvements were continual, data in Tables 4-5 and 4-6 imply an increase in the rate of ghetto expansion during the 1960s, evidenced by an increase in the speed of racial transition in border areas.

The population trends in Table 4-5 suggest that there was a fairly large increase during the 1960s in the rate at which blacks entered previously white or border neighborhoods and an accompanying rise in the rate at which whites evacuated those areas. These aggregate trends probably reflect a more rapid integration and resegregation of border tracts. In the first decade, the average concentration of blacks in incorporated tracts increased by a factor of five; and in the second decade, by a factor of ten. Indeed, during the 1960s, seven times as many whites as blacks lived in tracts that experienced substantial racial transition, where "substantial transition" is defined as an increase of 3 percent or more in the fraction black in a neighborhood.

Several factors might explain this apparent shift in the rate of ghetto expansion. One possible source is the general loosening of the central-city market between 1950 and 1960, a development that presumably reflects the rapid rate of white suburbanization, especially through migration from tracts near the ghetto border. During the 1950s, the black sector incorporated tracts whose average vacancy rate was under 1 percent; this unusually tight market may have hindered racial transition by reducing the opportunity costs of overt discriminatory behavior. By 1960, vacancy rates within the central city had increased to an average of 3 percent. This general weakening of the market may have undermined private and institutional resistance to integration, and may have facilitated black entry into previously all-white neighborhoods.

A second factor that might explain the apparent acceleration of ghetto expansion is the initiation of legislative reforms that were designed to ameliorate institutionalized discrimination in housing. If effective, such legislation would increase the ability of blacks to bid against whites in predominantly white neighborhoods and would encourage the initial integration of previously segregated tracts. In the absence of pronounced shifts in the racial attitudes of households, such legislation would probably not promote racial balance in neighborhoods, but instead would simply accelerate the black sector's rate of peripheral expansion.

Finally, the increased rate of racial transition might also reflect systematic differences in the characteristics of border neighborhoods at the beginning of the two decades. If, for example, some housing were particularly suited to the needs of the black community, it could be incorporated with little or no modification. On the other hand, if housing in the immediate path of expansion were particularly inappropriate, expansion would involve a significant degree of conversion or leapfrogging, and would become both cumbersome and expensive. Characteristics of the border residents—particularly socio-economic status and ethnicity—can also affect the speed of racial transition, given that different groups have different attitudes toward race and toward the overall desirability of their neighborhoods. Thus, it is possible that in 1960, conditions in border neighborhoods were more amenable to expansion than they were in the previous decade, and that as a result, transition occurred at a somewhat faster rate.

Although our data do not enable us to accept or reject this hypothesis, a comparison of type 2 neighborhoods in 1950 and 1960 does not reveal any strong evidence of an effect of this sort. From a relative standpoint, there was no significant difference in border neighborhoods between the two years. The concentration of various ethnic groups remained about the same, and although incomes and the overall quality of the stock increased between 1950 and 1960, they did not appear to increase relative to the average quality and income levels within the predominantly black sectors of the market. As a result, we suspect that this third factor had relatively little impact on the overall rate of neighborhood transition, and that the other sources noted above were the principal vehicles of the apparent change.

Thus, while the various trends described in this section result in a somewhat fragmentary image of the growth and composition of Boston's black housing market, and while the source of many of these developments is far from clear, the market data are generally consistent with our hypothesis that the observed reduction in the relative price of ghetto housing stemmed from an alleviation of the excess demand for quality housing in predominantly black areas. That same data suggest several possible reasons for this response. The first is an accelerated rate of ghetto expansion, due perhaps to the legislative reforms of the 1960s or to the generalized increase in vacancy rates between 1950 and 1960. The second possible reason is associated not so much with developments in the black sectors of the market, but rather with the decreased rate of white out-migration from white neighborhoods located beyond the path of ghetto expansion. This change accentuated differences in vacancy rates between white and black neighborhoods, and may have created a relative housing shortage in the predominantly white sectors of the city.

Pittsburgh

In Pittsburgh during the 1960s, the total population showed no growth and the black population very little. In Boston, by contrast, the white population showed little growth, but the black population grew very rapidly. Thus, in Pittsburgh the only source of increased demand for housing was through increases in real income. The demand from this source resulted in the construction of 109,000 new units during the 1960s, or about 14 percent of the 1970 housing stock. These units were predominantly owner-occupied and suburban, the latter being in part due to major highway improvements. The accompanying movement of white households from the central city (Table 4-3), where the majority of blacks lived, should have greatly increased the availability of housing to the latter. Indeed, a potentially substantial abandonment problem in the city was offset in two ways: First, the combination of an aggressive urban renewal program coupled with private actions resulted in the demolition of approximately 7 percent of the 1960 central-city stock; and second, an increase in household formation during the decade produced a decline in average household size in the city from 3.21 to 2.92 persons.

An important distinction between Boston and Pittsburgh is in the pattern of black residential location. In Boston, as noted, black residences were generally in contiguous census tracts located overwhelmingly in the central city. In Pittsburgh, by contrast, there were four main black residential areas in 1970 with several additional, smaller concentrations. Only two of the four, which include about 70 percent of the black population, are exclusively in the central city.[7] Our analysis is restricted to the four principal areas.

Also unlike Boston, the extent of racial transition of neighborhoods was really quite modest during the 1960s. We used a classification scheme similar to one used for the Boston analysis: Each of the four main black residential areas included in our analysis tracts is classified as being either in the core enclave, in the area of racial transition around the core, or in a ring of essentially white tracts around the second group.[8] As in the Boston analysis, the neighborhood types are coded 3, 2, and 1. The main pattern from 1950 through 1970 was for the black population to displace the white population in those areas in which blacks as of 1950 amounted to at least a measurable share of the population. This pattern is reflected in the entries in the first row of Table 4-7, which shows the fraction of population accounted for by blacks in each neighborhood type for the three census years; the black fraction of the population in the predominantly black neighborhood (type 3) rose steadily from 0.52 to 0.72. In all four residential areas during the 1950s, the number of census tracts with populations 30 percent or more black doubled (from 16 to 32); during the 1960s only nine more shifted, and these were spread over three of the four residential areas.[9] Hence

Table 4-7.   Housing and Demographic Trends in Pittsburgh, by Tract Type, 1950-1970

	1950[a]			1960			1970		
	Type 1	Type 2	Type 3	Type 1	Type 2	Type 3	Type 1	Type 2	Type 3
Percent population black	2	12	52	2	13	61	2	13	72
Percent units vacant	2	2	1	4	4	4	6	06	9
Percent units owner-occupied	39	44	30	49	43	46	48	43	38
Percent units in single-unit structures	35	46	32	52	53	50	47	46	49
Percent units in structures with 5 or more units	18	11	20	20	16	19	26	24	24
Percent units with									
Complete plumbing[b]	60	54	44	87	83	80	93	90	92
Central heat	65	61	55	81	72	60	85	84	76
1-3 rooms	NA	NA	NA	29	32	34	30	30	26
7 or more rooms	NA	NA	NA	15	11	11	14	12	13
Percent units in sound condition[c]	NA	NA	NA	.82	.70	.63	NA	NA	NA
Mean income (thous. dol.)[d]	3.22	3.07	2.32	7.54	5.84	4.82	11.85	9.30	7.64
Percent households living in dwelling									
2 years or less	NA	NA	NA	27	25	29	28	30	26
2-5 Years	NA	NA	NA	25	29	28	32	30	39
Over 5 years	NA	NA	NA	48	51	44	40	39	36

NA = not available.

[a]Tracts included in 1950 differ slightly from those for 1960 and 1970 due to noncomparability of tract boundaries.

[b]Includes piped hot and cold water and exclusive use of toilet and tub or shower.

[c]Not available for 1950 and 1970.

[d]For 1950, income of families and unrelated individuals; for 1960 and 1970, income of families.

the number of "transitional tracts" out of the 130 included in the analysis was quite small during the 1960s.

The explanation for the decrease in housing premiums paid by blacks in Pittsburgh, documented earlier, would seem logically to lie in the supply of housing available to blacks—both the number of units and their quality. The factors leading to higher rates of housing availability have already been noted, and the net effect of these factors is evident in the vacancy rates shown in Table 4-6. The Pittsburgh area went from an extremely tight market in 1950 to a fairly loose one by 1970. Similar to the Boston experience, in the predominantly black neighborhoods the pattern was accentuated by the high (9 percent) vacancy rates in 1970; unlike Boston, fairly high rates were also present in the type 1 neighborhoods. The overall softness in the market, of course, increases the choice not only of blacks but also of whites, making it easier for the latter to move away from blacks if they so choose. Likewise, higher vacancy rates impose additional costs on landlords, as well as on owner-occupants selling their homes who prefer not to deal with blacks, especially in those areas where blacks represent a sizable portion of the population.

An important question, though, concerns the quality of housing made available during the 1960s through the suburbanization of white households. This is especially critical because the real income of the black families rose by 28 percent from 1960 to 1970. (In Boston the increase was less than half this amount.) Data included in Table 4-7 provide some information on this point. In terms of the crude indications afforded by the fraction of units with complete plumbing facilities and central heat, there has been a massive improvement in basic dwelling unit quality since 1950; in 1970, for example, 92 percent of the units in the predominantly black neighborhood had full plumbing compared with 44 percent in 1950.[10] By 1970 the dwellings in the type 3 neighborhoods were remarkably similar in a number of characteristics to units in "all-white" (type 1) neighborhoods.

It has already been noted that the amount of housing made available to blacks through the expansion of predominantly black neighborhoods into all-white tracts was relatively unimportant. It is nevertheless of interest to contrast the "quality" of housing made available in this way with that already found in predominantly black neighborhoods. The data in Table 4-8 contrast the 1960 characteristics of nontransitional tracts (designated 1:1, 2:2, and 3:3) with tracts in transition (designated 1:2 and 2:3) over the decade. An examination of the data reveals no clear pattern; and on balance we conclude that the stock in the transitional and nontransitional areas was roughly similar. The more general conclusion following from this and several prior statements is that much of the improvement in the stock of housing in predominantly black neighborhoods over the decade involved upgrading of part of the existing stock and demolition of some of the worst stock through urban renewal.

To amplify this last point somewhat, it could be argued that the very tight market conditions of the 1950s, which could have made price and other types of discrimination against blacks fairly inexpensive to those so discriminating, produced the premiums blacks paid in 1960. During the 1960s the softer market conditions helped to

Table 4-8. Comparison of 1960 Characteristics of Nontransitional Tracts in Pittsburgh with Tracts in Transition during 1960-1970 (fractions of units having the stated characteristic)

| | Type of Tract[a] | | | | | |
	1:1	1:2	2:2	2:3	3:3[b]	3:3+[c]
Vacant	.04	.05	.05	.02	.04	.04
Owner-occupied	.50	.44	.46	.45	.36	.36
In 1-unit structures	.52	.49	.55	.61	.49	.51
In units in structures of 5 or more units	.20	.20	.16	.16	.19	.23
With complete plumbing	.88	.85	.83	.90	.80	.85
With central heat	.81	.82	.78	.77	.59	.69
In sound condition	.82	.84	.72	.70	.63	.68
With 1-3 rooms	.29	.30	.30	.26	.33	.29
With 7 or more rooms	.15	.14	.12	.14	.13	.12

[a]Nontransitional tracts are designated 1:1, 2:2, and 3:3; the others are transitional. The numbers 1, 2, and 3 refer to the neighborhood types as defined earlier.

[b]All tracts in type 3 neighborhoods in 1960.

[c]In tracts designated 3+, the black fraction of the population increased by 0.20 during 1960-1970.

dissipate the premiums; nevertheless, prices had to remain high enough to induce improvements black households sought to have made in the available stock. The higher demand was a product of rising real incomes combined with the higher social housing standards generally evident in the postwar era. The long response time of housing suppliers to the high prices is consistent with the fragmentary evidence on the price elasticity of supply of existing units (de Leeuw and Ekanem 1971; Ozanne and Struyk 1976; and de Leeuw and Struyk 1975, Chap. 5). In transitional neighborhoods, where housing suppliers' uncertainty is greater, even slower response would be likely. The primary importance of the improvement of the stock already largely occupied by black households seems to be worth emphasizing, since its role in alleviating pressure at the boundary of the black neighborhood has received very little attention in prior analyses. The marked reduction of housing premiums to blacks in Pittsburgh, then, seems to be attributable to a decrease in the competition for central-city and near-suburban housing stock caused by the outmovement of white households and to the response of housing suppliers in predominantly black neighborhoods to the demand by blacks for higher-quality units.

SUMMARY AND CONCLUSIONS

In this analysis we used data from the 1960 and 1970 census of Population and Housing to estimate the relative price of ghetto housing in Boston and Pittsburgh in each of the two sample years. For the decade considered, the experiences of the two cities were remarkably alike. In Pittsburgh, the markups in all-black tracts dropped from 20 percent in 1960 to 7 percent in 1970, while in Boston a 12 percent premium was replaced by a 5 percent ghetto discount.

Although the estimated differentials in price could be explained by a number of factors, we hypothesized that in both cities the 1960 markups reflected a shortage of quality housing in predominantly black neighborhoods and that the subsequent reduction of the markups stemmed from an alleviation of that initial excess demand. In the remainder of the study, we examined twenty-year trends in the characteristics of census tracts in both Boston and Pittsburgh to determine if market developments were consistent with our basic supply hypothesis. We also explored alternative sources of the hypothesized supply response.

In Boston, the overall price decline was consistent with a deceleration in the rate of white evacuation from white neighborhoods not adjacent to the ghetto, and with certain other developments that occurred within the black and border sectors of the central-city housing market. Since the growth in black demand was fairly constant between 1950 and 1970, the decline in the relative price of ghetto housing during the 1960s suggests a distinct shift in supply. Although the qualitative nature of the supply response was essentially the same in each decade—rising vacancy rates in predominantly black neighborhoods accompanied by significant increases in the overall quality of housing—its quantitative nature did appear to change, reflecting an acceleration in the rate of ghetto expansion. This change could be attributed to a variety of factors, including increased vacancy rates at the beginning of the decade and open housing reforms of the late 1960s.

Pittsburgh exhibited many of these same general patterns. In each decade, there was a fairly substantial rise in the overall quality of housing in predominantly black tracts; and these gains were once again accompanied by rising vacancy rates within the ghetto. In Pittsburgh, however, the increase in black demand between 1960 and 1970 was probably modest, given the relative stability of the black population. As a result, the observed price decline could simply reflect movements along a relatively stable supply curve for housing, rather than shifts in the way or in the rate at which units were supplied to blacks.

The similarities between the experiences of our two cities, despite their widely different patterns of demand, suggest possible declines in the relative price of ghetto housing in other metropolitan areas. Again, since many factors could affect the relative price of ghetto housing, different cities could easily display a noticeably different pattern. Nevertheless, our analysis does illustrate the need to reassess the evidence of the early 1960s in light of recent market developments which might facilitate the ability of the black sector to adjust to an excess demand for housing. In the end, the question is essentially an empirical one, and definitive answers await the arrival of similar analyses applied to a fairly large number of housing markets.

APPENDIX 4A

Table 4A-1. Stage I Boston Regressions,[a] 1960 and 1970 (figures in parentheses are *t* ratios)

Independent Variables	Regression for *ln Value*		Regression for *ln Rent*	
	1970	1960	1970	1960
Structural variables				
ln rooms[b]	.36	.46	.30	.29
	(16.20)	(21.89)	(23.49)	(24.82)
Central heat[c]	.07	.34	.09	.23
(yes=1)	(2.17)	(11.34)	(5.72)	(21.23)
Units in structure				
Duplex		.11	−.09	−.02
(yes=1)	d	(3.35)	(3.84)	(1.12)
Three or more	d	.21	−.11	−.04
(yes=1)		(5.42)	(4.97)	(2.75)
Central air conditioning	.10	e	.32	e
(yes=1)	(2.24)		(9.43)	
Sound condition	d	.26	d	.06
(yes=1)		(11.08)		(5.28)
Basement	.09	.11	.06	.03
(yes=1)	(3.91)	(4.24)	(3.15)	(1.17)
Number of bathrooms				
One and one-half	.16	e	.14	3
(yes=1)	(12.38)		(4.70)	
Two or more	.32	e	.25	e
(yes=1)	(19.40)		(7.39)	

Table 4A-1 (cont.)

Independent Variables	Regression for ln Rent 1970	Regression for ln Rent 1960	Regression for ln Rent 1970	Regression for ln Rent 1960
More than one (yes=1)	−	.30 (23.27)	−	.27 (8.80)
Age of structure				
Built 1960-1970 (yes=1)	.21 (12.44)	−	.18 (10.52)	−
Built 1950-1959 (yes=1)	.17 (11.63)	.28 (18.60)	−.13 (6.77)	−.07 (3.60)
Built 1940-1949 (yes=1)	.11 (6.15)	.20 (10.26)	−.06 (3.42)	−.11 (4.92)
Complete plumbing[f] (yes=1)	.18 (2.94)	.21 (4.95)	.25 (10.58)	.23 (16.19)
Household Variables Crowding				
Less than 0.5 persons per room (yes=1)	.01 (0.32)	.04 (3.55)	−.06 (6.16)	−.06 (6.41)
More than one person per room (yes=1)	−.07 (2.87)	−.06 (2.33)	−	−.02 (0.95)
Length of residence				
7-20 years (yes=1)	−.07 (5.52)	−.04 (3.08)	−.14 (12.05)	−.08 (8.07)
Over 20 years (yes=1)	−.11 (6.67)	−.08 (4.81)	−.18 (9.92)	−.10 (6.94)
Neighborhood variables Accessibility				
Central city location (yes=1)	−.13 (6.01)	−.17 (13.81)	.05 (3.77)	−.08 (8.47)
Proportion of units in single-family structure	−.08 (2.33)	g	−.12 (3.90)	g
Proportion of units in structures with 5 or more units	.01 (0.18)	g	.10 (3.09)	g
Demographic variables Average neighborhood income (thous. dol.)	.01 (1.83)	g	.01 (1.54)	g
Proportion high status[h]	.07 (0.60)	g	.19 (2.52)	g
Proportion black	−.04 (2.01)	g	.08 (1.91)	g
Black household head (yes=1)	−.04 (0.54)	−	.02 (0.64)	−
White household head (yes=1)	−	.12 (2.15)	−	.02 (1.04)
Proportion Puerto Rican	−.98 (2.15)	g	−.09 (0.37)	g

Table 4A-1 (cont.)

Independent Variables	Regression for In Rent		Regression for In Rent	
	1970	1960	1970	1960
Puerto Rican household head (yes=1)	.08 (0.67)	–	.01 (0.09)	–
Proportion high-valued units[i]	.54 (8.95)	–	.57 (11.65)	–
Proportion vacant units	−2.06 (5.13)	g	−.78 (3.90)	g
Constant	8.67 (102.9)	7.58 (93.42)	3.96 (87.16)	3.57 (93.57)
F	179.87	208.75	140.80	189.97
R^2	.57	.44	.48	.40
Number of observations	3,364	4,284	3,985	4,651

[a]The 1960 sample includes all SMSAs in Massachusetts; the 1970 sample includes the Boston urbanized area. The housing unit values are from the Census Bureau, which lists reported values in intervals that range from $0-$5,000 to $50,000 or more. Units were assigned values equal to the midpoint of these intervals except that units in the $0-$5,000 range were assigned the value of $3,500 and units in the $50,000 or over range were assigned values of $60,000. This procedure corresponds to that used by the Census for calculating average values of housing units.

"Rent" refers to gross monthly rent, which equals the contract rent of the unit plus the value of all utilities purchased by the tenant. For 1970, gross rent data are continuous.

[b]A value of 12 was assigned to units classified as having nine or more rooms.

[c]Includes steam or hot water or a central warm air furnace of a built-in electric unit.

[d]All owner-occupied units were one-unit structures.

[e]Data not included in public use sample.

[f]Includes each of the following: piped hot and cold water inside the structure, a flush toilet, and a bathtub or shower inside the structure which is used only by the occupants of that structure.

[g]Neighborhood data are available only from the 1970 Neighborhood Public Use Sample for the New England Census Division.

[h]This is a composite variable that measures the occupation and education of households residing in the unit's neighborhood: $X = 0.5 (0 + E)$, where 0 = proportion of workers who are professional, technical, and kindred workers, and managers and administrators except farm; and E = proportion of persons 25-54 years old with four or more years of college.

[i]Weighted average of the proportion of units with above-average values and gross rents: $X = p_0(HV) + p_r(HR)$, where HV is the proportion of owner-occupied units with values of $25,000 or more; HR is the proportion of renter-occupied units with gross rents of $150 or more; and p_0 and p_r are the proportions of the neighborhood's dwelling units that are owner-occupied and rented, respectively.

Table 4A-2. Stage I Pittsburgh Regressions,[a] 1960 and 1970 (t statistics in parentheses)

Independent Variables[b]	Regression for ln Rent		Regression for ln Value	
	1960	*1970*	*1960*	*1970*
Constant	3.15 (145)	3.46 (57.8)	7.67 (282)	7.24 (69.6)
ln rooms	.241 (27.4)	–	.423 (32.8)	.837 (16.6)
No. of rooms	–	.106 (14.3)	–	–
Private toilet (yes=1)	.136 (8.52)	–	–	–
Hot water (yes=1)	.232 (12.3)	–	–	–
Complete plumbing (yes=1)	–	.184 (5.25)	.283 (16.8)	–
Basement (yes=1)	.145 (10.8)	.122 (4.16)	.152 (11.6)	–
Central heat (yes=1)	.108 (10.6)	.251 (10.2)	.284 (23.6)	.443 (7.62)
Sound condition (yes=1)	.072 (7.46)	c	.219 (17.2)	c
Built 1960-1970 (yes=1)	–	.188 (5.90)	–	.587 (19.1)
Built 1950-1959 (yes=1)	.272 (15.7)	.176 (5.76)	.508 (53.3)	.577 (24.5)
Built 1940-1949 (yes=1)	.097 (6.44)	.070 (2.68)	.345 (30.8)	.418 (13.5)
1-unit structure (yes=1)	–	–.329 (10.8)		d
2-unit structure (yes=1)	.029 (2.54)	–.307 (10.3)	.278 (8.34)	d
3-4-unit structure (yes=1)	.011 (.90)	–.203 (6.69)	.309 (6.00)	d
5-9-unit structure (yes=1)	.024 (1.62)	–.147 (4.82)	.292 (3.96)	d
10+ unit structure (yes=1)	.224 (14.0)	–	–.094 (.75)	d
Number of bathrooms More than 1 (yes=1)	.244 (13.0)	–	.376 (43.4)	–
One and one-half (yes=1)	e	.175 (4.39)	e	.154 (6.51)

Table 4A-2 (cont.)

	Regression for $\ln$ Rent		Regression for $\ln$ Value	
Independent Variables[b]	1960	1970	1960	1970
2 (yes=1)	e	.125 (2.54)	e	.218 (6.47)
Over 2 (yes=1)	e	.255 (2.66)	e	.557 (14.3)
Window air conditioner (yes=1)	e	.256 (10.5)	e	.112 (4.43)
Central air conditioner (yes=1)	e .	.557 (13.4)	e	.221 (5.14)
Moved in 1968-1970 (yes=1)	−	.221 (5.85)	−	−
Moved in 1965-1967 (yes=1)	−	.083 (2.11)	−	−
Moved in 1960-1964 (yes=1)	−	.098 (2.39)	−	−
Moved in 1955-1960 (yes=1)	.119 (12.9)	−	.072 (6.71)	−
Moved in 1940-1954 (yes=1)	.060 (5.89)	−	.057 (6.42)	−
Children per room	−	−	−.091 (8.04)	−
Black household head (yes=1)	−.025 (1.15)	−.116 (4.86)	−.108 (6.43)	−.175 (3.65)
Nonwhite household head (yes=1)	−	.161 (1.49)	−	−
Central city location (yes=1)	.035 (4.26)	c	−.090 (11.5)	c
Unrelated person present (yes=1)	.064 (3.09)	−	−	−
$\bar{R}^2$	.328	.554	.478	.493
F	205	90.4	873	235

[a]The 1960 sample includes all SMSAs in Pennsylvania; the 1970 sample includes Allegheny and Westmoreland Counties. Housing unit values and rent are the same as for Table 4A-1 (see note a).

[b]$\ln$ rooms, plumbing, and central heat are defined as in Table 4A-1.

[c]Data not available.

[d]All owner-occupied units were one-unit structures.

[e]Data not included in the public use sample.

Table 4A-3. Stage II Boston Regressions, 1960 and 1970 (t statistics in parentheses; dependent variable is ($1n\ R_i - 1n\ \hat{R}_i$), the difference between the average log of rent for the tract and the predicted average $1n$ rent, where rents are average of gross rents and housing values)

Independent Variables	1960	1970
$1n$ (distance)[a]	.0223	−.0515
	(2.089)	(3.649)
Tax rate[b]	.0014	.0015
	(3.980)	(4.574)
(Tax rate) × (proportion owner-occupied)	−.0053	−.0041
	(10.54)	(9.463)
Per pupil school expenditures (hund. dol.)	.0048	.0206
	(0.755)	(7.025)
Average family income (thous. dol.)	.0444	.0153
	(18.27)	(10.40)
Proportion low status[c]	−.9257	−1.434
	(12.24)	(12.39)
Proportion other nonwhite	.6745	.2210
	(6.710)	(−.904)
Proportion black	−.1166	−.0488
	(1.490)	(1.471)
(Proportion black)^2	.2392	−
	(2.280)	
Proportion Italian[d]	.2032	.3347
	(5.568)	(4.914)
Proportion Puerto Rican[d]	.0716	.2006
	(0.076)	(1.032)
Proportion vacant	−.3564	−1.017
	(1.916)	(4.396)
Proportion public housing	−.3176	−.2704
	(10.08)	(5.274)
Proportion of land devoted to commercial activity	−.1176	−
	(1.476)	
Proportion of land devoted to manufacturing	−.5963	−
	(3.862)	
Air pollution[e]	−	−2.116
		(4.097)
Constant	−.1176	.0612
	(2.971)	(1.154)
R^2	.87	.79
F	194.95	137.9
No. of observations	436	478

[a]"Distance" is a weighted variable defined as:

Table 4A-3 (cont.)

$$\ln\ (\text{distance}_t) = \ln\ (a_1 x_{1t} + a_2 x_{2t} + \ldots + a_5 x_{5t})$$

where x_{it} is the straight-line distance between the tract and the ith employment center, and a_1 is the proportion of total SMSA manufacturing, wholesale, retail, and service employment contained in that center. Five employment centers were selected: Boston, Cambridge, Lynn, Quincy, and Waltham.

[b]The tax rate is the equalized (or full-valued) rate, obtained by multiplying the nominal rate by the municipality's average assessment-sales ratio.

[c]The socioeconomic status of the tract was measured by the following variable: $s = 0.5 \times (E + L)$, where E is the proportion of the tract's residents over twenty-five years of age who have not attended high school, and L is the proportion of male workers over fourteen years of age who are classified as laborers.

[d]"Italian" ("Puerto Rican") refers to individuals who were born in Italy (Puerto Rico) or whose parents were born in Italy (Puerto Rico).

[e]The air pollution variable measures the concentration of particulates in milligrams per cubic meter.

Table 4A-4. Stage II Pittsburgh Regressions, 1960 and 1970 (t statistics in parentheses; dependent variable is $\ln R_i - \ln \hat{R}_{i'}$ as for Table 4A-3)

Independent Variables	1960	1970
Proportion population black	.219 (4.02)	−.344 (4.16)
(Proportion population black)^2	–	.416 (4.57)
Proportion population Italian-born	.232 (1.83)	.346 (2.96)
Proportion population German-born	.963 (3.82)	.725 (2.43)
Proportion population first- or second-generation American	1.186 (3.13)	.507 (4.58)
Proportion population foreign-born	.163 (2.04)	–
Mean family income (thous. dol.)	.039 (8.30)	–
Mean income, families and unrelated individuals (thous. dol.)	–	.023 (7.23)
Proportion population over age 25 with 8 years or fewer of school	−.493 (6.20)	−.223 (3.18)
Time to CBD by bus	–	−.003 (3.04)
(Time to CBD by bus)^2	–	.00002 (2.88)
Average travel time to work	.172[a] (3.13)	.0004 (2.07)

Table 4A-4 (cont.)

Independent Variables	1960	1970
Percent of land undeveloped	.179	−.028
	(4.96)	(.60)
Percent of land in residential land use		.021
		(.53)
Property tax rate		.0031
		(4.07)
(Property tax rate) × (proportion of units owner-occupied)		−.0036
		(6.03)
Total per capita expenditures in jurisdiction (× 100)	.001	
	(1.88)	
Head tax rate		.005
		(.52)
Earnings tax rate in jurisdiction	−.019	
	(1.31)	
Capital school expenditures per student		.0001
		(2.82)
Proportion of units vacant	.618	.152
	(1.67)	(.35)
Proportion of population in non-institutional group quarters		.800
		(5.84)
Proportion of population in institutions		.169
		(1.27)
Proportion owner-occupied units in condominiums		−.885
		(10.6)
Constant	−.633	−.126
	(3.38)	(1.19)
$\bar{R}^2$	.604	.568
F	61.2	27.0

[a]Variable is the log of average travel time.

NOTES TO CHAPTER FOUR

1. Detailed analyses of the effects of group preferences on racial premiums have been done by Bailey (1959), Muth (1974), Pascal (1969), and Schnare (1976).

2. This is the usual form of a so-called hedonic index; for a full discussion of its properties, see Rosen (1974) and Griliches (1971).

3. Schnare (1976) provides details on this test, as well as on the overall econometric procedure.

4. The complete set of Stage I and Stage II parameters is presented in the appendix to this paper.

5. The nonrace variables included in these models are discussed in Schnare (1976).

6. The definition of type 3 neighborhoods for Boston and Pittsburgh was based on the observed pattern of neighborhood racial tipping; i.e., once a tract's proportion black reached about 20 percent, there was a large increase in the probability that its proportion black would increase significantly by the end of the decade.

7. The neighborhoods encompassed by each of the four areas are Manchester-Northside, Hill District-the Strip, East Liberty-Homewood-Brushton-Wilkensburg, and Rankin-Braddock. The third area is partially outside Pittsburgh City, and the fourth is completely outside.

8. The definitions of these areas in terms of percent of the population that is black are: type 1, 1-10 percent; type 2, 11-30 percent; type 3, over 30 percent. These definitions were selected after studying racial patterns over the two decades. For a more detailed discussion of racial transition in Pittsburgh see Darden (1973).

9. "Tracts" here refer either to individual tracts or to groups of two or three that were considered together in order to match the tract boundaries. In this regard it might be noted that sets of tracts included in the 1950-1960 and 1960-1970 analyses are not identical. The two sets differ by a few tracts because of problems of matching tract boundaries while retaining racial homogeneity, i.e., we did not want to join together tracts belonging to differing neighborhood types.

10. For a longer historical perspective on housing conditions in Pittsburgh see Lubove (1969).

REFERENCES

Bailey, Martin. 1959. "Note on the Economics of Residential Zoning and Urban Renewal." *Land Economics*, August.

_____. 1966. "Effects of Race and Other Demographic Factors on the Values of Single-Family Homes." *Land Economics*, May.

Becker, Gary. 1957. *The Economics of Discrimination*. Chicago: University of Chicago Press.

Berry, B.J.L., and R.S. Bednarz. 1975. "A Hedonic Model of Prices and Assessments for Single-Family Homes." *Land Economics*, February.

Darden, J.T. 1973. *Afro-Americans in Pittsburgh*. Lexington, Mass.: Heath.

de Leeuw, F., and N. Ekanem. 1971. "The Supply of Rental Housing." *American Economic Review*, December.

de Leeuw, F., and R. Struyk. 1975. *The Web of Urban Housing*. Washington, D.C.: The Urban Institute.

Gillingham, R. 1973. *Place to Place Rent Comparisons Using Hedonic Quality Adjustment Techniques*. Processed. U.S. Bureau of Labor Statistics, Office of Prices and Living Conditions, Research Discussion Paper No. 7.

Griliches, Zvi, ed. 1971. *Price Indices and Quality Change*. Cambridge, Mass.: Harvard University Press.

Haugen, Robert A., and A. Jones Heins. 1964. "A Market Separation Theory of Rent Differentials in Metropolitan Areas." *Quarterly Journal of Economics*, November.

Kain, John F. 1969. "Theories of Residential Location and Realities of Race." Mimeographed. Harvard University Program on Regional and Urban Economics, Discussion Paper 47.

Kain, J.F. and J.M. Quigley. 1970. "Measuring the Value of Housing Quality." *Journal of the American Statistical Association*, June.

_____. 1974. "Housing Markets and Racial Discrimination: A Microeconomic Analysis." Processed. New York: National Bureau of Economic Research.

King, T., and P. Mieszkowski. 1973. "Racial Discrimination, Segregation and the Price of Housing." *Journal of Political Economy*, May-June.

Lapham, V. 1971. "Do Blacks Pay More for Housing?" *Journal of Political Economy*, November-December.

Lubove, Roy. 1969. *Twentieth Century Pittsburgh: Government, Business, and Environmental Change*. New York: Wiley.

Muth, R.F. 1969. *Cities and Housing*. Chicago: University of Chicago Press.

_____. 1974. "Residential Segregation and Discrimination." In G.M. von Furstenburg, B. Harrison, and A.R. Horowitz, eds. *Patterns of Racial Discrimination* vol. I. Lexington, Mass.: Heath.

Ozanne, L., and R. Struyk. 1976. *Housing from the Existing Stock*. Washington, D.C.: Urban Institute.

Pascal, Anthony II. 1969. "The Analysis of Residential Segregation." In J.P. Crecine, ed. *Financing the Metropolis*. Beverly Hills: Sage Publications.

Rapkin, Chester. 1966. "Price Discrimination Against Negroes in the Rental Housing Market." In *Essays in Urban Land Economics*. Real Estate Research Program, University of California at Los Angeles.

Ridker, R.G., and J.A. Henning. 1967. "The Determinants of Residential Property Values with Special Reference to Air Pollution." *Review of Economics and Statistics*, May.

Rosen, S. 1973. "Hedonic Prices and Implicit Markets: Product Differentiation in Price Competition." *Journal of Political Economy*, January-February.

Schnare, A.B. 1976. "Racial and Ethnic Price Differentials in an Urban Housing Market." *Urban Studies*, June.

Sorensen, A.; K. Taeuber; and L. Hollingsworth. 1974. "Indices of Racial Residential Segregation for 109 Cities in the United States, 1940 to 1970." Processed. University of Wisconsin, Institute for Research on Poverty, Discussion Paper 200-74.

U.S. Bureau of the Census. 1972. *The Social and Economic Status of the Black Population in the United States, 1971*. Current Population Reports, Series P-23, no. 42.

Wihry, D. 1971. "Racial Price Discrimination in Metropolitan Housing Markets." Ph.D. dissertation, Syracuse University.

Comments on Chapter Four

Peter Mieszkowski

This is a very carefully done study. I can find little to criticize or disagree with. The authors are very well acquainted with the literature and with the difficulties associated with isolating and interpreting the relationship between rent levels and the racial composition of neighborhoods. One could quibble about the quality of the census data at their disposal, but this hardly seems appropriate, as Schnare and Struyk have used the data with care and imagination.

The basic quantitative proposition put forth is that various estimates of rent premiums (discounts) paid by black minority group members may be quite specific to the time and place of measurement. Using census data, Schnare and Struyk estimate rent relations for 1960 and 1970 for Boston and Pittsburgh and find that in both cities the rent differentials paid by blacks have declined significantly. In Boston, the 1960 differentials were U-shaped: minimum rents were found in areas that were 25 percent black; in the all-black ghetto, rents were some 12 percent higher than in all-white zones. In 1970 these premiums disappeared. Prices declined steadily as the concentration of blacks in a tract rose, with ghetto rents at least 5 percent lower than rents in the white interior.

In Pittsburgh in 1960 rents rose steadily with black concentration, reaching a maximum premium of 20 percent in all-black areas. In 1970 the relationship was U-shaped, with tracts that were 40 percent black having rents 7 percent lower than all-white tracts, while in 100 percent black tracts there was a 7 percent premium relative to all-white tracts.

As a result of their examination of population growth and movements within each of the two SMSAs, Schnare and Struyk in essence attribute the change in racial price differentials between 1960 and 1970 to the following factors: Rapid suburbanization in both Boston and Pittsburgh was accompanied by a rapid expansion of black areas into transitional neighborhoods in both central cities. In Boston, whites moved to the suburbs and became further concentrated in all-white areas in central-city Boston. In Pittsburgh, the rate of growth of the white and black populations was more modest, and rapid construction in the suburbs led to an increase in both the quality and quantity of housing available to blacks in the central city. In Pittsburgh, the vacancy rate in all central-city neighborhoods rose during the 1960s, reflecting general market weakness in that city. Similarly, in central-city Boston the vacancy rate rose in black neighborhoods.

The reasons for the more rapid neighborhood transition are not altogether clear. In Pittsburgh, slow population growth and new construction seem to explain the general softness in the central-city submarket. In Boston, where the population growth of whites and blacks was more rapid, the explanations of changes in black-white price differentials seem to depend on suburbanization and the movement of whites out of transitional, racially integrated neighborhoods. The authors several times mention institutional changes, most notably the inactment of the open-housing laws in the late 1960s, but it is doubtful whether these formal changes could have had much of an impact by the time of the 1970 census.

The analysis presented by Schnare-Struyk seems to confirm the housing models of Bailey and Muth, who placed stress on the market incentives for racially transforming neighborhoods in decentralized housing markets and on the aversion of whites to living in racially integrated neighborhoods and sharing integrated public facilities such as schools. As the white population has continued to decline in many central cities and whites appear to be isolating themselves in suburban communities, it is very likely that similar results will be obtained in other cities.

Some observers, myself included, will be skeptical that this study and others like it have fully controlled for neighborhood quality, and they may explain the lower housing prices in black neighborhoods in terms of low-quality schools, high crime rates, and so forth. Yet it is easier to raise the point on neighborhood quality than to control for it, and it does not really go against the main point made in this study: relative to whites, black Americans are now paying less for housing than they have in the past.

The regression results and the more informal analysis presented in the paper strongly suggest that the housing choices available to blacks have improved during the decade of the 1960s. What we do not know, however, is what restrictions remain and how severe they are. I believe that it is important to note the limitations of the analysis of racially determined rental differentials:

First, there always is some ambiguity of interpretation. Any differential measured at a given moment in time may be the outcome of a transitional shortrun shock that will soon work itself out. As noted, an estimated differential will rarely be net of neighborhood effects; also, it will rarely be net of household characteristics or "tenant quality." It *may* be that a typical black tenant will be less attractive than a typical white tenant because of economic status and characteristics of behavior (real or imagined) that bear on production costs.

Second, differentials do not get at the costs of market segregation and restrictions on the choice of housing bundle that an unregulated market mechanism may impose on black members of the population.

Finally, the estimated rent differentials have only a general, indirect bearing on housing market policies.

It seems to me that from the viewpoint of policy discussion and social action, the marginal benefits of further work on rent differentials may be quite low. More promising is the possibility of extending and formalizing the use of the audit approach to the investigation of racial discrimination in housing markets. In this approach, which is used by various social action groups in the United States, attempts are made to determine, by direct observation and market experience, the differential treatment of minority group members relative to whites by rental agents, real estate brokers, and so forth. Such an experiment, if carefully designed, could in principle provide useful information concerning the effects on the probability of "success" (getting an apartment, say) of such varied household characteristics as race, income status, occupation, family structure, education, appearance, as well as the effects of differences in the type of landlord, the neighborhood, and so forth.

Such an approach would isolate the effects of race and could have a direct bearing on the more effective enforcement of open-housing laws. The audit does not indicate how discrimination translates itself into price differentials, but it has become increasingly evident that rent differentials are only one (albeit the most important) of the dimensions of discrimination and segregation. Restrictions on access to various neighborhoods, types of housing, and better-quality schools may also be very important to increasingly more affluent minority group members.

Chapter Five

Census Data and Housing Analysis: Old Data Sources and New Applications

William C. Apgar, Jr.

INTRODUCTION

The supply of current, accurate, and detailed information on individual metropolitan areas has been increasing rapidly in recent years. While numerous agencies are responsible for this fortunate development, the Bureau of the Census has led the way with its expanded program of data collection and release, especially the Small Area Data Program of the Decennial Census of Housing and Population. The decennial census collects information on numerous housing attributes as well as the exact location of each residential dwelling unit. In addition, the census also gathers information on the economic and demographic characteristics of the occupants of each dwelling unit, including detailed place-of-work information for each employed member of the household over the age of fourteen.

The tremendous value of currently available Census Bureau data is evidenced by the vast quantities of social science research utilizing this important national resource. The Bureau of the Census has closely monitored the data needs of social science research and has responded to those needs by developing a series of sophisticated data

Note: This study is based on research funded by the Department of Housing and Urban Development under contract H-1843 to the urban studies group of the National Bureau of Economic Research. The author wishes to acknowledge the helpful comments of his colleagues in the study group, and especially John F. Kain and Gregory K. Ingram, who made extensive comments on an earlier draft.

summaries. For the 1960 census, in a major departure from previous practice, individual interview schedules were made available for a 1/1,000 sample of the population, identified by region of residence and city size. For the 1970 census, this program was expanded substantially with the release of a variety of 1 percent Public Use samples, which identified areas as small as individual counties. In addition, the Bureau of the Census has greatly expanded its program of data release for small areas and has made available a series of machine-readable data files which provide summary statistics and cross tabulations for a number of different levels of spatial aggregation, including census tracts, blocks, and minor civil divisions.

Further advantages of using Census Bureau information are its low cost and the extent and uniformity of its coverage. Few data sources can compete with available census data in these areas. To design and execute a special-purpose survey of housing consumption is a costly and time-consuming enterprise. Even when suitable data have been collected for other purposes, they are usually difficult and time consuming to use. More important, special-purpose data sources often provide information on only part of the urban housing market. For example, samples of sale prices of owner-occupied dwelling units, used in a number of recent studies of urban housing markets, exclude both renter and owner-occupied multiple units. Of equal importance is the difficulty or even impossibility of replicating analyses based on these highly specialized data sources. The use of nonuniform sources of data produces confusing and often unintelligible differences in results that may be specific to the location of the study, to the techniques of analysis, or to the data used.

By contrast, Census data are collected in a uniform manner for all owner- and renter-occupied and vacant housing units in the United States. This massive coverage permits the release of detailed complete-count housing information for states, counties, and large metropolitan areas as well as statistically reliable summary data for areas as small as individual city blocks. As a result, models estimated with Census data for one metropolitan area easily can be replicated for other metropolitan areas, and often can be replicated for spatial configurations ranging from individual census tracts or minor civil divisions to counties or entire states. Such flexibility is the unique strength of the decennial census.

Despite these numerous advantages, little systematic attention has been given to the efficient utilization of Census data for the analysis of urban housing markets. In part, this results from the exacting data needs of urban analysis. Recent theoretical and empirical work on urban housing markets has illustrated the need for large samples of data on the physical characteristics, location, and price of residential dwelling units. If housing consumption is best described in terms of a large number of diverse attributes, as this research suggests, models of urban spatial structure must address the possible impact of the interaction of structure attributes, neighborhood, and location on both housing supply and demand. Since neighborhood attributes are likely to vary over space, and since the linkages between spatially separated housing submarkets are likely to be quite subtle, many issues cannot be resolved unless the tests are conducted with large samples containing microspatial detail.

At first glance, Census data seem ill-suited for such detailed microspatial analysis. Despite numerous requests, the Bureau of the Census refuses to release sample data identified by small areas for fear that such a procedure could result in the exact identification of the responses of an individual household or otherwise undermine the confidentiality of the Census program. While it is true that guidelines followed by the Census in its publication program to insure the confidentiality of individual responses make it more difficult to use its data, I will demonstrate that researchers have seriously underestimated the potential value of existing Census data for urban analysis. In fact, currently available Census products include all the summary statistics required to estimate a wide range of spatially detailed housing market models.

The estimation of empirical models from summary statistics is hardly a new idea, but the implications of this concept for Census data use have been generally overlooked. In practice, most social science empirical research utilizes samples of observations on a set of variables. Since any distribution or interaction present in the data could be generated from this raw sample data, the minimum information actually required for the estimation of a model is of little practical concern. In actual practice, few empirical models use all or even a large fraction of the information available in such samples. Typically, the methods employed to estimate these models use aggregate or summary statistics obtained from the raw data. Depending on the exact properties of the estimating technique used, alternative sets of summary statistics are calculated as intermediate steps in the estimation of the parameters of the model. In ordinary least squares models, for example, it is common to ignore many three-way or higher-order interactions present in the raw data. The majority of ordinary least squares models utilize only the simple pairwise correlations between the variables in the equation.

In the analysis of Census data, recognition of the minimum information required for the estimation of an empirical model is of tremendous importance. Since both cost and considerations of confidentiality limit the amount and form of Census data, the efficient use of available data requires a precise statement of the model to be estimated and an exact enumeration of the required summary statistics. Needed summary data not contained in any single Census release often can be assembled by combining information from different published or machine readable sources. Additional summary statistics can be obtained directly from the Bureau of the Census through its program of special tabulations. In either case, the vast potential of Census data should be investigated before an empirical analysis is abandoned entirely or the analysis is recast to fit the specific nature of a non-Census data source.

In an effort to demonstrate the potential usefulness of Census housing data, I present an ordinary least squares model of housing price variation. The example was chosen for several reasons. First, the estimation of a single-equation model of the variation of housing prices over structure and neighborhood characteristics is a standard exercise in urban analysis. The example demonstrates that the replication of many spatially detailed models of price variation can be achieved without resort to special housing surveys. Second, the example presents a clear, yet simple illustration of the use of a number of Census data sources in the estimation of a single econometric model. Finally, an ordinary least squares model was chosen to demonstrate the potential usefulness of the release of raw product moments or simple correlation matrices of variables for blocks, tracts, or minor civil divisions. Such correlation matrices could vastly improve the quality of small-area data without further expanding the massive set of small-area cross tabulations already available.

Following this introduction, I summarize several recent empirical studies of urban housing markets concerned with the analysis of the spatial variation of housing prices and with the testing of alternative theories of housing market segmentation. Rather than emphasize the detailed and often conflicting findings of these studies, I concentrate on the difficulties inherent in applying available non-Census data sources to such an analysis.

I then present an ordinary least squares model of housing price variation estimated with Census data for the Pittsburgh SMSA. The empirical results both demonstrate the richness of the technique and provide a limited test of the extent of housing market segmentation in the Pittsburgh SMSA. A more general discussion of the estimation of alternative housing market models using Census data and a broad overview of the use of summary statistics in other forms of discrete multivariate analysis follow. Finally, I make suggestions for the future release of Census data and offer a few concluding comments.

ECONOMIC ANALYSIS OF URBAN HOUSING MARKETS: AN OVERVIEW

In recent years, members of the urban studies group at the NBER have published a series of econometric analyses of urban housing markets (see Kain and Quigley 1975 for an excellent overview). Each of these studies employed a relatively large body of home interview data, which permitted extensive microeconomic analysis of urban housing markets in St. Louis, San Francisco, and Pittsburgh (Kain and Quigley 1975, Quigley 1972, and Straszheim 1975).

While the details of these studies differ, they share a common core of theory and method and their findings are broadly consistent. In each of these studies it is documented that individual households demand specific housing attributes or bundles of attributes. Some of these attributes are produced by individual housing suppliers, using land, durable capital goods, and less durable operating inputs. Other housing services, including neighborhood amenities and disamenities and public goods, are selected simultaneously with the choice of a dwelling unit. The production of these elements of housing consumption, however, are beyond the control of any single housing supplier, but rather depend on the collective action of large numbers of housing suppliers, demanders, and public officials.

Researchers have responded to the great complexity of housing markets in a variety of ways. The most common response is to assume it away. If housing markets are in long-run equilibrium, it is possible to ignore many aspects of heterogeneity in housing outputs and treat housing services as a single homogeneous commodity. As Olsen (1969, p. 614) contends: "In long run competitive equilibrium, only one price per unit applies to all units of housing stock and another price to all units of housing service regardless of the size of the package in which these goods come."

Given the empirical findings of the NBER econometric studies it seems unlikely that the treatment of housing output as a single homogeneous commodity selling in a single unified housing market is tenable. It is equally unlikely that at any instance housing markets are at or near long-run equilibrium or that prices for comparable components of housing service are uniform throughout a metropolitan area. Rather, as Straszheim (1975, p. 22) observes: "Heterogeneity in the existing stock, other differences in neighborhood desirability and the existence of discrimination imply that the urban housing market is, in fact, a set of compartmentalized and unique submarkets delineated by housing type and location. Consequently, a great many markets must be considered, with complex interrelationships over time and space."

Straszheim was fortunate in having access to a data base with sufficient spatial and structural detail to test the implications of this theory of market segmentation and disequilibrium. Indeed, one distinguishing feature of the NBER econometric studies is their use of large samples of home interview data on households and dwelling units. These large samples permit the highly disaggregated micro analysis of housing prices and housing demand required to test hypotheses concerning a heterogeneous housing stock. It is of major importance that in these household surveys, information was collected on individual dwelling units, their location, and their occupants. Finally, these home interview data are especially useful because they cover both renter- and owner-occupied dwellings located throughout a metropolitan area.

Typically, the home interview data used by these NBER studies were obtained originally for other purposes. Each survey is unique unto itself, and each presents its own set of strengths and weaknesses. While these data have supported an impressive array of housing market studies, their unique features make generalizations across urban areas difficult.

In addition to NBER-sponsored activities, related analyses of housing markets have been presented by several other researchers, using relatively large samples of sales data generated by local property tax assessors, metropolitan mortgage bureaus, and local realtor groups (see Peterson 1974), and by the Federal Housing Administration (FHA) and other federal agencies.[1] These samples are often quite large and provide information on housing characteristics, location, and price. Property tax assessment data seem quite promising. Very often, for each parcel in the taxing jurisdiction, the assessor maintains a file on the characteristics of the lot and structure. For single-family homes, this is often accompanied by recent sales price and building permit information. Typically, all or part of this information is either on the public record or available to researchers subject only to appropriate assurances of confidentiality (see Peterson et al. 1973, Chap. 8). Given the improved quality of assessment techniques and the growing use of computerized retrieval systems, assessment data are likely to become an increasingly important source of housing market information.

This improved data on the sales price of owner-occupied housing are of considerable interest to both prospective home buyers and public officials. Since home ownership represents a major source of wealthholding for middle-income families, evaluation of the impact of alternative government actions on the purchase price of single-family homes is an important public issue.

Tests of many theories of urban spatial structure, however, require data on rents as opposed to values. Knowledge of the relationship between employment accessibility and land values gives only approximate information on the relationship between accessibility and land rents. Even in a simple monocentric model of urban spatial structure, current land rents do not necessarily bear a simple relationship to current land values. The former depends on current transportation costs, population characteristics, and subjective evaluations of time, while the latter depends on these plus a market evaluation of their likely changes over time. As a result, sales data must be analyzed with great care. This point, however, is overlooked by most analysts of sales data, who readily compare values to rents, using simple real estate rules of thumb.

One common approach is to assume that the imputed rents for owner-occupied dwelling units are 1 percent of the total value of the property. For example, Polinsky and Rubinfeld present an elegant theoretical model of the benefits of environmental improvements; they then proceed to an empirical test of their theory which uses both renter- and owner-occupied dwelling units. To convert the price information they have for these two groups into comparable units, they multiply monthly rents by a factor of 100 (Polinsky and Rubinfeld 1975).

Similar rough approximations appear throughout the literature on housing demand and housing price formation. Recently, A. Thomas King (1972, 1973) developed a model of housing demand based on a household's maximization of a branched utility function. King formulated the theoretical approach in terms of income and housing rents, but he tested the theory using the sales prices and attributes of a sample of single-family homes located in the New Haven area. He recognized this discrepancy; yet, he concluded it was a trivial matter to convert values into rents (King 1972, p. 19, especially footnote 9).

While this assumption is convenient, it is unlikely that the treatment of the multiperiod investment aspects of housing purchases is as simple as the analyses by King and by Polinsky and Rubinfeld suggest. If housing markets are in long-run static equilibrium, the market price per unit of time for any piece of housing capital will be equal to the long-run supply price of capital. This in turn depends on the purchase price of capital, the rate of depreciation, and rate of interest. If alternative housing investments are equally risky and have the same rate of depreciation and the same construction costs per unit, then in equilibrium, the value of any piece of housing capital will be a constant multiple of the annual rents generated by that capital stock.

There is considerable evidence, however, that the ratio of housing value to rent is not constant over structural type or location. Structures located in blighted areas often sell for only three or four times their annual rental receipts, while buildings in more desirable neighborhoods often sell for seven or eight times annual rents. Even within the same neighborhood type, the relationship between value and rent often differs by structural type (Peterson et al. 1973).

These problems make sales data particularly inappropriate for analysis of market segmentation. For any particular attribute, there could exist a well-defined pattern of spatial variation in current rents, reflecting excess supplies in some areas and excess demands in others. Yet depending on the extent to which these excess supplies and demands are expected to persist, the market value for the particular attribute could exhibit differing degrees of variation from its long-run supply price.

In addition to the problems of interpreting market value information, sales data also suffer from lack of uniform coverage. The typical analysis of housing sales data covers only single-family, owner-occupied dwelling units. In most areas these units are newer and more highly suburbanized than the rental housing or owner-occupied multiple stock. Thus, much of the great diversity of housing-structure types is ignored in analyses which concentrate on single-family, owner-occupied units.

Ann B. Schnare and Raymond Struyk (1974), for example, have recently completed a series of analyses using a sample of 2,200 single-family, owner-occupied houses located in thirteen suburban communities in the Boston SMSA. Using the standard regression approach, they attempted to explain sales price as a function of structure, neighborhood, and locational attributes. They concluded that there was no significant spatial variation in the sales price of individual housing attributes, and that substitution on the part of housing consumers and housing demanders in this submarket was adequate to prevent "widespread and pervasive market segmentation" (Schnare and Struyk 1974, p. 40). This could well be the case. It is impossible to determine, of course, whether their results are an indication that the market values have already discounted existing differentials in current rents, or whether, in fact, no current rent differentials exist within this relatively homogeneous subsample of dwelling units.

Despite the difficulty of analyzing housing markets, many researchers are attracted by the apparent simplicity of single-equation models of price variation and long-run equilibrium models of housing supply and demand. While model simplicity is often a virtue, the value of ignoring many crucial short-run-disequilibrium aspects of urban housing markets is less than obvious. Schnare and Struyk suggest that only simple models can be calibrated with available data and that data are not available to support empirical models of housing markets that incorporate the notions of housing market segmentation outlined above. They conclude (p. 2) that "the possibility of distinct market segmentation poses a real threat to the viability of statistical analyses of housing prices."

Their view of the possibilities for empirical analyses of housing markets seems overly pessimistic. As I illustrate in the next section, currently available Census Bureau data will permit many interesting tests to be made of housing market segmentation and the spatial variation of housing prices. Furthermore, these examples give only an inkling of the many analyses that can be conducted with Census data. While it is tempting to abstract from real-world complexities and present a simplified theory consistent with the most readily available data, it is often more rewarding to probe for ways to expand the capabilities of existing data sources for testing more realistic theories.

THE USE OF CENSUS SUMMARY STATISTICS IN AN ORDINARY LEAST SQUARES MODEL OF GROSS MONTHLY RENT

The census Public Use Sample Program has stimulated a great deal of empirical research based on Census data.[2] This program made available large samples of household interview data identified by subareas as small as individual counties or county groups with populations of 250,000 or more.[3] Unfortunately, the Bureau of the Census has concluded that confidentiality requirements prohibit the release of sample data identified by small areas of residence. Such microspatial detail would, of course, greatly expand the usefulness of the data for the analysis of many aspects of urban housing markets.

Fortunately, many forms of analysis do not require sample data. It is widely recognized that a raw product moment matrix provides the information needed for the estimation of the coefficients of an ordinary least squares model. Many available statistical packages provide the capability for processing a sample of observations, calculating the summary statistics needed to estimate the model, and retaining this information for subsequent analysis. As a result, individual observations are not required to estimate a variety of ordinary least squares models. Instead, they can be estimated directly from Census data aggregated at different levels and obtained from a number of separate Census publications and computer tapes. For example, available Census tables permit estimation of housing market models that measure the effect of neighborhood and structural characteristics on the price of housing services.

This general proposition can be illustrated by Equation (5-1):

$$R_{ij} = \sum_{k=1}^{K} X_{ijk} A_k + \sum_{h=1}^{H} L_{ijh} B_h + e_{ij} \tag{5-1}$$

which states that the rent of the ith dwelling unit in the jth subarea or neighborhood is a linear function of K attributes of the dwelling unit and its structure and H attributes of the neighborhood and location. The ordinary least squares (OLS) estimates of the coefficients require only information on the relationship between each of the variables taken two at a time. These moments can be obtained from data summarized at different levels of aggregation and spatial detail.

Consider, for example, the raw product moment between two of the structural variables. This calculation does not require information on the location of the dwelling unit, but only the joint distribution of the two variables over the entire study area. This can be obtained from samples of Census files containing no subarea information. In the case where the two attributes are defined in discrete terms, the moment can be obtained directly from a cross tabulation of the two variables aggregated to the areawide level. If the first variable is a dummy for the presence or absence of full plumbing and the second is a dummy for the presence or absence of central heating, then the raw product moment of the two variables is simply the count of dwelling units that have both attributes.

Most census variables are collected and presented in terms of a limited number of categories. Since many structural attributes can best be described in terms of the presence or absence of certain physical features, this categorization is adequate. In other instances, attributes are inherently continuous and their conversion to discrete categories results in a loss of information, particularly for open-ended categories. It should be observed that this shortcoming is not unique to census data and that the extensive pretesting of questionnaires by the Census enables it to use categories which minimize the loss of information.

For certain variables, continuous information is collected. Rent is one such variable. Even so, the continuous distribution of rent is not needed to estimate the linear rent equation. As long as all the structural variables are represented in discrete terms, then the raw moments involving those variables and rent can be exactly determined using the mean rent and the count of all rental dwelling units in the entire area for each level of the discrete structural variables.

An estimate of the variation of rent does require continuous information. While an approximation can be made by assigning values to each of a number of discrete intervals, this procedure produces an unknown loss of accuracy which affects measures of goodness of fit, including, of course, R^2. It should be observed, however, that since the variation of rent is not required for the calculation of the individual coefficients of an ordinary least squares model, the impact of the lack of continuous rent information in an ordinary least squares framework is greatly reduced.

Unlike structural attributes, locational detail is needed to obtain the product moments involving neighborhood attributes. If the neighborhood attribute is assumed to hold for the entire subarea, the only subareal structural information required is a summation of the attributes over all dwelling units in the subarea. The raw product moments involving both structural and neighborhood variables are weighted sums of the aggregate structural characteristics for each neighborhood, where the weights are the values of the neighborhood attribute in question.

Moments involving only neighborhood attributes can be obtained in a similar fashion. Since the neighborhood attributes are assumed constant within a subarea, the raw product moment between two neighborhood attributes can be exactly estimated by taking a weighted sum of the product of the two variables. In this instance the weights are the total number of observations in each subarea or neighborhood.

The locationally specific data required for neighborhood moment calculations can be obtained from a number of sources. For 1970, the Bureau of Census computer tapes contain the distributions of structural variables required to estimate rent functions for metropolitan areas at the census tract and block level. If parts of the study area are not tracted, the minor civil division or enumeration district can be used to form the subareas. The appropriate delineation of subarea depends on the nature of the neighborhood data used. These neighborhood variables can be obtained from land use planning studies, transportation surveys, and similar sources. If the data reveal that broad sections of the study area are highly homogeneous, census tract aggregates could suffice as subareas. In other instances individual tracts or even block data might be needed to capture subtle spatial variations in neighborhood amenities.

The preceding discussion has been rather general and was intended to introduce the notion that the estimation of a linear rent equation does not necessarily require sample data with locational detail, but can be estimated with aggregate and subareal data of a special nature. In the next section I present an example to further illustrate this technique. I then discuss other similar models that can be estimated using aggregate census data.

A RENT EQUATION FOR THE PITTSBURGH SMSA

The statistical approach outlined in the preceding section can be applied to any urban place. To illustrate these techniques, I use Census tables for the Pittsburgh SMSA. Data published in the Metropolitan Housing Characteristics (MHC) series and available on the Fourth Count Summary tract tapes for Pittsburgh in 1970 were used to estimate Equation (5-2).

$$R_{ij} = A_0 + \sum_{k=1}^{9} X_{ijk} A_k + \sum_{h=1}^{6} L_{ijh} \qquad (5\text{-}2)$$

where

j designates a census tract (702 in all) in the Pittsburgh SMSA.

i designates the individual occupied renter units in each tract.

X_1 to X_4 are dummy variables for structure. X is 1 if the dwelling unit is in a two-family house and 0 otherwise. The other three categories are 3-4 units, 5-9 units, and 10 or more units; single-family units are represented in the constant term.

X_5 to X_7 are age dummy variables. X_5 is 1 if the dwelling unit was built during 1950-1959 and 0 otherwise. The other two categories are: 1940-1949 and before 1940. Units built since 1959 are represented in the constant term.

X_8 is a dummy variable for plumbing. X_8 is 1 if the dwelling unit has only partial plumbing facilities and 0 otherwise.

X_9 is the number of rooms in the dwelling unit.

L_1 is a measure of accessibility for each tract in minutes of one-way travel time. It was calculated using a matrix of zone-to-zone travel time and employment location and a standard exponential decay weighting function. The travel times are based on 1967 data. (See Ingram 1971, App. A, for a fuller discussion of this variable.)

L_2 is the average income of all families in the tract, in thousands of dollars.

L_3 is the black population as a percent of the total population in each tract.

L_4 is net residential density of each tract in units per residential acre.[4]

L_5 is a dummy for tract location. L_5 is 1 for tracts located in the City of Pittsburgh and 0 otherwise.

L_6 is a dummy for race of the head of household residing in the unit. L_6 is 1 for black-occupied units and 0 otherwise.

Data from Metropolitan Housing Characteristics (MHC) and Fourth Count do not permit an exact estimation of Equation (5-2). There are three minor sources of error. First, there are minor inconsistencies between the Fourth Count and MHC data. For five census tracts with fewer than fifty rental units, only the total number of renter-occupied dwelling units is provided. All the other variables for these tracts were suppressed. For several other tracts, some of the required variables were suppressed. In the Pittsburgh analysis, some or all of the tract level variables had to be imputed for approximately 0.3 percent of all rental dwelling units.

Second, the total number of renter-occupied dwelling units obtained from the Fourth Count and MHC differed by 0.5 percent. Since the two sources were released at different times, this discrepancy could reflect differences in error editing. In any event, it was a minor matter to adjust for these differences by scaling the tract level data to agree with the published aggregates.

The most difficult problem arises from the Census definition of the renter-occupied subsample. For the Pittsburgh SMSA, 5.3 percent of all renter households were enumerated as paying "no cash rent." Another 1.6 percent were units located on lots with ten or more acres. No rental information was collected for these units. Unfortunately, both groups are included in the cross tabulations of the structural attributes. To adjust for this problem, the product moments involving the rental information were scaled to reflect the differential coverage of the structural and rental data.

In Table 5-1, I present the means and standard deviations for gross monthly rent and fifteen explanatory variables for the entire Pittsburgh SMSA. In 1970, Pittsburgh had 245,085 renter-occupied

Table 5-1. Rent Regressions for Total SMSA Sample, Pittsburgh, 1970: Means and Coefficients of Individual Variables (number of observations = 49,017; figures in parentheses below means are standard deviations; figures below coefficients are standard errors)

	Mean	Regression Coefficient
Constant		−32.25
Structure-type dummies[a]		
2 units	0.21	−1.24
	(0.41)	(0.45)
3-4 units	0.15	0.18
	(0.36)	(0.52)
5-9 units	0.12	4.84
	(0.32)	(0.57)
10 or more units	0.19	14.52
	(0.39)	(0.56)
Year-built dummies[a]		
1950-1959	0.10	−29.07
	(0.30)	(0.67)
1940-1949	0.12	−41.68
	(0.33)	(0.65)
Before 1940	0.65	−47.69
	(0.47)	(0.54)
Plumbing dummy: partial plumbing[a]	0.07	−17.21
	(0.26)	(0.63)
No. of rooms per dwelling unit	4.12	12.97
	(1.47)	(0.13)
Accessibility (minutes of one-way travel time)	22.47	2.09
	(4.37)	(0.48)
Average tract income (thous. dol.)	9.20	8.04
	(2.65)	(0.74)
Tract percent black	11.59	0.01
	(24.36)	(0.01)
Net residential density (units per acre)	15.31	0.20
	(24.48)	(0.01)
Location dummy, Pittsburgh	0.36	1.21
	(0.48)	(0.46)
Race dummy, black[a]	0.13	−2.91
	(0.34)	(0.69)
Rent per unit	108.35	
	(52.25)	
R^2		0.557
Standard error		34.689
Number of observations		49.017

Source: Means are from U.S. Census of Population and Housing, 1970, *Metropolitan Housing Characteristics for the Pittsburgh SMSA,* and Fourth Count Summary Tapes for the Pittsburgh SMSA.
[a]See text for explanation of dummies.

dwelling units. Both the tract data and the SMSA level data used to estimate the model summed to this total. Data were collected from only a sample of the population except for a few variables, for which complete-count estimates were obtained by scaling a 20, 15, or 5 percent random stratified subsample. Since the census variables used in this model were all drawn from the 20 percent sample, it was assumed in calculating sample statistics and degrees of freedom that the actual sample for the entire SMSA contained only 49,017 renter-occupied dwelling units (e.g., 49,017 = 0.2 × 245,085).

With the exception of these minor problems of internal consistency, the estimates obtained are the same as those that could have been obtained using a sample of Census households identified by Census tract of residence. While Equation (5-2) could have been estimated for any metropolitan area, the Pittsburgh SMSA was used because data for several useful neighborhood characteristics such as measure of accessibility, tract net residential density, percent nonwhite, and mean tract family income were readily available. While there is no limit to the number of neighborhood variables that could have been used in the analysis, additional neighborhood variables would have turned out to be highly correlated with the four variables included, and would have needlessly complicated this illustration of technique. In addition, it would have been possible to use the moment matrices generated for this example and ridge regression techniques to investigate the effect that multicollinearity has on the stability of the coefficient estimates; but again, this would tend to confuse the central methodological thrust of the paper (see Hoerl and Kennard 1970).

Also shown in Table 5-1 are the estimated coefficients for Equation (5-2) and their standard errors for the entire Pittsburgh SMSA. Overall, the model performs reasonably well, explaining 55 percent of the variance, and each of the coefficients is highly significant. This second result is hardly surprising, however, given that the regression is based on nearly 50,000 observations.

The individual coefficients conform fairly well to expectations. Older dwelling units rent at a discount, as do units with only partial plumbing. Additional rooms rent for an extra $12.97 each. As compared to a single-family unit, large multiple units appear to rent at a premium. This finding in part reflects the fact that large multiples are newer on average than single-family renter units and provide services not measured by the structural variables included in the equation.

The neighborhood coefficients also have plausible value. Greater accessibility, central location, higher mean tract income, and higher density are all associated with higher rents. The percent black coefficient is small and insignificant, but the dummy variable for black occupancy is significantly negative.

Perhaps more important than the test results of this exercise for the particular model is the illustration that a linear rent equation can be estimated by using census data obtained from two sources. The problems discussed previously, i.e., suppression of some tract data, release of MHC and Fourth Count data at different times, and apparent differences in error editing and in the treatment of no cash rent, could have created insurmountable problems. Fortunately, the inconsistencies that did exist were small. The two sources had virtually identical means and variances for the common structural characteristics, often differing in only the fourth or fifth significant digit. In addition, in those few instances where tract level cross tabulations were available, the moments available from tract data were virtually identical to those derived from published SMSA level data. Those differences that did appear seem to result from a difference of approximately 0.5 percent in the total number of renter-occupied dwelling units enumerated on the Fourth Count tapes compared to MHC. An adjustment for this discrepancy was made by scaling the tract level data by the appropriate ratio.

While the results shown in Table 5-1 are interesting in their own right, their more important value is that they illustrate the wide range of analyses possible using aggregate Census data. In the next section the analysis presented in the table is extended by presenting additional OLS estimates for several stratified samples.

TEST OF INTERACTION FOR THE OLS FRAMEWORK

One central empirical and theoretical issue in the analysis of housing markets is the extent to which particular housing attributes rent for equal amounts across space or across types of occupants. Tests of this market segmentation hypothesis have proliferated in recent years. In this section I illustrate how available Census data can be used to test that hypothesis in metropolitan housing markets.

In addition to the SMSA-wide data used in the previous section, the Metropolitan Housing Characteristic series also presents the same contingency tables for all households and for black-headed households for each city over 50,000 and the suburban ring. In the Pittsburgh SMSA, only the central city and the suburbs are identified, but in other SMSAs numerous non-central-city locations are identified as well. This further stratification permits estimation of Equation (5-2) for black- and white-occupied rental units located in the central city and the suburbs. Table 5-2 contains the means and

Table 5-2. Means and Standard Deviations of Structural and Neighborhood Variables for Renter-occupied Dwelling Units, by Race and Location, Pittsburgh, 1970 (figures in parentheses are standard deviations)

	White-occupied		Black-occupied	
	City	*Suburbs*	*City*	*Suburbs*
Structure-type dummy				
2 units	0.21	0.22	0.15	0.18
	(0.41)	(0.41)	(0.35)	(0.39)
3-4 units	0.17	0.14	0.16	0.14
	(0.37)	(0.35)	(0.37)	(0.34)
5-9 units	0.12	0.10	0.19	0.11
	(0.32)	(0.31)	(0.39)	(0.32)
10 or more units	0.29	0.15	0.17	0.16
	(0.45)	(0.36)	(0.38)	(0.36)
Year-built dummies				
1950-1959	0.07	0.12	0.07	0.11
	(0.26)	(0.32)	(0.25)	(0.31)
1940-1949	0.10	0.13	0.18	0.16
	(0.30)	(0.33)	(0.38)	(0.37)
Before 1940	0.74	0.61	0.64	0.64
	(0.44)	(0.49)	(0.48)	(0.48)
Plumbing dummy: partial plumbing	0.10	0.06	0.10	0.09
	(0.30)	(0.24)	(0.29)	(0.28)
No. of rooms per dwelling unit	3.72	4.29	4.09	4.34
	(1.53)	(1.43)	(1.45)	(1.29)
Accessibility	26.08	20.38	26.36	20.34
	(1.13)	(4.15)	(1.33)	(3.81)
Average tract income (thous. dol.)	9.63	9.58	6.09	7.80
	(3.21)	(2.08)	(2.04)	(1.81)
Tract percent black	7.75	3.13	70.32	2.77
	(16.49)	(7.46)	(29.63)	(2.61)
Net residential density (units per acre)	27.60	8.59	23.58	13.94
	(39.45)	(10.98)	(14.75)	(19.17)
Rent per unit	116.47	108.69	90.69	89.19
	(60.91)	(50.18)	(35.83)	(33.40)
Number of observations	13,182	29,362	4,573	1,900

standard deviations for each of the variables. Again, the sample size has been adjusted to reflect the fact that the underlying data were based on only a 20 percent enumeration.

Tables 5-3, 5-4, and 5-5 contain estimated coefficients for the stratified subsamples. Table 5-3 contains estimates for the central-city and suburban subsamples, and in Tables 5-4 and 5-5, the sample is stratified by both race and location.

Table 5-3. Coefficients of Individual Variables in Rent Regression for City and Suburban Samples, Pittsburgh, 1970 (figures in parenthese are standard errors)

	City-Sample Coefficients	*Suburban-Sample Coefficients*
Structure-type dummies		
2 units	1.683	−1.961
	(0.916)	(0.511)
3-4 units	7.392	−3.522
	(0.982)	(0.594)
5-9 units	14.713	−0.879
	(1.050)	(0.662)
10 or more units	24.724	8.333
	(1.031)	(0.659)
Year-built dummies		
1950-1959	−27.570	−30.932
	(1.429)	(0.734)
1940-1949	−34.814	−45.254
	(1.286)	(0.726)
Before 1940	−40.188	−51.692
	(1.091)	(0.605)
Plumbing dummy: partial plumbing	−17.683	−16.695
	(1.060)	(0.791)
No. of rooms	13.341	12.909
	(0.234)	(0.148)
Accessibility	0.210	2.196
	(0.251)	(0.047)
Average tract income	7.950	8.229
	(0.116)	(0.110)
Tract percent black	−0.050	0.152
	(0.153)	(0.020)
Net residential density	0.174	0.339
	(0.009)	(0.018)
Location dummy, Pittsburgh	−	−
Race dummy, black	2.248	−7.695
	(1.106)	(0.889)
Constant	6.556	−32.098
R^2	0.569	0.617
Standard error	37.241	30.656
Number of observations	17,755	31,262

Table 5-4. Coefficients of Individual Variables in Rent Regression for White-occupied Dwelling Units, by Location, Pittsburgh, 1970 (figures in parentheses are standard errors)

	SMSA Coefficients	*City-Sample Coefficients*	*Suburban-Sample Coefficients*
Structure-type dummies			
2 units	−1.23	2.79	−1.90
	(0.49)	(1.08)	(0.53)
3-4 units	0.37	10.20	−3.20
	(0.56)	(1.18)	(0.61)
5-9 units	5.91	21.20	−0.16
	(0.62)	(1.33)	(0.68)
10 or more units	17.44	32.70	9.68
	(0.61)	(1.26)	(0.69)
Year-built dummies			
1950-1959	−30.95	−35.56	−31.20
	(0.72)	(1.71)	(0.75)
1940-1949	−45.92	−48.19	−46.65
	(0.71)	(1.62)	(0.75)
Before 1940	−52.51	−56.15	−53.12
	(0.58)	(1.35)	(0.62)
Plumbing dummy: partial plumbing	−18.79	−20.01	−17.22
	(0.70)	(1.26)	(0.83)
No. of rooms	13.45	14.68	13.19
	(0.14)	(0.28)	(0.15)
Accessibility	2.09	−0.37	2.21
	(0.04)	(0.31)	(0.04)
Average tract income	7.67	7.01	8.15
	(0.10)	(0.13)	(0.11)
Tract percent black	−0.11	−0.31	0.10
	(0.02)	(0.02)	(0.03)
Net residential density	0.20	0.15	0.37
	(0.01)	(0.01)	(0.02)
Location dummy, Pittsburgh	2.07		
	(0.49)		
Constant	−26.92	38.80	−32.32
R^2	0.615	0.602	0.629
Standard error	33.42	38.46	30.56
Number of observations	42,544	13,182	29,362

Table 5-5. Coefficients of Individual Variables in Rent Regression for Black-occupied Dwelling Units, by Location, Pittsburgh, 1970 (figures in parentheses are standard errors)

	SMSA Coefficients	City-Sample Coefficients	Suburban-Sample Coefficients
Structure-type dummies			
2 units	−0.29 (1.11)	0.09 (1.36)	−1.15 (1.86)
3-4 units	−2.04 (1.15)	−0.09 (1.37)	−7.30 (2.07)
5-9 units	−2.68 (1.14)	0.01 (1.32)	−7.76 (2.31)
10 or more units	0.54 (1.20)	1.85 (1.39)	−9.24 (2.34)
Year-built dummies			
1950-1959	−11.35 (1.66)	−12.29 (2.01)	−13.54 (2.96)
1940-1949	−8.50 (1.42)	−6.70 (1.64)	−12.72 (2.83)
Before 1940	−11.13 (1.23)	−8.03 (1.46)	−19.74 (2.60)
Plumbing dummy: partial plumbing	−11.98 (1.29)	−10.89 (1.52)	−14.43 (2.39)
No. of rooms	10.98 (0.29)	11.42 (0.35)	9.33 (0.55)
Accessibility	1.05 (0.15)	−1.38 (0.35)	1.50 (0.18)
Average tract income	6.39 (0.23)	6.63 (0.26)	4.44 (0.53)
Tract percent black	0.01 (0.02)	−0.02 (0.02)	0.12 (0.03)
Net residential density	0.25 (0.02)	0.33 (0.03)	0.12 (0.04)
Location dummy, Pittsburgh	6.40 (1.22)	−	−
Constant		41.95	−0.56
R^2	0.380	0.428	0.325
Standard error	27.70	27.14	27.71
Number of observations	6,473	4,573	1,900

Again, most of the coefficients are highly significant. The major exceptions are structure-type dummy variables in the black-occupied equations. For the black-occupied city subsample, none of the dummy variables has coefficients that are twice their standard errors. In general, the black renter equations do not perform as well as those for white renters. The R^2's are only 0.43 and 0.33 for the black-occupied city and suburban subsamples compared to 0.60 and 0.63 for the comparable white subsamples.

Finally, the coefficients of the basic equation seem to vary from one sample to the next. The rent paid for each additional room ranges from $14.68 for white households living in the city to $9.33 for black households living in the suburbs. The discount for buildings built before 1940 is $56.15 for white-occupied units in the city. The discount for black-occupied units is only $8.03 for units located in the city and $19.74 for black-occupied suburban dwelling units.

F tests on the equality of coefficients, shown in the tabulation below, confirm the finding that the coefficients of individual attributes are statistically different for blacks and whites living in the central city and the suburbs:

	R^2	Stand. Error	Degrees of Freedom	F Test
Pooled model	.554	34.69	–	–
Stratified models				
Race	.608	32.73	15;48,987	404.7
Location	.597	33.18	15;48,987	302.5
Race and location	.615	32.50	14;48,961	491.6

The hypothesis that the coefficients of the four subsamples differ by only a location and a race dummy can be rejected at the 0.01 level of confidence. Similarly, attempts to pool the data by race or location were rejected at the same level of confidence.

The foregoing table also demonstrates that the stratifications significantly improve the explanatory power of the model. The pooled model explains 55 percent of the variance in monthly gross rent. One-way stratification by location increases the explanatory power of the model by five percentage points, and one-way stratification by race increases the explanatory power by six percentage points. Two-way stratification increases the explained variance by nearly seven percentage points—to 62 percent. Similarly, stratification of the equation by location and race reduce the aggregate standard error by approximately 7 percent.

As was noted earlier, there has been considerable debate in recent literature over the empirical importance of alternative market segmentation hypotheses. The central concern is the extent to which a single hedonic index for housing consumption can be identified, or whether market segmentation undermines the usefulness of the hedonic approach or any other unidimensional description of housing services. The issues take on added significance when it is realized that the validation of several major policy planning models is heavily dependent on the assumption that a single hedonic index can be identified using a single metropolitanwide or cross-metropolitan model of observed market rents; for example, important aspects of the calibration of the Urban Institute Housing Market Simulation Model are based on the single-equation hedonic approach (see de Leeuw and Struyk 1975).

Given the limited number of variables included in the illustrations presented in this study, it would be inappropriate to assign too much significance to the reported test statistics. It is likely that many of the differences observed in the coefficients reflect measurement problems and the omission of relevant variables. The inclusion of a more detailed set of dummy variables to represent the age and number of units in the structure should reduce these measurement problems, as should the inclusion of other indicators of structural quality such as the presence of central air-conditioning, the type of heating system, the number of bathrooms, and the nature of the available kitchen equipment. In addition, improved specification variables that measure the quality of local services and the attractiveness of the neighborhood would undoubtedly help. Finally, additional stratifications and tests for interaction should be performed before any set of equations is given much credence.

With these caveats in mind, it does seem that the results presented in these illustrations are consistent with the hypothesis of housing market stratification. While this interpretation could well be altered in light of additional estimation, it should be stressed that unlike models estimated with single-source data bases, the models presented here can be replicated for any SMSA, major city, or group of counties in the United States. Moreover, unlike many alternative analyses of housing prices, which utilize samples of sales prices, the equations estimated in this study are based on a sample of renter-occupied dwelling units. This frees the analysis from complications introduced by the consideration of the multiperiod investment aspects of the purchase of a dwelling unit. Finally, it is also possible both to expand the list of individual structural attributes and enrich the neighborhood definition and stratification schemes. As I illustrate in the next section, these refined models can also be estimated by using Census housing data.

ALTERNATIVE MODELS OF HOUSING PRICES

The 1970 Census survey contained thirty-five housing questions. Of these, fifteen were collected for all dwelling units in the United States. Other housing questions were obtained for samples of 20, 15, or 5 percent. In each instance, the results of the sample surveys were scaled to complete-count control totals.[5] In addition to the data for number of rooms, structural type, year built, and partial plumbing, which were used in the previous sections, information was also gathered on the number of bedrooms and bathrooms; the type of bathroom, kitchen, cooking, heating, and air-conditioning facilities available for each dwelling unit; and the source of water sewage disposal, number of stories, and presence of elevators in each structure or building.

Extension of the OLS models presented in the previous section requires aggregate cross tabulations, or two-dimensional contingency tables of the included variables, as well as one-way frequency distributions at the neighborhood level. All the needed one-way frequency distributions are available on the Fourth Count Summary Tapes for census tracts and minor civil divisions. The Bureau of the Census has also announced plans to release similar data for census blocks and enumeration districts (Census 1973c). The usefulness of this data in the linear rent model depends, of course, on the level of data suppression and the consistency of this new data source with previously released Census data.

Obtaining the required contingency tables for extension of the linear rent model is somewhat more difficult. In addition to data published in the Metropolitan Housing Characteristics series, many contingency tables can be found on the Sixth Count Summary Tapes, which provide summary housing data for states, SMSAs, metropolitan counties, nonmetropolitan counties of 50,000 inhabitants or more, cities of 50,000 inhabitants or more, and central cities. For each of these areas, the Sixth Count tapes provide 109,061 cells of housing market data in 348 tables (Census 1972). Of these, 164 tables involve one or more population items, while the other 184 involve only housing characteristics.

Using Sixth Count data, it is possible to further stratify the rent equation presented in the previous sections by counties or by cities of 50,000 or more. For large SMSAs, this would represent a significant improvement over the central-city and suburban stratifications used in the previous Pittsburgh examples. Because of the large number of tables and diverse levels of stratification, the Sixth Count Summary information for a single state may occupy as many as fourteen reels of computer tape. While the size of the Sixth Count files makes the extraction of the required tables somewhat difficult, the improvement in model specification should be well worth the effort.

Even though a large number of tables are on the Sixth Count Summary tapes, the required information for use of all thirty-five housing variables in a single linear rent equation is not on these tapes or in other published Census information. Such an equation would require the calculation of 630 raw product moments, and only a fraction of the needed contingency tables are contained on the Sixth Count tapes. Thus, for example, in addition to testing for the impact on rent of age, structural type, plumbing, and number of rooms, it would also be possible to test for the impact of either the type of heating or air-conditioning equipment. All the required cross tabulations are available on Sixth Count. The inclusion of both the heating and air-conditioning variables in a single equation, however, requires the joint distribution of these two variables, information not contained on those tapes.

The lack of Sixth Count information should pose no real problem to the specification of more complicated rent equations. The missing contingency tables or product moments could be obtained from a special tabulation of the Census data. This, of course, is a costly activity requiring careful planning and allowance for sufficient time to permit the bureau to program and process the initial request. Once this has been done, subsequent requests for similar data for other metropolitan areas should prove less difficult and less expensive to obtain.

Somewhat less precise estimates of the required moments can be obtained directly from the Public Use Sample tapes. These tapes contain a 1/100 sample of all Census questionnaires and include all the housing information collected. As was noted earlier, however, the Public Use Sample tapes do not present detailed spatial information. This is no obstacle to the estimation of linear rent equations, since calculation of the raw product moments involving only structural attributes does not require information on the location of the dwelling unit.

The main difficulty with using Public Use Sample data in the estimation of product moments results from possible sampling errors and inconsistencies between sample and complete-count information. For example, estimates of variance of each of two variables obtained from complete-count data and similar estimates of the covariance between these two variables obtained from sample data could well produce an estimate of simple correlation between the variables which falls outside the zero-one interval, a disconcerting prospect, indeed.

Yet a simple adjustment of the sample data will eliminate possible inconsistencies. Consider, for example, the estimation of the raw moment between type of heating equipment and type of air-conditioning equipment available in the dwelling unit. The joint distribution of these two variables obtained from the sample data can be scaled to satisfy the known complete-count one-way distribution of each variable. This procedure preserves the cross-product ratios present in the sample data while ensuring that the sample cross tabulation is consistent with the complete-count data.[6] Finally, it should be observed that scaling the data also improves the efficiency of the sample estimate of the raw product moment involving the two variables, since the procedure is equivalent to creating a random stratified sample of observations.

Further improvement in the efficiency of the sample estimates of the raw product moments can be achieved by scaling the sample data to satisfy multiple-dimension contingency tables. For example, each observation of the sample tapes could be classified by type of structure, heating equipment, and air-conditioning equipment. The observations could then be adjusted to satisfy both the complete-count joint distribution of structural type and type of heating equipment and the complete-count joint distribution of structural type and type of air-conditioning equipment. This scaling requires an iterative technique, since adjusting the data to satisfy the first joint distribution may produce results inconsistent with the second joint distribution. As was true of the simple two-dimensional problem, this three-way scaling problem is equivalent to the formation of a random stratified sample and should further improve the efficiency of the sample estimates of raw product moments or other statistics.

By following the above procedures it should be possible to convert Public Use Sample data into usable estimates of raw product moments not available from complete-count data. This permits the estimation of rent equations using all of the housing variables collected by the Census Bureau, while still considering the potential impact of neighborhood and locational characteristics. While it is possible that sampling error present in the estimated product moments will result in biased estimates of the coefficients of the model, careful stratification and scaling of the sample data along the lines previously suggested should greatly reduce the remaining error. In general, the value of the Public Use Sample data for any type of analysis will be enhanced by scaling that data to match available complete-count, one-way, or joint frequency distributions. Indeed, the Public Use Sample of the U.S. Census is one of the few sources of sample data for which complete-count control totals for each variable are available.

As the above discussion illustrates, Census data can support a very rich ordinary least squares analysis of housing price variation and market segmentation. The estimation of the regression equation required only raw product moments for each pair of variables. Although it is possible to use available Census data to perform tests of market segmentation by race and a crude stratification by location, other dimensions or market segmentations are also of interest.

Assuming that Census tracts correspond roughly to homogeneous neighborhoods, it is possible to estimate individual equations for each tract. In addition to the one-way frequency distributions used in the earlier analysis, the Fourth Count Summary tapes also present a number of useful tract-specific cross tabulations. For each tract in the Pittsburgh SMSA, for example, information is available on the joint distribution of rent payments and structural type, rent payments and age of structure, and age of structure and structural type. By assigning values to each of the rent categories it is possible to calculate the raw product moments needed to estimate the coefficients of a model in which it is assumed rent is a linear function of structural type and age for each tract.

Lack of available cross tabulations severely limits the possibilities for tract-specific rent equations. In an earlier paper, Apgar and Kain presented a series of tract-level regression equations. Data considerations, however, limited the analysis to four housing variables, i.e., structural type, age, plumbing, and number of bedrooms (see Apgar and Kain 1972). Even at this reduced level of detail, several of the required raw product moments could not be obtained from the data. Rather, it was necessary to estimate values for these missing moments that were consistent with the known tract-level one-way distributions of the variables.[7]

Despite these difficulties, the tract-specific regressions for the Pittsburgh metropolitan area did reveal some significant differences in the variation of attribute prices over neighborhood and location. It is of more importance to the current discussion that the analysis of Pittsburgh tract data demonstrated the ease of estimating regressions directly from raw product moments. Three separate functional forms of the basic equation were estimated for owners and renters stratified by race and located in each of the 702 Census tracts in the Pittsburgh area. In all, sufficient data were available for the estimation of nearly 4,000 separate equations. If software development costs are excluded, the average computer cost for estimating each equation and printing out the results were approximately four cents. It is unlikely that an analysis using raw sample data could have been completed at any lower cost.

It should be clear, then, that the ability to estimate an OLS model of housing price variation is limited only by the detail of available summary data. As a result, the release of cross-product matrices for housing variables aggregated by block, tract, or minor civil division would do much to offset the lack of spatially detailed Census sample data. These matrices would be the building blocks for numerous regression analyses based on Census data and would greatly improve the quality of Census housing analysis. Indeed, such a program for improved quality of small-area data would have significant value for other areas of social science research; and in the final section of this study I briefly consider some of these alternative applications.

CENSUS SUMMARY DATA AND DISCRETE MULTIVARIATE ANALYSIS

I have presented a detailed discussion of the estimation of a series of OLS models of housing prices. This emphasis on housing prices should not obscure the fact that the techniques presented are equally applicable to other areas of research. Nor should it be assumed that the approach is limited to OLS analysis. Indeed, given the current availability of Census cross tabulations, many types of discrete multivariate analysis can be conducted with Census summary data. In an effort to underscore the potential richness of census-based econometric analysis, I present some alternative uses of the summary data.

The importance of home ownership as a vehicle for wealth accumulation is well documented. Yet it is clear that black households are systematically excluded from the benefits of owner occupancy (Kain and Quigley 1972). Two explanations come quickly to mind. First, it is likely that racial discrimination limits black residential choice to portions of the housing stock which are inappropriate vehicles for home ownership. Second, it is likely that even if black residential areas do expand to include suitable housing stock, racial discrimination by lending institutions could prevent black households from achieving owner status.

It is possible to evaluate these two explanations with a logit model of home ownership. Consider, for example, the basic logit model, which equates the log of the odds of home ownership with a linear function of race, family income, family type, and neighborhood type. Related models could include the interaction between family income, neighborhood, and race, or other higher-order interactions.

As was the case with the OLS models, tests for the presence of interaction in this spatially detailed logit model of home ownership could be conducted with sample data identified by small areas. Assuming that the census tracts correspond to a desired typology of neighborhoods, it is also possible to estimate these logit models using a more limited set of neighborhood-specific cross tabulations. In this problem the parameters of the simple linear logit model can be obtained by combining the four-way cross tabulation—race by family income by family type by neighborhood type—and each of the two-way cross tabulations involving tenure into a single estimate of the full five-dimensional array—race by tenure by family type by family income by neighborhood type. Using an iterative procedure, an estimate can be obtained of the unknown five-dimensional array that satisfied the known set of marginal distributions or interaction assumptions. In this instance, the assumption is that the five-way array can be fully described with one four-dimensional marginal summary and four two-dimensional marginal summaries. All other possible higher-order interactions are assumed to be absent. By using the values produced from this estimated array, coefficients can be constructed for the linear logit model described above. While the procedure is somewhat complicated to describe, it is in fact computationally quite simple. The approach follows directly from Leo Goodman's demonstration that certain hierarchical hypotheses concerning the interaction structure of a multivariate contingency table correspond to the logit analysis of a dichotomous variable (Goodman 1970).

Hypotheses concerning the presence of interaction terms in the logit model can be tested by fitting more complex models. The only matrix not present in the Census tract summary data is the five-way cross tabulation involving all of the variables in the problem. This precludes the possibility of fitting the so-called saturated model, i.e., the model that corresponds to the hypothesis that all possible interactions are represented in the data in a statistically significant manner. If it is correct to reject this hypothesis, then it is possible to test for the presence of other interactions in the logit framework. The tests are based on the usual chi-square goodness-of-fit statistic and follow directly from Goodman's observations on the partitioning of hierarchical hypotheses on multidimensional contingency tables.

Since the preceding discussion was somewhat terse, the reader is referred directly to the growing literature on discrete multivariate analysis, for example, the excellent textbook by Bishop et al. (1974). It is hoped, however, that this presentation has been sufficiently detailed to establish one rather simple point. Just as was true with OLS models of housing markets, available small-area Census Bureau summary data can support detailed logit analyses. As the above discussion illustrates, use of Census data in a logit analysis of home ownership could be quite rewarding. It is likely that such analysis would lead to the rejection of the simple hypothesis that each of the variables affects the log of the odds of home ownership in a linearly additive fashion. More complex specifications could be tested, however—a process that would undoubtedly enhance our understanding of the relationship between race and home ownership.

Numerous other examples of discrete multivariate analysis based on Census summary data could be presented. Literally thousands of multiple-dimension contingency tables are presented in the First to the Sixth Count Summary Tapes for 1970. In addition, for both 1960 and 1970, a number of other cross tabulations have been released as a byproduct of the publication of the special Census Subject Reports. These present the most detailed information available from Census sources on such diverse topics as modal choice, journey to work, intrametropolitan mobility of households, and the occupational and geographical mobility of workers. Each of these separate Census products is a potentially rich source of the summary statistics needed to perform useful logit, OLS, or other discrete multivariate analyses of important issues.

CONCLUSION

Although confidentiality requirements may prohibit the Bureau of the Census from releasing sample data identified by detailed geographic area, many empirical tests of important hypotheses do not require information on individual households, but rather a much reduced set of summary statistics aggregated at different levels. Such exercises will succeed only if these summary statistics are internally consistent; yet as this study has illustrated, current procedures generate data with several minor inconsistencies. Correction of these problems would greatly increase the accuracy and ease of estimation of Census-based econometric models.

First, the Census should attempt to reconcile the differences between the alternative sources of housing data. As was noted earlier, the total number of renter-occupied dwelling units obtained from the Fourth Count and Metropolitan Housing Characteristics do not agree. Since these two sources were released at different times, this discrepancy could reflect differences in error editing. While the desire for the prompt release of Census data is understandable, the need for their internal consistency is an equally important objective. If errors are discovered during the early phases of census processing, subsequent release of the adjusted data would be of considerable importance.

Second, the Census policy of data suppression should be reassessed. There is no apparent advantage in defining a Census tract with so few households that summary statistics for all households are suppressed. These small tracts should be aggregated with larger ones so that tract-level summary statistics can be presented that are consistent with similar statistics published for an entire county or metropolitan area.

Third, the Bureau of the Census should reassess its treatment of households who pay "no cash rent" and rental units located on lots with ten or more units. Unfortunately, both groups are included in the cross tabulations of the structural attributes. Since both types reflect special situations, it would be good sense to exclude them from all tabulations of renter-occupied housing units. Separate tabulations for those two situations could be presented instead. The current procedure does not provide sufficient information for analysis of those special cases but does increase the difficulty of using all rental data.

In addition to reviewing the procedures used to ensure data consistency, the Bureau of the Census should also review its programs of release of summary statistics and sample data. As was noted, the Public Use Sample of the U.S. Census is one of the few sources of sample data for which complete-count control totals for each variable are available. In addition, the Sixth Count Summary tapes provide information required to scale the sample data to satisfy a series of multidimensional contingency tables. Even if the bureau is reluctant to release Public Use Sample data with additional small-area detail, it should consider expansion of the Fourth and Sixth Count Summary tape program. This would greatly improve the efficiency of the summary statistics generated with existing Census sample data.

While sample data are required for many types of analysis, I have outlined a generally overlooked use for complete-count aggregate Census summary statistics. Increased availability of Census summary statistics for tract, minor civil division, or metropolitan levels would enhance use of the data for ordinary least squares, logit, or other discrete multivariate analysis. These additional summary statistics could be provided as new contingency tables, but the creation of product moment matrices of individual Census variables for a variety of levels of aggregation would be a more compact way of releasing similar information. Other summary statistics could be released for individual tracts or blocks. Such procedures would permit small-area analysis of Census data while preserving the confidentiality of individual responses.

Finally, it should be observed that the confidentiality requirements of the Bureau of the Census do not represent a needless obstacle to research but rather, an important aspect of the Census program which should be rationalized and improved. The success of the Census in gathering complete and accurate information on millions of households rests in part on its ability to make a meaningful pledge of confidentiality. In a time of growing skepticism concerning governmental invasion of privacy, these pledges assume even greater importance. The tremendous nonresponse rates in many non-Census special surveys underscore the importance of the confidentiality issue.

Given the difficulty and expense of collecting any household interview information, an attempt by the Bureau of the Census to improve the quality of available small-area summary data should be well worth the effort. For 1970, the major costs of data acquisition and processing have already been incurred. For a small additional expenditure, considerable benefits could be obtained by reformating existing small-area information and creating new small-area summary statistics. For future censuses, possible improvement in question design should be considered as well. This would be especially important for housing analysis, which presents many difficult measurement problems.

The Bureau of the Census is in a unique position to gather and disseminate small-area data. Researchers would do well to develop analytical methods compatible with the requirements of the agency. Substantial empirical research can be conducted without infringing on the privacy of individuals. The Bureau of the Census already provides many valuable summary statistics, and I hope it will continue to expand its program of data acquisition and release.

NOTES TO CHAPTER FIVE

1. For a discussion of sales data gathered by federal agencies, see Musgrave (1969).

2. See, for example, *Review of Public Data Use* (December 1972), which contains a series of articles about Public Use Sample research.

3. For a complete description of the Public Use Sample data and other Census products see Census (1973a).

4. These land use data were obtained from the Southwest Pennsylvania Regional Planning Commission.

5. For a discussion of sampling procedures, see Census (1973a).

6. For a discussion of the implications of scaling a multidimensional contingency table see Bishop (1969). Also see Goodman (1970).

7. See Apgar and Kain (1972, appendix) for a complete discussion of the procedure used to estimate the missing moments.

REFERENCES

Apgar, William C., Jr., and John P. Kain. 1972. "The Residential Price Geography of the Pittsburgh SMSA." Paper presented at winter meetings of Econometric Society of America. Toronto, Canada. December.

Bishop, Yvonne M. 1969. "Full Contingency Tables, Logits, and Split Contingency Tables." *Biometrics*, June.

Bishop, Yvonne M., et al. 1974. *Discrete Multivariate Analysis*. Cambridge, Mass.: M.I.T. Press.

Census. 1972. U.S. Bureau of the Census. Social and Economic Statistics Administration. *Data Access Description*. Computer Tape series, CT-7. August.

_____. 1973a. U.S. Bureau of the Census. *A Procedural History of the 1970 Census of Population and Housing*.

_____. 1973c. U.S. Bureau of the Census. *Small Area Data Notes*. September. mnmnmnmnmnm

de Leeuw, Frank, and Raymond J. Struyk. 1975. *The Web of Urban Housing*. Washington, D.C.: Urban Institute.

Goodman, Leo. 1970. "The Multivariate Analysis of Qualitative Data: Interactions Among Multiple Classifications." *Journal of the American Statistical Association*, March.

Hoerl, Arthur E., and Robert W. Kennard. 1970. "Ridge Regression: Biased Estimation for Nonorthogonal Problems" and "Ridge Regression: Applications to Nonorthogonal Problems." *Technometrics*, February.

Ingram, Gregory K. 1971. "A Simulation Model of an Urban Housing Market." Ph.D. dissertation, Harvard University.

Kain, John F., and John M. Quigley. 1972. "Housing Market Discrimination, Homeownership, and Savings Behavior." *American Economic Review*, June.

_____. 1975. *Housing Markets and Racial Discrimination: A Microeconomic Analysis*. Urban and Regional Studies 3. New York: National Bureau of Economic Research.

King, A. Thomas. 1972. "Land Values and the Demand for Housing." Ph.D. dissertation, Yale University.

_____. 1973. "Households in Housing Markets: The Demand for Housing Components." Working Paper. Processed. Bureau of Business and Economic Research, University of Maryland. March.

Musgrave, John C. 1969. "The Measurement of Price Changes in Construction." *Journal of the American Statistical Association*, September.

Olsen, Edgar. 1969. "A Competitive Theory of the Housing Market." *American Economic Review*, September.

Peterson, George E. 1974. "The Effect of Zoning Regulations on Suburban Property Values." Working Paper. Processed. Washington, D.C.: Urban Institute.

Peterson, George E., et al. 1973. *Property Taxes, Housing, and the Cities.* Lexington, Mass.: D.C. Heath and Company.

Polinsky, A. Mitchell, and Daniel L. Rubinfeld. 1975. "Property Values and the Benefits of Environmental Improvements: Theory and Measurement." Discussion Paper 104. Processed. Institute of Economic Research, Harvard University. March.

Quigley, John M. 1972. "Residential Location: Multiple Workplaces and a Heterogeneous Housing Stock." Ph.D. dissertation, Harvard University.

Review of Public Data Use; December 1972. Entire issue was devoted to Public Use samples.

Schnare, Ann B., and Raymond J. Struyk. 1974. "Segmentation in Urban Housing Markets." Paper presented before Committee on Urban Economics of Conference on Housing Research. Washington University, October 4-5.

Straszheim, Mahlon. 1975. *An Exonometric Analysis of the Urban Housing Market.* Urban and Regional Studies 2. New York: National Bureau of Economic Research.

Comments on Chapter Five

Eric A. Hanushek

Apgar's study has three distinct aspects. First, there is a methodological discussion about the best ways to use available data on urban housing. Second, there is an implicit research strategy for future analyses of urban structure. And, third, there is a set of implications for the Bureau of the Census pertaining to methods of providing "more information" without sacrificing guarantees of confidentiality.

The first two topics—methodology and research strategy—are best considered within the context of the actual empirical analysis presented by Apgar. This is an analysis of relative rental prices of housing units within a metropolitan area—in this case the Pittsburgh metropolitan area. The motivation for this analysis comes from three sources: First, the empirical analyses of housing prices which have been done in the past have generally used unique data sources and model specifications, making it difficult to compare the results across studies. Second, past studies (and projected future ones) have concentrated more on sales of owner-occupied units, and these units might not adequately reflect the total housing market. Third, if because of market segmentation different prices are in effect for similar housing services in different locations, large bodies of data are called for to sort out the "linkages between spatially separated housing submarkets."

The thrust of Apgar's study is that the Census provides a large and consistent body of micro data which can be used to learn more about

Note: In preparing these comments, I benefited from discussions with John Quigley.

urban form and the spatial aspects of urban housing markets. It is his contention that the richness of the published Census data has been largely overlooked and that the tabulations provide all the information needed to estimate models of housing prices for individual units and not just aggregations such as housing prices for Census tracts.

The starting point for Apgar's analysis is a presumption that the Census Bureau collects and reports in various forms all the data about attributes of housing structures that would be needed for a properly specified model of housing prices or rents. To summarize his methodology, let us then begin with the presentation of Census housing data and the information requirements for estimation of ordinary least squares coefficients. For each metropolitan area, the Census publishes a number of cross tabulations of aspects of housing units (such as structural type, dwelling unit age, rent, and value). These are published for an entire SMSA, for all cities over 50,000 in population, for the suburban ring, and by race of the occupant. Additionally, Census publications provide frequency counts of these attributes and others for individual Census tracts.

Two basic analytical schemes, then, can be followed to analyze prices of housing units. First, if we observe that the required cross-product information for least squares estimation where the independent variables are categorical is simply the information contained in the two-way cross tabulations, we see that a model based upon estimation from individual units can be developed for any geographical area (or set of households) for which a complete set of two-way tabulations is available. Alternatively, we could estimate a model of housing prices based upon aggregate Census tract data, that is, using Census tracts as the observational units. There are two problems with the first method: First, the Census does not publish all of the cross tabulations of variables that might be desired; and second, there are differences among geographic subareas, for example, in neighborhood, accessibility and public services, which we would like to include in a housing price model but for which we do not have the needed cross-product data. The second method—estimation based upon aggregate Census tract data—suffers from possible aggregation biases and losses of efficiency because none of the within-Census tract variation in housing attributes is used in estimation.[1]

Apgar proposes to combine these two methods into a mixed estimation technique. The essence of the technique is to estimate the parameters of housing prices partly on the basis of individual data for the whole area and partly on the basis of aggregate Census tract variables. (As a footnote, I would add that the tract variables do not have to be provided by the Census but can be taken from other sources as long as the measurements are consistent with the tract boundaries.) Although it builds upon the fairly well known "pure" alternatives, this is an interesting methodological development. As Apgar points out, there is a considerable history of empirical analyses which appear to overlook such a mixed estimation strategy. Nevertheless, judgments on this technique must be based upon its empirical usefulness.

Apgar has provided us with an example of how this methodology can be applied by estimating a series of rental price models for the Pittsburgh metropolitan area. These are hedonic indexes of rental prices based upon structural type, age of the structure, plumbing, number of rooms, tract-specific accessibility, net density, income, and racial composition. Similar models are estimated for the entire SMSA, for the central city and suburban ring, and for blacks and whites in the central city and ring. He further suggests, on the basis of availability and consistency of the data and the costs of doing such estimation, that a profitable research strategy is to replicate this analysis for each of the other tracted SMSAs in the United States. My remarks relate directly to these conclusions.

To begin, let us consider what we have learned from the analysis of the Pittsburgh data. The basic hedonic approach has been followed in a wide variety of circumstances,[2] although none of those previous attempts has been based upon 50,000 observations. Several possible uses have motivated past applications and provide some justification for the enterprise. First, the hedonic index can be used to develop standardized bundles of housing services or different aspects of those services. Since housing services are multi-dimensional, including dwelling unit attributes, neighborhood attributes, and locational attributes such as accessibility and public services, it is necessary in many analyses of urban housing markets and urban form to standardize the bundle. However, we do not have good ways of treating multi-dimensional goods when we do not have any price information linking the individual attributes. In the hedonic approach, estimates are made of the price associated with particular underlying components of housing services. When the market is in equilibrium, these estimates can be interpreted as shadow prices for the individual attributes. Use of these indexes, or portions of them, facilitates analyses of the supply and demand of different quantities of housing services and the interrelationships of housing bundles with urban form. Second, hedonic indexes provide a framework within which it is possible to consider the effects of accessibility, various externalities in price determination, and racial discrimination. By standardizing carefully for different attributes of dwelling units, we can then concentrate on these issues. Third, we can look at market segmentation where the term is meant to imply differences in the relative valuations of different underlying housing attributes for identifiable sub-markets such as geographical areas or racial groups. Apgar wishes to concentrate mainly upon this third use, but presumably this type of analysis of the Census would be applicable to the other purposes also.

Data from the decennial census for individual dwelling units provides not only a very large sample, which can be used for the estimation, but also the possibility of replication in other cities. These aspects are not without costs, however. We must trade these advantages against an equivalent investment in obtaining more detailed and richer data about individual aspects of structure, neighborhood, and location for one or more metropolitan areas. In using the Census data, there seem to be considerable costs in terms of the quality of the data. To begin with, the information available is very rudimentary. There are data for five structural types, four age groupings, a measure of completeness of the plumbing, and the number of rooms. This is certainly not a very complete description of an individual dwelling unit. Most important, there is no information about the quality of the unit (except, perhaps, for the plumbing variable). It is doubtful that we would want to rely upon this portion of the model to provide the foundation for a further or more detailed analysis of relationships involving structural attributes. However, it is important to note that *all of the potential gains* obtained from using this mixed aggregation method consist of efficiency gains in the estimation of the coefficients for the four structural attributes measured. Further, these efficiency gains (compared to estimation using Census tract variables) accrue only to the extent that the model is properly specified, that is, that it is linear in terms of those four attributes of the housing stock. Apgar suggests that more complete models than the ones he presents can be estimated. However, limitations arising from the presentation of data by the Census (i.e., missing cross tabulations of variables) imply that models cannot be much more extensive than those estimated.

Apgar's neighborhood measures are also very crude. They pertain only to the tract level, and this is probably a very poor level of aggregation for the purpose of uncovering neighborhood effects. In these measures, one again finds a lack of qualitative information except perhaps in the measure of accessibility, a variable not found in basic Census data. There is no information about public services. Thus, it appears that the Census provides a large amount of not too detailed data, and that data base does not take us very far in addressing two of the possible uses of hedonic price indexes for housing, namely, providing a good method for standardizing housing bundles or allowing detailed analysis of neighborhoods or externalities. In passing, I note that on the question of racial discrimination, Apgar's results (in terms of the dummy variable for black households) indicate that whites are discriminated against in the SMSA as a whole and, when division by central city-suburb is made, whites are discriminated against in the suburbs. However, we are not likely to take these estimates of discrimination seriously in a model which so imperfectly measures the housing attributes. Apgar does not seem to take this seriously since he does not even mention it.

One area of investigation remains, and that one—the test of market segmentation—Apgar addresses most directly. While for many analyses these models may not be complete enough in terms of the individual components, they might still be useful in making some overall statements about market segmentation or about differences in relative prices over different submarkets. However, for those purposes, this type of research also seems to fall somewhat short of what might be desired. As noted before, the maintained hypothesis is that there are subtle interactions between structural attributes, neighborhood characteristics, and location. Apgar then notes that the large Census samples provide a data base that can be used to test such interactions. However, the only interactions between submarkets and various prices that he can analyze are those between central city and suburb and between racial groups similarly divided. Within each of these four cells, he can only look at linear models in which there is no interaction between housing characteristics and neighborhoods. He cannot, for example, determine if there is any interaction between neighborhood quality and housing size. If we had not become conditioned by the Census presentation of data, we would probably not define submarkets as simply central city and suburb. Note that this submarket definition is imposed on the mixed estimation strategy, but it is not mandatory in an estimation strategy based upon Census tract aggregates; tracts may be divided in a variety of ways to test market segmentation hypotheses with aggregate data. Apgar does find statistically significant differences between the individual models. But there is a question about how to interpret them, particularly since the measures of structure and neighborhood are poor and public services are not measured at all.

Finally, let us return to the overall issue of the implicit research strategy. In the end, Apgar cites the cheapness of the regression analyses (although that significantly understates the costs of replication) and implies that we should replicate this analysis for other SMSAs.[3] What would we learn from such an analysis? In all likelihood we would find that there were significant differences in the shadow prices of different attributes. Such cross-sectional differences are already known to exist (see Ball's work, cited earlier). Further, recent research by Alan Goodman indicates that the hedonic indexes for a single location show considerable change over even short periods of time.[4] For example, obtaining estimates of the effect of a race dummy variable in 150 cities probably would not increase our understanding of racial submarkets for housing services. This is at least my view because I am unwilling to accept the specification dictated by the housing attributes currently available from the Census—and especially those four structural attributes that are completely cross-tabulated.

Since hedonic indexes represent reduced form models of the housing market, we would be tempted to explain observed differences among areas in terms of a variety of structural differences in either specific supply or demand conditions. However, it would be difficult to do this in a systematic manner without knowledge of the underlying supply and demand relationships within the different housing markets. Therefore, it would seem better to concentrate attention on a single housing market, where we could hope to isolate either more information about structural aspects or more precise information about some aspect of the housing market.

A more appealing research design than this Census strategy would call for a more intensive analysis of a given city. If the money for this analysis were spent on a carefully designed survey that addressed, say, the issue of neighborhoods, or public services, or market segmentation, I would speculate that we could increase our knowledge of urban structure more than by following the Census route. The appeal of using specialized data samples in the past has been that they often contain particular information about one aspect of urban housing markets. Indeed, the analytical design of many such studies has revolved around capitalizing on one or two particularly rich features of a body of data. Certainly, it would be helpful to replicate some of these studies with consistent data from other sources. However, consistency is not an absolute virtue, particularly when consistency implies losing all of the richness of any given analysis and imposing a maintained hypothesis which we would not in general be willing to accept.

A key point is that we are very uncertain about the correct specification of the housing price model. Even with the use of specialized data, there are many uncertainties about the specification of various aspects of the total housing bundle. Replication of the Census analysis, based upon its minimal number of measures of housing attributes, cannot give us much guidance in terms of appropriate specification. The goal of comparisons across different estimates of hedonic indexes has mainly been to learn about model specification, and that issue has little to do with the efficiency of estimation of a few structural parameters. In fact, the questions of micro data and efficiency have meaning only within the context of reasonably well-specified models. There seems to be little one can say about the virtue of "efficient" estimates of possibly highly biased coefficients.

It also seems important to note one other aspect of the research design in this area. Data availability is not the only problem. There are some serious conceptual problems that have not been adequately addressed. For example, neighborhood is a concept that has received considerable attention. Yet there are few discussions of how one should go about measuring neighborhoods. In another area, the appropriate measurement and treatment of public services is unclear. Should we measure levels of services? Value added in public provision of services? Value added adjusted for costs? Or should we assume that all differences in public services are reflected in price differences for given housing units? Apgar completely ignores the issue, but even those who have considered it do not seem to have made much progress. In short, our conceptual and measurement tools need some refining. Also, our methods of analysis need some further consideration. Should we continue to analyze the reduced form models implied by the hedonic indexes or should we move toward more structural demand and supply relationships?

These issues take us considerably beyond the scope of this particular paper. However, they do suggest that at our current state of knowledge a continuation of smaller-scale analyses that focus upon particular smaller issues may not be a wasteful strategy. Thus, in terms of methodology and research strategy, it appears that Apgar makes a very valid point that Census housing data have not been fully exploited by their users. However, the generalization of this point in terms of research strategy is a bit misleading. The prime shortcoming of current models of housing prices and urban structure does not seem to be efficiency of parametric estimates but reasonableness of model specification.

The final point of Apgar's study—implications for the Bureau of the Census—is very well taken. The presentation of published Census data is not the best possible. Inconsistencies in data and missing detail appear to be introduced unnecessarily. Through consideration of research needs and uses of the Census data, improvements could be made at virtually no cost.

As preparations are made for the 1980 census, design considerations obtained from potential research uses should be brought in. An important suggestion that is developed by Apgar is that the Census could routinely present cross-product information. As a practical matter, this would not have to be available in hard copy; machine-readable information would be sufficient. This step would expand the value of the data without compromising the policy of confidentiality. (It would probably have the added advantage of forcing the Census Bureau to provide consistent data.) Nevertheless, perhaps a more important issue to take to the Census Bureau is a better understanding of the specific data that they should collect. In other words, even here the importance of model specification should not be underestimated.

NOTES TO COMMENTS ON CHAPTER FIVE

1. Note that the efficiency gains of using the micro data might be offset by biases that arise from incomplete data in the cross tabulations or by errors resulting from the use of two different published sources.

2. See Michael J. Ball, "Recent Empirical Works on the Determinants of Relative House Prices," *Urban Studies*, June 1973.

3. Apgar's current model includes measures of accessibility by tract and net residential density by tract. Obtaining similar information for other cities could be very expensive. Furthermore, this does not include any estimate of the costs that would be involved in sorting out the results for 150 cities.

4. Alan C. Goodman, "Neighborhood Effects, Hedonic Prices, and the Residential Housing Choice" (Ph D. dissertation, Yale University, 1976).

❋ *Chapter Six*

Habitability Laws and Low-Cost Rental Housing

Werner Z. Hirsch and
Stephen Margolis

INTRODUCTION

In 1970, 8.5 million households in the United States—one
in every eight—inhabited substandard housing as defined
by the Census, mostly rental housing.[1] Yet, as long ago as
1949, Congress had established a national goal of "a decent and
suitable living environment for every American family."[2] We can
identify a number of legislative responses to this challenge, including
such federal programs as urban renewal, public housing, Model Cities,
and rent subsidies. In addition, and often in isolation, state legislatures and the courts have instituted laws with the same purpose in
mind. These laws have sought to modify the venerable one-sided
relationship between landlord and tenant. Such modifications, be
they common law or statutory, have been along two major lines of
approach—habitability laws and continued tenure laws.

A substantial literature exists on landlord-tenant relations, but
little work has been done to examine the economic implications of
housing laws on landlords and tenants.[3] In this study, we provide a
model for the evaluation of the costs and benefits of various
habitability laws. In particular, we will evaluate laws on repair and
rent deduct, receivership, rent withholding, and rent abatement, as
well as laws for combating retaliatory eviction; all these are measures
that reduce the risk borne by the tenant in procuring housing. Our
objective is to determine the costs imposed by these laws and their
distribution between landlord and tenant, as well as the resulting net
costs or benefits.

181

We first present the major laws that regulate the relationship between landlord and tenant. We then offer some concepts and definitions designed to facilitate the analysis of the impact of habitability laws on rents paid by low-income groups. Next, we examine the allocation process for housing services within a demand-supply framework. We model the rental housing consumption process as well as the supply process. Finally, we develop an empirical methodology and present our results. In our empirical work we use a data file on landlord-tenant legal relations specially constructed by us and household data from the University of Michigan Panel Study of Income Dynamics for 1968-1972.

LANDLORD-TENANT LAWS

Historically, most of the American states have subscribed to the early common law rule that landlords are under no duty to repair and maintain residential premises leased to tenants[4] or to deliver residential premises in a habitable condition. Moreover, since the rules of property law solidified before the development of mutually dependent covenants in contract law, a lessee's covenant to pay rent was considered independent of the lessor's covenant to provide housing. As a result, for example, if a tenant's home became uninhabitable, even though it was through no fault of his own, he could neither demand that repairs be made by the landlord nor escape liability for the rent due for the remainder of the term. Thus, the tenant had to pay rent regardless of whether he received any benefits from the residential premises.

A major modification of this traditional common law landlord-tenant relationship began soon after World War II. Basically, two approaches have been pursued, mainly through laws that assure tenants habitable housing and, to a lesser extent, continued tenancy (Hirsch et al. 1975).

In the first line of approach, many large American cities, by means of housing codes, shifted to the landlord the responsibility for repairing leased premises and maintaining them in habitable condition. The codes impose the burden of repair and maintenance on the landlord, while placing responsibility for cleanliness of the dwelling and specified minor items of maintenance on the tenant. Usually, the owner remains ultimately responsible for having housing code violations corrected. Parallel to these housing codes and in furthering their enforcement, courts and legislatures have created rights of actions of tenants. To this end, a number of legal remedies have been fashioned; they increase the property rights that are purchased by tenants while concomitantly reducing those retained by landlords. These remedies, designed to provide a minimum level of housing quality to tenants, include repair and rent deduction, rent withholding and abatement, and receivership. They are often supplemented by provisions that prohibit retaliatory eviction, facilitate return of the tenant's security deposit, and legalize rent strikes. Furthermore, courts have recently begun to imply a warranty of habitability into urban residential leases.[5]

These recent changes in landlord-tenant relations, by implying and extending a warranty of habitability, automatically revise the doctrine of caveat emptor. Since certainty about the law has declined, previously nonexistent legal risks have arisen and the distribution of risks between landlord and tenant has been altered. For example, in the presence of caveat emptor, the landlord's obligations to repair and maintain premises are clear and, therefore, he faces few risks regardless of how little repair and maintenance he provides. At the same time, tenants face many risks, all of which change when the doctrine of caveat emptor is modified.

Without a warranty of habitability, there is considerable potential for variation in the level of service delivered to the tenant. Thus, the tenant's lease agreement is, for him, a source of risk. There are two sources of that variability:

First, there is the risk that the tenant has not correctly assessed the attributes of the dwelling before leasing. Here, the law would appear to economize on the cost of acquiring information, since the landlord is in the best position to evaluate his own property. Therefore, the law may be seen as requiring more complete disclosure of information, so that the tenant cannot claim that services he might reasonably have expected under the lease were not forthcoming.

Second, there is the risk that some damage to the dwelling will occur and reduce the flow of services during the period of the lease. When a habitability law is passed, the risk is transferred from tenant to landlord. In the absence of such a law, the tenant would be responsible for repair if he wished to derive the full benefits from his residence. To the extent that maintenance can vary, the tenant's consumption is subject to risk. Under the habitability law, risk is transferred to the landlord, whose profit is now subject to the variability of maintenance expenditures. The transfer of risk does raise serious questions as to who is the efficient risk bearer. Since the landlord may control many units, he therefore may have a smaller expected variation per unit. On the other hand, if the landlord's assets are specialized in housing, the total risk he bears may represent a relatively large part of his total wealth. The poor tenant may be less averse to risk than the wealthier landlord. Thus, there seems to be no clear a priori basis for determining whether landlord or tenant will have a larger evaluation of the cost of avoiding the risk associated with the rental dwelling unit.

Let us next examine the major habitability laws. In Table 6-1, we indicate which laws were in force in early 1972 in the twenty-five states included in our sample.

Repair and deduct laws offer tenants a self-help remedy by permitting them, upon their own initiative, to repair defects in their

Table 6-1. Habitability Laws, by States, 1972

States in Sample	Repair and Deduct	Withholding	Receivership	Eviction
Alabama	no	no	no	no
Arizona	no	no	no	no
California	yes	no	no	yes
Colorado	no	no	no	no
Washington, D.C.	no	yes	no	yes
Florida	no	no	no	yes
Georgia	yes	yes	no	no
Illinois	no	yes[a]	yes	yes
Indiana	no	no	no	no
Kansas	no	no	no	no
Kentucky	no	no	no	no
Louisiana	yes	no	no	no
Maryland	no	yes	no	yes
Massachusetts	no	yes	yes	yes
Michigan	no	yes[a]	yes	no
Mississippi	no	no	no	no
Missouri	no	yes	yes	no
New Jersey	yes	yes	yes	yes
New York	no	yes[a]	yes	yes
Ohio	no	no	no	no
Oregon	no	no	no	no
Pennsylvania	no	yes	no	yes
South Carolina	no	no	no	no
Texas	no	no	no	no
Washington	no	no	no	no

[a]Welfare departments are authorized to withhold rent.

premises and deduct repair charges from their rent.[6] By 1972, this remedy was available in four states in our sample. It is basically limited to relatively minor defects.[7] Wide application of this remedy in a large multiple-unit dwelling could be inefficient compared to the result if the landlord undertook the repair and benefited from scale economies.

A second form of remedy is rent withholding, through either escrow or rent abatement. In the first case, the tenant pays rent into a court-created escrow account. Rental income is withheld from the landlord until violations are corrected.[8] Illinois, Michigan, and New York even authorize rent withholding by the state welfare department or some other agency. An alternative is rent abatement, which is more consistent with the application of contract rather than property law principles.[9] Rent abatement permits the tenant to remain in possession of the premises without paying rent or by paying a reduced amount until the housing defects are remedied. The condition of the premises constitutes a defense either to an action of eviction or to an action for rent. In most situations, the actual differences between withholding and abatement are very small. Even under abatement, rent is usually also placed into escrow, either as a good faith gesture by the tenant or because courts so order pending a full investigation of the existence and correction of code violations. Therefore, in this paper we lump abatement and withholding together as withholding laws. By 1972, such laws were in existence in ten of the states included in our sample.

A third remedy is receivership, i.e., appointment by the court of a receiver who takes control of buildings and who corrects hazardous defects, after the landlord has failed to act within a reasonable period. By 1972, this remedy had become available in six of the states included in our sample. If large-scale repairs are needed and cannot be financed through rental payments, some statutes permit the receiver to seek additional loans. When this is done, old first liens are converted into new second liens, imposing particularly heavy costs on lenders and, therefore, ultimately on landlords. Initiation of receivership is usually preceded by a hearing in which the court determines whether the landlord has failed to provide essential services. If the court so rules, the rent is deposited with the court-appointed receiver until the violation is corrected. As long as the tenant continues to pay rent into escrow, his landlord cannot evict him for nonpayment.

Altogether, courts increasingly imply warranties of fitness and habitability in urban residential leases. This implied warranty of habitability may be used as a defense in both actions of eviction and actions for rent, if the tenant is able to show that a "substantial" violation of the housing code existed during the period rent was withheld. In addition, the tenant may have an affirmative cause of action against the landlord for breach of contract, while remaining liable for the reasonable value of the use of the premises.

Of the three remedies listed, receivership is potentially the most costly to the landlord. It results in a complete stoppage of rental income to him, since all tenants in the building, not only the aggrieved ones, pay rents into escrow. Moreover, the landlord altogether loses control over his building. Instead, control is temporarily transferred to a receiver who may be enthusiastic about fixing up the building, possibly even above minimum standards established by housing codes. The repair decisions are thus made without due consideration of their potential profitability. Finally, contrary to most repair and deduct and withholding laws, receivership is usually initiated by government, which has vast legal resources behind it.

The three major remedies are often supplemented by laws that can reinforce them. One is retaliatory eviction, which is designed to protect tenants from being penalized by landlords for complaining against housing code violations. Such laws, which usually freeze rents for ninety days after compliance, existed in 1972 in nine states of our sample. Furthermore, a number of states have laws that facilitate the return of the tenant's security deposit at the end of the tenancy. Finally, a few states have legalized rent strikes by tenants against a particular landlord.[10]

Laws that prohibit retaliatory eviction, facilitate return of the tenant's security deposit, and legalize rent strikes, like the other three remedies, impose costs on landlords. Parts of these costs may result from reduced flexibility given landlords, imposition of high repair and maintenance levels, and possibly legal costs. Of these remedies, retaliatory eviction laws resembling temporary rent controls tend to be the most costly to landlords.

In addition to these habitability laws, state legislatures have begun to pursue a second line of approach by assuring tenants continued tenancy, mainly through just-cause eviction statutes.[11] Under the latter, tenants can only be evicted for just cause, which is explicitly stipulated in the legislation. For example, such statutes in New Jersey (New Jersey Stats. 1974) delineate a limited number of legal grounds which would constitute the sole basis for eviction: failure to pay rent; disorderly conduct; willful damage or injury to the premises; breach of express covenants; continued violation of landlord's rules and regulations; landlord wishes to retire permanently; or landlord wishes to board up or demolish the premises because he has been cited for substandard housing violations and it is economically unfeasible for the owner to eliminate the violations.

Like habitability laws, just-cause eviction statutes reduce the property rights of landlords, particularly their flexibility in renting out their apartments. We do not deal with just-cause eviction statutes in this paper, but we note that such laws impose costs on landlords both because the statutes extend the warrant of habitability and its enforcement and because tenants assured of continued occupancy can feel free to use all available legal remedies to obtain from landlords relatively high levels of repair and maintenance.

Habitability laws can be viewed as rules of contract that change the nature of the permissible contract. One simple interpretation is that the habitability law constrains actors to contracts in which the landlord bears the risks associated with repair and maintenance, while without that law the form of the contract is not constrained. If such an interpretation were correct, then a strong a priori case could be made for the inefficiency of habitability laws. However, it is equally likely that under caveat emptor, the consumer is constrained from purchasing a desired bundle of housing services that includes warranties. Such would be the case if high transaction costs interfered with an efficient reallocation of rights. The reasons are that deviations from a standard contract are costly and enforcement of any warranties purchased would be difficult under general application of caveat emptor. Finally, it may be that a contract that obligates the landlord to maintain the premises is efficient and has already evolved as the standard relationship between landlord and tenant, and that the habitability law merely provides legal recognition of this so as to reduce enforcement costs. These alternative interpretations each imply a different conclusion regarding the efficiency of habitability laws, and therefore provide the motivation for the empirical investigation undertaken below.[1,2]

CONCEPTS AND DEFINITIONS

Of central importance in the housing market analysis is the time period allowed for landlords and tenants to respond to changes in prices or other circumstances. Thus, attention must be given to the time period relevant to housing demand and supply. Clearly, the answers to hypothetical questions such as how much housing a group of households would consume at different rents, and how many rental units a group of landlords would put on the market at different rents, will depend on the amount of time that the decision maker has to react to changes. For example, if prices go up, by tomorrow the landlord can offer for rent only the units he owns today; by next year, he can acquire facilities and convert them to a particular application. At present, there appear to be two polar treatments of the supply of housing in the legal literature, an extreme long-run case by Komesar (1973) and a short-run case by Ackerman (1971).

The time period has a bearing on the expected distribution of costs. Thus, for example, traditional long-run models provide an easy answer to questions about the distribution between landlord and tenant of costs that might result from compliance with additional housing laws. In the competitive case with infinite time to make adjustments by means of new construction, the supply of housing is a horizontal or near-horizontal line at the price equal to the cost of providing housing services (de Leeuw 1974). Thus, in this simple case, the supply shifts upward ·to reflect the additional costs associated with the law. The effect on rental price is then equal or approximately equal to the change in costs. This would occur whether or not any benefits were received by the tenant. The traditional long-run case leaves us with only the question of evaluating the benefits and costs. The distribution of costs is unambiguous, i.e., the tenant pays all additional costs.

However, this absolute long-run model, while perhaps useful for analyzing investment decisions, is less than satisfactory for our analysis of housing markets. One of the aspects of housing that qualifies it for a more distinct analysis is the durability of the commodity. For assets as long lived as housing structures, full adjustment to a change in environment may take more time than any particular set of circumstances lasts. The durability of housing structures leads to a second approach to the problem, where the supply of housing is treated as being perfectly inelastic. For example, in Ackerman, the assumption is made that the structures are in place and that they will be rented at some price rather than allowed to remain vacant. If a new law results in losses, the properties are simply revalued downward with a once-over loss to the landlord; but the property will remain in the rental market.[13]

This short-run model might be applied to certain pricing decisions, but it begs most of the important questions of concern to us. Clearly, if we assume no possible reaction by landlords, we will have no trouble concluding that the landlords' reactions will not lead to higher rents. It can, however, be argued that changes in the number of units will be small in the short run. This is particularly true for low-quality housing, if the appropriate response of supplies to the change in the law should be to withdraw units from this submarket, since upgrading to a higher quality is often quite expensive. Filtering down of higher-quality categories may be curtailed, but the effect will be small, since it is the consequence of construction and maintenance decisions made many years in the past and of environmental factors not under the control of landlords. For these reasons, it is not unrealistic to define, for the purpose of analysis here, a quasi-long-run period in which both the number and character of structures vary, but in which adjustment in the construction of new units has no bearing on the stock of low-quality structures. We are seeking a housing quality model that will allow the landlord to react by varying either housing quality or, as we will show below, the quantity of housing services, while not actually changing the number of dwelling units. Such a change will occur for the low-quality range primarily by varying the maintenance effort, which is the primary form of adjustment in our quasi-long-run model. It is widely observed that the type of management that an apartment building has will have an important impact on the quality of housing services and on the neighborhood as well if management practices are similar within the area (Sternlieb 1966). Much of the effect of management relates to the making of needed repairs and the frequency and quality of routine maintenance.

In summary, then, we will seek to build a model to evaluate the effects of a change in the legal environment on the housing market, particularly the low-cost rental housing market. It is a realistically quasi-long-run model in which the total low-cost housing stock is not completely free to vary, but other dimensions of landlords' behavior, mainly housing quality changes, are unconstrained.

We turn now to the quantity and quality dimensions of housing. Above, we used the word "quality" as we believe it to be conventionally understood; that is, as describing the essential character, the goodness or badness, of the commodity. Thus, a higher-quality unit is somehow "better," i.e., imparts greater service, than a lower-quality unit of equivalent size. Nonetheless, such a definition is far too vague and, to a degree, misleading. Any particular aspect of a dwelling, be it paint, heat, size, location, etc., can be regarded as a distinct economic commodity, and variations in these commodities are variations in the amount of goods being consumed by the individual occupying the dwelling. We aggregate over these commodities and summarize by denoting as "housing services" all of those characteristics taken together. Then a better dwelling, be it larger, in better condition, or both, is said simply to deliver more housing service (Muth 1969, and others). Given this definition, we can speak of quality as being the amount of housing service contained in a dwelling. In particular, the decision by a landlord to provide high or low quality in a particular dwelling is equivalent to the decision to provide more or less housing service.

Having defined the commodity with which we are concerned, i.e., housing service, we turn next to the problem of measurement. Measurement will be facilitated through the estimation of weights for the components of housing service, as shown below.

Rent payments represent a price multiplied by a quantity; in the market we observe expenditures rather than prices. For homogeneous commodities, this problem is solved by simply dividing observed expenditures by the quantity purchased. For housing there is no easily observable quantity. Rental payments can be regarded as the sum of payments for a number of characteristics, or,

$$R_j = \sum_{i=1}^{n} \alpha_i x_{ij} \qquad (6\text{-}1)$$

where R_j is the rental payment for the jth dwelling unit, α_i is the price of characteristic i, and x_{ij} if the quantity of the ith characteristic contained in the jth dwelling unit. The above represents a standard expression of the hedonic price approach. Unfortunately, this is not sufficient for our case. Hedonic prices represent outcomes of interactions of supply and demand. Because we are looking across cities, we have many supply and demand relationships and therefore we cannot expect uniform $\alpha_i's$ to apply for all observations. As a result, we must depart from the usual approach in order to incorporate those variables which enter the model through their differential effects on supply and demand across cities:

$$R_j = \sum_{i}^{n} \alpha_i x_{ij} + \sum_{i}^{m} \beta_i y_{ij} + \sum_{i}^{1} \gamma_i z_{ij} \qquad (6\text{-}2)$$

where y_{ij} is a factor determining the demands of the jth household and z_{ij} is a factor determining the supply of housing in the city in which the jth household is located. (The specific variables used will be discussed below, where the supply and demand processes are treated.)

Assuming that the values of the characteristics are successfully observed, what are the prices associated with individual observations for the analysis of supply and demand? The usual hedonic price approach would appear to summarize all prices, leaving us the same price for every unit in our set of observations. This difficulty is overcome when it is recognized that the coefficients of characteristics in our system are not prices, as they would be in the usual hedonic price approach, but merely weightings that explain a part of the variability in the observations of housing expenditures. In particular, the products of the hedonic price coefficients times their respective characteristics explain that part of the variability in the observations which is due to variations in the quantity of housing services received by each household. In evaluating prices for housing services, we wish to include the variation due to supply and demand and exclude variation due, for example, to differences in number of rooms, soundness of the building, etc. We can do this by dividing rent by the product of the weighting from Equation (6-2) multiplied by the characteristics present in an individual dwelling unit. Rothenberg (1974) does so, using actual rents, and calls the denominator "hedonic value." Then the quotient, which he expresses as the ratio of market value to hedonic value, is conveniently interpreted as the price per unit of hedonic value or, simply, the price per unit of housing service.

It is useful at this point to relate our formulation to current work by others on hedonic prices. In particular, we wish to show how the cross-cities setting that we must use is inconsistent with the usual hedonic price approach. However, the inapplicability of that approach is of no importance to our efforts; our objective is not to explore the different supply and demand environments for attributes of dwellings but simply to observe the supply and demand for housing services in general.

We have noted that the coefficients of characteristics are not prices. This qualification is not the same as the statement by Rosen that hedonic prices are not literally prices, since there exist no opportunities to trade characteristics at constant prices (Rosen 1974). In his setting, while the characteristics coefficients are not prices, the hedonic price equations are argued to contain the information that consumers and producers respond to. In this study no such argument can be made. First, no set of characteristics prices prevail for all cities. Second, the estimation process that we use precludes the observation of marginal price relationships, although they might exist within housing markets.[14]

Looking at residences in separate markets, we find that differences in market supply and demand variables are a major source of variation in expenditures for housing. To delete these variables from the first step of the estimation would bias the characteristics coefficients, in case characteristics were correlated with any of these other variables. However, by including the market supply and demand conditions in the equation, we remove the effect of these factors on those coefficients. Thus, the coefficients lose all similarity to prices. This is desirable, since we are interested only in the relative valuation generally placed on the characteristics by consumers.

We can demonstrate the constrasts of the two approaches with an example. Let us say that a locality has, over time, depleted nearby supplies of lumber. Consequently, increasing amounts are imported, resulting in price increáses. In the normal setting, this change would require an increase in the price or evaluation of structural attributes such as size, number of rooms, etc. In our setting, we would want the weightings of these characteristics to be unchanged as a result of the changing supplies of building materials. We want only to be able to determine "how much house" is present in the first step of the hedonic value computation. Later, we will use this information to conclude that indeed "this much house" is more expensive in that city, now that lumber is more costly, since we will observe a high ratio of price to hedonic value for dwellings there.

The underlying motivation of the two different approaches explains the difference in methods. Rosen seeks to disaggregate total payment by observing characteristics. We seek an aggregate measure of value, but we can observe only the disaggregate values of the characteristics, so we aggregate over these.

THE ALLOCATION PROCESS—SUPPLY AND DEMAND

In the above, we discussed two of the problems that are usually identified as sources of difficulty in dealing with housing: the problem of measurement and the durability of the housing stock. A further consideration is market structure.

Though we may speak in terms of homogeneous "value units," the consumer in fact is choosing among a set of heterogeneous commodities. That is, each particular dwelling unit has a unique set of attributes, especially with regard to its location. In fact, this has led to the observation that each landlord is a monopolist for the particular dwelling unit owned by him. In that case, no supply function relating housing service to prices will exist. Yet, the housing market is not monopolistic in the usual sense of the term; many producers provide commodities that are close substitutes for one another. It can be argued that under such circumstances the landlord will tend to accept the highest bid for his dwelling unit and will provide a package of housing attributes intended to maximize his profits. Given these considerations, we can diagram the quantity choice problem as presented in Figure 6-1.

The diagram is similar to that used in determining optimum

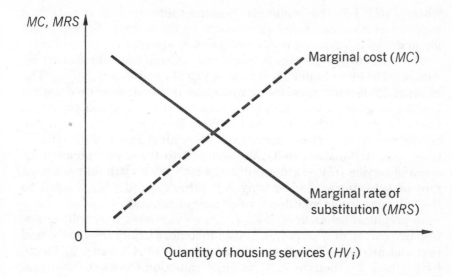

Figure 6-1.

output for a perfectly discriminating monopolist or for determining the net benefit maximizing output for a public agency. In short, the landlord will provide additional services so long as the tenant's marginal evaluation is greater than the marginal cost of the services. In what follows, we provide a more detailed explanation of the marginal cost and marginal evaluation functions. It is important to note that these are not conventional supply and demand functions, although they do reflect supply and demand processes. Furthermore, they can be used in much the same way as conventional supply and demand relationships to evaluate the market impact of housing laws.

The Housing Consumption Process

The consumption process of the household in this framework is somewhat different from that of traditional approaches. As discussed earlier, market prices and variable quantities of a housing commodity are not available to the household; thus, maximization of utility by the household with a linear budget constraint, given market prices and a level of income, is not possible.

Given the above derivation of a value measure and constraints on market information, the household consumption problem can be formulated as follows:

$$\max U(HV_i, X) \text{ subject to } Y = P_x X + [P(HV_i)] \qquad (6\text{-}3)$$

where $P(HV_i)$ is the nonlinear housing value or total bid; HV_i, a measure of housing; X, all other goods in the market; Y, household income; and P_x, price of nonhousing commodities.

The solution to the above problems follows that shown first by Alonso (1964) and later by Wheaton (1974) and Rosen (1974). The bid-rent framework involves a production decision, which we assume here to be given, and a consumption decision process. This process is tractable given the information problem discussed above, and it can be shown to have close theoretical ties with standard utility analysis.[15] Given Equation (6-3), the solution to the choice quantity of housing service (HV_i) is that point at which the household's marginal rate of substitution for housing and other expenditures is equal to the bid value for an additional value unit of housing.

In graphical terms, if $\Theta(HV_i; Y, u^*, \gamma)$ expresses the "willingness-to-pay" curves of a household, given income, a utility level (u^*), and personal attributes (γ), the optimal choice is at A (shown in Figure 6-2), where the household's marginal valuation equals the marginal cost of housing service (HV_i).

It should be noted that the bid-value curves hold income, the

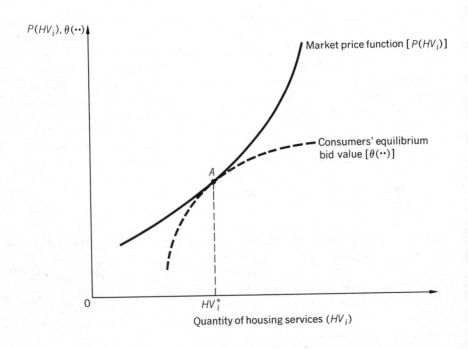

Figure 6-2. Solution for Consumer.

chosen level of houshold utility, and personal attributes constant.[16] Assumptions for achieving a solution include a high degree of independence in the bid-value process and convexity and regularity of $P(HV_i)$. (These assumptions are not modified in this discussion.)

An interesting variable in the willingness-to-pay function, Θ, is the set of personal attributes, γ. By varying γ, different Θ curves can be found for well-defined groups of individual households. By segmenting households in this way, the assumption can be eliminated that all households have utility functions of the same form. An assumption about personal attributes is stated later in this section.[17]

To interpret the bid-rent approach, the following factors are relevant. Households are assumed to be making a kind of offer on every rental housing unit that leaves them equally well off no matter which offer is accepted. This is consistent with the choice of a u^* in the Θ function. Equilibrium is obtained when the values are such that every unit is occupied by the highest bidder. If an individual household is the high bidder on more than one unit, it submits bids which are lower for all units, again such that it is indifferent as to which of the bids are accepted, thus obtaining a higher level of utility than it obtained with the previous bids. The bidder who is not high on any unit can reevaluate its needs and submit a set of higher bids, that is, it can bid along a lower indifference curve, each bid representing for it a choice between housing and nonhousing consumption.

Within the above setting, we regard the household's decision-making process as moving along an indifference curve as it exchanges housing services for nonhousing consumption. Doing so, the household pays according to its marginal rate of substitution of housing for other expenditures for each successive unit of housing service.

We assume that individuals with similar personal attributes can be identified and that landlords are aware of these attributes and react to them. (This view is not unrealistic, since landlords commonly do have some expectations about the income, family size, and ages of potential renters and tend to tailor their housing units to this clientele.)

As described, an optimal bid-rent function for an individual household will depend on the income and personal attributes of the household and the level of bids of other households in the locality. The bids of other households can be assumed to vary across cities primarily by differences in income, thus giving a nonuniform set of $P(HV_i)$ values. These values most likely reflect different marginal cost curves, and therefore, no clear tracing of a housing supply curve may result. This interaction could, however, be explained by the simultaneous decision processes of suppliers and consumers.

As described above, the observed value measure derived from the ratio of rental value to hedonic value is an average evaluation, *not* a marginal one. This does not, however, create an empirical problem, but does require a different interpretation of regression coefficients. Clearly, we can solve for a marginal evaluation, given a linear relationship between average evaluation and quantity. The empirical relationship to be estimated then becomes:

$$\frac{R_j}{HV_j} = f(HV_j, \text{household income, average income of other house-}$$

holds in the SMSA, laws applying to the SMSA) (6-4)

where R_j is the rent of the jth household and HV_j is the hedonic value of the dwelling occupied by the jth household.

Supply

Having introduced the bid-rent process in the previous section, we can demonstrate an analogous supply process quite briefly. Here, the supplier is viewed as confronting a fixed price function $P(HV_i)$, an assumption equivalent to the assumption that competitive firms confront constant prices. Obviously, the assumption cannot be literally true in either case, but probably reflects accurately the supplier's perception that individually he has little influence on market prices.

We can express the decision of the supplier as follows:

$$\max \pi = P(HV_i) - C(HV_i, P_i, D(M), L, B) \qquad (6\text{-}5)$$

where M is maintenance, $D(M)$ relates maintenance to depreciation, P_i is a vector of input prices, L is legal costs, and B is a vector of other characteristics of the producer.

In the supply setting, the bid curves represent equal willingness to supply. Thus, for each supplier, we can define the function that solves Equation (6-5) for any specified π for values of the exogenous variables appropriate to the supplier. We define $P = \phi (HV_i; \pi, T, P_i, D(M), L, B)$ as representing points of equal profit for the landlord. As before, equilibrium is attained where the bid function is tangent to the $P(HV_i)$ function, since higher ϕ ( ) are obtained for higher values of π while holding all other variables constant. The result is shown graphically in Figure 6-3. Since ϕ ($\cdot$) represents points of constant profit, any particular ϕ ($\cdot$) is simply the total cost function plus some constant. Therefore, where equilibrium is obtained, marginal cost must equal the marginal price of HV_i.

As in the usual competitive model, high profits are assumed to attract new entrants into the submarket, i.e., additional offerers are created at a point such as B along the $P(HV_i)$ curve. With this, consumers will resubmit bids so as to be high bidders on only one unit. This shifts $P(HV_i)$ downward, and producers will then obtain an equilibrium on lower isoprofit contours.

For an individual producer, the equilibrium relations can be shown more easily by differentiating $P(HV_i)$ and $C(HV_i)$ and using the marginal relationships as in Figure 6-4. $C'(HV_i)$ is the marginal cost of current housing services or marginal current expenditures net of their effects on future revenues and legal costs. $E(HV_i)$ is the total expenditure for providing current housing service H. Thus,

$$C'(HV_i) = E'(HV_i) - D'(M) - L'(HV_i) \qquad (6\text{-}6)$$

where, $L'(HV_i)$ relates legal costs to the level of services provided and

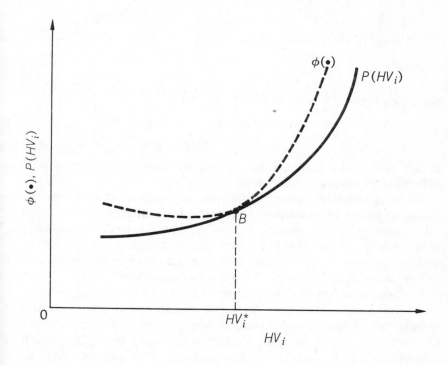

Note: For definition of variables, see Figure 6-2 and text.

Figure 6-3. Graphical Solution for Producer.

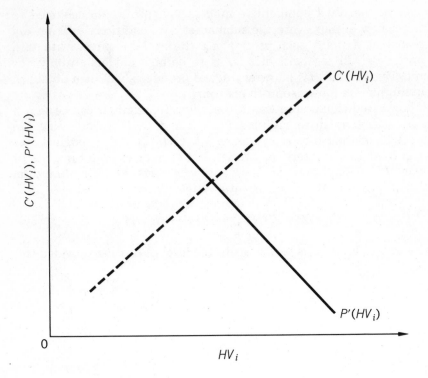

Note: For definition of variables, see Figure 6-2 and text.

Figure 6-4.

$D'(M)$ relates the future value of the structure to current capital expenditures on the dwelling unit.

$D'(M)$ is negative; hence $-D'(M)$ can be interpreted as the savings in depreciation attributable to a unit of maintenance input. The interpretation of the condition then is that the landlord increases maintenance up to the point where the marginal evaluation of quality derived from a unit of maintenance plus the savings in depreciation equal the price of the maintenance input.

The legal cost function would presumably be a decreasing function of maintenance. However, the relationship cannot be observed because we lack essential information on, for example, the number of cases filed and their cost. Furthermore, there are difficulties in associating the probabilities of case filing with various levels of maintenance. We estimate the differential impact of the legal environment by distinguishing between populations according to the laws implemented in each case. In this sense, the legal cost function provides the rationale for distinguishing between the two populations, those that have and those that do not have the particular law, and predicts the effect of laws on the supply of housing services. The legal cost function includes all costs imposed by the legal system, including any penalties that might result from noncompliance. Thus, the legal cost function reflects the incentives for provision of a higher level of service than the law might require.

Our expectation is that landlords supply less housing service at any particular price, if circumstances change so as to increase their costs or to make the supplying of housing a less desirable activity than it had been. Yet, the effect of the legal cost function itself acts to increase incentives to provide services. However, the law does affect the landlord's expectation that his property will continue to be used as a dwelling by altering its expected future profitability, and therefore the law affects the expected return to the landlord from any current maintenance expenditures.

In our investigation, we have so far been attempting to identify variables that would provide information regarding the comparative productivity of maintenance expenditure among cities. Our approach has been to identify the factors that probably have an impact on landlord's future returns from current maintenance expenditures. One factor, as discussed above, is the status of housing laws. A second important factor is the value of land: where land values in a city are high, one would expect that the remaining life of low-quality dwellings will be short, since it is likely that with further deterioration the structure will become more profitable in other uses. A third variable is the relative prices of dwellings in different quality categories. This should indicate the reduction in the landlord's revenues that would occur if the quality of the unit is allowed to decline. A final variable, the number of vacancies in the lower-quality categories per low-income renting household, also should indicate the opportunities confronting a landlord and, therefore, his willingness to allow units to filter down.

IMPLEMENTATION

The conceptual framework that has been presented allows us to formulate empirical supply and demand relationships. In this section, we provide a description of the data and basic structural relations of the model and some results.

Data and Structural Considerations
Most of our housing data, i.e., housing characteristics and house-

hold descriptions, were taken from the University of Michigan Panel Study of Income Dynamics (University of Michigan 1972). A primary advantage of these data over Census data is that the former provide current housing information that can be combined with current legal information. The University of Michigan sample is large enough to permit separation of low-income households from other types of households in the rental housing market. The variables are defined and their sources are given in Table 6-2.[18]

Several of the variables found in that table are based on observations for an SMSA. If, for example, several separate households are

Table 6-2

Table 6-2. Description and Source of Variables

Name of Variable	Description	Source
RTIL2	Sum of annual household rent plus utilities paid in 1972	1972 Michigan survey
ROOM2	Number of rooms in the dwelling	—Do.—
DIST2	Distance of housing structure to the center of the SMSA	—Do.—
STRU2	Structural type	—Do.—
AVGI	Average household income for a five-year period, 1968-1972	1968-72 Michigan survey
LOT	Average lot value of equivalent sites in SMSAs	FHA (1973)
DEPR	Ratio: tenth percentile rental unit price to median rental unit price	Census (1970)
RENTY	Median SMSA household income for renters	Census (1970)
SMSAY	Total per capita income for the SMSA	—Do.—
CONCOST	Costs of construction for brick-concrete apartments across cities	1972 Boeckh index
HEAT	Average annual heating cost per room for rental units in an SMSA	Apartment building income, expense analysis (IREM 1972)
REDUCT	Identifies states with repair and deduct housing laws	Hirsch et al. (1975)
RWHOLD	Identifies states with both retaliatory eviction and withholding laws	—Do.—
RECEIVE	Identifies states with receivership laws	—Do.—
VACPER	Number of vacancies below median divided by number of low-income renters	Census (1970)
PTAX	Property tax per household, average for the SMSA	Census (1970)
RPOP	Number of low-income tenants in the SMSA	Census (1970)

located in a particular SMSA, the data recorded for each observation will be equivalent. In a situation where differences in household rents in different SMSAs are observed, this is not important. However, when rental payments by households in one defined SMSA are being explained by such a measure, the explanatory power of the system will be small. Since both types of observation are included in the model's data base, the effects of this insensitivity may be important.

The use of dummy variables related to the law and housing variables is necessitated by the lack of data on the status, nature, and effects of laws. In particular, data on enforcement or direct legal costs and on knowledge of laws are unavailable. Dummy variables are therefore used to distinguish states and housing locations with habitability laws from those without such laws. These distinctions can also be used to indicate places where legal costs are imposed versus places where they are not, if we assume that knowledge and enforcement exist and realize that magnitudes of such costs are not distinguished.

The housing model described in the theoretical section has several components. The first is an estimation of a household rent equation. The dependent variable, rental payments (R), is regressed on four classes of variable:[19] housing characteristics (HC), demand factors (DF), market supply factors (SF), and landlord-tenant laws (L), i.e.,

$$R = f(HC, DF, SF, L) \tag{6-7}$$

This is a reduced form equation that has a direct relationship to other structural equations, i.e., to household consumption and landlord supply. Since differences between housing payments among and within cities are included in the data base, the purpose of the DF and SF variables is to take account of those market variables so that the estimated value of defined housing characteristics can be aggregated regardless of location.

A second purpose for estimating Equation (6-7) is to identify the effects of landlord-tenant laws on rental payments and to test the significance of the estimated coefficients of the law variables. Hypotheses related to both the impact and significance of such laws can be tested in terms of sign and values.

It is interesting to note that if

$$\hat{R} = \sum_{i=1}^{n} \alpha_i x_i \tag{6-8}$$

aggregate value of defined housing characteristics, where $\hat{R}$ is a quantity proxy for housing, and $R/\hat{R}$ is a price measure, there are two well-defined structural equations:[20]

$$\text{Consumption:} \quad R/\hat{R} = g(\hat{R}, HDF, L) \quad (6\text{-}9)$$

$$\text{Supply:} \quad \hat{R} = h(R/\hat{R}, HSF, L) \quad (6\text{-}10)$$

where HDF = housing demand factors and HSF = housing supply factors. These variables represent subsets of the larger vectors, DF and SF, in Equation (6-7). A nonsignificant relationship between rent and law variables may not reflect similar insignificance at the structural equation level. To guarantee a similar result on both levels of estimation a perfectly identified or specified system must exist—an unlikely condition.

The preceding statement is intuitively reasonable because the dependent variable is rental payments $[(R/\hat{R}) \cdot \hat{R}]$ in the rental payments equation, whereas the dependent variables are $R/\hat{R}$ and $\hat{R}$ in the structural equations.

Suppose rental payments for a defined housing quantity are $100 in a location without a tenant-landlord law and $104 in a location with a law. In a regression, there would be little significance to the law, but suppose that demanders were unaffected by the law (i.e., no demand curve shifts occur), but suppliers had increased marginal costs (reflected in a supply curve shift). In graphical terms, with inelastic demand, a shift in the supply curve with no shift in demand could reflect a significant effect of the law on suppliers and little effect on rental payments (see Figure 6-5).[20]

Two other factors that seem important in determining the significance of the hypothesized relationship between laws and rent are the definition of the law variable(s) and the subpopulation of households being investigated. For instance, if all housing laws were aggregated and a single law variable defined, different information would result than if various types of housing laws were defined and investigated.[21] Comparison between subpopulations, e.g., aged and young households, could lead to different results depending on mobility and other demand factors of the household. This may mean that the household's demand relationship for some groupings accounts for a dominant part of the rental payment-law relationship.

Results of the Rent Expenditure Equation
On the basis of the current understanding of the low-cost rental market, the following relationships in the reduced form rent equation are expected:

The *number of rooms* within a dwelling is expected to be positively correlated with annual rent (the larger the dwelling, the higher the expected rent).

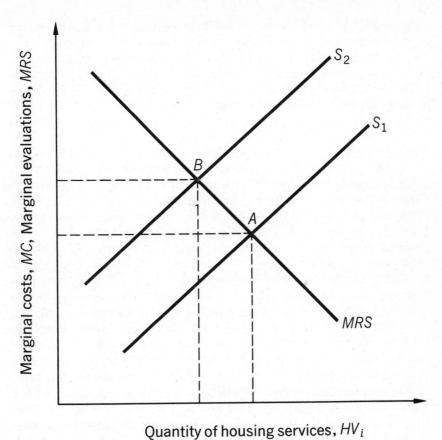

Figure 6-5.

The household's *distance* to the center of the SMSA is expected to have a negative relationship with rent (the further from the center the household, the lower the rent).[22]

Type of structure, a dummy variable with zero indicating less desirable and 1 more desirable dwelling types, is expected to have a positive relationship with rent.[23]

Vacancies reflect incentives for providing services as well as the total demand for dwellings. No particular hypothesis for the sign of this variable can be made.

Property taxes reflect the value of public expenditures, and thus should be positively related to rents.

Average household income for 1968-1972 is expected to have a positive relationship with rent.[24]

Median SMSA renter income is used to indicate the relative number of low-income tenants. No particular hypothesis is available.[2 5]

Lot value, intended to reflect the value of property in alternative uses, is expected to have a positive correlation with rent. High values for land in other uses would indicate small incentives to maintain the structure in its present form.

Depreciation, used to index the rate of decline in landlord revenue, is expected to be positively related to rent. When this ratio is relatively high, landlords will tend to allow their building(s) to depreciate, and rents for a given quality level will be higher.

Renting population reflects the scale of the housing service industry as a whole. No particular sign is predicted.

Construction costs designed to reflect differences in rents across cities, are expected to be positively related to rent.[2 6]

Average annual *heating cost* per dwelling in an SMSA is expected to be positively related to rent.

Finally, three *law* variables, indicating the status of habitability laws in an SMSA in early 1972, are introduced. They are repair and deduct, a combination of withholding and retaliatory eviction, and receivership. If enforced, they are likely to impose costs on landlords and, therefore, are expected to be positively correlated with rent.[2 7] Rather than introducing retaliatory eviction as a separate law variable, it has been combined with withholding laws. The withholding-retaliatory eviction variable is a dummy, with 1 indicating that both laws exist and zero indicating otherwise. Our formulation of the law variables is based on the presumption that today repair and deduct remedies are not very costly to landlords and, therefore, furnish little incentive to evict tenants. And, since unlike complaints under receivership laws, withholding laws tend to be tenant-initiated, the tenant often requires protection from retaliatory eviction.

An ordinary least squares regression was estimated, relating rent (*RTIL2*) to subsets of independent variables from Table 6-2 for 154 observations in fifty SMSAs. All variables which were not dummies or indiscrete intervals were put into logarithmic form. The results are given in Table 6-3.

All variables except LCONCOST (log of *CONCOST*) have the expected signs. The sign of *CONCOST* may indicate that fewer demolitions are carried out in places where construction costs are high. Of the housing characteristics in our equation, number of rooms per dwelling (*LROOM2*), structural type (*LSTRU2*), and average household income during 1968-1972 (*LAVGI*) were all

Table 6-3.   Rent Equation (dependent variable[a] is $LRTIL2$ = log of rent plus utilities; N = 154; figures in parentheses are t ratios; an asterisk denotes significance at the 95 percent level)

Independent Variables[a]	Coefficient	Independent Variables[a]	Coefficient
ROOM2	0.0836 (5.6520)*	REDUCT	−0.0611 (0.6599)*
DIST2	−0.0138 (0.3773)	RECEIVE	0.1671 (2.2571)*
STRU2	0.1502 (3.0004)*	RWHOLD	−0.0203 (0.1923)
LAVGI	0.3920 (7.4095)*	LPTAX	0.2282 (1.5757)
LRENTY	−0.0799 (0.2133)	LHEAT	0.1416 (1.2374)
LCONCOST	−0.8035 (1.7348)*	LVACPER	−0.0682 (1.2368)
LLOT	0.3032 (2.5345)*	LRPOP	−0.0562 (1.0442)
LDEPR	0.1899 (0.6142)		
Constant	5.2068		
R^2	0.61		
F statistic for equation	14.624		

[a]For identification of variables, see Table 6-2. The prefix L denotes log form.

significant at the 99 percent level. Lot value ($LLOT$) was also significant at the 95 percent level.

Turning next to the main concern of this study, we find that of the habitability laws, only receivership ($RECEIVE$) is statistically significant. The others have negative signs, but their values are quite small and not significantly different from zero. In the presentation of the habitability laws it was pointed out that receivership laws stop the flow of rental income to the landlord completely and take away control over his building. Further, because they are initiated by government, they are backed by its rather large resources. They are, therefore, the most costly to landlords.

Altogether, the equation taken as a whole is statistically significant (the F value is 14.06). It has, moreover, a relatively good explanatory value, accounting for about 61 percent of the variation in rents paid in 1972 by indigents in our sample. Hence, in 1972, indigents paid significantly higher rents in a statistical sense in states that had receivership laws than in those that did not. When the effects of all independent variables in the equation other than receivership are held constant, indigent tenants are found to have paid approximately $192 more in annual rent in 1972 in the presence of receivership than in its absence (average 1972 annual rent in our sample was $1,082).[28]

In the supply and demand estimation, heating cost and property taxes were included in the computation of $\hat{R}$. For the estimation we define two new variables:

$$RHAT = .0836\ ROOM - .0138\ DIST + .150\ STRU \qquad (6\text{-}11)$$

$$+ .228\ LPTAX + .142\ LHEAT$$

$$AVEEVAL = RTIL/RHAT \qquad (6\text{-}12)$$

In the supply equation, all variables except $LCONCOST$ and repair and deduct laws have the expected signs (see Table 6-4). $LHEAT$ is included in the supply equation since it represents a constraint on the landlord's behavior regarding the amount of housing service he may provide. Hence, its positive sign would be expected. The depreciation coefficient indicates that as the severity of the consequences of undermaintenance diminish, so does the willingness to provide any particular level of service. High lot values predict diminished willingness to provide service, as do high vacancy rates for the low-income categories. The income for the SMSA represents a variety of factors, but can be interpreted much like $LRENTY$: higher values for income would tend to indicate that relatively more higher-quality units are available to filter down. The coefficients of the law variables indicate a reduced willingness to supply at any given price in the presence of receivership and withholding. Repair and deduct has an incorrect sign, but its coefficient is quite small.

In the demand equation, all variables have the expected signs (Table 6-4). Average evaluations tend to rise with income, and fall where property taxes or heating costs are high. The price-quantity relationship is negative, but actually horizontal for all practical purposes. The law variable coefficients do indicate that tenants place some positive evaluation on the laws, as each of these are positive.

In evaluating the costs and benefits of habitability laws, we look at the vertical shifts of the supply and demand equations that include those laws. We note that, given the formulation of the supply equation, the vertical shift resulting from the law is the horizontal

Table 6-4. Supply and Demand Equations (sample size = 154; figures in parentheses are t ratios; an asterisk denotes significance at the 95 percent level)

Supply Equation; Dependent Variable[a] = LRHAT		Demand Equation; Dependent Variable[a] = LAVEEVAL	
Independent Variables[b]	Coefficient	Independent Variables[b]	Coefficient
LAVEEVAL	0.2613 (3.7539)*	LRHAT	−0.0414 (0.0787)
LHEAT	0.0472 (0.7364)	LAVGI	0.3919 (5.1813)*
LCONCOST	0.0781 (0.3215)	REDUCT	0.1045 (1.4761)
LDEPR	−0.2845 (1.6808)*	RWHOLD	0.1287 (1.8643)*
RWHOLD	−0.0211 (0.3739)	RECEIVE	0.1239 (2.1383)*
RECEIVE	−0.0497 (1.2627)	LHEAT	−0.1678 (1.8866)*
REDUCT	0.0072 (0.1428)	LPTAX	−0.0265 (0.1849)
LLOT	−0.1947 (2.9435)*		
LSMSAY	0.9025 (4.9726)*		
LVACPER	−0.0456 (1.6814)*		
F statistic for equation	7.1949	F statistic for equation	13.1363

[a]LRHAT is defined by Equation (6-11); LAVEEVAL, by Equation (6-12) (the prefix L denotes log form of the variable).

[b]The independent variables are defined in Table 6-1; L denotes log form.

shift times the negative reciprocal of the price coefficient. Further, we note the assumption that the shifts are parallel, an assumption that would likely be incorrect were it not for the limitation of our sample to low-income households.

For the one variable that has a significant coefficient in the rent equation, receivership (*RECEIVE*), the shift in the supply equation is larger than the shift in the demand equation. The shift in the former is about 19 percent, while in the latter it is about 12 percent. Hence, for receivership, it would appear that the costs outweigh the benefits;

however, it is important to note that these differences are not significant.[30]

It is interesting to note that receivership is the only law that seems to raise rents and has a substantial effect on the supply function. The explanation may be in the basic distinction between receivership and the other habitability laws. Receivership is undertaken by state and local governments; the others are all tenant initiated. Repairs made under receivership may be quite extensive and may be undertaken without consideration of profitability or the tenant's desires, thus imposing large costs on landlords. Repairs under the other habitability laws are tenant initiated and, therefore, would not be undertaken against the interests of the tenant. Tenant-initiated habitability laws may, therefore, represent a more effective compromise for attaining an efficient relationship between landlord and tenant.

CONCLUSIONS

We have attempted to develop a housing market model that permits an evaluation of legal sanctions designed to assure indigent tenants habitable dwellings. Of the major habitability laws, the most powerful one (providing for receivership) was found to be associated with a statistically significant increase in rental expenditures of indigent tenants. Our data further indicate that costs may outweigh the benefits imposed on such tenants. Thus, merely extending tenants' legal rights of action, and thereby shifting some of the power away from landlords, may not in fact enhance the tenants' welfare. The cost of providing habitable housing must be borne by someone. There is evidence that the cost imposed by receivership laws appears to be largely borne by tenants without their receiving fully compensating benefits.

One striking reason why a receivership law may hurt rather than help indigent tenants is related to the failure of habitability laws to provide enhanced financial means to pay for improved dwellings. Thus, to attain their objective of aiding indigent tenants, income transfers—perhaps in the form of rent subsidies—should supplement common and state statutory laws that tilt landlord-tenant relations in favor of the latter.

NOTES TO CHAPTER SIX

1. *Census of Housing*, 1970 Metropolitan Housing Characteristics, Final Report HC (2)-1.
2. Housing Act of 1949 § 2, 63 Stat. 413, as amended, 42 U.S. Code § 1441 (Supp. V, 1970).

3. There are some references in Martin (1971).

4. A lease at common law was considered to be the purchase of an interest in property, subject to the doctrine of caveat emptor. Since the lease agreement was considered a conveyance of property for a term, the tenant was deemed to have assumed the obligations and liabilities of ownership.

5. Key cases are *Pines* v. *Perssion*, 14 Wis. 2d. 590, 11 N.W. 2d 404, (1961); *Lemle* v. *Breeden*, 51 Haw. 426, 462 P. 2d 470 (1969); and *Javins* v. *First National Realty Corp.*, 138 U.S. App. D.C. 369, 423 F. 2d 1071, cert. denied, 400 U.S. 925, 91 S. Ct. 186, 27 L. Ed. 2d 185 (1970).

6. The landlord must be notified after the fact, and only after he has failed to take action within an appropriate time period can the tenant contract for repair. In most states, the statute permits tenants to deduct no more than one month's rent to finance repairs.

7. Repair and deduct laws can be applied relatively easily by tenants, since the laws can be invoked without a prior judicial determination. Should a judicial proceeding later determine that the tenant was not justified in taking action, he would merely be liable for the outstanding balance of the rent, i.e., the deducted repair bill.

8. As long as the violations continue, the welfare recipient is given a statutory defense to any action or summary proceeding for nonpayment of rent.

9. In utilizing a rent abatement scheme and refusing to pay rent, a tenant takes the risk that a court may later determine that his actions were unwarranted because, for example, housing code violations were not substantial enough. Should that turn out to be the case, the tenant may have to pay the rent due plus moving expenses, attorney fees, court costs, and even statutory penalties.

10. At the forefront of states legalizing rent strikes are New Jersey and New York.

11. Although initially designed to make habitability laws work by protecting tenants who complain about housing code violations, retaliatory eviction statutes can also be looked upon as devices to assure tenants of continued tenancy.

12. The interpretation of habitability laws made here is that they are different from, though not unrelated to, housing codes. Our emphasis here has been on the transfer of risk and responsibility for maintenance from the tenant to the landlord. Housing codes, however, disallow rental of low-quality units. While habitability laws may refer to housing codes as a standard of reasonableness, the housing codes typically represent very high standards, and therefore are enforced neither as a consequence of habitability laws nor by other means. Today many housing codes require, for example, that hot water be available at all taps, usually at 120 degrees Fahrenheit. Many require that every dwelling unit contain a lavatory, bath/shower, and kitchen sink. Virtually no housing code allows sharing of kitchens, and very few allow sharing of bathroom facilities between two units. Most housing codes require heating facilities capable of maintaining a temperature of 70 degrees Fahrenheit, though some do not require this between 10:00 P.M. and 6:00 A.M. The Uniform Housing Code (prepared by the International Conference of Building Officials), for example, requires that every dwelling unit have at least one room with no less than 150 square feet of floor area. Other habitable rooms except kitchens must have an area of not less

than 70 square feet; and when more than two persons occupy a room used for sleeping purposes, the required floor area must be increased at a rate of 50 square feet for each occupant in excess of two. It stipulates that habitable rooms, storage rooms, and laundry rooms shall have a ceiling height of not less than seven feet measured to the lowest projection from the ceiling. Furthermore, codes of many cities have stringent light and ventilation provisions. For example, according to the Uniform Housing Code, all guest rooms, dormitories, and habitable rooms within a dwelling unit must be provided with natural light by means of windows or skylights with an area of not less than one-tenth of the floor area of such rooms, with a minimum of ten square feet.

Many of the housing standards are perhaps so high because vested interests, e.g., the building industry, have often participated in their writing. Indigent tenants, therefore, often can find that their costs for dwellings that meet such inflated standards are very high, and in extreme cases they place a rather low value on these improvements. The courts have been cognizant of the possibility of these standards being higher than necessary. For example, in *Early Estates, Inc.* v. *Housing Board of Review*, 174 A. 2d 117 (1961), the court struck down a portion of an ordinance requiring hot water facilities as being beyond a city council's power to require facilities needed to make dwellings "fit for human habitation."

13. Ackerman (1971, p. 1103) states:

> Even if the investor originally purchased a building for $100,000 and is currently earning only one percent or $1000 per year in profit before code enforcement, the only financially relevant question for him is the value that the market places on the right to receive $1000. If a purchaser is willing to buy the future income stream for $5000, abandonment is irrational unless the anticipated stream of future code costs exceeds this amount after an appropriate discount rate is applied.

It should be pointed out that in the later parts of his article, Ackerman modifies his assumptions to allow code enforcement costs to force some dwellings to be either abandoned or converted to commercial establishments.

14. The differences in estimation procedures between the hedonic price approach and ours illustrate the contrasts between them. Rosen suggests that hedonic prices be dealt with by a two-stage estimation process. First, a simple regression of characteristics on observed prices is carried out using the best-fitting functional form. Next, the resulting characteristics equation is used to determine a marginal price of each characteristic in each of the observed commodities. Finally, these marginal price observations are used in the structural equations for the supply and demand for characteristics. All of this makes good sense in the usual setting, since the marginal price functions do determine consumers' and producers' behavior with respect to characteristics.

15. Market prices, which are constants to households, and bid rents or bid values are equal at optimal utility-maximizing levels of the household. Bid-value curves can be shown to be downward sloping, as are demand curves. Bid values are also affected by the level of income and other factors in the market. Finally, bid-value curves can be derived from indirect utility functions.

16. If there was only one set of P for all cities and all individual households had differing characteristics, the envelope process, which results from optimum solutions (such as A) by each household, would exactly trace out the supply (marginal cost curve) of HV_i values.

17. Market segmentation is one direct consequence of the bid-value approach. This is rationalized later in this paper where market segmentation is by suppliers and not by geographical subareas, which are often not segmented.

18. Many data sources, such as the Bureau of Labor Statistics and the Federal Housing Administration, record information on a "standard" or "equivalent" housing structure or household. These are often inconsistent and rarely reflect an emphasis on poor households. However, one disadvantage of the University of Michigan data is that their representativity could not be effectively calculated. Even if the 5,000 households are representative of the population in general, there are no guarantees that subpopulations in any one period are representative. In addition, several periods are examined and employed (for example, in the determination of household income). The use of time series data also could be nonrepresentative, but there is no evidence to indicate this.

Where appropriate, data from different sources were examined. In our selection process, we sought to maximize the inclusion of theoretically relevant variables without creating serious empirical problems. Of course, no definitive statement on including data from different sources can be made, since comparisons of biases resulting from omission of variables from the model and from use of proxy rather than consistent data are not possible.

19. The actual value used for rent was the total contract rent plus payment for utilities. The cost of utilities was included so that values would be comparable whether utilities were included in the contract rent or paid separately.

20. This argument would apply to any factor that had a shift in supply only.

21. As identified in Table 6-2, specification of different laws is possible. Signs of estimated coefficients and their significance depend on knowledge and enforcement which could reverse expected signs if such factors do not exist. Interpretation could also differ depending on whether the landlord or tenant initiates the proceedings.

22. Distance is an interval variable for distance from the center of the SMSA.

23. More desirable structural types are assumed to be the larger apartment buildings, where maintenance of low-cost units tends to be better than in duplexes and single-family dwellings.

24. Average household income rather than a current income measure was used because current housing expenditures are based on past decision making by the household in terms of previous as well as current income. It is also preferable to obtain some measure of *permanent* income in order to assess a relationship with a household rental expenditure.

25. Renter income levels reflect demand pressures in the particular housing market. The more segmented the housing market, the less important the pressure of other (nonpoor) households on the housing sector examined. Higher income for other renters may predict higher rents, if markets are not segmented and others bid higher, or lower rents, if more units can filter down to supply low-income tenants.

26. The construction costs variable is needed to describe differences in rents *across* cities. Such factors as variations in the costs of labor and materials are cited in the literature as important in cross-sectional models on housing. The Boeckh index includes such factors.

27. Since we do not have enforcement data, we must assume that once a law goes into effect, it provides signals to landlords and tenants, and they react rationally to the resulting incentives.

28. Since the regression line passes through the mean values of the variables, we evaluate the impact of receivership laws at this point:

Given: $\overline{RENT}$ = \$1,082 = mean value of annual rent

$RENT'$ = mean value of annual rent when a receivership law is in effect

$RENT''$ = mean value of annual rent in the absence of a receivership law

$\overline{REC}$ = 0.2662 = mean value of receivership law

$\overline{LRENT''}$ = $\overline{LRENT}$ $-$ 0.17 $\overline{REC}$; $RENT''$ = 1,038.

Since $LRENT' - LRENT'' = 0.17$, $RENT' = 1,230$. The difference is \$192.

29. Given the coefficients in the supply equation and a ceteris paribus assumption, we would have for supply, $LRHAT = A + 0.261\ LAVEEVAL$, where A is the intercept of the supply equation. Thus, if the presence of the habitability law changes A by χ then the vertical shift is the inverse of the original supply function: $LAVEEVAL = (1/0.261\ LRHAT) - (A/0.261)$ i.e., $-\chi/0.261$. Thus, the vertical shift of the supply equation is $0.497/0.261 = 19$ percent for receivership laws.

30. Withholding and repair and deduct laws indicate a slightly larger shift for demand; however, these differences are also not significant, and more important, these variables did not show significant effects on rents.

REFERENCES

Ackerman, Bruce A. 1971. "Regulating Slum Housing Markets on Behalf of the Poor: Of Housing Codes, Housing Subsidies and Income Distribution Policy." *Yale Law Review*, vol. 80, pp. 1093-1197.

_____. 1975. *Economic Foundation of Property Law*. Boston: Little, Brown.

Alonso, William. 1964. *Location and Land Use*. Cambridge, Mass.: Harvard University Press.

Boeckh. 1972. Building Costs Index Numbers (Brick/Concrete Apartments). *Boeckh Building Cost Index Numbers*. Bimonthly. Milwaukee; American Appraisal Company, Inc.

Census. 1970. U.S. Bureau of the Census. *Local Government Finances in Selected Metropolitan Areas and Large Counties*.

DeLeeuw, Frank. 1971. "The Demand for Housing: A Review of Cross-Section Evidence." *Review of Economics and Statistics*, February.

_____. 1974. "What Should U.S. Housing Policy Be?" *Journal of Finance* May.

De Leeuw, Frank, and Nkanta F. Ekanem. 1971. "The Supply of Rental Housing." *American Economic Review*, December.

FHA [Federal Housing Administration]. 1973. *FHA Homes 1972: Data for States and Selected Areas on Characteristics of FHA Operations under Section 203.*

Hirsch, Werner Z. 1974. "Reducing Law's Uncertainty and Complexity." *UCLA Law Review*, June.

Hirsch, Werner Z., Hirsch, Joel G., and Margolis, Stephen. 1975. "Regression Analysis of the Effects of Habitability Laws Upon Rent: An Empirical Observation on the Ackerman-Komesar Debate." *California Law Review*, vol. 63, pp. 1099-1143.

IREM [Institute of Real Estate Management]. 1972. *Income/Expenses Analysis: Apartments, Condominiums, and Cooperatives in 1971.* Chicago: National Association of Realtors.

King, A. Thomas. 1975. "The Demand for Housing: Integrating the Roles of Journey-to-Work, Neighborhood Quality and Prices." In *Household Production and Consumption.* Studies in Income and Wealth 40. New York: National Bureau of Economic Research.

Komesar, Neil K. 1973. "Return to Slumville: A Critique of the Ackerman Analysis of Housing Code Enforcement and the Poor." *Yale Law Review*, vol. 82, pp. 1175-1207.

Martin, Peter. 1971. *The Ill-Housed.* Mineola, N.Y.: Foundation Press.

Muth, Richard F. 1969. *Cities and Housing.* Chicago: University of Chicago Press.

New Jersey Stats. Ann., 2A: 18-53 (West Supplement, 1974).

Rosen, Sherwin. 1974. "Hedonic Prices and Implicit Markets." *Journal of Political Economy*, February.

Rothenberg, Jerome, *Housing Market Supply: A Model of Conversion and New Construction.* Paper presented at the Conference on Housing Research of the Committee on Urban Economics. St. Louis, Mo. October.

Sternlieb, George. 1966. *The Tenement Landlord.* New Brunswick, N.J.: Rutgers University Press.

University of Michigan. Survey Research Center. 1972. *University of Michigan Panel Study of Income Dynamics—1968-72.*

Wheaton, William C. 1974. *A Bid Rent Approach to Housing Demand.* Processed. Massachusetts Institute of Technology, Economics Department Working Paper 135. July.

Comments on Chapter Six

Robert Schafer

Housing codes and enforcement procedures are typical of the regulatory approach of lawyers to social problems and have received widespread attention in the legal literature. Until recently, economists have shown little interest in integrating the law and legal institutions into economic analysis. Fortunately, the subject of law and economics is a growing area of interest to both lawyers and economists. The Hirsch and Margolis study is part of this new thrust and is particularly noteworthy as one of the few economic analyses and the first empirical study of housing code enforcement. The repair and deduct, rent withholding, and receivership laws that they study are methods that the legal profession has devised to enforce housing codes.

Housing codes and their enforcement mechanisms transfer risks from the tenant to the landlord. Property law, until recently, has enforced the principle of cavaet emptor. In fact, it has gone even further, because covenants to pay rent were found to be enforceable by the landlord even if he had violated a covenant in the same lease to maintain the premises. These rules placed the risk of nonpayment of rent on the landlord and the risk of inferior maintenance (less than promised) on the tenant. If transaction costs were zero (or even very small), this allocation of rights would have had little effect on the ultimate allocation of resources because the parties could redistribute the rights (Coase 1960). However, transaction costs are not small, particularly for the tenant. Therefore, these rules could have a large impact on the operation of the housing market. Housing codes, repair and deduct laws, rent withholding schemes, rent receivership, and implied warranties of habitability create a new risk (renting substandard housing) and place this risk on the landlord. If a landlord persists in renting substandard housing, he (she) may have to give up income from the property for some period of time. Furthermore, these laws do not allow a redistribution of these risks, that is, the landlord cannot return the risk to the tenant via a covenant in the lease. Here we have two substantially different allocations of risks; yet we have very little to go by in deciding which is the best one or whether some intermediate allocation would be better.

Economists can contribute to the evaluation of a strategy of housing code enforcement by providing decision makers with guidance in their efforts to answer the following questions:

1. Will code enforcement lead to increased rents?
2. Will code enforcement put people out in the street?
3. What will happen if codes are selectively enforced in only part of the housing market?
4. What are the income distribution implications of code enforcement?
5. What are the welfare gains and losses?

There are, of course, several other administrative (including fairness) and political issues that must be studied in an evaluation of code enforcement. However, I discuss only the five itemized issues.

The teaching of economic theory is that when price falls below average variable cost, the firm will shut down or abandon the housing (Miller 1973). A simple set of cost and demand curves serves as an illustration. Following the work of Olsen (1969), we define an "unobservable theoretical entity," housing service per time period, which is assumed to be homogeneous. This facilitates the conceptual comparison of different dwelling units. Hirsch and Margolis make the same assumption. It is important to be aware of the limitations inherent in this approach; Olsen's framework ignores the durability of the stock, limitations on the extent to which existing units can be altered, indivisibility, neighborhood quality, the nonmarket provision of certain attributes of the housing bundle, and the spatial distribution of housing.

According to this approach, the number of units of housing services per dwelling unit per time period (q) increases with the quality of the dwelling unit. Let p be the price per unit of housing service per time period. Then Figure 6A-1 represents the cost curves of a firm and a tenant's (or the average tenant's) demand curve for

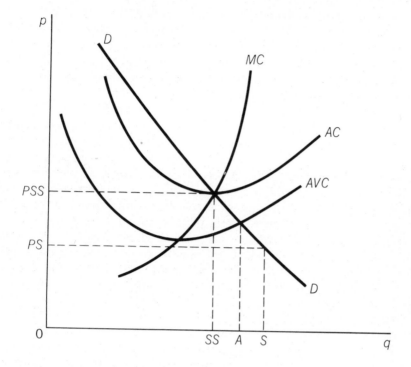

Figure 6A-1.

dwelling units of different quality. They are drawn so that the market would produce *SS* units of housing services per time period per dwelling unit for a price of *PSS* times *SS*. *S* indicates the minimum amount of housing services permitted by the housing code. If the code is enforced, the firm in Figure 6A-1 will abandon the building. If the minimum required by the code were to the left of *SS*, then this firm would not be affected. If it were between *SS* and *A*, the firm would continue to operate in the short run, but at a loss. As Komesar (1973) points out, the cost curves change with time (all costs become variable in the long run), and the firm may eventually close down. If the code requirement were to the right of *A*, the firm would abandon the housing and some people would end up on the street, assuming that the code includes occupancy criteria that are also enforced. We will return to this issue below.

The profitability of slum housing is a popular stereotype that is based more on mythology than fact. If slum landlords earned abnormal profits and if these abnormal profits were large enough, there would be no abandonment. This is readily illustrated for the case of a monopolist whose marginal revenue curve is below the demand curve. The point of production would then be a q less than *SS*. Then any code that required a minimum above this point but less than or equal to *SS* could be enforced without any effect on the firm's behavior (Miller 1973).

The empirical evidence on rates of return to slum ownership is mostly indirect. Researchers examine the concentration of ownership and if the ownership is not concentrated, draw an inference of competitive returns. Sternlieb's survey (1966) of rental properties in Newark showed that 42.8 percent of the surveyed parcels were owned by persons who owned no other rental properties; 21.2 percent, by owners of one or two other rental properties; 10.9 percent, by owners of three to six parcels; and only 15.8 percent, by owners of more than twelve other parcels. Ackerman (1971) points out a difficulty with this data; the shares are in terms of parcels and not dwelling units. This is a valid criticism, but at the same time it does not justify complete dismissal of the implication that the slum housing market is competitive.

A similar conclusion was reached by Peterson et al. (1973) in a study of four Providence neighborhoods. The neighborhoods represented three different market conditions, which were defined in terms of relative market prices and price trends. In the "blighted" neighborhood they found that 80.0 percent of the properties were owned by persons who owned no other property; and only 1.5 percent, by owners of five or more properties. As is indicated in the tabulation below (Peterson 1973, p. 56), this pattern remained virtually unchanged from one neighborhood to the next:

Neighborhood	Percent Owning Only One Property	Percent Owning 5 or More Properties
Upward transitional	78.5	3.3
Upward transitional	83.2	1.6
Downward transitional	85.8	1.0
Blighted	80.0	1.5
Total	82.2	1.6

In this study, which covered ten cities, they concluded (p. 55) that:

The lack of concentration of ownership in the low-income housing market in Providence clearly contradicts the image of a housing market dominated by several large slum lords. In other cities, the large slum lord was often talked about, and certainly individuals who owned several thousand units exist, but in each city we also found and talked to large numbers of smaller investors in blighted areas, including many black real estate operators, who specialized in buying and managing a limited number of low-income properties. While this topic deserves additional study, we conclude that there is considerable evidence that low-income areas are not the sole province of a [sic] few large investors.

Some of my own research at the National Bureau of Economic Research contradicts Ackerman's criticism that the previous studies dealt with the ownership of parcels and not dwelling units. For three neighborhoods in the city of Pittsburgh, the share of parcels held by small owners (fewer than four parcels) is just about the same as their share of dwelling units. In Table 6A-1, the data on ownership for each of these neighborhoods are summarized. Small owners owned 68.9 percent of the parcels and 63.1 percent of the dwelling units in the three neighborhoods. Large owners (more than twelve parcels) owned 11.5 percent of the parcels and 18.8 percent of the units. These data suggest that parcel ownership is a reasonable proxy for dwelling unit ownership in studying market power or concentration in the housing market.

Comparisons of rates of return on investment in real estate versus returns on other investments would throw some light on the extent of abnormal profits in housing markets. A few authors have attempted such studies with mixed success. Sternlieb (1966) found rates of return that averaged 8 to 12 percent for 32 slum properties in Newark. Sporn (1950) found a rather high average rate of return—19.8 percent—for 45 parcels in Milwaukee. These figures do not exhibit the consistently high returns that the popular belief in

Table 6A-1. Ownership of Parcels and Dwelling Units by Owner Size and Neighborhood: Pittsburgh, 1974

| Size of Owner's Holdings | Neighborhood | | | | | | Combined | |
| | A | | B | | C | | | |
	Parcels	Units	Parcels	Units	Parcels	Units	Parcels	Units
Small	76.9%	67.9%	56.3%	57.5%	68.4%	62.5%	68.9%	63.1%
Medium	11.5	15.1	37.5	32.5	15.8	10.7	19.7	18.1
Large	11.5	17.0	6.3	10.0	15.8	26.8	11.5	18.8
All Sizes	100.0	100.0	100.0	100.0	100.0	100.0	100.0	100.0
Sample size	26	53	16	40	19	56	61	149

the slumlord suggests. Sternlieb's figures for Newark are comparable to returns on corporate bonds. In addition, in none of these studies have the risk differentials been systematically assessed in relation to the rates of return.

There is no reason to believe that the minimum housing services required by the code will be related to the firm's cost curves in any specific way. At a minimum, we would expect some distribution of the firm's cost curves about the code requirement. In addition, the empirical evidence is inconsistent with very sizable abnormal profits. As a result, some firms would be expected to abandon dwelling units. Then, one of the important empirical questions is: How many dwelling units might be abandoned under code enforcement?

Abandonment could also be avoided if tenants were willing to pay the price demanded by landlords for providing code-standard housing. As was shown in Figure 6A-1, for the low-income housing market, the interaction of supply and demand for housing services per dwelling unit (q) results in a housing quality that is below code standards (SS). If a code is enforced at S, the supply price per unit of q will increase or remain the same depending on the price elasticity of the supply of q. However, the supply price of the dwelling unit (p x q) will always increase, even with a perfectly elastic supply of q, because q is being forced up. Households will have to choose between paying this increase and living on the street. This choice is dipicted in Figure 6A-2 in terms of a budget transformation line (TB) and indifference curves (I and I'). Most of the budget line is curved because the supply price per unit of q may change with the amount of q. If a housing code is enforced at a minimum amount of q equal to S, the household has two choices: pay the higher price and consume S or move to the street. The budget transformation line has been drawn with a vertical portion (line segment AB) that represents no cash expenditures for housing; this segment amounts to living on the street. If the indifference curve that passes through the point on the budget transformation line at S does not also intersect AB, then the household will choose to pay the higher price of a dwelling unit with S units of housing service per time period. If the indifference curve intersects AB, the household will choose the street. If the code's minimum q is above T, the household will be forced to the street because its income would be insufficient to pay for this much housing. The demand curve that is implied by the choices under code enforcement has a kink at q equal to S. For q's that are greater than S, the demand curve is unchanged. The demand curve below S, however, disappears and is replaced by a vertical line rising from the point on the original demand curve that corresponds with S. As a

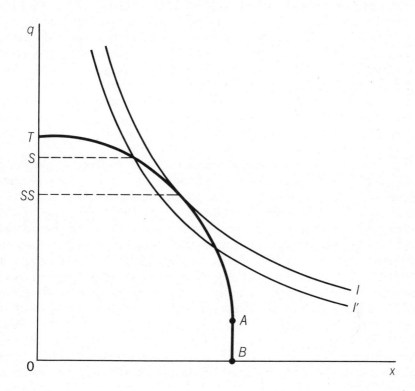

Figure 6A-2.

result, price elasticities of demand in the low-income submarket should be less elastic in the presence of code enforcement.

In the preceding analysis, it has been assumed that the code, which includes occupancy standards, is enforced throughout the housing market. If that is not the case, then households will have a third option—moving to an area where the code is not enforced. They would undoubtedly elect this option whenever it is available because it would maximize their satisfaction, i.e., restore them to a tangency position. Under a fully enforced housing code the household would be obliged to sacrifice some satisfaction. This is a deadweight welfare loss to society unless the other members of the society reap substantial gains in their utility because no one lives in substandard housing (Daly and Giertz 1972, Aaron and von Furstenberg 1971).

In practice, it is likely that the parts of the housing code covering facilities and the level of maintenance will be enforced while the occupancy restrictions, e.g., persons per room, will be relaxed. If that happens, tenants will have the option of doubling up in dwelling units that meet code standards except for the occupancy restrictions. This alternative will undoubtedly appeal to many tenants. As in the case of enforcement in only part of the geographical area comprising the submarket, partial enforcement of the code provisions will lead tenants to take advantage of the loophole to move toward their higher levels of precode satisfaction.

In view of the preceding discussion and review of empirical evidence, economists would be inclined to answer the five questions posed earlier as follows: Rents will probably increase, but the amount of the increase will depend on the price elasticity of the supply of housing services per dwelling unit. Although the supply will probably decline, the result will depend on the extent of abnormal profits and the choice of households between accepting code housing or living on the streets. If codes are selectively enforced in only some geographical parts of the market, code enforcement will probably have little effect on households other than generating a move to a new area, and might result in the abandonment of some physical capital in the area of enforcement (Ingram and Kain 1973). The tenants will bear the burden of rent increases above any abnormal profits. Any income redistribution will be from landlords to tenants, but only to the extent of abnormal profits. After the abnormal profits are absorbed, the tenants will suffer a deadweight welfare loss. There are better ways of achieving income redistribution objectives (Komesar 1973, Posner 1972). If, however, Congress decides to enact and fund a housing allowance program, tenants would have the income to pay the increased cost associated with code enforcement, i.e., a national housing allowance would make an effective code enforcement program possible.

Ackerman (1971) has presented an argument that under certain circumstances, which he seems to believe are highly probable, rents will not increase, supply will not decline, and housing code enforcement will be a better income redistribution device than a negative income tax. Although he carefully discusses his assumptions, the limits of his conclusions are often lost in the midst of a lengthy brief on behalf of his general conclusion. A comment by Komesar (1973) undermines much of Ackerman's analysis, especially on the issue of the preferred measures of income redistribution. However, Komesar's attachment to the long-run supply curve is as unrealistic as Ackerman's assumptions. Studies of the housing market suggest that the price elasticity of supply is more inelastic than elastic. At the same time, it is not inelastic enough to justify Ackerman's assumptions, which amount to an extremely inelastic supply curve. Muth's analysis (1960) indicates that the housing market as a whole requires six years to absorb 90 percent of a shift in demand. De Leeuw and Ekanem (1971) have estimated the price elasticity of the supply of housing services per dwelling unit to be 0.3 to 0.7. There is nothing paradoxical or surprising about Ackerman's conclusion, because it follows directly from his assumptions. In essence he assumes that there are abnormal profits in Slumville and that, for nearly all firms, price is greater than average variable cost at the point on the firm's cost curves that corresponds to code-standard housing. Whether Ackerman's scenario is correct is an empirical question. What are the profit levels in the low-income housing market? What are the price elasticities of supply and demand?

Hirsch and Margolis present an elegant theoretical discussion, but it does not add to the reader's understanding of the specification of the estimated equations. Their central purpose is to analyze whether the reallocation (and creation) of risks due to habitability laws shifts the supply and demand curves. The potential contribution of the study lies in its empirical analyses.

The theoretical discussion adds confusion rather than clarity, since it is a questionable modification of Rosen's analysis (1974) of hedonic price indexes. The difference between the two formulations arises from the addition of supply (e.g., the construction cost index), demand (e.g., household income and median income for renters in the SMSA), and legal variables to the housing characteristics normally found in an hedonic price index. Hirsch and Margolis justify this on grounds that their observations are distributed across many different cities, each of which may be facing very different supply and demand equations. This justification seems to be relevant for the SMSA-level variables but not for each household's income (average over 1968-1972).

The coefficients of the housing characteristics (number of rooms, distance to the central business district, structural type, property tax, and heating cost) are employed as the implicit prices of these attributes to calculate a measure of the amount of housing services in each dwelling unit ($\hat{R}$). The latter is then used as the quantity variable in the supply and demand equations. The five housing characteristics are an inadequate description of the attributes normally associated with housing. There are no characteristics that capture neighborhood attributes or level of public services or building attributes—lot size, floor area, kitchen facilities, heating systems, and bathrooms, to name but a few. Property taxes per household for the SMSA is a wholly inadequate representation of the amount of public services associated with any particular dwelling unit, since services vary widely between governments and even within jurisdictions. There is also no measure of the quality dimension, even though the Michigan Survey contains information on the repair needs of each dwelling unit. That measure, although inadequate in terms of the heterogeneous nature of housing, would have been better than none. The interpretation of structural type as a cost-related variable instead of a housing attribute such as density indicates an inadequate understanding of the hedonic technique. The limited characterization of the housing bundle makes the use of these coefficients to construct a quantity measure for housing highly questionable. Such use is further questionable on conceptual grounds because the inclusion of the so-called supply and demand variables obfuscates the meaning of the housing characteristic coefficients (Rosen 1974). It may be the case that the operation of housing markets in different SMSAs can only be effectively examined by estimating a separate hedonic price index for each SMSA. The estimate could be made from micro data, using the Public Use Sample from the 1970 Census. Although the Michigan Survey is more recent, a check of the states that have receivership laws shows that all of these laws were in force prior to the 1970 Census. The laws were enacted in 1962 (two states), 1965, 1966, 1968, and 1969. Therefore, the Michigan Survey does not have a major advantage over the Census for the most important legal variable. A sample of 154 observations is too small to study what amounts to fifty different housing markets.

The legal variables consist of three dummies, one each for states that have repair and deduct laws, rent-withholding and retaliatory eviction laws, and rent receivership laws. Receivership laws are believed to be the most effective enforcement measure of the three, and rent-withholding laws are believed to be more effective than repair and deduct laws. Only six of the twenty-five states in the sample have rent receivership laws: Illinois, Massachusetts, Michigan, Missouri, New Jersey, and New York. It is quite possible that these dummy variables could represent other factors, such as urbanization or a propensity to pass progressive social legislation, that those states have in common. With these reservations in mind, Hirsch and Margolis estimate that tenants pay significantly higher rents in states that have rent receivership laws. The other two legal variables have negative signs and are not statistically significant at the 5 percent level. Although Hirsch and Margolis describe their rent equation as being in reduced form, it is not clear what it is a reduced form of. It certainly is not a reduced form of the supply and demand equations. As a result, the meaning of these estimates and their bearing on an evaluation of housing code enforcement remains unclear.

One would hope that the supply and demand equations would provide more useful information. However, they are beset with specification problems, and perform unsatisfactorily. The proxy for quantity is the hedonic value $(\hat{R})$ and that for price is the ratio of the actual rent to the hedonic value $(R/\hat{R})$. As in the case of the hedonic equation, the supply and demand equations differ in substantial respects from those recommended by Rosen (1974).

The supply and demand equations are asserted to be well-defined structural equations. If we accept the Hirsch and Margolis proxies for quantity and price, we would expect two structural equations that had quantity as the dependent variable, namely, $\hat{R} = f(R/\hat{R}, HDF, L)$ for demand and $\hat{R} = k(R/\hat{R}, HSF, L)$ for supply. Instead, Hirsch and Margolis switch $\hat{R}$ with $R/\hat{R}$ only in the demand equation. They are not the first to do this; others have entertained similar specifications with no more explanation than that "it is convenient" (de Leeuw and Ekanem 1971). It may be convenient, but why should this be the specification? It will affect the empirical estimates because in one case the sum of the squared errors of quantity $(\hat{R})$ is minimized, and in the other, that of price $(R/\hat{R})$. These procedures will give different estimates of the price elasticity of demand. In the Hirsch-Margolis formulation this price elasticity is the inverse of the coefficient of $\hat{R}$, and the coefficients of HDF and L variables would have to be transformed (multiplied by the negative of the price elasticity) to arrive at estimates of their effects on demand. A further estimation problem arises because $\hat{R}$ appears in the dependent variable and one of the independent variables in both equations.

In appropriately specified supply and demand equations, the legal variables contribute to an evaluation of housing code enforcement by providing information on the allocation of risks between landlords and tenants. If code enforcement shifted risks from tenants to landlords, the supply curve would be expected to shift to the left (negative coefficients for the legal variables in the supply equation), and the demand curve would be expected to shift to the right (positive coefficients for the legal variables in the demand equation). The shift in the supply curve would probably not be parallel; the curve would shift further at lower values of $\hat{R}$ than at higher ones because code enforcement will have less effect on the risks of supplying housing above the code standard. The Hirsch-Margolis estimates indicate that the supply curve shifts as expected in response to rent receivership and rent-withholding laws but shifts in the opposite direction for repair and deduct laws. The legal coefficients in the Hirsch-Margolis "demand" equation must be multiplied by the negative of the inverse of the coefficient of $\hat{R}$ to obtain the coefficients corresponding to the standard demand and supply equations. As a result, the legal variables would have the expected signs and would represent the expected shifts. All the coefficients of the legal variables in the supply equations are highly insignificant by conventional statistical tests, and the repair and deduct variable is insignificant in the demand equation.

The estimate of the price elasticity of supply (0.2613) compares reasonably well with prior estimates. At the same time, I am hard pressed to explain the role of *LSMSAY* (average income for the SMSA) in a supply equation. This demand variable appears to be in the wrong place; yet it plays a prominent role in the estimated equation. Such an income variable would be appropriate in the demand equation, but there is none there. (A measure of each household's income, however, is appropriately included.)

The demand equation is beset by a similar problem of suitability: *LHEAT* (average annual heat cost per structure) is a prominent, but inappropriate, variable in that equation. *LHEAT* could be interpreted as a proxy for climatic variations in demand, but temperature would be better suited for the purpose. As a supply variable, *LHEAT* could represent an input cost differential or some regionally varying constraint on the production function. In the former role, we would expect a negative sign. The estimate, however, is positive, and Hirsch and Margolis explain that *LHEAT* is a constraint on the amount of service a landlord can provide.

These empirical and conceptual inadequacies in the estimated equations and the statistically weak and inconsistent results for the legal variables cast considerable doubt on the reliability of the estimates. I certainly do not have a great deal of confidence in the comparison of costs and benefits. In fact, the comparison is troubling because it is inappropriately framed in terms of a cost-benefit analysis at the same time that such important elements as administrative costs are ignored. The shifts are interesting, but they do not contain enough information to evaluate housing code enforcement.

In summary, the important empirical questions remain without any clear-cut answers. The most that can be said is that the Hirsch-Margolis results are inconsistent with Ackerman's world because the supply curve shifts more than the demand curve for rent receivership, which is the most effective enforcement procedure of the three under study. Rent increases and welfare losses are likely to accompany code enforcement.

REFERENCES

Aaron, Henry J., and George M. von Furstenberg. 1971. "The Inefficiency of Transfers in Kind: The Case of Housing Assistance." *Western Economic Journal*, June.

Ackerman, Bruce A. 1971. "Regulating Slum Markets on Behalf of the Poor: Of Housing Codes, Housing Subsidies and Income Distribution Policy." *Yale Law Journal*, vol. 80, pp. 1093-1197.

_____. 1973. "More on Slum Housing and Redistribution Policy: A Reply to Professor Komesar." *Yale Law Journal*, vol. 82, pp. 1194-1207.

Coase, Ronald. 1960. "The Problem of Social Cost." *Journal of Law and Economics*, October.

Daly, George, and Fred Giertz. 1972. "Welfare Economics and Welfare Reform." *American Economic Review*, March.

de Leeuw, Frank, and Nkanta F. Ekanem. 1971. "The Supply of Rental Housing." *American Economic Review*, December.

Ingram, Gregory K., and John F. Kain. 1973. "A Simple Model of Housing Production and the Abandonment Problem." *American Real Estate and Urban Economics Association Journal*, June.

Komesar, Neil K. 1973. "Return to Slumville: A Critique of the Ackerman Analysis of Housing Code Enforcement and the Poor." *Yale Law Journal*, vol. 82, pp. 1175-1193.

Miller, L. Charles, Jr. 1973. "The Economics of Housing Code Enforcement." *Land Economics*, February.

Muth, Richard F. 1960. "The Demand for Non-Farm Housing." In A. Harburger, ed. *The Demand for Durable Goods*. Chicago: Chicago University Press.

Olsen, Edgar O. 1969. "A Competitive Theory of the Housing Market." *American Economic Review*, September.

Peterson, George E.; Arthur P. Solomon; Hadi Madjid; and William C. Apgar Jr. 1973. *Property Taxes, Housing and the Cities*. Lexington, Mass.: Heath.

Posner, Richard A. 1972. *Economic Analysis of Law*. Boston: Little, Brown.

Rosen, Sherwin. 1974. "Hedonic Prices and Implicit Markets." *Journal of Political Economy*, January/February.

Sporn, Arthur D. 1960. "Empirical Studies in the Economics of Slum Ownership." *Land Economics*, November.

Sternlieb, George. 1966. *The Tenement Landlord*. New Brunswick, N.J.: Rutgers University Press.

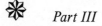 *Part III*

**Modeling the Housing Market
and Selected Housing Policies**

Chapter Seven

Analyzing Housing Policies with the Urban Institute Housing Model

Frank de Leeuw and
Raymond J. Struyk

INTRODUCTION

An urban housing market is a network of interrelated parts. The decision to tear down a block of houses in one neighborhood forces the occupants to seek housing elsewhere and sets in motion a chain of moves that can affect communities throughout an area. The decision to restrict growth in a suburban area has similar far-flung effects, stimulating new construction in other suburbs and perhaps stimulating redevelopment of older housing as well. A decision to pay housing allowances to the low-income households of an urban area may decrease the demand for the lowest-quality stock, increase the demand for somewhat better housing, and could eventually produce changes in the entire structure of housing prices and locational patterns of the area.

The housing market is, of course, not unique in being composed of many interrelated parts. It is true of housing, however, that many policy controversies have centered to an unusual extent on exactly how this network of interrelations works—on the relocation effects of urban renewal, on the price effects of housing allowances, on the population redistribution caused by local no-growth policies. A model capable of analyzing these issues must deal in some detail with

Note: Sue Marshall, Larry Ozanne, and Ann Schnare worked with us on the model and share full credit for the results reported here. Dennis Eisen and Andrew Struik also made important contributions to the model. The entire project was sponsored by the Office of Policy Development and Research, U.S. Department of Housing and Urban Development. We, however, bear full responsibility for statements made and views expressed.

submarkets for different levels of housing quality and different geographic locations.

Besides dealing with submarkets and their interrelations, a realistic housing model must reflect two special characteristics accounting for much of the distinctive behavior of housing markets: "durability" and "neighborhood effects." Durability of housing refers not only to the long time period over which the housing stock yields its services but also to the unalterable nature of many of the characteristics of a dwelling once it is built. Whether a dwelling is a detached house or an apartment in a twenty-story building, whether it is downtown or in a suburb, whether it is on a large or a small lot—these are among the many characteristics largely fixed at the time of construction. The second feature of housing markets—neighborhood effects—refers not just to the dependence of the value of one dwelling upon the physical appearance of neighboring dwellings but, even more important, to the strong influence of neighborhood racial composition and socioeconomic status on the choice of where to live.

The Urban Institute housing model is an attempt to quantify the interrelationships among the parts of an urban housing market while emphasizing the two special characteristics of durability and neighborhood effects. It represents an urban housing market composed of thirty to forty "model" dwellings and households, a new-construction industry, and numerous possibilities for government intervention. Households choose which dwelling to occupy on the basis of the utility function, while owners of existing dwellings choose levels of housing services they will provide on the basis of expected profit maximization. Durability enters the model through the distinction between new housing, which is assumed to be perfectly elastic in supply, and existing dwellings, whose specific characteristics are among the initial conditions of the model and whose supply elasticity is one of the principle objects of empirical investigation. Neighborhood effects are captured by having each household's decision to occupy or not to occupy a particular dwelling depend not only on the characteristics and price of that dwelling but also on characteristics of other dwellings and occupants in the geographic zone in which that dwelling is located.

Development of the model has been under the sponsorship of the Department of Housing and Urban Development. HUD's particular interest in sponsoring the model has been the analysis of the possible effects of housing allowances, but the model has been designed so that a variety of housing policies and other economic or demographic developments can be analyzed within the same framework. Work on the model began in the fall of 1971, with the first year being devoted primarily to developing the theoretical model and a procedure for its computer simulation. The second year of work emphasized empirical applications to U.S. metropolitan areas during 1960-1970. Initial empirical work led to some changes in the structure of the model and in the computer algorithm simulation procedure. The most recent period has been taken up with these changes plus additional empirical work and the beginnings of policy analysis.

The remainder of this study is in three parts. We describe the model, beginning with a nontechnical account of the general structure, then proceed to a mathematical description of the key relationships, and summarize the empirical results of applications to six metropolitan areas. We deal with model results, first introducing the useful analytical device of a price-structure curve and then describing results of simulating a rise in new-construction costs, a slowdown of population growth, and two housing policies. In the final section, we appraise some of the strong and weak points of the model.

MODEL DESCRIPTION

The Theoretical Model in Brief

The Urban Institute housing model deals with ten-year changes in housing quality and household location within a metropolitan area. The four key phrases of this capsule description are "ten-year changes," "housing quality," "household location," and "within a metropolitan area." Each of them serves to distinguish the model from other models or studies, for example, from short-run explanations of housing market dynamics, from location-free theories of the filtering process, or from macroeconomic analyses with a national focus.

As mentioned earlier, a metropolitan housing market is represented in the model by a few dozen "model" households, a few dozen "model" dwellings, a building industry, and possibilities for a variety of government restrictions or programs. The four "actors" in the model are, therefore, households seeking a place to live, owners of existing dwellings offering housing services at various prices, a building industry meeting demands at an acceptable rate of return, and governments able to regulate the housing-location process at many different points. The model searches for a "solution"—a situation in which no one can improve his position according to the rules of behavior and constraints he obeys—through a matching of households with new or existing dwellings. In the nontechnical description of the model in this section, we take up each of the four actors in turn and describe the nature of the solution process. We then introduce a price-quantity diagram illustrating the interaction of households, owners, and builders.

"Model" Households. Each "model" household represents several hundred or thousand actual households, the exact number depending on the size of the metropolitan area to which the model is being applied. A household belongs to one of several household types and is characterized by two measures of its income. The household types with which we have worked in applying the model to specific metropolitan areas include white, nonelderly families; white, elderly, single-person households; black, nonelderly families; and black, elderly, single-person households; in the case of Austin, the types also include Chicano, nonelderly families, and Chicano, elderly, single-person households. Some of the parameters of the model, as we shall indicate in the next section, differ by household type.

The two income measures for each model household are an actual income figure—the estimated mean actual income of the households represented by the model—and a "model" income figure—a weighted average of actual income and median income for the household type to which it belongs. Although we initially experimented with one "permanent" income figure for each model household, we finally decided that two income figures were necessary. An actual income figure was necessary because certain of the programs the model is intended to analyze—for example, housing allowances—operate on actual income rather than any transformed version of income. The assumption of unitary income elasticity embedded in the utility function of the model, however, is inappropriate to measured single-year incomes; a second, smoothed version of income was required.[1] The model thus uses actual income as the variable directly affected by certain housing, tax, or transfer programs, and model income in actually determining the choice of location and quality which each household makes. A change in actual income—owing to a housing allowance, for example—is of course translated into a change in model income, but the latter change is smaller than the former.

Household behavior in the model consists of deciding which of all possible dwellings to occupy, including a new dwelling with any desired level of services (subject to any government-imposed minimum standards for new construction) or any of the existing dwellings in the model. The household makes its decision on the basis of the quantity of housing services offered by each dwelling, the price per unit of the housing service offered, the household's model income, and three characteristics of the zone in which each dwelling is located.

The three zonal characteristics are average travel time to and from work, average net rent per dwelling, and the proportion of residents in the zone who belong to the same racial group as the household making the choice. Travel time is simply introduced into the model as a piece of exogenous information about each zone. Average net rent and racial composition are determined by the model itself, with the result that there is a two-way interaction between household choice and the zonal characteristics. This interaction, incidentally, is the source of considerable complexity in the solution process for the model, since it introduces the possibility of multiple solutions meeting the criterion of utility maximization by each household.

All the variables influencing household choices are combined into a utility function which the household is attempting to maximize. The function has four parameters whose values decisively influence what the model predicts about the effects of housing policies. One of the principal goals of the application of the model to specific metropolitan areas is to obtain estimates of these parameters.

"Model" Dwellings. Each model dwelling, like each model household, represents several hundred or thousand actual cases; in fact, the number of actual cases per model unit is (apart from minor statistical adjustments) the same for dwellings as it is for households. Each model dwelling belongs to one of several zones (five or six so far) differing in accessibility, initial wealth, or initial racial composition. Each model dwelling is also characterized by the quantity of housing services supplied—a flow of output per month—at the beginning of the ten-year interval to which the model applies. The quantity of housing services of a dwelling, one of the basic concepts of the model, refers to an index of all the things of value which a physical structure provides—space, shelter, privacy, pleasing design, and a host of others. It does not refer to the neighborhood characteristics associated with each dwelling; these are measured by the various attributes of the zone in which a dwelling is located.

The behavior of the owners of existing dwellings consists of making price-quantity offers with the goal of maximizing expected profits. Each price-quantity offer consists of a quantity of housing services to be provided at the end of the decade to which the model refers and a price at which that quantity will be provided. The offers thus resemble rental advertisements specifying services provided and monthly cost. The price-quantity offers for each dwelling must lie along a supply curve whose position depends on the initial quantity of housing services offered by the dwelling and two parameters of the model, one related to a depreciation rate and the other to an elasticity of supply with respect to price. It is these two parameters which determine the supply elasticity of the existing housing stock.

The owner of each existing dwelling seeks to locate as high up along his supply curve as he can, for his expected profits are an increasing function of his position along the supply curve. Competition among the owners of actual dwellings making up each "model" dwelling is assumed sufficient to keep landlords from making offers above their supply curves.

The model includes a minimum price per unit of service, defined as that price which is just sufficient to cover the cost of operating a dwelling. If the owner of a dwelling is unable to find an occupant at any price at or above the minimum, then he withdraws his dwelling from the stock of housing. Withdrawal can take the form of long-term vacancy, demolition, conversion to nonresidential use, or abandonment. The model does not distinguish among these different kinds of withdrawal.

Builders. The third actor in the model, the building industry, plays a more passive role than model households and model dwellings. The industry is characterized by a horizontal supply curve, that is, it is prepared to offer new dwellings at a monthly total cost which is proportional to the level of services the dwelling provides. The price per unit of service at which new dwellings are available is taken as exogenous for each housing market. Empirically, it is measured on the basis of FHA data on the cost and square footage of new dwellings; it tends to set a ceiling for the price structure of all the existing stock, although existing dwellings with especially favorable zonal characteristics can command prices above the new-construction price. In the present model, newly constructed dwellings are assumed to be concentrated in a single "zone of new construction."[2]

For a time span much shorter than ten years the assumption of a perfectly elastic supply of new housing would be inappropriate. The mortgage market and building supply industries are subject to capacity limitations which sometimes strongly influence the course of new construction in the shortrun. Even over a ten-year span, the supply of land is limited and the effect is to make the supply of new housing less than perfectly elastic. Muth (1968) has argued convincingly, however, that the increase in land prices due to the bidding away of land from other users by residential users has only a neglible effect on the long-run supply elasticity of new housing.

Governments. The final factor of the model, "government," can influence the housing-location process at so many different points that it is impossible to describe its behavior succinctly. Tax charges, subsidy payments, transfer payments with or without earmarking for housing, minimum new-construction requirements, and the specification of minimum quantities of housing services in a particular zone are among the ways through which governments can affect housing markets in the model.

An income tax can be represented by replacing a household's actual income by income less the tax (and making a smaller reduction in its model income) before it enters the housing market. Tax rates and other parameters of tax formulas—for example, exemption levels—can be set separately for each household type, or even for each model household. Transfer payments are represented by using the same procedure as for taxes. A transfer earmarked for housing—a housing allowance—can be represented by requiring an eligible household to consume at least some minimum level of housing services or spend some minimum amount on housing in order to receive the transfer; the household then determines its utility-maximizing choice without the allowance, its choice with the allowance (including the minimum requirements), and the larger of these two maxima. A restrictive zoning ordinance can be represented by setting a minimum quantity of housing services for all of the dwellings in a zone. The model is exceptionally rich in the variety of government policies it can analyze.

The Solution Process. The solution of the model, as mentioned earlier, is a situation in which none of the four actors has any incentive to change its position. Each household is the unique occupant of one dwelling, the one which maximizes its satisfaction given all the price-quantity offers facing it. The owner of each existing dwelling is as high up along his supply curve as he can be without finding his dwelling vacant. (If a dwelling is vacant even at the lowest point on its supply curve, it is withdrawn from the stock.) The building industry is supplying the number of new dwellings households are willing to purchase. Government regulations are strictly enforced.

The computer program to solve the model searches for a solution with these properties through a process of trial and error. Departures from solution conditions in one trial govern the way in which the solution is modified for the next trial. The steps in the search process have no theoretical or empirical significance; it is only the final solution of a problem which is of interest. Although the solution algorithm is a time-consuming and complex computer program with a number of still unresolved difficulties, it works well for the great majority of problems we have been interested in solving.

A Price-Quantity Diagram. The model deals with both the quality (or level of housing services) of dwellings and with location. Figure 7-1 illustrates the treatment of quality but not the locational aspects of the model.

The horizontal axis in Figure 7-1 measures the quantity of housing services (a weighted index of all the separate services) provided per month by an individual dwelling. The vertical axis measures price *per unit of service*, that is, the monthly gross cost of occupancy of a dwelling divided by its index of housing services. The total cost of a dwelling on a monthly basis is its price times its quantity.

The diagram represents supply conditions in an urban housing market during a ten-year interval. In a very short period—say, a month or a year—the supply of housing services is virtually determined by the stock inherited from the previous period, and the supply provided by an individual dwelling could be represented on the diagram by a vertical line. In a very long period—say, half a century—the influence of the inherited stock is quite small, and

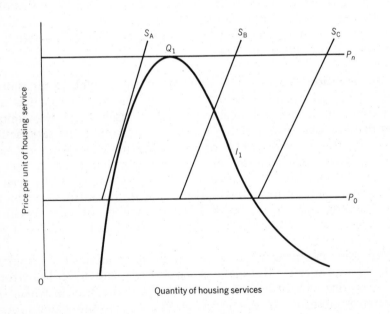

Note: For identification of variables, see accompanying text.

Figure 7-1. Housing Supply over a Ten-Year Span.

supply possibilities could be represented by a single, close-to-horizontal curve representing the price per unit of newly constructed dwellings, along which builders can supply any desired number of new dwellings. In an intermediate period, the representation of supply must reflect both the inelastic character of the existing stock and the elastic conditions of new supply.

Line P_n in Figure 7-1 depicts the price per unit at which new dwellings are available. It is the sum of capital costs per month (including land costs), operating costs per month, and developers' normal profits, all per unit of service. Any number of new dwellings can be built along the line, each one represented by a dot corresponding to its quantity of services.

Lines S_A, S_B, and S_C depict the relation between quantity and price for three existing dwellings, a "luxury" dwelling (C) providing a high level of services, a "slum" dwelling (A) providing a low level of services, and a dwelling (B) providing a level of services between the other two. The slope and position of the three supply curves depend on the time span to which they refer—ten years in Figure 7-1. Each dwelling produced along the new supply line acquires its own supply curve for the decade following initial construction. When the model is run for two or more decades, then the position of each dwelling's supply curve shifts from decade to decade as its start-of-decade level of services changes.

Line P_0 depicts the minimum price per unit of service at which it pays the owner of a dwelling to keep it in operation. P_0 corresponds to the concept of average variable costs in the theory of the firm. In the model, if an occupant cannot be found for a dwelling at a price at or above P_0, the dwelling is dropped from the housing stock.

Finally, I_1 represents an indifference curve for one household. The point of tangency (Q_1) between I_1 and the new-construction price (P_n) represents the level of housing services that maximizes that household's utility at price P_n. If that household, in other words, is forced to occupy a new dwelling, but at any level of services it wishes, it will choose one with a level equal to Q_1. Curve I_1 depicts all other price-quantity combinations that are just as attractive to the household as the one at point Q_1. The precise shape of I_1 will not be derived here; it is sufficient to note that in order to persuade household 1 to depart in *either* direction from its optimum choice (Q_1), it is necessary to offer it a price reduction below P_n. Faced with any offer involving a price at or above P_n, the household would prefer Q_1 at P_n.

The area inside I_1 represents price-quantity combinations preferred over a new dwelling; the area outside I_1 represents outcomes less satisfying than a new dwelling at Q_1. Among the three existing dwellings depicted in Figure 7-1, only B has any chance of being preferred to a new dwelling by household 1. Dwelling B will be preferred to a new dwelling at Q_1 if it makes a price-quantity offer inside I_1. Dwellings A and C would not be preferred to a new dwelling at any price above the minimum P_0. If a housing market consisted solely of household 1, dwellings A, B, and C, and a building industry, then the market outcome would be, according to the model, occupancy of dwelling B at a price just below the intersection of S_B and I_1, withdrawal of dwellings A and C from the market, and no new construction.

As we add households and dwellings to Figure 7-1, households have an increasing number of closely substitutable existing dwellings from which to choose, and dwellings have a wider range of potential occupants. Instead of one or two isolated price-quantity points at which housing services are sold, a relatively smooth set of points forming a price-structure curve tends to emerge. These price-structure curves are a useful device for understanding the operation of the model and will be described at the beginning of the section on simulation results.

Mathematical Specification

Two kinds of behavior drive the model: utility maximization by households and profit maximization by owners of existing dwellings. The household utility function and the landlord-owner supply functions used in the empirical work are specified below.[3]

Household Utility Functions. Each household evaluates each dwelling by means of a utility function. The utility of dwelling j to household i, U_{ij}, can be represented as

$$U_{ij} = HXZ_1 \, Z_2 \, Z_3 \qquad (7\text{-}1)$$

H represents the utility of housing services and is defined by:

$$H = [Q_j - \alpha_i \gamma_i (Y_i^m / P_n)]^{\alpha_i} \qquad (7\text{-}2)$$

where Q_j is the quantity of housing services offered by dwelling j, α_i is a parameter expressing the strength of housing preferences (versus preference for other goods) for households of type i, γ_1 is a parameter expressing the degree to which households will alter their housing choice in response to a price discount, Y_i^m is household i's model income after adjustment for taxes and transfers, and P_n is the price per unit of service of newly constructed dwellings.

The term in the utility function described by Equation (7-2) is an elaboration of the idea underlying the so-called linear expenditure system, namely, that observed demand behavior is best approximated by making utility depend on the excess of quantities consumed over some minimum acceptable levels. Unlike the linear expenditure system, however, Equation (7-2) makes the minimum acceptable level itself a function of income. The importance of the minimum depends on the parameter γ_1, which is determined empirically. For γ_1 equal to zero, Equation (7-2) reduces to a simple Cobb-Douglas expression for the utility of housing services.

X represents the utility of nonhousing goods and is specified in a manner analogous to H. The budget constraint facing the consumer is used to define nonhousing goods as $(Y_i^m - P_j Q_j)$, where Y_i^m is the household's model income and P_j and Q_j are the price and quantity of services of dwelling j.[4] X is defined as

$$X = [(Y_i - P_j Q_j) - (1 - \alpha_i)\gamma_1 Y_i^m]^{1-\alpha}i \qquad (7\text{-}3)$$

Three zonal characteristics are represented by the Z's: accessibility (Z_1), wealth (Z_2), and racial composition (Z_3) and are defined in Equations (7-4), (7-5), and (7-6).

$$Z_1 = (200 - T_j)^{0.5 + \alpha_i - \alpha_1} \qquad (7\text{-}4)$$

where T_j is average travel time (in hours per month) in the zone in which dwelling j is located, α_i is a parameter expressing the strength of housing preferences of households of the type of household i, and α_1 is the value of α_i for white, nonelderly families.

The term in parentheses, $200 - T_j$, is an approximation to monthly hours of leisure time available to an average worker in the zone in which dwelling j is located. The exponent of this term is based on the value households place on travel time and on analysis of how we might expect this value to vary with strength of housing demand.

$$Z_2 = [(\overline{P}_j - P_0)\overline{Q}_i / (P_j' - P_0)Q_j']^{0.01\gamma_2} \qquad (7\text{-}5)$$

where P_j represents price per unit of housing services; P_0, minimum operating costs per unit of housing services; Q_j, quantity of housing services; and γ_2 is a parameter expressing the strength of preferences for a wealthy zone. P and Q refer to zonal averages (the zone in which dwelling j is located); and P' and Q', to SMSA averages. Hence, the expression represents the average net rent (gross rent less operating costs) of dwellings in a zone relative to the average net rent in an SMSA, and serves as an indicator of zonal wealth.

Finally,

$$Z_3 = R_{ij} + [1,000/(100\gamma_3 + 1)] \tag{7-6}$$

where R_{ij} is the proportion of households located in the same zone as dwelling j and belonging to the same racial group as household i, and γ_3 is a parameter expressing the strength of household preferences for racial homogeneity. The larger γ_3, the more sensitive is Z_3 (and hence U_{ij}) to variations in R_{ij}. With γ_3 equal to zero, Z_3 can vary only between 1,000 and 1,001, a range of 0.1 percent. With γ_3 equal to 1.0, Z_3 can vary between approximately 10 and 11, a range of 10 percent.

Supply Functions for Existing Dwellings. The supply curve for existing dwelling j is specified as follows:

$$Q_j = \left[\beta_1 + \beta_2 \left(\frac{2}{3} \right) \left(\frac{P_j - P_0}{P_c} \right) \right] Q_0 \tag{7-7}$$

where Q_j is the level of housing services currently provided by dwelling j; Q_0, the level of housing services provided by dwelling j ten years ago; P_j, the price per unit of service offered by dwelling j; P_0, operating costs per unit of service; and P_c, capital costs per unit of service for a new dwelling. β_1 and β_2 are empirically determined parameters. Prices are all on a flow basis, that is, they are costs per unit of service per month, not costs per unit of capital stock.

Equation (7-7) is derived from the maximization of an expression for expected profits, subject to a production function for housing services. The production function is given by:

$$Q = \left\{ \beta_1 + \left[2\beta_2 \left(\frac{C}{Q_0} \right) \right]^{0.5} \right\} Q_0 \tag{7-8}$$

where C is the quantity of capital invested in a dwelling during a decade. The properties of this function and the derivation of the supply curve are discussed in de Leeuw and Struyk (1976).

Empirical Results

The model has been applied to six metropolitan areas for the decade of 1960-1970. The areas are Austin, Chicago, Durham,

Pittsburgh, Portland (Oregon), and Washington, D.C. They represent a wide range of sizes, growth rates, racial compositions, incomes, and housing costs. Each application involved several man-months of data gathering and estimation. Space permits only the briefest summary of results.

The first major step in applying the model to an area was to specify zonal boundaries and to construct model dwellings and households. Each area was divided into four or five zones on the basis of 1960 data so as to maximize within-zone homogeneity in racial composition and rental values but subject to the constraint that boundaries of major political jurisdictions had to be retained. Thus, in most areas, there was an inner-city, low-income, high-minority zone, a "rest of the central city" zone, and two or three suburban zones separated on the basis of income.

Next, a hedonic index technique was used to construct a value and rent deflator for each zone. Each deflator was applied to the distribution of housing values and rents in order to obtain a distribution of housing services for each zone. This distribution of services was then subdivided into model dwellings. In an area with 1,200 actual dwellings per model dwelling, the 1,200 dwellings providing the lowest level of services in Zone 1 were averaged to obtain one model dwelling for Zone 2, the 1,200 with the next highest level of services were averaged to obtain a second model dwelling of Zone 1, and so forth. Model households were obtained in an analogous way from separate income distributions for each of the household types of the model (white, nonelderly families, black, nonelderly families, and so forth).

Econometric analysis of rent-income and value-income ratios was used to obtain one set of key parameters of the model, the alphas expressing the strength of preference for housing versus other goods for each of the household types of the model. Analysis of the household utility function shows that the alphas are closely related, although not identical to, the proportion of income which households of a given type devote to housing.

To estimate the other behavioral parameters, the model was simulated under a variety of assumptions about these parameters, and values were selected that gave the best fit to actual zonal distributions of incomes, racial composition, rent, and withdrawals from the initial stock of housing. This estimation by simulation proceeded in two steps. First, 1960 households were matched with 1960 dwellings under the assumption of a perfectly inelastic 1960 supply in order to obtain the best-fitting gammas of the utility function. Then, using those gammas, the model was simulated for 1960-1970, to obtain the best-fitting betas of the supply function.

The results of this lengthy and complex estimating procedure are summarized in Table 7-1. For most of the parameters there are clear central tendencies in the estimates. For example, the values of alpha for white, nonelderly families cluster around 0.8, while those for elderly, white families cluster around 0.25. For the parameters of the supply function (the β's), however, the distribution appears to be bimodal. For three of the cities, β_2 is estimated at 0.9, and β_1 ranges from 0.4 to 0.6; for two others, β_2 is estimated at only 0.4, and β_1, at 0.7. A number of empirical and sensitivity tests we have conducted lead us to conclude that (a) we cannot at present reduce this range of uncertainty about the supply function parameters and (b) some of the policy simulation results depend on which end of the range of estimates we use. Consequently, we have used two different pairs of beta estimates, an "elastic" set and an "inelastic" one, in most of our policy analyses. Even the elastic set, however, implies a price elasticity of supply in the neighborhood of 1.0, or far below the supply elasticity of new dwellings.

SIMULATION RESULTS

In this section we analyze the effects on the housing stock and household location of four economic or demographic changes: an increase in the cost of new construction, an especially topical subject in light of the experience of the past few years; a decrease in the rate of growth of urban areas, another subject suggested by recent U.S. trends; a housing allowance program with a payment formula that makes 22 percent of the population eligible; and a subsidy payment for the construction of new units, a housing strategy pursued to some extent in this country and especially interesting in comparison with housing allowances. Before reporting the results of these analyses, we introduce the concept of a "price-structure curve," which offers a way of obtaining an intuitive grasp of the effects of housing policies and other developments on various sectors of the housing market.

The Structure of Housing Prices
One way of thinking about the model is as a set of demand and supply functions for closely related submarkets. There is a demand for, and supply of, low-quality model dwellings in the inner city; high-quality dwellings in the inner city; and so on for many levels of housing services and many geographic locations and for new dwellings as well as existing dwellings. The prices per unit of housing services for all these model dwellings—and for the actual housing

Table 7-1. Estimated Parametric Values for Six Metropolitan Areas

Parameters	Metropolitan Areas					
	Durham	Austin	Portland	Pittsburgh	Washington	Chicago
α's: ratios of housing expense to income						
α(1): white, nonelderly families						
1960	.19	.18	.17	.16	.19	.18
1970	.17	.20	.18	.15	.19	.17
α(2): white, elderly, single households						
1960	.25	.27	.28	.22	.24	.26
1970	.26	.27	.28	.19	.25	.27
α(3): black, nonelderly families						
1960	.20	.18	.17	.19	.19	.21
1970	.19	.19	.18	.25	.20	.20
α(4): black, elderly, single households						
1960	.26	.27	—	.25	.24	.26
1970	.27	.28	—	.27	.27	.27
α(5): Chicano, nonelderly families						
1960	—	.18	—	—	—	—
1970	—	.18	—	—	—	—
α(6): Chicano, elderly, single households						
1960	—	.27	—	—	—	—
1970	—	.25	—	—	—	—
γ's: other parameters of household behavior						
γ(1): price responsiveness	.8	.8	.9	.9	.9	.7
γ(2): attitude toward zonal wealth	.4	.2	.6	.3	.3	.4
γ(3): attitude toward zonal racial mix	.7	.9	.9	.7	.6	.1
β's: supply parameters						
β(1)	.7	.4	.4	.5	.6	.7
β(2)	.4	.9	.9	.6	.9	.4

submarkets they represent—need not be the same, because one model dwelling is not a perfect substitute (in either demand or supply) for another. Prices of various model dwellings cannot differ too much, however, because substitution in demand is strong enough to cause vacancies or overoccupancy if the price of one dwelling is out of line with prices of closely related dwellings.

A price-structure curve provides a useful way to summarize housing market results in the model. Figure 7-2 illustrates two price-structure curves based on actual runs of the model; the quantity of housing services produced by each dwelling is measured along the horizontal axis; and the price per unit of housing service for each of these dwellings, along the vertical axis. The total monthly amount the occupant pays for housing services is the quantity multiplied by the price per unit of service. Each point on the curves

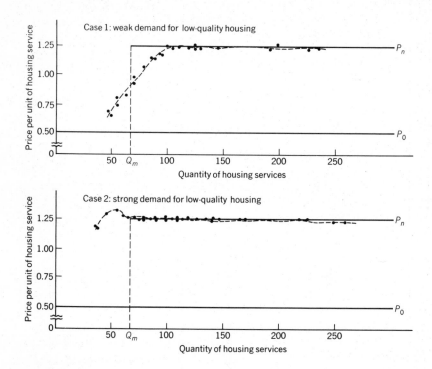

p_n = new-construction price.

p_o = minimum operating price of existing dwelling.

Q_m = minimum legal level of new-housing services.

Figure 7-2. The Structure of Housing Prices.

represents one model dwelling and can be thought of broadly as representing the intersection of a demand curve and a supply curve for one submarket.

Generally, prices per unit of service tend to lie between lines P_n and P_0 on the price axis. As in Figure 7-1, P_n is the price per unit at which new dwellings are available, and P_0 represents minimum costs per unit of service necessary to keep a dwelling in operation. If a unit remains vacant even after its price has been lowered to P_0, then the dwelling (according to the model) will be withdrawn from the occupied residential stock through conversion to nonresidential use, prolonged vacancy, or abandonment.

P_n tends to serve as an upper limit to housing prices because a household is very unlikely to pay more per unit of service for an existing dwelling than for a new dwelling with an identical level of services. One important exception to this ceiling role of P_n occurs because in most metropolitan areas, building codes, zoning requirements, and other regulations effectively prevent construction of new dwellings with a low level of services. For example, large parts of most metropolitan areas exclude or carefully regulate mobile homes. Below the minimum permitted level of new-housing services, represented by Q_m in Figure 7-2, there is no reason why prices per unit of service cannot exceed P_n—as in fact they do in the bottom panel of the figure.

Dynamic forces within most housing markets tend to keep prices close to the P_n ceiling for moderate- and high-service dwellings. These dynamic forces include growth in real income over time, growth in population over time, and depreciation of dwellings over time. All three forces tend to create excess demand for housing at the high-service end of the range, with the result that prices of existing dwellings in that range tend to be driven up toward the P_n ceiling and that is the range within which new construction usually takes place.

In the low-service end of the range the three forces do not act in the same direction. At that end, growth in real income and depreciation of the housing stock probably tend to create an excess supply of dwellings and, hence, lower prices. On the other hand, population growth, especially in the form of an influx of low-income households, tends to increase the demand for services. Where the excess-supply forces dominate, the result may be a situation like case 1 in Figure 7-2, in which low-service dwellings sell at a discount per unit of service. Where population growth is rapid and where there is an effective minimum Q_m near the low-service end of the scale, the result may be the curve depicted for case 2 in Figure 7-2, in which housing fairly near the low-service end of the scale sells at a premium.

Besides Q_m, the other reason prices may exceed P_n is the desirability of certain locations. Since household choices depend in part on characteristics of the zone in which a dwelling is located, a zone with especially desirable characteristics can command a premium above new-construction prices. Variations in zone characteristics account for much of the departure from smoothness in the two price-structure curves of Figure 7-2.

The device of a price-structure curve will prove useful in understanding simulations of a variety of market developments and housing policies. We shall introduce each of the four developments to be analyzed below with a discussion of how we would expect that development to change price-structure curves for different kinds of initial housing market situations. While these discussions fall far short of rigorous analyses, they provide valuable intuitive guidance to the way major housing market forces interact in the model.

Before we present actual model results, we again indicate what the policy simulations do and do not represent. The simulations trace through both the direct effects on households or dwellings of a subsidy or a higher new-dwelling price, and those indirect effects on other households or dwellings that are due to the interrelations of different sectors of the housing market. In the case of housing policies, the simulations take account of both subsidies and any taxes levied to finance them. The simulations stop short, however, of a full general equilibrium model of all interrelations in the economy; they deal only with interrelations of demands and supplies within an urban housing market. The simulations are also limited, with the exception of a few references to twenty-year runs, to ten-year changes; there are no suggestions as to the monthly or annual path that housing prices, services, or locational patterns might follow in moving from start- to end-of-decade positions. In the case of housing policies, finally, results refer to "idealized" policies in which program provisions are fully known and obeyed by each participant.

A Rise in the Cost of New Construction

In the short run, the greatest impact of a rise in new-construction costs would appear to be on those with a high probability of occupying new dwellings—generally speaking, on affluent rather than poor households, on young rather than old households, on white rather than black households. However, ten-year impacts taking full account of interrelationships among housing submarkets can be, as we shall see, quite different. A rise in new-construction costs is therefore a good example of the value of the model in improving our understanding of housing markets.

For an understanding of model simulation results, the price-structure curves just described are a useful starting point. A rise in new construction costs is equivalent to a rise in line P_n in Figure 7-2. In the middle and upper ranges of housing quality, where P_n serves as an effective upper limit to the prices of existing dwellings, we would expect the latter to rise by approximately the same amount as the rise in new-construction costs. At these higher prices, however, households will presumably choose to consume smaller amounts of housing services. This downward shift in demand can have two effects. One, which we shall not observe in the simulation and which would in general require a large price increase, is that prices of some high-quality dwellings could fall below the P_n ceiling. The second effect, very much in evidence in the simulations, is that this shift will increase the demand for low- and moderate-quality dwellings and, hence, raise their prices. Thus, even in ranges where P_n is not an effective upper limit to the price structure, an increase in P_n can cause a rise in prices.

The increase in demand for low- and moderate-quality housing can cause not only an increase in prices, but an increase in housing "conservation" as well—that is, some dwellings that would otherwise be withdrawn from the stock remain occupied. In a housing market in which very few dwellings are being withdrawn from stock even without high construction costs, this conservation effect is necessarily limited. In fact, in a tight market of this kind it can even happen that higher construction costs cause some low-income households to be left literally without housing; the existing dwellings they would have occupied at a lower price structure are demanded by households that can outbid them, while the cost of a minimum-standard new dwelling $(P_n Q_m)$ is higher than they can afford. In less extreme market situations, however, an increase in new-construction costs can cause a significant drop in withdrawals from the stock and result in correspondingly fewer new dwellings.

These results of higher new-construction costs are sketched in the top panel of Figure 7-3, which refers to one of the two actual cases to be analyzed below. Prices of existing dwellings in the upper quality ranges rise by almost exactly the amount of the increase in P_n, and prices of low-quality dwellings rise by somewhat more than the increase in P_n. Careful examination of the figure reveals that one additional existing model dwelling withdrawn from the stock in the low-P_n case is retained and occupied in the high-P_n case.

In Table 7-2, we summarize the numerical results for two areas,

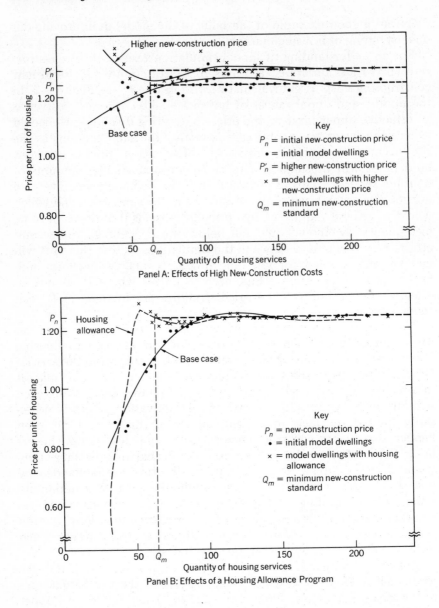

Panel A: Effects of High New-Construction Costs

Panel B: Effects of a Housing Allowance Program

Figure 7-3. New-Construction Costs, Housing Allowances, and the Structure of Housing Prices.

each designed to be representative of a fairly large group of U.S. metropolitan areas in the 1960s. Urban Area A is characterized by a high rate of growth, a relatively high proportion of minority households, and a relatively elastic supply of existing dwellings. Urban Area B is also characterized by a high rate of growth but has a low minority proportion and an inelastic supply of existing dwellings. While these areas are just two of the eight sets of initial market conditions we used in our work, they are sufficient to give an accurate impression of our simulation results.

Results for prices and quantities generally follow the pattern suggested by the discussion of price-structure curves. Prices for high-income households (roughly, those with incomes above the median) are close to the P_n ceiling and rise by almost exactly the 5-cent increase in P_n. Prices for moderate- and low-income households for whom the P_n ceiling is not necessarily effective also rise, but by slightly less than 5 cents in some cases and slightly more in others. Quantities consumed generally fall, and the implied rise in elasticity of demand relating the fall in quantity to the rise in price is generally close to -1.0, the value which is built into the household utility functions.

The one exception to this quantity response shows up on Urban Area A for low-income households and for the inner-city zone. For these (heavily overlapping) categories, quantities are unchanged or higher in spite of higher prices. The clue to these exceptions lies in the next block of figures in the table, summarizing new construction and withdrawals. In Urban Area A there are no withdrawals from stock even in the "standard" case, and so there is no possibility of responding to higher prices by conserving dwellings which would be dropped out of the stock in the standard case. In effect, the increasing demand for moderate- and low-quality dwellings encounters a completely inelastic supply in terms of numbers of dwellings. The supply in terms of dwelling quality is not completely inelastic, however, with the result that the increase in demand permits some landlords to move up along their supply curves and offer bigger quantities at higher prices. The large price increase in the central city of Urban Area A reflects this movement along supply curves. In Urban Area B, where there are withdrawals from stock in the standard case, the supply of low-quality dwellings is not completely inelastic, and low-income households, by increasing the conservation of existing dwellings, succeed in responding to higher prices by reducing quantities consumed.

Table 7-2.   Simulation Results[a] for Changes in Construction Costs and Population Growth (prices are in dollars)

Quantities[b] and Prices	Urban Area A (rapid growth, high minority, elastic supply)			Urban Area B (rapid growth, low minority, inelastic supply)		
	Standard Case	High-P Case[n]	Slow-Growth Case	Standard Case	High-P Case[n]	Slow-Growth Case
High-income households						
Aver. housing quantity	157.8	151.5	163.0	161.0	154.3	159.7
Aver. housing price	1.236	1.287	1.224	1.241	1.292	1.244
Moderate-income households						
Aver. housing quantity	89.2	87.7	90.9	86.3	82.1	89.2
Aver. housing price	1.242	1.275	1.205	1.218	1.263	1.194
Low-income households						
Aver. housing quantity	55.8	55.8	58.7	54.5	50.5	58.6
Aver. housing price	1.210	1.267	1.095	1.009	1.053	.858
Zonal averages (occupied dwellings)						
Inner-city zone						
Aver. housing quantity	101.6	103.2	110.9	100.9	100.1	108.0
Aver. housing price	1.219	1.296	1.206	1.184	1.220	1.119
Other zones						
Aver. housing quantity	130.4	125.0	130.3	130.8	126.9	133.0
Aver. housing price	1.232	1.278	1.186	1.184	1.247	1.167

Housing stock changes						
New construction (model dwellings)	9	9	5	15	14	10
Withdrawals (model dwellings)	0	0	3	3	2	6
Minority "model" households						
Inner-city zone	5	6	4	1	1	2
Other zones	3	2	3	1	1	0

aIn the high P_n case, capital costs per unit of quantity are raised from $0.72 to $0.77, which raises new-construction costs per unit of quantity from $1.24 to $1.29. In the slow-growth case, the number of end-of-decade model households is reduced from 40 to 33 for Urban Area A and from 42 to 35 for Urban Area B. The number of existing dwellings (before withdrawals or new construction) is 31 in all cases.

bThis is an index of housing quantity. The smallest new dwelling that can be built in conformity with building codes would provide 65.0 units of service per month.

The zonal average prices in the table indicate that the Urban Institute housing model—at least the version we use in this study—does not necessarily yield a price gradient in which inner-city housing prices are higher than housing prices in less accessible portions of urban areas. The relation in the model between inner-city prices and prices elsewhere depends on three sets of zonal characteristics: accessibility, average dwelling quality, and racial composition. Accessibility makes for higher inner-city prices in our model as in theoretical models or urban structures generally; but the other two attributes can work in either direction (as the discussion of Figure 7-2 illustrated in the case of dwelling quality). In the results shown in Table 7-2 the three sets of attributes result more or less in a standoff; average prices differ very little between the inner city and the rest of the urban area.[5]

The final block of figures in Table 7-2 indicates very little change in the pattern of minority household occupancy. Price-structure curves do not permit us to form any expectations about racial occupancy patterns, and it is indeed difficult to make any generalizations about simulation results based on our model. A great deal seems to depend on whether the distribution of demand by minority group households closely matches the distribution of services in a particular zone; the latter, in turn, is quite sensitive to minor variations in the initial conditions of a problem.

A Decline in the Rate of Population Growth

The high rates of growth that characterize the two urban areas analyzed in this study enter the model in the form of a high number of "model" households in the final year of the decade relative to the number of "model" dwellings existing in the initial year. It is easy to simulate lower rates of growth in population by reducing the number of "model" households—from 40 to 33 for Urban Area A and from 43 to 35 for Urban Area B. The same distributions of income by household type are assumed under both sets of growth rates, with the result that average income is almost the same for the rapid-growth and slow-growth cases.

In terms of price-structure curves, low population growth can be thought of as reducing demands in a wide range of submarkets. For middle- and upper-quality housing, where P_n is an effective ceiling to prices of existing dwellings, the critical question about lower growth is whether it reduces demand enough to make the ceiling no longer effective. For moderate declines in growth, such as the cases analyzed here, we would expect the model to yield simply a decline in the number of new dwellings, with very little change in prices of existing dwellings. For drastic reductions in growth, the entire structure of existing housing prices may begin to slip below P_n. For low- and moderate-quality housing, a reduction in demand cannot have very much of its impact in the form of fewer new dwellings, since there are few or no new dwellings to begin with. We would therefore expect the impact of low demand to fall on existing dwellings, pushing down their prices and quantities of services and causing some of them to be withdrawn from the stock. The possibility of withdrawal from stock means that low-income households need not reduce the quantities they consume as prices fall; rather, they can respond to price reductions by moving into higher-quality dwellings and consuming the higher quantities they prefer.

The results shown in Table 7-2 bear out these expectations. For high-income households prices hardly change, while quantities rise slightly in one area and fall in the other, a random variation due to small differences in the distribution of incomes among high-income households. For moderate- and even more for low-income households, however, average prices fall and average quantities rise. The combination of lower prices and higher quantities requires an increase in withdrawals from stock, and this takes place on a large scale in both areas. Geographically, it is especially evident in the inner city, where a significant price reduction causes dwellings to move down along their supply curves; but increased withdrawals at the low end of the quality spectrum nevertheless permit the average quantity of services per occupied dwelling to increase. As in the case of higher new-construction costs, effects on the location of minority households are small and do not provide any basis for generalization.

A Housing Allowance Program

The proposal of housing allowances for low-income households was the impetus for construction of the Urban Institute model, and the policy is currently being tested in a number of urban areas. The allowance simulations reported are in the form of a negative income tax combined with a stipulated minimum level of housing consumption as a condition of receiving an income subsidy. The minimum requirement is the means of inducing households to spend a large proportion of the subsidy on housing rather than on other goods and services.

Subsidies under these plans are equal to the difference (when positive) between 20 percent of gross income and $66.40 for elderly households and single persons and $82.70 for all other family units. The corresponding annual breakeven incomes implied by these schedules are just under $4,000 and $5,000. A tax rate of approximately 1 percent of income, after deducting exemptions, finances the subsidy. In order to receive the subsidy, elderly households and singles must consume at least 54 units of housing services, and all other eligible households must consume at least 65 units. These requirements approximately equal the levels of service which the "guarantee" subsidy levels ($66.40 and $82.70) would buy at the new-construction price per unit of service ($1.24).

In terms of price-structure curves, housing allowances reduce demand for the very poorest quality of housing, increase demand for quantities just above the minimum requirements, and slightly reduce demand (because of the tax) for high-quality housing. The effect on the poorest-quality housing ought to be a decline in price and, hence, an increase in withdrawals, with the final result that very few households may end up actually paying the lower prices.

For housing just above the minimum, results ought to depend critically on the initial price-structure curve. If there is an initial discount for this type of housing, then a housing allowance can cause a significant price increase before households will be induced to move into new dwellings. If there is no initial discount, the price effects could well be much more moderate. The bottom panel of Figure 7-3 depicts the first of these cases, in which a housing allowance causes significant price increases for quantities above the required minimum. For high-quality housing, an allowance program ought to reduce quantities consumed slightly and affect prices very little.

As Table 7-3 indicates, the results of high-income households in the two urban areas show the expected slight decline in quantities and stability in prices. Moderate-income households also experience little change in quantities and prices. For low-income households, however, there is a sharp contrast between the two areas, illustrating the two cases just discussed. In Urban Area *A*, where the supply of existing dwellings is relatively elastic and there is initially very little discount for low-quality housing, a housing allowance causes only a minor increase in prices, and most of the subsidy paid goes into higher quantities of housing services purchased by the recipients. In Urban Area *B*, on the other hand, where there is a substantial discount for low-quality housing in the standard case, an allowance causes sharp price increases for recipients in the housing allowance case. Here, about half of the increased expenditure on housing goes into higher prices, with only the remaining half going into consumption of higher quantities of services.

The figures in the table relating to moderate-income households are of greater interest than their stability might indicate, since one of the questions about housing allowances has been whether they would drive up prices facing households with income just above the eligibility limits. In the cases analyzed in the table, as well as in other cases we have analyzed, the answer is no: price effects of housing allowances are very largely confined to the income range from which eligible households are drawn.

The contrast between the two areas carried over into inner-city changes in housing stock developments. In Area *A*, with little initial price discount, allowances cause a significant shift out of the poorest-quality housing, with the result that average quantity prices for occupied dwellings in the inner city rise and withdrawals increase sharply. In Area *B*, while some existing model dwellings are upgraded, and their prices approach the new-construction price, the price of one dwelling with quantity far below the program minimum is reduced enough to tempt a low-income household to refuse the allowance and occupy an extremely low-rent dwelling. Average prices in the inner city consequently fall in Area *B*, and only one additional dwelling is withdrawn. In neither area is there any effect on racial composition.

In addition to the results shown in Table 7-3, we have analyzed a variety of other housing allowance and income transfer programs for these two cases and a number of others. Our conclusions based on this work include the following:

1. A full-scale housing allowance would, in many locations, significantly increase housing prices by participants.
2. The inflationary danger of a housing allowance varies with background circumstances. It is most severe where prices per unit of housing service initially are especially low relative to new-construction costs—where low-quality housing, in other words, is relatively cheap. The danger is least where prices initially are above new-construction costs.
3. Point 2 notwithstanding, the allowance is most cost-effective in areas with an initial price discount for lower-quality units because existing dwellings there, even after moving up their supply curves, are cheaper than dwellings providing equivalent quantities of services in no-discount areas.
4. Income redistribution without any earmarking for housing would drive up housing prices but by significantly less than allowances.
5. Most of the upward price movement due to a housing allowance affects participants directly. Households above eligibility levels suffer only minor price increases.
6. Price effects of a housing allowance are much greater over a ten-year span than over twenty years.

Table 7-3.   Simulation Results[a] for a Housing Allowance and a Construction Subsidy (prices are in dollars)

Quantities[b] and Prices	Urban Area A (rapid growth, high minority, elastic supply)			Urban Area B (rapid growth, low minority, inelastic supply)		
	Standard Case	Housing Allowance	Construction Subsidy	Standard Case	Housing Allowance	Construction Subsidy
High-income households						
Aver. housing quantity	157.8	157.4	167.3	161.0	159.2	171.3
Aver. housing price	1.236	1.238	1.153	1.241	1.241	1.153
Aver. monthly tax (−) or subsidy (+)	—	−$10	−$10	—	−$10	−$10
Moderate-income households						
Aver. housing quantity	89.2	88.8	97.0	86.3	86.9	91.3
Aver. housing price	1.242	1.238	1.142	1.218	1.235	1.108
Aver. monthly tax (−) or subsidy (+)	—	−$3	−$3	—	−$3	−$3
Low-income households						
Aver. housing quantity	55.8	66.4	62.0	54.5	60.9	59.1
Aver. housing price	1.210	1.259	1.003	1.009	1.154	0.819
Aver. monthly tax (−) or subsidy (+)	—	$31	0	—	+$27	0
Participation rate	—	100%	—	—	88%	—
Zonal averages						
Inner-city zone						
Aver. housing quantity	101.6	114.0	104.9	100.9	99.1	104.5
Aver. housing price	1.219	1.246	1.149	1.184	1.123	1.067
Other zones						
Aver. housing quantity	130.4	130.1	132.1	130.8	134.1	135.2
Aver. housing price	1.232	1.240	1.135	1.184	1.240	1.087

Housing stock changes					
New construction (model dwellings)	9	12	14	15	16	17
Withdrawals (model dwellings)	0	3	5	3	4	5
Minority "model" households					
Inner-city zone	5	5	6	1	1	1
Other zones	3	3	2	1	1	1

aThe housing allowance program pays the difference (when positive) between $82.70 (for nonelderly families) or (for other households) $66.40 and 20 percent of monthly income, subject to a minimum housing consumption requirement (see text). The new-construction subsidy lowers P_n from 1.24 to 1.15. It does not affect capital costs for improvement of existing dwellings. Both programs are financed by a tax equal to 1 percent of monthly income less $213 for nonelderly families and 1 percent of monthly income less $92 for other households.

bSee Table 7-2, note b.

This last point is particularly worth emphasizing.[6] The structure of the model implies that the price effects of housing policies should become less severe as time passes. The reason is basically that the longer the time span the more elastic the supply of housing. A price that causes the services from an existing dwelling to decline by 10 percent in one decade will cause services to decline by approximately 20 percent in two decades; conversely, a price causing a rise in services by 10 percent in one decade will cause a rise of about 20 percent in two decades. Furthermore, the longer the time span under consideration, the larger generally will be the share accounted for by new construction, the supply of which is assumed to be perfectly elastic. Our simulation results suggest that ten years is too short a period in which to attain the highly elastic response to housing subsidies we would eventually expect, but twenty years' time suffices.

A New-Construction Subsidy

The policy of a supply subsidy to all newly constructed dwellings corresponds to what is often called the "filtering" strategy of encouraging high levels of new-housing starts with the expectation that these will eventually benefit occupants of existing housing through a chain of moves.

The specific policy is one which lowers the price of new dwellings from $1.24 to $1.15 per unit of housing service. The subsidy is financed out of general income taxes; the tax rate is identical to the one used to finance the full-scale housing allowance just discussed. This identity of tax rates and hence of program costs facilitates comparison between the two policies.

In terms of price structure we would expect a new-construction subsidy to have effects in many respects just opposite to those of an increase in new-housing costs. In the portion of the price-structure curve where the new-construction price is the effective ceiling, prices of existing dwellings should decline by roughly the amount of the subsidy. At these lower prices the demand for relatively good quality housing should shift upward (the tax to finance the subsidy will moderate but not eliminate this shift), with a corresponding downward shift in the demand for low-quality dwellings. The downward shift should in turn cause prices of low-quality dwellings to fall and withdrawals to increase.

In our two urban areas, as Table 7-3 shows, the decline in prices facing high-income households closely matches the depth of the subsidy, while the price decrease for low-income households is nearly twice as large. Low-income households are thus major, if indirect, beneficiaries of the construction subsidy.

Like housing allowances, construction subsidies lead to increasing withdrawals from the housing stock. For those existing dwellings not withdrawn from the stock, however, construction subsidies lead to declines in prices and services provided, while housing allowances generally lead to increases in both factors. The zonal averages in Table 7-3 illustrate the contrast in prices, although they mask the contrast in quantities because of differences in withdrawals and new construction between the two policies.

The household utility function underlying the model provides a way of summarizing costs and benefits of the two programs to different groups of the population. Using the utility function, it is possible to calculate an average change in monthly income (positive or negative) equivalent to each policy for each of the three groups of households distinguished in Table 7-3, taking account not only of taxes and transfers but of market effects as well. These "cash equivalents" are in simple cases closely related to consumer surpluses. In some more complex cases, as when minimum participation requirements push households off their demand curves, the cash equivalents remain operative, whereas measures of consumer surplus do not.

There are serious conceptual problems in any such calculation of a "cash equivalent" of a given policy even for a single household, let alone a group of households. Nevertheless, the comparison among households of differing incomes seems interesting enough to warrant presenting the results shown in Table 7-4. The income definitions are the same as those used in Table 7-3; households labeled low income are those eligible for the housing allowance; moderate income, those with incomes between 100 and 150 percent of eligibility; and high income, all other households.

Two principal conclusions are suggested by the data in Table 7-4. The first, hardly a surprise, is that housing allowances are of more benefit to low-income households and of greater cost to the other two groups of households than new-construction subsidies. Thus, in the first column, a housing allowance policy is the equivalent of a $26 increase in monthly income for the average low-income household, while a new-construction subsidy is the equivalent of only $5 per month. For the average moderate-income household, the allowance is the equivalent of a $2 decrease in monthly income, while the construction subsidy is the equivalent of a $5 increase. For middle-to-high income households both policies are equivalent to decreases in average income, with a greater decrease for the allowance plan (−$10) than for the new-construction subsidy (−$3).

The second, and perhaps unexpected, conclusion is that both policies in effect redistribute income from high-income to low-

Table 7-4.   Cash Equivalence of Two Housing Policies (dollars per household per month)

	Urban Area A (rapid growth, high minority, elastic supply)	Urban Area B (rapid growth, low minority, inelastic supply)
Low-income households (eligible for allowance)		
Full-scale allowance	+26	+16
New-construction subsidy	+5	+14
Moderate-income households (near-eligible for allowance)		
Full-scale allowance	−2	−3
New-construction subsidy	+5	+2
Middle- to high-income households		
Full-scale allowance	−10	−4
New-construction subsidy	−3	−4

Note: The "cash equivalent" figures in this table are derived from individual household utility levels before and after the introduction of each policy, which is carried out in three steps. The first step is the translation of utility changes for each household into income or cash equivalent changes. In this step prices and certain other market variables are held constant at an average of their no-policy and policy levels. The second step is the averaging of cash equivalent changes over groups of households. The third step is the correction of the group averages in step 2 so that their average over all households for any one city and policy equals zero. The correction is accomplished by adjusting each group average cash equivalent by the same fraction of group average income. Essentially, this correction is a way of distributing the increased profits on existing dwellings in the case of a housing allowance and the reduced profits on existing dwellings in the case of a new-construction subsidy. The distribution of profits in both cases is assumed to be proportional to group average income. While this assumption is plausible, it has not been tested, nor is the restriction that cash equivalents average to zero the result of any empirical or theoretical work.

income households. That a housing allowance works out that way is not of course surprising, but that a new-construction subsidy should have that effect is something of a surprise. The reason for the result is the close substitution in demand between new and existing dwellings. Although the direct price subsidy goes only to occupants of new dwellings—and their incomes are well above the average—the indirect price effects of the subsidy extend the benefits to low-income households. Taxes to finance the subsidy are paid by high-income and "near-eligible" households, and not by low-income households.

Some caveats are in order with respect to this final result. A different tax structure could of course substantially alter the progressivity of either program. Furthermore, while the calculations in the table take detailed account of market changes as they affect housing consumption, they deal only crudely, as the note to the table indicates, with the feedback of market changes to income via changes in landlord and homeowner profits. Nevertheless, the comparisons in the table are of some value in themselves and perhaps even more valuable as an indication of the potential of the model in comparing costs and benefits of a wide range of housing programs to different groups of households.

THE RELIABILITY OF RESULTS

The aim of the Urban Institute housing model has been to quantify the broad interrelations among sectors of a metropolitan housing market. Without such quantification there is invariably a great deal of uncertainty about the effects of housing and land-use policies, including housing allowances, construction subsidies, restrictive zoning, and urban renewal. But while quantification is highly desirable, a detailed tracing of all linkages, short run and long, among the many neighborhoods and structural types of a large metropolitan area would be an enormously complex and expensive undertaking. The model has therefore focused on "broad" interrelations, restricting itself to five or six geographic zones, a single quantitative index of physical housing services for each of a few dozen model dwellings, and a small number of parameters expressing the behavior of households and owners.

There are two ways of looking at the model that may be helpful in judging how well it meets our objective. The first is a brief listing of its principal strengths and weaknesses. The second is a capsule summary of its essential structural features—an attempt to answer the question, What ingredients of a model are necessary to obtain policy results like the ones in this study?

On the strengths and limitations of the model, three strong points deserve special emphasis. First, the model is grounded in a well-developed theory of housing market behavior. Because of its relatively tight theoretical framework, the model is rich in the range of empirical information that can be related to it and of exogenous developments or behavioral changes it can analyze. Further, model solutions, while obtained through a fairly complex and not always automatic algorithm, can be understood and analyzed quite easily through graphic devices such as new-housing indifference curves and price-structure curves.

The second point has to do with validation. The model has been fitted to six metropolitan areas displaying a wide variety of housing conditions and has produced a distinct clustering of most of the major estimated parameters. The results for all six areas as a group have been analyzed for the sensitivity of the errors of fit to slight changes in the parameters. Only for the parameters measuring the supply behavior of the existing stock does the range of uncertainty remain large enough to have important policy implications. For the six areas to which it has been applied, the model is a distinct improvement over a simpler model in which housing depreciates at a fixed rate and neighborhood effects are ignored. In addition, the model has performed respectably when used to predict 1970 market outcomes for one area on the basis of parametric values obtained by applying the model to other areas. On balance, the present model has received much more extensive empirical testing than other existing urban models.

The third strong point is that the model is capable of analyzing a broad range of detailed policy changes. Many of the qualitative policy implications derived from the model hold up under a range of initial conditions, but the variation is often systematic and the results suggest broad generalizations about the effects of housing policies in different markets. The model should generate many ideas about the consequences of housing policies and the design of optimal policies, especially if the range of uncertainty about supply behavior is narrowed.

Regarding limitations, four points deserve some emphasis. First, the model is restricted to ten-year intervals and in fact in work so far, to the single ten-year interval 1960-1970. Much public concern over the market effects of housing policies relates to periods shorter than ten years; but the model conveys no information about the annual or monthly path from the initial position to its ten-year results. Much could be done by way of applications to urban areas outside the United States, time spans other than a decade, and historical periods other than the 1960s.

A second limitation is that the model is too aggregative to serve as a reliable predictor of the detailed consequences of policy changes or exogenous developments for particular zones or household groupings. For example, because the number of model dwellings and households means is small, only restricted confidence can be placed in the spatial shifts of minorities associated with the introduction of housing subsidy policies. Policy implications by broad groupings— high-quality versus low-quality housing, central city versus suburb, or rich versus poor households—are probably the finest level of detail for which serious attention to model results is warranted.

Less obvious than these points are the third and fourth limitations of the model, arising from its restricted range of behavior. On the household side, behavior consists of choosing between housing and other goods and among various housing submarkets. The possible effects of housing allowances and other housing policies on work incentives or family formation are ignored. Furthermore, it does not deal with noncompliance with policy regulations or with "noneconomic" influences on household responses—for example, psychological reasons that might lead a household to decline participation in an allowance program even if it stands to gain economically by enrolling.

On the business side, the model is restricted to markets for new and existing housing. There is no treatment of the basic determinants of land costs, although an extension of the basic model does contain implications about the effects of housing programs on relative land costs in different portions of a metropolitan area, given the overall average cost of land for new construction. Nor is there any treatment of markets for other inputs into housing services, such as maintenance, labor, or construction materials, or of the feedback of market changes to the distribution of household incomes.

We conclude with a list of "essential features of the model" which, taken together, imply a theory of urban housing markets with implications resembling, at least qualitatively, the simulation results presented in this paper. Of the seven features listed below, some are bases for classifying or disaggregating the housing stock, some are historical characteristics of metropolitan areas, and some are empirical values of key parameters. The seven features are these:

1. *Market segmentation*—the segmentation of a metropolitan housing market into submarkets defined by location and quantity of services.
2. *Imperfect substitution*—the empirical finding that these submarkets are close but not perfect substitutes in demand, the imperfection being due both to strong preferences regarding quality level and to strong neighborhood effects.
3. *Durability*—the separation of housing supply into new and existing supply, with the latter accounting for most of the supply even in a ten-year span.
4. *Elastic new supply*—the assumption, based on past empirical work, that the supply of new housing is extremely elastic in a period as long as ten years.
5. *Inelastic existing supply*—the empirical finding that the supply of housing services produced from existing dwellings is far from perfectly elastic over a ten-year span.

6. *Supply trends*—the empirical finding that at stable (over time) relative prices, existing dwellings change their level of services very slowly.
7. *Demand trends*—the historical fact of growth of real income per household over time in almost every metropolitan area (but great variation among areas in growth of population).

The presence of market segmentation makes it possible for prices to differ in various sectors of the market and for policies to have heavier impacts on some submarkets than on others. Differential prices, however, also require the presence of imperfect substitutability in demand and inelastic supply of at least some portion of the stock. Without these additional conditions, responses to price signals by households and suppliers would work to eliminate price variations. Thus, the next four characteristics are all also necessary conditions for differential policy impact in different segments of the market.

The last two factors are responsible for the normal excess demand for high-quality units, which is met by new construction, and the more variable outcome at the low end of the quality spectrum, with price discounts under some conditions but not under others. These determinants of price structure in turn govern the differences among submarkets and among metropolitan areas in the impact of housing policies. Judgments about the reliability of the policy results in this study (at least as to the direction and general magnitude) should depend on how well these seven features of the model are thought to constitute an accurate characterization of urban housing markets.

Our own judgment is that the estimates are the best currently available and that they are reliable enough to merit serious consideration in discussions of housing policies, at least as to direction and general magnitude. We are aware, of course, of the value of more testing and research. But we feel that further exploration of the "space" of policies, city types, and parametric estimates should be encouraged along with developmental work. Even the present model, we feel, can be exploited to suggest a great deal about the possible consequences of alternative housing subsidy forms, land-use policies, mixed policy strategies, least-cost ways of achieving policy goals, and a number of other matters that go well beyond the results in this study.

NOTES TO CHAPTER SEVEN

1. Pioneering studies of the income concept appropriate to housing demand are those of Muth (1960) and Reid (1962). The proposition that a single year is

much too short for measuring the effect of income on housing demand, strongly supported by these two studies, is by now generally accepted even though controversy about other aspects of housing demand continues.

2. Ann Schnare has developed a version of the model in which the assumption of a single zone of new construction is dropped and new dwellings are allocated geographically.

3. A detailed justification of functional forms chosen and an analysis of their mathematical properties will be found in de Leeuw and Struyk (1976).

4. In an expanded version of the model developed by Ann Schnare (but not used here) money costs of transportation as well as housing expenditures are deducted from model income.

5. The standoff, however, is apparently sensitive to our simplifying assumption that all new dwellings are located in a single, relatively inaccessible "zone of new construction." In a version of the model developed by Ann Schnare in which this assumption is dropped, there is a much more pronounced tendency toward above-average prices in the central city.

6. To simulate the model for two decades, model dwellings occupied at the end of the first decade become the existing stock for the second decade. Model households for the second decade are derived by extrapolating growth rates in population and average income.

REFERENCES

de Leeuw, F., and R. Struyk. 1976. *The Web of Urban Housing.* Washington, D.C.: The Urban Institute.

Muth, R.F. 1960. "The Demand for Nonfarm Housing." In *The Demand for Durable Goods,* edited by A. Harberger. Chicago: University of Chicago Press.

Reid, M. 1962. *Housing and Income.* Chicago: University of Chicago Press.

Comments on Chapter Seven

Edwin S. Mills

This is an important study. The Urban Institute housing model is as imaginative, elaborate, careful, and sophisticated as any extant urban model. This study reports on use of the model for some painstaking analysis of government housing policies and of changes in other exogenous variables in the model. The policy analysis is as carefully done as any I have seen with an urban model, and is much more carefully done than most policy analysis in any substantive specialty in economics.

No one interested in the housing problems of the poor can fail to be instructed by the simulations of the effects of housing allowances and construction subsidies. They shed light on those issues that have been important in the debate about government housing policy: the extent to which a subsidy for construction of new houses might improve low-income housing by the filtering down process; the extent to which housing allowances might result in more expensive rather than better housing for recipients; and the effect of housing allowances on housing costs of those not eligible for the allowances.

But suppose I ask myself how this study affects my views about government housing policies, or how it might have affected my views if the numbers had been different but still consistent with the underlying model. I want to defend the conclusion that it is unlikely that these simulations will tell us anything that will affect our views about housing policies.

The most fundamental question that can be asked about government housing programs is: Why have them? More specifically, suppose the decision has been made to redistribute income by taxing the nonpoor and using the money to benefit the poor. Why do it through housing programs rather than by a negative income tax or some other cash grant? There is nothing here that would justify use of housing programs to redistribute income. The reason for redistribution via housing programs is presumably the existence of an external economy or neighborhood effect from housing consumption. But no such externality is mentioned. That is to say, if we calculate the sum of gains and losses in consumer surplus from the housing allowance (or the construction subsidy) and the taxes to pay for them, the sum must be negative. In this model, housing subsidies either create or widen gaps between prices and costs whose equality is necessary for efficient allocation of housing resources. Whether one ought to favor housing programs or cash grants to redistribute income depends on the existence or nonexistence of market failure in housing, not on details about how elastic housing supply is to low-income people. Yet the paper concentrates entirely on the latter kind of issue and says nothing about the former.

Next, suppose that it has been decided, on grounds not discussed in the study, to redistribute income by housing programs. How might the simulations affect my views as to the choice between a housing allowance and a construction subsidy. It seems to me that simple economic common sense tells us that the housing allowance is to be preferred. A construction subsidy benefits the poor only indirectly in that new housing in the model (and in reality, except for public housing) is constructed only for the nonpoor and the poor benefit by acceleration of the filtering down process. The housing allowance, however, goes directly to the poor. Only if the housing allowance is badly designed, for example, by forcing the poor to consume much more housing than they want, could a construction subsidy benefit them more than a subsidy provided to them directly. Any model that suggested otherwise would be suspect. In fact, this one does not. Table 7-4 shows that, dollar for dollar, the poor benefit more from the housing allowance than from the construction subsidy. It is hard to imagine a simulation that would change my belief that the poor will benefit more from a dollar spent on a housing allowance than from a dollar spent subsidizing new construction.

Of course, the numbers are nevertheless interesting. Even though the poor benefit less from a construction subsidy than from an equally costly housing allowance, the nonpoor are likely to prefer the construction subsidy since they receive some benefit from the program. This is certainly important to officials who must face the electorate, but it is also a kind of information the political process is likely to bring to their attention forcefully.

In conclusion, I feel that the simulations are very interesting, but that they do not, and probably could not, change my mind on important matters.

Chapter Eight

The Production of Housing Services from Existing Dwelling Units

Gregory K. Ingram and
Yitzhak Oron

INTRODUCTION

Despite the fact that the bulk of housing services in urban areas is provided by existing dwelling units, our empirical and theoretical understanding of how existing dwelling units are operated over time to produce housing services is meager. Early analyses of this topic focused on the change in quality or in relative quality ranking of existing dwelling units. This change, termed filtering, is typically represented in early studies as a reduced form combination of supply and demand behavior (Lowry 1960; Smith 1964). Recently, models that more fully specify the supply and demand side of the market for existing units have been developed, some of which use simulation techniques to represent the supply and demand decisions of housing producers and households (de Leeuw 1972) while others apply the optimal control theory approach (Sweeney 1974).

An alternative model of the housing market's supply side focuses not on the production of housing services from combinations of existing units and operating inputs, but on the production of dwelling units from combinations of land and capital. Partial empirical tests of that model have been made by examining residential

Note: This study is based on research funded by the Department of Housing and Urban Development under contract H-1843 to the Urban Studies Group of the National Bureau of Economic Research. The authors wish to thank their colleagues in the group for many thoughtful comments. In particular, John F. Kain made extensive comments on an early draft, and William Apgar and Herman Leonard helped clarify several conceptual issues.

density gradients in urban areas (Muth 1969; Mills 1970). That model is used to analyze long-run investments in housing stocks, whereas our concern in this study is with the shorter-run operations of existing units.

The model presented here differs from most other analyses of the supply side of the housing market in its treatment of housing services produced by existing units. The model allows more than one structure type; and existing housing capital as well as housing outputs are assumed to be structure-type-specific. In addition, substitution between housing capital and operating inputs is incorporated in the production of structure quality. This approach can be contrasted with other recent work on housing supply that either treats housing capital as homogeneous or does not allow for substitution between capital and operating inputs (de Leeuw 1972; Sweeney 1974).

The model's major focus in on how housing producers operate existing dwelling units to produce housing services. Existing units are described in terms of three summary characteristics—structure quality, structure type, and neighborhood quality—that differ by mode of production or supply elasticity. The production of structure quality is treated in terms that parallel the choice of optimal plant size in the theory of the firm, and structure quality is produced by heterogeneous capital and operating inputs. Decisions about structure type follow the usual assumptions of investment theory. Neighborhood quality is assumed to be a local public good not produced by housing entrepreneurs. The model also includes some determinants of supply response, such as cash flow constraints, that may have significant impacts upon short-run adjustments in the housing market.

The analytic framework of the model is outlined and estimates of the supply parameters are given. Numerical experiments are performed with the supply model to determine likely values for the magnitude and duration of the increases in short-run average costs of structure quality that might accompany a housing market policy, such as a housing allowance, that suddenly increased the demand for structure quality. The supply model is combined with a demand model in a primitive market-clearing framework, and several comparative static equilibrium sensitivity analyses of model parameters are carried out. Appendix 8A contains a brief description of the estimation of the elasticity of substitution between capital and operating inputs in the production of structure quality.

CHARACTERIZATION OF HOUSING PRODUCTION

In this model, housing is a composite of several characteristics, and dwelling units are available with specific combinations of these characteristics. We define the housing services produced by dwelling units in terms of their characteristics as:

$$\text{Housing services}_s = (Q_s, N, A)$$

where Q_s is the quality of structure services produced by a unit of structure type s; N is the quality of the neighborhood of the unit; and A is the accessibility of the unit. The rents for particular dwelling units are determined by all three characteristics; but for existing units, only Q_s, the structure quality, can be varied. In this analysis we ignore accessibility and incorporate neighborhood quality to the extent that it affects the production of structure quality. We focus on the supply of structure quality, the one characteristic of existing units that is under the control of housing producers.

Structure services are produced from three components—land, capital, and operating inputs—which differ significantly in their durability. At the extremes, land is infinitely durable, and operating inputs are completely consumed during production. The capital that is used to produce structure quality has a range of durabilities. Many basic capital components of a dwelling unit are very durable, while the interior finish of a unit, its mechanical subsystems, and many of its exterior features have relatively short lives. Although an average depreciation rate can be calculated for the capital in a given dwelling unit, that rate is a function of the mix of capital stocks in the unit. It is apparent that a variation of the index number problem exists for the representation of housing capital depreciation.[1]

Besides having a variety of durabilities, the capital in a dwelling unit also differs in terms of its substitutability in the production process that yields structure quality. Structure quality is subscripted by structure type, and we assume some minimum stock and configuration of capital is required in order to produce structure quality of a particular structure type. Minimum stock includes the unit's foundation and shell, and is essentially an entry requirement on the supply side. Once this minimum stock is available, a housing producer can produce structure quality with operating inputs and additional capital. This restriction on production can be summarized as

$$Q_s = \begin{cases} \text{zero}; KT_s < C_s \\ \\ f(K_s, O); KT_s > C_s \end{cases}$$

where C_s is the minimum stock of capital required for the production of structure quality of structure type s, O represents operating inputs, and KT is a unit's total capital.

Categorizing a dwelling unit's capital in terms of its durability and substitutability in the production of structure quality is an interesting topic for research, but one we will not pursue here. Instead, we assume that a dwelling unit's capital can be separated into two categories, as we have done in the foregoing equation. The first category, termed "structure capital," or C_s, is extremely durable and has an (assumed) depreciation rate of zero. The second category, termed "quality capital," or K_s, is the capital required for the production of structure quality of structure type s. Quality capital is not very durable; it depreciates at an annual rate, d; and it can be changed readily by incremental investment, termed "maintenance" (M). Structure capital will not affect the production of quality by existing units and will only be a factor in decisions about new construction or the conversion of a unit from one structure type to another. This categorization of a dwelling unit's capital implies that its depreciation rate, averaged over both capital categories, increases with the level of structure quality the unit produces.

Within this framework we assume that housing producers operate individual dwelling units and try to maximize their profits. During each time period they pick a level of operating inputs for their unit, determine the expenditure on maintenance, and calculate whether it would pay them to alter the structure type of their unit. We assume that in making these decisions, the housing producer is familiar with the operating requirements and debt structure of his building; that he knows the prices of the inputs he uses; and that he has well-defined expectations about the structure of rents in his neighborhood and the way in which rents would vary with the quality of his unit.

In many respects the model we set forth parallels the analysis of optimal plant size in the theory of the firm. In our model the dwelling unit is the "plant," and the housing producer must invest or disinvest in this plant over time so that he produces his "output," dwelling unit quality, in a least-cost way. In addition, housing producers can have different kinds of plants (structure type) and buy and sell in different markets (neighborhoods).

ANALYTICS OF THE SUPPLY MODEL

Time in this model is treated as a series of discrete periods of one year's duration. We assume the housing producer revises his operating strategy at the beginning of each time period on a contracting or market day. At this time he makes three decisions. The first deals with the level of quality he will produce this period and how to do it. The second involves the amount he will invest in the building this period. The third is whether he should transform his unit into some other structure type. We consider each of these decisions in turn.

The Current-Period Operating Decision
During the current period the housing producer's unit has a stock of quality capital, K_t, embodied in it (for clarity, the subscript for structure type is omitted). We assume that any maintenance expenditure this period will not alter the stock of capital until the next period, so K_t is fixed in the current period. In addition, we assume that rental receipts and expenditures on operating inputs are concurrent, with the result that no within-period discounting is required. These two assumptions let us separate the housing producer's choice of operating inputs from his choice of maintenance expenditures in the current period.

The housing producer's opportunities for producing structure quality with various combinations of operating inputs, O_t, and quality capital, K_t, are summarized in a production function,

$$Q_t = f(O_t, K_t) \qquad (8\text{-}1)$$

where Q_t is the level of structure quality produced in period t. In addition, the housing producer knows how gross rents will vary with structure quality for his unit, and he knows P_o, the price per unit of operating inputs. Since K_t, the unit's stock of quality capital, is fixed for the current period, the housing producer chooses operating inputs to maximize his short-run profits or cash flow, defined as the difference between gross rents and expenditures on operating inputs. The solution involves the usual first-order conditions:

$$\frac{dR(O; K, t)}{dO} = P_o \qquad (8\text{-}2)$$

where $R(O; K, t)$ is the relation between gross rents and operating inputs obtained by substituting the production function in Equation (8-1) into the relation between gross rents and quality which is known to the housing producer.

The Current-Period Maintenance Decision

The current-period maintenance or investment decision is more complicated than the choice of operating inputs because maintenance expenditures made this period will affect the stock of quality capital of the unit in subsequent periods.[2] Moreover, there are constraints on the rate at which a housing producer can alter the stock of quality capital in his unit. We assume, for example, that maintenance must be non-negative: the housing producer cannot reduce his stock of quality capital at a pace that exceeds the rate of depreciation. In addition, if a housing producer wants to purchase maintenance inputs in amounts that exceed his cash flow, he must pay a higher interest rate than the opportunity cost of his cash flow, a requirement that will tend to reduce his rate of investment. Given these constraints, the housing producer's objective is to pick a maintenance and operating input stream that maximizes the present value of his net revenues. This objective can be stated as

$$\text{maximize} \sum_{t=0}^{\infty} (R_t - P_o O_t - P_m M_t - F_t) \frac{1}{(1+r)^t} \qquad (8\text{-}3)$$

subject to the production function for quality and the accounting relation for capital, maintenance, and depreciation:

$$K_{t+1} = K_t - dK_t + M_t \qquad (8\text{-}4)$$

In Equation (8-3), R_t is the gross rent of the unit, P_m is the price per unit of maintenance, F_t are the fixed costs exclusive of financing, and r is the interest rate. If the relation between rents and dwelling unit quality is known over time, a housing producer can calculate his optimal time path for maintenance and operating inputs within the framework of optimal control theory.[3] However, this supply model does not follow the formal optimal control procedure, but rather represents the housing producer's decision about maintenance in a simpler framework.

The major simplification we make is to relax the assumption that a housing producer has perfect knowledge of the relation between rents and quality over time. Instead, we assume he has an expectation about that relation over a planning interval of five periods. After that time, he projects a relation between rents and quality that does not change. This simplification is based on the premise that housing producers have some knowledge or expectation about how prices in their neighborhood will be changing over the next few periods, and what the relation bween rent and quality is likely to be after these changes have occurred. Beyond his planning interval, however, a housing producer's information about prices is poor, and he merely projects his expectations for the fifth year into the future without change.

This assumption about housing producers' price expectations fixes the relation between rents and quality in future periods. By making this relation fixed or stationary beyond the planning interval, we can derive the optimal stock of quality capital that corresponds to the future stationary state without using optimal control techniques, and then choose a maintenance policy that will move the dwelling unit toward the optimal capital stock. This approach may correspond more closely to the way in which housing producers actually behave while still being closely related to the behavior implicit in the optimal control theory representation.

In the stationary state, where the expected relation between rent and quality, the production function, and the input prices do not change, the landlord's choice of O_t, M_t, and K_t will also be unchanging. This stationarity assumption implies, therefore, that maintenance inputs exactly offset depreciation losses. Furthermore, with the stationarity assumption, the optimal stock of quality capital satisfies the usual first-order condition,

$$\frac{d(R - P_o O)}{dK} = P_k \tag{8-5}$$

where P_k is the price of a unit of quality capital for one period, essentially the price of a capital *flow*. Since maintenance inputs augment the stock of quality capital, we know that the price for a unit of quality capital *stock* is P_m. If we keep the unit of capital for one period, we must pay the going rate of interest on the capital, r. In addition, we have assumed that quality capital depreciates at a constant rate, d, during each period. Hence, to keep a unit of quality capital for one period, a landlord must pay $P_m r$ in interest and $P_m d$ in depreciation. The one-period price of quality capital is therefore $P_m(r + d)$, and this is the price that must satisfy the first-order conditions in Equation (8-5). By combining the first-order conditions in Equations (8-5) and (8-2) with the production function in Equation (8-1), we can derive the optimal stock of quality capital, the optimal fow of operating inputs, and the optimal quality level to be produced at the end of the planning interval.

Having determined the optimal capital stock in the future stationary state, we now turn to the maintenance decision. Each dwelling unit has an existing stock of quality capital, K_t, and the unit's maintenance policy should lead to the optimal capital stock, K^*, during the planning interval. Let us consider first a situation in which a unit's current stock of quality capital exceeds its optimal level. Since we have assumed that maintenance inputs cannot be negative, the unit's stock of quality capital cannot be reduced more rapidly than the depreciation rate. That is, over the planning interval of T periods, no maintenance inputs will be purchased this period if

$$\frac{K_t}{(1 + d)^T} \geqslant K^* \tag{8-6}$$

for in that case the purchase of maintenace inputs would slow the rate at which the optimal level of capital stock is approached. If Equation (8-6) does not apply, then some maintenance inputs will be provided over the planning interval. In that case, the housing producer determines what the most efficient stock of capital would be for the quality level he has decided to produce during the current period, and he attempts to move to that capital stock by the next time period. If the most efficient stock of capital for quality level L is $K^e(L)$, a housing producer who is producing L this period will have a desired level of maintenance,

$$M = K^e(L) - K_t(1 - d) \tag{8-7}$$

Since the most efficient capital stock for any quality level is a function of the interest rate, the desired maintenance will also be a function of the interest rate. In our discussion thus far we have used r as the interest rate, implicitly assuming that this rate is r_g, the opportunity cost of internally generated funds. This assumption will hold in the stationary state if the building is viable. When a housing producer is adjusting his stock of quality capital in the short run, however, maintenance expenditures may exceed cash flow for one or more periods. We assume that there is an external interest rate, r_x, greater than r_g, at which additional funds can be borrowed.[4] In the short run, therefore, a housing producer's interest rate is related to his cash flow, and his supply curve of funds resembles S, shown in Figure 8-1, where CF is available cash flow. This available cash is gross rents less expenditures on operating inputs and other fixed obligations such as taxes. Since fixed costs can vary, otherwise similar units may have different cash flows. Desired maintenance expenditures can be represented as a demand curve on Figure 8-1, and curves M_1, M_2, and M_3 illustrate possible outcomes.

Another constraint on the level of current maintenance expenditures is its consistency with the optimal capital stock at the end of the planning interval. That is, the maintenance for the current period, M_t, must satisfy the condition

$$K_0(1-d)^T + M_t(1-d)^{T-1} \leqslant K* \tag{8-8}$$

Of course, when the housing producer's decision on maintenance is made within a dynamic framework, the end of the planning interval is never attained. During each time period the planning interval covers the next T periods. This rolling interval is merely a device that lets us represent the more distant future, when expectations are poorly defined, as a stationary state. In each current period the housing producer reformulates his operating and maintenance strategy.

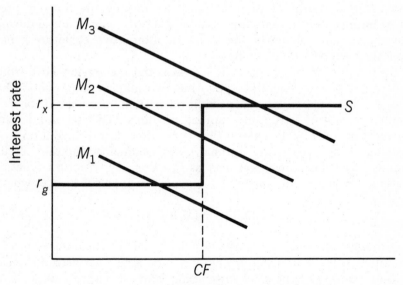

Figure 8-1. Interest Rates, Cash Flow, and Current-Period Maintenance Decisions.

The Structure-Type Decision

The housing producer's decisions about operating inputs and maintenance are conditional on his decision concerning the structure type of his unit. We consider the structure type decision last because its prerequisites are the current period's optimal operating and maintenance decisions. We assume that a housing producer decides to convert a unit from one structure type to another by comparing the value of alternative types with the value of the current type and its conversion cost. In this case, the value of a unit, V, is equal to the discounted sum of net revenues from the unit, or

$$V = \sum_{t=0}^{\infty} (R_t - P_o O_t - P_m M_t - F_t)\frac{1}{(1 + r)^t} \tag{8-9}$$

where F denotes fixed costs associated with the unit exclusive of financing costs. In order to calculate the maximum value of a unit, the optimal maintenance and operating strategy must be determined. This is required for the structure type the housing producer has now, as well as for alternative types he considers. For his existing unit, the housing producer determines his expected net revenues during the planning interval and during the postplanning-interval stationary state. For alternative structure types, we assume the housing producer immediately attains the optimal level of quality capital during conversion and calculates the value of alternative structure types from their expected net revenues.

Abstracting from changes in lot size, the conversion cost from structure type i to structure type j has two major components: The first is the expenditure for additional structure capital or for removing existing structure capital, or both. The second is the expenditure on quality capital that is required to produce a unit of structure type j with the optimal stock of quality capital. Let us denote this total conversion cost as C_{ij}. For all j structure types, a housing producer will convert from type i to type j if $Z_j > 0$, where

$$Z_j = \max_j [V_j - (V_i + C_{ij})] \tag{8-10}$$

Although we will not consider it in detail in the model, at any instant in time, a housing producer will be able to construct a new unit of structure type j by purchasing land, structure capital, and quality capital. If we represent the cost of new construction by NC_j, then construction will occur if

$$V_j > NC_j \tag{8-11}$$

and NC_j will ultimately limit V_j. Of course, NC_j will vary over time if land prices or the optimal quality level of a unit change. The costs of conversion and new construction can limit possible values of V_i and V_j, but many combinations of the two will produce neither structure-type conversions nor new construction.

Change in Neighborhood Quality

We assume that housing producers do not have direct control over the production of neighborhood quality. They may have expectations about how neighborhood quality will change over time, however, and these expectations might influence their behavior. For the moment we will not specify precisely the determinants of neighborhood quality, although it is undoubtedly some amalgam of the characteristics of dwelling units and households in an area. At this point we will merely assume that neighborhood quality is a neighborhood-specific public good.

SPECIFYING THE SUPPLY MODEL

In this section we specify the dimensions and parameters of a housing supply model that incorporates many of the features described in the previous sections. For the sake of simplicity the model employs only two levels of neighborhood quality and two structure types. Input prices vary by neighborhood, and the production function for quality varies by structure type. Dwelling unit quality can be produced at eight possible levels; so its representation is more continuous than neighborhood quality or structure type.

Although the supply model includes neighborhoods, it does not include location in this simple version. The model can be envisioned as representing the housing market in a metropolitan area that has been stratified into zones according to neighborhood quality level. The model refers to aggregates of zones of each quality level and otherwise ignores the location of particular units.

Since the major goal of the supply model is to represent the operation of existing units, the construction of new units and the conversion from one structure type to another are not endogenous. Accordingly, the major parameters that must be determined in the supply model are those in the production function for structure quality. The data for determining these parameters are not as good as we would like, but the available data do permit us to obtain reasonable estimates of parameter values. We obtain production function parameters for two structure types: a high-rise elevator building and a small multiple unit building.

A CES (constant elasticity of substitution) production function is employed. This is flexible, yet simple, with properties that are attractive for representing the production of structure quality. Using K for quality capital, O for operation inputs, and Q for structure quality, the CES function is

$$Q = A[\alpha K^{-\beta} + (1-\alpha)O^{-\beta}]^{-1/\beta} \qquad (8\text{-}12)$$

in the case of constant returns to scale. The parameters of this function are A, the scaling or efficiency factor; α, the distribution factor; and β, the substitution factor, which determines $1/(\beta + 1)$, the elasticity of substitution between the factor inputs.

The Elasticity of Substitution

The elasticity of substitution between operating inputs and quality capital can be estimated by regressing the log of the ratio of dwelling unit quality to operating inputs on the log of the ratio of their prices (Arrow et al. 1961). We estimated this elasticity from a time series sample compiled for small multiple units in the Boston area (Key 1973). This sample, which covers the period 1942-1969, includes annual rental and expense information for twenty-nine apartment buildings, the majority of which have fewer than fifty dwelling units. These apartment buildings are operated by large real estate firms that provide good quality middle-income housing and follow conscientious maintenance practices. For this sample structure quality was proxied by the annual average rent per room divided by the Boston-area rent index; operating inputs are measured by the price-adjusted operating expense per room. Both the consumer price index and a fuel and utility index were used as measures of the price of operating inputs.[5] One difficulty with these data is that rent control was in effect from 1942 until March 1956.

Using the data in combination with various post-rent-control dummy variables, we obtained estimates of the elasticity of substitution ranging from 0.32 to 0.65; the results of the regressions are shown in Appendix 8A. Although these estimates left much to be desired, we concluded that the elasticity of substitution for these units was approximately 0.5, and we used this value as the elasticity of substitution for the small, multiple-unit building. We lacked the data for estimating the elasticity of substitution for the high-rise structure, but we assumed that it had a higher elasticity than the small, multiple unit buildings. This stems from our belief that a large "plant" offers more possibilities for substitution than a small "plant." Accordingly, we set the elasticity of substitution for the high rise at 0.6, a value that is still within the range of estimated elasticities for small multiple units. These elasticities of substitution imply values for β of 1.0 for small structures and 0.67 for large ones.

The Distribution Factor

The distribution factor, α, in a CES production function is an important determinant of the share of output that each input factor receives. Applying the usual first-order conditions to Equation (8-12), we obtain the following ratio of factor shares:

$$\frac{P_o \cdot O}{P_k \cdot K} = \frac{P_k}{P_o}^{-\beta/(\beta+1)} \left(\frac{1-\alpha}{\alpha}\right)^{1/\beta+1} \tag{8-13}$$

which shows that β and the input prices also play a role in determining relative factor shares. Having determined β for the two structure types, we went on to specify the prices of the inputs. We set both P_o and P_m equal to unity. Since $P_k = P_m(r+d)$ we also had to specify the interest and depreciation rates. We assumed that the depreciation rate for quality capital was 10 percent per year and that the interest rate was 5 percent per year.[6] Hence, the ratio of P_k to P_o was 0.15.

The ratio of factor shares specified in Equation (8-13) is not directly observable because operating statements do not report $P_k K$, the payment to quality capital, but they do contain enough information to determine the ratio of operating expenses to maintenance expenses. Moreover, we know that the ratio of maintenance expenditures to total expenditures on quality capital is $d/(r+d)$; so we can write the expression for factor shares in terms of observable quantities as

$$\frac{P_o O}{P_m M} = \left(\frac{r+d}{d}\right) \left(\frac{P_k}{P_o}\right)^{-\beta/(\beta+1)} \left(\frac{1-\alpha}{\alpha}\right)^{1/(\beta+1)} \tag{8-14}$$

Operating data were available to us from two sources: the time series on Boston units used to estimate the elasticity of substitution and a recent study of rent control in the Boston region (Sternlieb 1974). These data are shown in Table 8-1, and the ratios of expenditures on operating inputs to expenditures on maintenance are similar for comparable time periods and structure types. The ratio for high-rise units is approximately 1.33 and the ratio for smaller buildings seems to be somewhat lower. During the most recent time periods 1.25 is a representative ratio for our small multiple unit structures. Using these ratios of input shares we obtained values for α of 0.906 for the latter and 0.812 for the high rises.

Other Parameters of the Supply Model

We can calculate the optimal stock of quality capital and the optimal level of operating inputs using the production function in Equation (8-12) and first-order conditions in Equation (8-13). The optimal levels of each input are

$$K^* = \left[\alpha + (1-\alpha) \left(\frac{P_k}{P_o} \frac{1-\alpha}{\alpha} \right)^{-\beta/(1+\beta)} \right]^{1/\beta} \frac{Q}{A}$$

$$ (8\text{-}15) $$

$$O^* = \left[(1-\alpha) + \alpha \left(\frac{P_k}{P_o} \frac{1-\alpha}{\alpha} \right)^{\beta/(1+\beta)} \right]^{1/\beta} \frac{Q}{A}$$

Table 8-1. Operating and Maintenance Expenditures as Ratios to Gross Rents and to Each Other,[a] 1942-1969 and 1971-1973

Expenditure Item	Time Period or Structure Type					
	Uncontrolled Rents			Controlled Rents		
	'65-'69	'60-'64	'55-'59	'50-'55	'45-'49	'42-'44
	Key Data (1973, p. 45)					
Operating inputs (O)	0.26	0.27	0.31	0.32	0.33	0.30
Maintenance and repair (M)	0.21	0.18	0.21	0.15	0.14	0.15
Total	0.47	0.45	0.52	0.47	0.47	0.45
Ratio of O to M	1.24	1.50	1.48	2.13	2.36	2.00

	Period of Uncontrolled Rents		Period of Controlled Rents	
	High Rise	Other	High Rise	Other
	Sternlieb Data (1975, pp. 39-43)			
Operating inputs (O)	0.16	0.20	0.19	0.21
Maintenance and repair (M)	0.12	0.16	0.14	0.16
Total	0.28	0.36	0.33	0.37
Ration of O to M	1.33	1.25	1.36	1.31

[a]The data from Key are for 29 buildings. The Sternlieb data are for 12,068 units and cover the period 1971-1973.

Moreover, in the CES production function, minimum levels of each input are required to produce a given level of output. In our case this means that the quality isoquant of each dwelling unit is asymptotic to nonzero values of quality capital and operating inputs. For any level of structure quality, Q, the minimum input requirements are

$$K_{min} = \alpha^{1/\beta} (Q/A)$$ (8-16)

$$Q_{min} = (1 - \alpha)^{1/\beta} (Q/A)$$

These conditions imply that dwelling units with specific levels of quality capital will not be able to produce quality levels above a certain point in the short run, a very plausible restriction for a model of the housing market.

The final values we specified to complete our supply side model were the prices of factor inputs across neighborhoods and the values of dwelling unit quality to be produced. We assumed that all factor prices across neighborhoods were equal except for the interest rate, r, which we assume is 5 percent in good neighborhoods and 7 percent in bad ones. This interest rate difference reflects differences in risk between the two neighborhoods. Setting the eight levels of dwelling unit quality that will be produced was arbitrary; so we assumed A equalled unity, and we scaled our eight quality levels to increase logarithmically from the lowest to the highest quality level.

The parameters and dimensions of the supply model are summarized in Table 8-2; in Table 8-3, we show the eight quality levels and the long-run annual average cost of supplying each quality level by each structure type in each neighborhood. The factor share data in Table 8-1 show that expenditures on maintenance and operating inputs claim from 28 to 47 percent of gross rents, and they imply that the total cost of supplying quality (using our assumed values of r and d) ranges from 34 to 62 percent of gross rents. Using these ratios as rough guides, the annual rents for the dwelling unit quality levels shown in Table 8-3 will be from 1-2/3 to 3 times the cost of quality for each quality level. That is, a typical gross rent for quality level 8 might range from \$32 to \$72 per month, and a typical gross rent for quality level 1 might range from \$190 to \$430 per month. The factor share data in Table 8-1 also suggest that owners devote a lower share of gross rents to dwelling unit quality in high rises than in small multiple unit structures. Structure capital and land costs are presumably higher for high-rise units than for low-rise ones.

The data that are available for estimating parameters of the

Table 8-2.   Supply Model Parameters[a]

Parameter	Structure Type	
	High Rise	Small Multi
Elasticity of substitution	0.6	0.5
β	0.67	1.0
α	0.812	0.906
A	1.	1.

	Good Neighborhood		Bad Neighborhood	
	High Rise	Small Multi	High Rise	Small Multi
K^*	$1.90Q$	$1.66Q$	$1.83Q$	$1.61Q$
O^*	$0.25Q$	$0.21Q$	$0.26Q$	$0.22Q$
K_{min}	$0.73Q$	$0.91Q$	$0.73Q$	$0.91Q$
O_{min}	$0.08Q$	$0.09Q$	$0.08Q$	$0.09Q$
Long-run marginal cost per unit of Q	0.54	0.46	0.57	0.49
r	0.05	0.05	0.07	0.07
d	0.10	0.10	0.10	0.10
$P_o(O/P_m)M$	1.33	1.25	1.42	1.32

[a]Variables are defined infra.

Table 8-3.   Quality Levels and Long-Run Average Cost of Quality per Dwelling Unit per Year

Quality Level No.	Q	Good Neighborhood		Bad Neighborhood	
		High Rise	Small Multi	High Rise	Small Multi
1	3,000	$1,605	$1,377	$1,713	$1,481
2	2,322	1,242	1,066	1,326	1,146
3	1,798	962	825	1,027	888
4	1,392	745	639	795	687
5	1,078	577	495	616	532
6	834	446	383	476	412
7	646	346	297	369	319
8	500	268	230	286	247

production function for structure quality are not perfect, but they do suggest that different structure types are likely to have different production functions. An alternative interpretation would be that the various parameters and input prices constitute a partial sensitivity test of the production function over a reasonable range of values.

SHORT-RUN ADJUSTMENT PATHS

In this section we perform some experiments with the production functions estimated in the previous section. In these experiments we examine the rate at which housing producers can alter the levels of structure quality produced by their units and the paths of short-run average costs during the adjustment period. We concentrate on cases where changes in patterns of demand will lead housing producers to increase the level of structure quality they produce. This type of demand shift is likely to accompany the introduction of a housing allowance program in a metropolitan housing market. We limit our analysis to the adjustment of structure quality and ignore possible changes in the demand for structure type or neighborhood quality. These latter two characteristics will be dealt with in the next section.

We begin by reviewing market conditions when the supply of structure quality in the housing market is in equilibrium. Since this characteristic is elastic in supply in the long run and is produced by a constant-returns-to-scale technology, the long-run supply curve will be horizontal. All levels of quality produced will be equally profitable; the rent for structure quality will equal the long-run average cost of production; and housing producers at each quality level will have the optimal stock of quality capital. If demands for structure quality suddenly increase, housing producers will immediately be able to increase the quality level they produce by increasing operating inputs. In the short run, however, housing producers will no longer have optimal capital stocks, and their short-run average costs of producing structure quality will rise above long-run average costs. Since the rents for quality will be determined by the costs of marginal producers at each quality level, the rents will rise in those levels with increased demand. Over a number of periods, housing producers will invest in quality capital until their stock of quality capital attains its new optimal level. At this time, rents for structure quality will again equal long-run average costs. In such a scenario at least two questions are of interest: How much will rents for structure quality increase in the short run? How long will it take for these rents to return to their equilibrium levels?

Using our production functions we can estimate rent changes from cost changes under certain pricing rules. It is apparent that the answers to these questions depend on several factors, including the magnitude of the increase in demand and the amount of cash flow available to the housing producer for investment. The cash flow available is in turn related to the pricing rule followed. We will assume that housing producers price their structure quality at short-run average cost. An average cost pricing rule is used because the marginal housing producer in each quality level has an alternative use for his unit: producing a lower quality level.

Short-Run Rent Increases from Demand Shifts

When a unit with the optimal stock of quality capital for quality level L is used to produce quality level $L + i$, operating inputs must be increased because the stock of quality capital is fixed in the short run (the current period). In addition, operating inputs are not perfect substitutes for quality capital; as shown in Equation (8-16), some quality levels may not even be attainable in the short run. The data in the following tabulation were computed using the short-run average cost pricing rule. The figures show the percent increase in the rent for structure quality that would be demanded by a housing producer whose unit was used to produce structure quality with the stock of quality capital that is optimal for a lower quality level:

Type	0	*Number of Quality Levels Above That for Which Capital Stock Is Optimal*			
		1	*2*	*3*	*4*
High rise					
Good neighborhood	0	8.1	50.2	312.5	–
Bad neighborhood	0	9.2	56.3	415.0	–
Small multi					
Good neighborhood	0	12.4	162.1	–	–
Bad neighborhood	0	13.5	235.0	–	–

For example, if a high-rise unit in a good neighborhood has an optimal stock of quality capital one level lower, the rent charge for quality will be 8.1 percent above the long-run equilibrium rent for quality. The data also illustrate that high-rise units, with their higher elasticity of substitution, can move up three quality levels in the short run while small multiple units can move up only two levels in the same period. Finally, we see from the table that the cost of having the incorrect capital stock is somewhat greater in bad neighborhoods than in good ones because of the former's higher interest rate.

It is clear that the magnitude of the short-run increase in rents for quality will depend on the size of the demand shift and the distribution over quality levels of the existing stock. For example, if the increase in the demand for quality is moderate, dwelling units might only shift to the next higher quality level, and the data in the table suggest that quality rents would rise only from 8 to 13 percent in the short run. If some units shifted two quality levels, quality rents would rise much more, from 50 to 235 percent, and it would be surprising if the increase in demand from a housing allowance would be large enough to sustain a price rise of that magnitude. We will investigate this question further when we operate the supply model in conjunction with a demand model.

The percent change figures in the foregoing table remind us that even in the very short run the production of dwelling unit quality from the existing stock is not inelastic. Our production functions for dwelling unit quality allow some substitution between inputs and allow a range of adjustments of outputs. At the same time, however, we see that sudden changes in demand are likely to produce rent increases in some quality levels because some housing producers will have nonoptimal capital stocks. These rent increases are not merely income transfers to landlords; they represent payments for production costs that are incurred by housing producers who suddenly find themselves out of equilibrium. These short-run rent increases will continue until housing producers can adjust their capital stocks to new optimal levels. We now try to determine how long this adjustment might take.

Length of the Adjustment Period

To reach a higher level of quality capital, a housing producer must make net investments over time, and the time it takes him to reach the new quality level will be a function of the resources he can devote to investment. We analyze two options for financing net investment that might be available to a housing producer: First we assume that only cash generated by the unit is available for investment and that he cannot borrow; and second, we assume he can borrow funds to finance his investment and that he must pay off his loan with his cash flow.

To simplify the case where investment is paid for directly out of cash flow, we assume that the cash flow available for net investment can be represented as a proportion of the stock of quality capital. If

p is the proportion of quality capital available for net investment, then the rate of change of quality capital, $\dot{K}$, will be

$$\dot{K} = p\,K_t \qquad (8\text{-}17)$$

which is a simple differential equation. Solving it yields the result,

$$T_{ij} = \frac{1}{p}\,1n\,\frac{K_j}{K_i} \qquad (8\text{-}18)$$

where T_{ij} is the time required to move from capital stock K_i to capital stock K_j, and p is the proportion of the capital stock devoted to net investment.

It will be recalled from Table 8-3 that the quality levels we use in our model are scaled logarithmically; ratios of quality levels are therefore constant multiples. Since the optimal stock of quality capital is a linear function of quality, the ratios of optimal capital stocks for different quality levels will also be constant multiples. As a result, from Equation (8-18) we can see that the time required to move a unit's capital stock up two levels will be twice that required to move it up one level.

These properties of the adjustment period are illustrated in the table below, where we show the number of time periods (in years) required to increase the stock of quality capital of a dwelling unit by one, two, or three quality levels as a function of p, the proportion of quality capital invested each year. (Note that, given the parameters of the model, the optimal stock of quality capital will range from one to two times the annual gross rents.)

Number of Quality Levels Moved		Proportion of Quality Capital Invested Each Year						
		0.01	*0.03*	*0.05*	*0.07*	*0.09*	*0.11*	*0.15*
1	1	25.7	8.7	5.2	3.8	3.0	2.5	1.8
2	2	51.4	17.3	10.5	7.6	5.9	4.9	3.7
3	3	77.2	26.0	15.7	11.3	8.9	7.4	5.5

For example, a housing producer with 5 percent of his quality capital available for net investment (roughly 5 percent of gross rents) will take approximately five years to attain the optimal stock of quality capital for the next higher quality level. Note that these time periods of adjustment are independent of structure type and neighborhood quality and depend only on the funds available for investment.

A sense of the path of rents during the adjustment period can be conveyed by examining a particular unit. Figure 8-2 shows the path of quality rents for a high-rise unit in a good neighborhood where the net investment is 7 percent of quality capital. The rent paths are percent increases over long-run levels for a unit that is being shifted one, two, or three quality levels. The short-run rent levels decay exponentially to their long-run equilibrium levels.

In calculating the length of the adjustment period, we have assumed thus far that housing producers try to pay for their increased investments in quality capital on a current basis from their net revenues. This may correspond to the way in which some housing

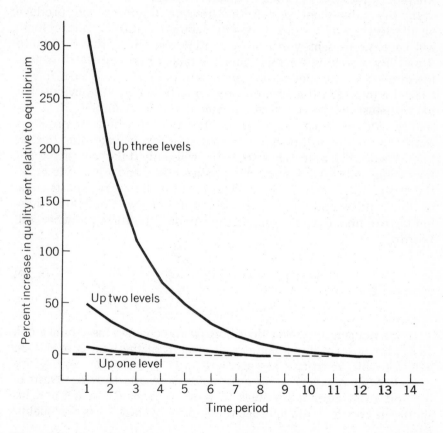

Figure 8-2. Time Path of Rent for Quality during Adjustment with No Borrowing (high rise unit; good neighborhood; $p = 0.07$).

producers behave, but others may borrow and finance expenditures on additional quality capital.

We now assume that housing producers can borrow money at a rate r_x, that is higher than their long-run opportunity cost of capital, r. Since r_x exceeds r, a housing producer who borrows to increase his stock of quality capital to a level appropriate for quality level j must calculate a new desired capital stock, K_j^x, that reflects r_x. During the current period, a housing producer can invest $p\,K_t$ in additional quality capital. If he wishes to attain his new desired capital stock, he must also borrow

$$B = K_j^x - (K_i' + p\,K_i') \tag{8-19}$$

where K_i' is his existing stock of quality capital.

In the subsequent period the housing producer will produce quality level j with a stock of quality capital equal to K_j^x; hence, there will be some present-worth factor for interest rate r_x that is equal to B/pK_j^x. By searching for this value in a table of present-worth factors for rate r_x, we can determine how many periods it will take to pay back the loan. For the term of the loan to be finite, it is obvious that pK_j^x/r_x must be greater than B. Since we are examining only the supply side of the market we assume that the housing producer wants to minimize the short-run average costs of providing quality level j with his unit. Therefore, he will only take out a loan if borrowing reduces his short-run average costs, and we define B_0 as the largest loan amount that will yield short-run average costs equal to those he would incur if he did not borrow. Combining these limits, we find that the amount of funds a housing producer will borrow is

$$B = \min[K_j^x - (1 + p)K_j'; \frac{pK_1^x}{r_x}; B_0] \tag{8-20}$$

If the housing producer does borrow and changes his capital stock to K_j^x, the latter will remain at that level until the loan is repaid. In addition, his short-run average cost will be constant during this period. After repayment, his cost of funds reverts to r; he invests in his unit from current revenues to move it from K_j^x to K_j^*, and his short-run average costs approach long-run coverage costs for quality level j.

Let us look at these calculations for the same unit we considered earlier: a high-rise unit in a good neighborhood with cash flow available for investment and amortization equal to 7 percent of quality capital. In addition, let us assume that r_x is 10 percent. In this case, illustrated in Figure 8-3, we find that it does not pay to borrow at all to move up one quality level. However, to move two or three quality levels, borrowing does pay, although the length of the adjustment period is virtually unchanged in both cases.

THE SUPPLY MODEL IN A MARKET-CLEARING CONTEXT

In this section we combine the supply model for dwelling unit quality with household demands for housing. Demand equations in which the independent variables are rents and the neighborhood,

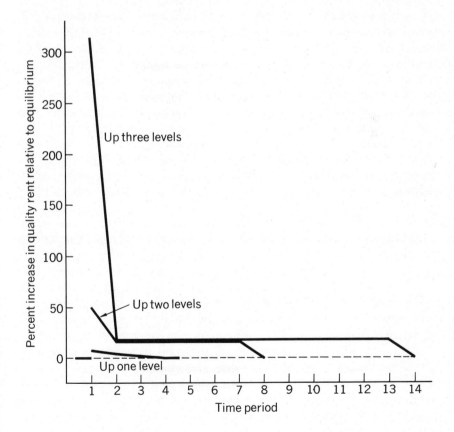

Figure 8-3. Time Path of Rent for Quality during Adjustment Period with Borrowing (high rise unit in good neighborhood; $P = 0.07$; $r_x = 10$ percent).

structure, and quality attributes of dwelling units represent the housing demands of households. Housing producers supply dwelling unit quality with existing units using operating and quality capital inputs as described in earlier sections. We assume that neighborhood quality levels are fixed. New construction and conversions between structure types are not endogenous in the supply sector of the model, but we have carried out some experiments with the model in which new units are added exogenously in response to price changes.

This combination of supply and demand behavior can be envisaged as representing a market for dwelling unit quality over time. At the beginning of each time period 200 households distributed over six income classes face a fixed stock of dwelling units and choose a unit in which to reside for the current period. The market-clearing procedure operates in two steps: First, using current-period expected rents for structure quality, we alter the combined rents for neighborhood and structure type until the market for these two (fixed) attributes is cleared. Once the households are allocated among neighborhoods and structures, a second market-clearing procedure is used to clear the market for dwelling unit quality in each neighborhood-structure combination. Since housing producers can alter the level of dwelling unit quality they produce in the current period, this second market-clearing procedure iterates between demand and supply until the demands of households match the quality levels supplied by housing producers at common rents for dwelling unit quality. On the basis of established rents for dwelling unit quality, housing producers form expectations about what the rents for dwelling quality will be in future time periods, and they use these expectations to determine their maintenance expenditure this period. During the succeeding period, households and housing producers recontract for quality levels, prices are revised, expectations are reformulated, and maintenance decisions are made. When this process has continued for several time periods and no changes have been made in supply or demand parameters, an equilibrium is reached. In addition, model parameters can be altered to generate different equilibriums, which can be analyzed in terms of price and quantity elasticities or other summary statistics.

In this section we present several partial equilibrium analyses or sensitivity tests that involve changing various parameters of the model and determining the effect these changes have on model outcomes. In addition, we test an approximation to a housing allowance program by altering the income distribution of households. Before describing the model experiments, we outline the decisions of households and housing producers as represented in the model.

The Household's Choice of Dwelling Unit

On a given market day 200 households distributed over six income classes participate in the model's market for neighborhoods, structures, and dwelling unit quality. The number of households is equal to the number of available dwelling units in the market. A housing bundle is characterized by the neighborhood, structure type, and quality level it provides. The households have demand equations that are of the form

$$PR(N, S, Q, I) = \frac{\exp\,[\alpha_I N + \beta_I S + \gamma_I Q + \delta_I R(N, S, Q)_t]}{\underset{N,S,Q}{\Sigma}\{\exp\,[\alpha_I N + \beta_I S + \gamma_I Q + \delta_I R(N, S, Q)_t]\}} \quad (8\text{-}21)$$

where

$PR(N, S, Q, I)$ = proportion of households in income class I choosing a unit of quality level Q, structure type S, and neighborhood N;

$R(N, S, Q)_t$ = rent for a dwelling unit of quality level Q and structure type S in neighborhood N;

$\alpha_I, \beta_I, \gamma_I, \delta_I$ = coefficients of neighborhood quality, structure type, dwelling unit quality, and rent for income class I.

This demand equation is of the logit type, and its exponents can be thought of as utility functions.

The market clearing is done in two steps. In the first step demand and supply classified by neighborhood and structure are equated by changing the rents for these attributes. The rent term, $R(N, S, Q)$, in Equation (8-21) is separated into two components: the expected rent for dwelling unit quality, $R(Q)$, and the rent for neighborhood and structure type, $R(N, S)$.[7] Since the supply of units by structure type and neighborhood is fixed, $R(N, S)$ is adjusted in the first stage of market clearing until household demands are matched up with the dwelling units available with these two attributes. In the second stage of market clearing, $R(N, S)$ is fixed, and demand and supply are iterated within each neighborhood and structure type submarket until the market for dwelling unit quality is cleared.

The Provision of Dwelling Unit Quality

Given a schedule of demands for each of the eight possible quality levels, housing producers must determine the least costly means of meeting the demands at each level. Since each dwelling unit has a different amount of capital associated with it, in terms of operating inputs it is always less costly to produce units at the highest quality level in buildings with the largest amounts of quality capital; to produce the second highest quality level in units with the next largest amounts of quality capital; and so forth. This assignment of dwelling units to quality levels according to the amounts of quality capital embodied in the units maximizes the total cash flow of landlords subject to the constraint that the demand schedule of households must be met.

Given this technique of determining a production schedule that minimizes the total cost of producing the quality levels demanded, each quality level's marginal unit in the supply function can be determined by inspection. Because dwelling units are assigned to quality levels according to the stock of quality capital they embody, the marginal unit in each quality level is the one with the least amount of capital supplying that quality level. The full cost of providing the given quality level with the marginal unit sets the rent for quality, $R(Q)$, in that quality level and is the sum of the cost of the required operating inputs plus the one-period costs of capital embodied in the unit:

$$P_o O' + P_m (r + d)K' \tag{8-22}$$

where O' are the required operating inputs for the quality level and K' is the unit's capital stock. Of course, each quality level will have a different marginal unit and a different cost for its marginal unit.

After the household demands have been matched to the supplies of quality levels and market-clearing rents for quality are formulated, each housing producer revises his rent expectations for the future and determines his maintenance expenditures for the current period. A housing producer expects the long-run equilibrium rents for quality to equal his long-run marginal costs. He must form expectations about rents in the next few periods because these expected rents are the basis for his decision to produce a certain quality level and to purchase additional capital this year. He knows the current and past rents and the expected long-run rent. We assume that the housing producer believes that rents will reach their long-run equilibrium by the end of a planning interval T periods long (in the program we assume that $T = 5$). We believe that the housing producer expects the change in rent next year to be some weighted average of the change in rent this year and the average yearly change needed to achieve the long-run value after T periods. The particular formulation is

$$R(Q)_{t+1} = R(Q)_t + \mu [R(Q)_t - R(Q)_{t-1}] + (1 - \mu) \frac{R(Q^*) - R(Q)_t}{T}$$

$$(8\text{-}23)$$

where

$R(Q)_t$ = rent for quality level Q for a given neighborhood and structure type;

$R(Q^*)$ = long-run rents of quality level Q; and

μ = parameter of expectations.

Housing producers may have different α's and T's. In the numerical solution we assume they may have different α's only.

After forming his expectations concerning next year's rents, the housing producer calculates his expected profit for each quality level and invests to produce the quality level which he expects will be most profitable to him in the next period. Since it is assumed that a housing producer cannot sell his quality capital, maintenance will be set at zero if his depreciated capital stock will be above the optimal level in the next period.

Parameters for the Dynamic Model

In order to run the dynamic model, parameters must be specified for the demand side of the model. This specification is difficult because we have little empirical evidence about the parameters of demand for quality. Measures of dwelling unit quality are crude, inconsistent, or poorly defined in most data that describe dwelling unit characteristics. The demand parameters we have to choose are the α's, β's, γ's, and δ's in the household demand functions defined in Equation (8-21). One way to insure that the parameters are reasonable is to derive the choice elasticities implicit in Equation (8-21). The elasticity of the probability of choosing a particular quality level can be determined for changes in neighborhood, structure, quality, and rents, as follows:

$$N_N = N\alpha_I (1 - PR) \qquad (8\text{-}24)$$

$$N_S = S\beta_I (1 - PR) \qquad (8\text{-}25)$$

$$N_Q = Q\gamma_I (1 - PR) \qquad (8\text{-}26)$$

$$N_R = R\delta_I (1 - PR) \qquad (8\text{-}27)$$

where PR is the probability of choosing a particular combination of dwelling unit attributes; and N_X is the elasticity of the probability with respect to X.

The model has six income classes, and the parameters of demand can differ by income class. The parameters we used, shown in Table 8-4, are somewhat arbitrary but they produce reasonable distributions in the model. Table 8-4 also shows representative choice elasticities of the probabilities of each attribute, and the parameters were chosen with some consideration for what would be reasonable elasticities.

Table 8-4. Demand Parameters and Elasticities of Probabilities

Class No.	Income Class	α	β	γ	δ
		Parameter Values			
1.	Over $15,000	2.0	2.00	.002	−.00225
2.	$10,000-15,000	2.0	1.90	.002	−.00285
3.	$7,000-10,000	2.0	1.85	.002	−.00345
4.	$5,000-7,000	2.0	1.80	.002	−.00405
5.	$3,000-6,000	2.0	1.75	.002	−.00465
6.	$0-3,000	2.0	1.70	.002	−.00525
		Elasticity Range for $PR = 0.2$			
1.	Over $15,000	1.6-3.2	1.6-3.2	1-6	0.5-5.0
2.	$10,000-15,000	1.6-3.2	1.5-3.0	1-6	0.6-6.3
3.	$7,000-10,000	1.6-3.2	1.5-3.0	1.6	0.7-7.6
4.	$5,000-7,000	1.6-3.2	1.4-2.9	1-6	0.8-8.9
5.	$3,000-6,000	1.6-3.2	1.4-2.8	1-6	0.9-10.2
6.	$0-3,000	1.6-3.2	1.3-2.7	1-6	1.1-11.2

Note: In calculating elasticities, the range of the attributes used was N: 1 to 2 (1 = bad neighborhood; 2 = good neighborhood); S: 1 to 2 (1 = small multiple; 2 = high rise); Q: $500 to $3,000; and R: $250 to $2,750.

In addition to demand parameters, the distribution of households by income and of dwelling units by N, S, and Q must be determined. The distributors used in the model were derived from 1970 Census data for the Boston SMSA. In order to generate these distributions we assumed that the City of Boston represented the low-quality neighborhood; and the suburbs, the high-quality neighborhood. In addition, we classified buildings with three to nine units as the small, multifamily structure type, and buildings with ten or more units as high rises. The resultant percent distribution of renter families by income class is shown in the following tabulation; the number of households in each class in the model is shown in parentheses:

Over $15,000	$10,000-$15,000	$7,000-$10,000	$5,000-$7,000	$3,000-$5,000	$3,000 or Less
11.3%	19.4%	20.3%	14.6%	13.4%	21.0%
(22)	(39)	(41)	(29)	(27)	(42)

The percent distribution of dwelling units by neighborhood and structure type and the number of units in each category in the model are as follows:

	Boston City		Boston Suburbs	
	Small Multi	High Rise	Small Multi	High Rise
	26.4%	20.2%	33.3%	20.0%
	(53)	(40)	(67)	(40)

The Basic Case

When operated together the demand and supply portions of the housing market model produce an equilibrium outcome that we term the "basic case." In this equilibrium the rents expected by housing producers and households equal the short-run market rents, and all dwelling units have their long-run equilibrium capital stocks. In Table 8-5 some results from the equilibrium basic case are summarized.

The first part of Table 8-5 shows that high-income households are more likely to reside in the more desirable structure type ($S = 2$) and the more desirable neighborhood ($N = 2$) than are low-income households. The rents shown for neighborhood and structure type, $R(N, S)$, are essentially demand-determined quasi-rents for the fixed supplies of structure and neighborhood attributes. These quasi-rents obviously would play a key role in determining either the construction of new structures in each neighborhood or the conversions from one structure type to another.

The second part of Table 8-5 shows that the equilibrium distribution of dwelling quality varies across the neighborhood-structure type combinations, a result we would expect given that these combinations attract income classes differentially. The column labeled $r(Q)$ displays the rent per unit of dwelling quality in each neighborhood and structure combination. This per-unit rent is constant across all levels of dwelling quality because we have assumed dwelling quality is produced by a constant returns to scale

Table 8-5. Summary Results from the Equilibrium Solution of the Basic Case

			Neighborhood and Structure Type by Income Class						
			Income Class[a]						Total No.
N	S	R(N,S)	1	2	3	4	5	6	of Households
1	1	17.2	2	6	9	8	10	18	53
1	2	415.7	4	8	9	6	5	8	40
2	1	560.1	6	13	15	10	9	14	67
2	2	1038.1	10	12	8	5	3	2	40
	Total		22	39	41	29	27	42	200

			Dwelling Unit Quality by Neighborhood and Structure Type								
			Quality Level[a]								Total No.
N	S	r(Q)	1	2	3	4	5	6	7	8	of Households
1	1	.49	7	6	6	7	6	7	7	7	53
1	2	.58	5	4	5	4	5	5	6	6	40
2	1	.45	13	10	9	7	7	7	7	7	67
2	2	.54	8	6	5	5	4	4	4	4	40
	Total		33	26	25	23	22	23	24	24	200

	Percent Distribution of Dwelling Unit Quality by Income Class for High Rise Dwelling in Bad Neighborhood (N = 1, S = 2)								
Income	Quality Level[a]								
Class	1	2	3	4	5	6	7	8	Total
1	32%	19%	13%	10%	8%	7%	6%	5%	100%
2	21	16	14	12	10	10	9	8	100
3	14	13	13	12	12	12	12	12	100
4	7	9	11	12	14	15	16	16	100
5	4	6	9	11	14	17	19	20	100
6	2	4	7	10	14	18	21	24	100

[a]The income class equivalents are given in Table 8-4; the quality equivalents, in Table 8-3. $N = 1$ designates a good neighborhood; $N = 2$, a bad one. $S = 1$ designates a small, multiple-unit dwelling; $S = 2$, a high rise.

technology. The per-unit rent of dwelling quality differs by neighborhood and structure type because of the specification of the model: Recall that the parameters of the dwelling quality production functions differ by structure type and that the price of capital differs by neighborhood.

The third part of Table 8-5 shows the percent distribution across quality levels by income class for a particular neighborhood and structure type combination. Note how these distributions change from the highest income class (=1) to the lowest (=6) and that the distribution exhibits some evidence of diagonality.

Although the actual numbers shown in Table 8-5 are primarily illustrative of how the housing market model works when the demand and supply sides are integrated, they do remind us of the implications of the model specifications we have employed. Many other models that represent quality change or the production of housing services over time assume that incremental investment or maintenance applied to existing units is less efficient than new construction, has decreasing returns to scale, or has decreasing returns over time (de Leeuw; Sweeney). Since the supply model presented here assumes constant returns to scale for incremental investment in existing units, a decline in the quality of existing units over time has not (in effect) been specified on the supply side. In this model some changes on the supply side, e.g., an increase in the prices of factor inputs, can change the quality of dwelling units over time, but a more important cause of such changes is likely to be shifts in the demand for the structure and neighborhood attributes of dwelling units. Changes in the composition of demand within neighborhood and structure type submarkets will alter the equilibrium quality levels produced, and the latter can either increase or decrease depending on the demographic or real income changes that occur. If some heterogeneity is introduced into the representation of housing stocks, changes in the quality of particular dwelling units over time can result from demand changes as well as from possible decreasing returns on the supply side. If housing is represented as a homogeneous good, however, quality change over time typically must stem from the specification of diminishing returns to investment in existing units.

Sensitivity Analyses of the Model

In addition to examining the basic case, we made several runs in which parameters were changed and new equilibriums were attained. Elasticities with respect to the parameter changes were calculated to see how sensitive various equilibrium outputs of the model were to such changes. In Table 8-6 we summarize seven sensitivity runs of the model. The columns display the overall average of dwelling quality, the average rent per unit of dwelling quality, the average quasi-rent for neighborhood and structure type, and the average total expenditure on housing. In all sensitivity runs the distribution of households by income class and the distribution of dwelling units by neighbor-

Table 8-6. Sensitivity Tests: Results Aggregated over All Households

Item	$\overline{Q}$	$\overline{r(Q)}$	$\overline{R(N,S)}$	Average Total Expenditure
1. Basic Case				
Level	1,533	0.504	463	1,235
2. Increase P_Q by 50% (1.0 to 1.5)				
Level	1,312	0.611	459	1,260
Elasticity	−0.29	0.42	−0.02	0.04
3. Increase Interest Rates 50% (7.0 to 10.5; 5.0 to 7.5)				
Level	1,423	0.554	471	1,259
Elasticity	−0.14	0.19	0.03	0.04
4. Reduce Interest Rate in N = 2 by 50% (5.0 to 2.5)				
Level	1,596	0.480	496	1,262
Elasticity	−0.08	0.09	−0.14	−0.04
5. Raise Elasticity of Substitution in S = 2 by 10% (0.6 to 0.66)				
Level	1,575	0.486	484	1,250
Elasticity	0.27	−0.36	0.45	0.12
6. Raise α for S = 2 by 10% (0.812 to 0.893)				
Level	1,626	0.453	531	1,268
Elasticity	0.60	−1.0	1.5	0.26
7. Demand Coefficient of Q Reduced 25% (0.002 to 0.0015)				
Level	1,244	0.504	470	1,096
Elasticity	0.75	0	−0.06	0.45
8. Demand Coefficient of Rent Reduced 10%				
Level	1,549	0.504	509	1,287
Elasticity	0.07	0	0.99	0.43

Note: Elasticities are calculated with respect to parametric changes.

hood and structure type remain fixed. Runs 2 through 6 alter parameters of the supply side: runs 2 and 3 change the costs of producing quality in all units, and runs 4, 5, and 6 alter supply costs in only one neighborhood or one structure type. Runs 7 and 8 alter demand coefficients for all households.

A comparison of runs 2 through 6 with the basic case shows that average total expenditure is fairly constant, increasing by a maximum of 2 percent. In these runs households respond to changes in $r(Q)$ by varying the amount of quality they purchase. This is shown in Figure 8-4, which displays what is esentially a demand curve for dwelling quality. Of course, this relation is complicated somewhat by changes in $R(N, S)$, the quasi-rents for N and S. Runs 7 and 8, in which demand coefficients are altered, produce somewhat larger changes in total expenditures and $R(N, S)$. In these runs the supply side is

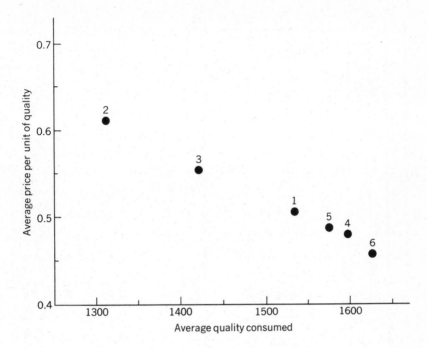

Note: Numbered points refer to runs in Table 8-6.

Figure 8-4. Quality versus Rent for Quality from Sensitivity Tests of Supply Parameters.

unaltered; and $r(Q)$ keeps its basic case value, but the altered demand parameters produce changes in the average level of quality consumed.

Table 8-7 displays average values and elasticities for model outputs by structure type and neighborhood. Supply changes limited to one structure type or neighborhood (runs 4, 5, and 6) tend to produce their largest effects on units with the attributes affected by the altered parameters. Note, for example, that in run 4 the first neighborhod results are very similar to those of the basic case, and in run 5 the structure 1 results are little changed from the basic case. In these two runs supply changes are made in neighborhood 2 and structure 2, respectively.

The sensitivity tests show that model results are, indeed, responsive to parameter values. The importance of the demand parameters, while not surprising, compounds the problems on the demand side of the model, which is especially difficult to estimate.

Table 8-7. Sensitivity Tests: Results by Neighborhood and Structure Type

		Good Neighborhood						Bad Neighborhood					
		Small Multi			High Rise			Small Multi			High Rise		
Item		Q	r(Q)	R(N,S)	Q	r(Q)	R(N,S)	Q	r(Q)	R(N,S)	Q	r(Q)	R(N,S)
1. Basic Case													
	Level	1,429	0.487	17.2	1,381	0.576	415.7	1,635	0.454	500.1	1,654	0.538	1,038.1
2. Increase P_Q by 50%													
	Level	1,201	0.587	17.7	1,173	0.699	408.4	1,416	0.551	498.0	1,424	0.657	1,026.3
	Elasticity	-0.32	0.41	0.6	-0.30	0.42	-0.04	-0.26	0.42	-0.01	-0.28	0.18	-0.02
3. Increase Interest Rates 50% (7.0 to 10.5; 5.0 to 7.5)													
	Level	1,298	0.542	16.4	1,268	0.638	415.5	1,539	0.495	515.3	1,552	0.585	1,054.5
	Elasticity	-0.18	0.22	-0.09	-0.16	0.21	0	-0.12	0.18	0.06	-0.12	0.18	0.03
4. Reduce Interest Rate in $N=2$ by 50% (5.0 to 2.5)													
	Level	1,429	0.487	14.2	1,381	0.576	409.6	1,754	0.412	563.0	1,768	0.18	0.61
	Elasticity	0	0	0.3	0	0	0.03	-0.15	0.18	-0.25	-0.13		
5. Raise Elasticity of Substitution in $S=2$ by 10% (0.6 to 6.6)													
	Level	1,429	0.487	15.1	1,477	0.532	469.9	1,635	0.454	496.0	1,764	0.494	1,101.5
	Elasticity	0	0	-1.22	0.70	-0.76	1.30	0	0	-0.08	0.67	-0.81	0.61
6. Raise α for $S=2$ by 10% (0.745 to 0.820)													
	Level	1,413	0.487	11.8	1,721	0.454	578.3	1,629	0.454	490.4	1,806	0.409	1,240.2
	Elasticity	-0.11	0	-3.1	2.5	0	-8.6	-0.04	0	-0.19	0.92	-2.4	1.95
7. Demand Coefficient of Q Reduced 25% (0.002 to 0.0015)													
	Level	1,156	0.487	16.4	1,121	0.576	441.7	1,334	0.454	494.1	1,335	0.538	1,056.5
	Elasticity	0.76	0	0.19	0.75	0	-0.25	0.74	0	0.05	0.77	0	-0.08
8. Demand Coefficient of Rent Reduced 10%													
	Level	1,372	0.487	13.1	1,402	0.576	458.4	1,622	0.459	548.0	1,781	0.538	1,199.9
	Elasticity	-0.40	0	-2.3	0.15	0	1.03	-0.08	0	0.95	0.77	0	1.08

Experimenting with Housing Allowances

The final exercises performed with the model incorporate a representation of a housing allowance program, which is simulated by altering the income distribution of households in the model. The top portion of Table 8-8 displays changes made in the income distribution of the model that roughly correspond to the implementation of a housing allowance program. Two runs were made with the altered income distribution. In the first run no other changes were made, and in particular the distribution of dwelling units by neighborhood and structure type was unchanged. In the second run this distribution was changed by adding two units in the neighborhood 2, structure type 2 category and subtracting two units in the neighborhood 1, structure 1 category; this change is intended to represent new construction that might occur in response to increase in quasi-rents for neighborhood and structural type in the first run.

The lower section of Table 8-8 summarizes results from the two housing allowance runs and presents comparable figures from the basic case run. When the supply is held fixed the change in income distribution produces higher quasi-rents for N and S, an increase in

Table 8-8. Housing Allowance Simulations[a]

Income Distribution Changes for Housing Allowance (number of households)

	Income Class					
Run	1	2	3	4	5	6
Basic Case	22	39	41	29	27	42
Allowance	22	39	41	37	42	19
Change	0	0	0	+8	+15	−23

Summary of Results from Allowance Simulations

		Basic Case			Fixed Supply			Altered Supply		
N	S	$\bar{Q}$	$R(N,S)$	Av. Tot. Expend.	$\bar{Q}$	$R(N,S)$	Av. Tot. Expend.	$\bar{Q}$	$R(N,S)$	Av. Tot. Expend.
1	1	1,429	17.2	713	1,458	15.8	726	1,456	16.6	726
1	2	1,381	416	1,211	1,413	430	1,244	1,413	420	1,234
2	1	1,635	500	1,242	1,672	514	1,273	1,672	505	1,264
2	2	1,654	1,038	1,928	1,654	1,060	1,950	1,620	1,029	1,901
Weighted average		1,533	463	1,235	1,560	474	1,258	1,553	463	1,243

[a]The income class limits are given in Table 8-3. $N = 1$ designates a good neighborhood; $N = 2$, a bad one. $S = 1$ designates a small, multiple-unit dwelling; $S = 2$, a high rise.

average quality levels consumed, and a slight rise in total housing expenditures. It appears that the higher incomes are used to bid up rents for the fixed attributes (N and S) and to raise quality in three of the four N and S categories. The slight alteration in supply in the second run returns the quasi-rents nearly to their levels in the basic case, raises the average quality level consumed, and increases total housing expenditures relative to the basic case.

A more detailed description of the two housing allowance runs and a comparison with the basic case are presented in Table 8-9, which shows the distribution over dwelling quality levels for each neighborhood and structure type. In the run with the stock of units

Table 8-9. Housing Allowance Runs and Quality Levels[a] (number of households)

N	S	1	2	3	4	5	6	7	8	Total
					Quality Level					
1	1	7	6	6	7	6	7	7	7	53
1	2	5	4	5	4	5	5	6	6	40
2	1	13	10	9	7	7	7	7	7	67
2	2	8	6	5	5	4	4	4	4	40
	Total	33	26	25	23	22	23	24	24	200
				Allowance with Fixed Supply						
1	1	7	7	6	7	6	6	7	7	53
1	2	5	5	4	5	5	5	5	6	40
2	1	14	10	9	7	7	7	7	6	67
2	2	8	6	5	5	4	4	4	4	40
	Total	34	28	24	24	22	22	23	23	200
	Change from basic case	+1	+2	−1	+1	0	−1	−1	−1	
				Allowance with Altered Supply						
1	1	8	7	6	6	5	6	6	7	51
1	2	5	5	4	5	5	5	5	6	40
2	1	14	10	9	7	7	7	7	6	67
2	2	7	6	5	4	5	5	5	5	42
	Total	34	28	24	22	22	23	23	24	200
	Change from basic case	+1	+2	−1	−1	0	0	−1	0	

[a]Quality levels are described in Table 8-3; N and S in note to Table 8-4.

fixed by N and S, the quality levels consumed increase relative to the basic case, but in a complicated manner as households shift among quality levels. When the stock of units is altered in the second run, the average level of quality consumed still exceeds that in the basic case, but the same number of households consume the lowest quality level, as in the basic case. In addition, the number of units of the lowest quality level has increased in the most desirable neighborhood and structure type.

Although these runs are merely illustrative of the changes that may occur under a housing allowance regime, they do suggest that households may use increased dollars to buy structure or neighborhood attributes they desire rather than dwelling unit quality. In fact, housing allowances might in some cases encourage households to trade off dwelling unit quality for these other attributes. It is obvious, however, that we must have more data to support the demand equation parameters before we can project impacts of housing programs with any confidence.

CONCLUSION

In this study we presented a theoretical representation of housing supply that emphasizes the operation of the existing stock of dwelling units. Three major characteristics of dwelling units were distinguished: structure quality, structure type, and neighborhood quality. The production of dwelling unit quality was treated in terms that parallel the choice of optimal plant size in the theory of the firm; decisions about structure type, although treated less completely, were made in accordance with the usual assumptions of investment theory.

A production function having constant elasticity of substitution was specified for the production of structure quality, and parameters for it were estimated from available data on the operation of dwelling units. The quantitative version of the model distinguished two structure types and two levels of neighborhood quality. Numerical experiments were performed with the model to determine likely ranges of values for short-run increases in rents, as well as their duration, that might accompany any housing market policy that increases demands for structure quality. Although increases in rents could be quite large in the very short run, moderate increases in the demand for structure quality would probably increase gross rents by from 4 to 7 percent in the short run, and these rent increases would likely dissipate in less than six years.

The supply representation was combined in a market-clearing

framework with demand equations for housing attributes. Several sensitivity analyses were performed with this market model, and some preliminary housing allowance experiments were reported on. These experiments suggested that housing allowances increase the average quality of housing consumed, but may lead some households to substitute neighborhood quality or structure attributes for dwelling quality.

We stressed the role of operating inputs and maintenance in short-run adjustments of existing units. Expenditures on these factors constitute an important component of the costs of producing housing, and they typically receive little attention in analyses of housing markets.

Finally, we gave much attention here to the short-run dynamics of housing market adjustment processes, not only because of their importance in gauging the response of the housing market to specific policy proposals, now under consideration, but also because more complete representation of these adjustment mechanisms will increase our ability to judge the appropriateness of equilibrium assumptions in the housing market.

APPENDIX 8A: ESTIMATES OF THE ELASTICITY OF SUBSTITUTION BETWEEN OPERATING INPUTS AND CAPITAL

The estimation of the elasticity of substitution between operating inputs and capital in the production of structure quality depends on several assumptions, which we describe here. We begin by deriving the first-order conditions of the CES production function in Equation (8-12) as

$$\frac{dQ}{dO} = \frac{P_o}{P_Q} = -\frac{1}{\beta}[\alpha K^{-\beta} + (1-\alpha)O^{-\beta}]^{-1/(\beta-1)}(1-\alpha)(-\beta)^{-\beta-1}$$

(8A-1)

which with substitution leads to

$$\frac{dQ}{dO} = \frac{P_o}{P_Q} = (1-\alpha)(Q/O)^{\beta+1}$$

(8A-2)

By rearranging terms, we obtain the equation to be estimated:

$$\frac{Q}{O} = (1-\alpha)^{-1/(\beta+1)}(P_o/P_Q)^{1/(\beta+1)}$$

(8A-3)

where P_o and P_Q are the prices (or price indexes) of operating inputs and structure quality, respectively. Estimating Equation (8A-3) is impossible because we do not observe Q directly. However, we do have data on rent payments and expenditures on operating inputs, and we can obtain price indexes for rents and operating inputs, O, over time. We then estimate the equation

$$\frac{R/P_R}{\text{Op.Exp.}/P_o} = \frac{S}{O} = c(P_o/P_R)^b \qquad (8A\text{-}4)$$

and obtain b, which is an estimate of the elasticity of substitution if S is a good proxy for Q. S would be a good proxy if, for example, the ratio Q/S were constant. Such constancy is unlikely throughout the entire period covered by our data, perhaps most notably because rent control was in effect until March 1956. The major control for variations in Q/S used in the estimation is a dummy variable that distinguishes years with rent control from years without, a technique that assumes Q/S was constant within the two periods.

The price index for rents used in the estimation is the Boston rent index drawn from Bureau of Labor Statistics, *Consumer Price Indexes in Selected SMSA's*, and it is available from 1944 to the present. Two price indexes reported in the same publication were used for operating inputs: the Boston consumer price index, available over the whole time span of the sample; and a price index for utilities and fuel, which can be readily constructed from 1953 on. Separate estimates of the elasticity of substitution were made using these two indexes for the price of operating inputs, and a graphical display of the data is shown in Figures 8A-1 and 8A-2. It is clear from Figure 8A-1, in which the CPI is used as the price index of operating inputs, that the sample seems to be broken into a rent control and post-rent-control period, except that both 1956 and 1957 appear to be part of the former period. Both 1956 and 1957 appear to be in the rent control period in Figure 8A-2 as well, where the index of utilities and fuels is used as the price of operating inputs. Because of the difficulty of defining the post-rent-control period with a dummy variable, two definitions were used: $D1$, which covers 1958-1969; and $D2$, for 1956-1969. Regression estimates of the elasticity of substitution using these dummy variables are shown in the following tabulation (figures in parentheses are t statistics):

Constant	Elasticity of Substitution	D1 (1958-1969)	D2 (1956-1969)	R^2
\multicolumn{5}{c}{Based on Consumer Price Index (sample = 1944-1969)}
−1.14	0.65 (7.59)	0.11 (8.04)		.77
−1.13	0.49 (3.83)		0.08 (3.63)	.43
\multicolumn{5}{c}{Based on Utility and Fuel Index (sample = 1953-1969)}
−1.13	0.63 (6.65)	0.08 (3.9)		.80
−1.09	0.32 (3.15)		−0.01 (0.03)	.57

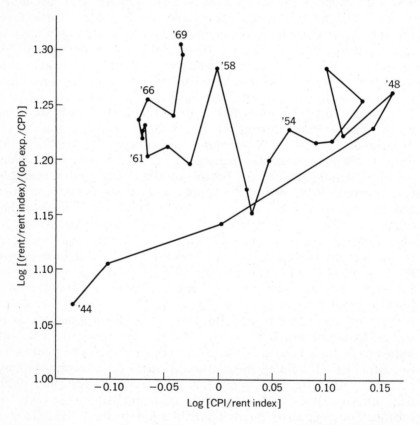

Figure 8A-1. Elasticity of Substitution Using Consumer Price Index (CPI).

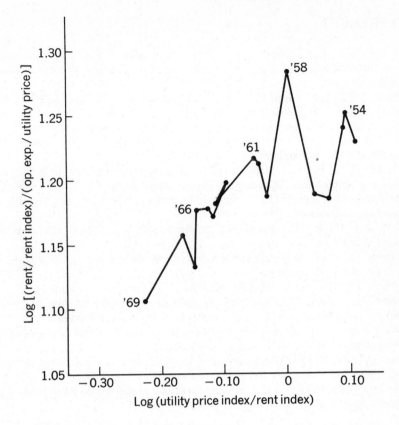

Figure 8A-2. Elasticity of Substitution Using Utility and Fuel Index.

NOTES TO CHAPTER EIGHT

1. Of course, this problem is not limited to housing capital; see Feldstein and Rothschild (1974).

2. Note that maintenance is defined as gross investment in quality capital and excludes operating inputs.

3. An exposition of this approach is given in Dildine and Massey (1974).

4. Alternatively, r_x might increase with the amount borrowed.

5. Operating expenses do not include property taxes. Details of the estimation are presented in Appendix 8A.

6. Since only quality capital depreciates, if the average depreciation rate for housing is 2 percent, we are assuming that quality capital amounts to one-fifth of the value of a unit.

7. Household expected rent for dwelling unit quality this period is $R(Q)$ of the previous period.

REFERENCES

Arrow, K.J.; H.B. Chenery; B.S. Minhas; and R.M. Solow. 1961. "Capital Labor Substitution and Economic Efficiency." *Review of Economics and Statistics*, August.

Brown, H.J.; J.R. Ginn; F.J. James; J.F. Kain; and M.R. Straszheim. 1972. *Empirical Models of Urban Land Use: Suggestions on Research Objectives and Organizations.* New York: National Bureau of Economic Research.

de Leeuw, F. 1972. "The Distribution of Housing Services." Processed. Washington, D.C.: Urban Institute. June.

Dildine, L.L., and F.A. Massey. 1974. "Dynamic Model of Private Incentives to Housing Maintenance." *Southern Economic Journal*, April.

Feldstein, M.S., and M. Rothschild. 1974. "Towards an Economic Theory of Replacement Investment." *Econometrica*, May.

Key, S.J. 1973. "The Economics of Rental Housing." Ph.D. dissertation, Harvard University.

Lowry, I.S. 1960. "Filtering and Housing Standards: A Conceptual Analysis." *Land Economics*, November.

Mills, E.S. 1970. "Urban Density Functions." *Urban Studies*, February.

Muth, R.F. 1969. *Cities and Housing.* Chicago: University of Chicago Press.

Smith, W.F. 1964. *Filtering and Neighborhood Change.* Research Report 24. Center for Real Estate and Urban Economics, Institute of Urban and Regional Development, University of California, Berkeley.

Sternlieb, G. 1975. "The Realities of Rent Control in the Greater Boston Area." Processed. Center for Urban Policy Research, Rutgers University.

Sweeney, J.L. 1974. "A Commodity Hierarchy Model of the Rental Housing Market." *Journal of Urban Economics*, July.

Comments on Chapter Eight

Jerome Rothenberg

This study by Ingram and Oron is ambitious, imaginative, and quite skillfully carried out. Its subject has up to now been only very slightly examined. It is highly suggestive, indicating useful directions for further work.

PRODUCTION INPUTS

The authors concentrate on the supply behavior of owners of existing rental housing. Their chief emphasis is on a distinction among three types of housing structure inputs with notably different longevities: structural capital, quality capital, and operating inputs. The three have different depreciation rates: essentially zero for structural capital, which is assumed to have an indefinite lifetime; one-period durability for operating inputs; and in-between for quality capital. Moreover, structural capital has a discontinuous cost function; and quality capital and operating inputs are deemed to have smooth substitution possibilities with one another.

What is gained from this trichotomy? First, a clear basis for generating the distinction between short- and long-run supply adjustments. Second, an interesting discussion of the transition adjustment process. There is an illuminating simulation application to a demand-supply interaction, with both policy runs and sensitivity analysis that carry a reasonably realistic ring. Thus, the distinctions are instructive; they highlight some important issues in supply—mostly relating to individual production and cost functions, and individual supplier behavior.

But the treatment does at the same time slight other important issues in housing supply: for example, questions about market structure, the aggregate supply behavior of different groups, competing types of supply, and the impact of different forms of competition—across tenure classes, structure types, neighborhoods, different quality levels, and between new construction and conversion. It excludes custom suppliers, i.e., those who are simply direct agents of users. Moreover, the emphasis on rental housing is too insulated. There is no note taken that market opportunities in the rental sector—the relation between rents and quality—depend on what is happening to demand *and supply* for ownership units: households can trade off across tenure classes.

PRODUCTION FUNCTION

Assuming the structural capital of existing units to be fixed, the authors treat the production of structural *quality* as a process involving quality capital and operating inputs in a CES production function. This entails continuous tradeoffs with constant elasticity of substitution and constant returns to scale over an indefinite range of structural quality. While there is some ambiguity as to what is included in the category of quality capital, this treatment reflects what may be a serious misrepresentation of the technical opportunities of changing the quality of existing structures. I shall begin by briefly characterizing what I take to be some salient features of such opportunities, and then relate these to the present treatment.

A given housing structure constrains future changes in quality in a variety of ways: (1) through size, general layout, materials, plumbing; (2) through more specific architectural features, such as number of rooms; (3) through particular installations, decorations, appliances; (4) through a given state of condition (repairs, etc.); (5) through a set of current services associated with occupancy, such as heating, garbage removal, cleanliness, etc. These groups are ordered in terms of the degree of constraint each exercises on future changes in quality. Groups 1 and 2 especially exert important technical, as well as aesthetic, complementarities that are absent, or must be violated, under significant conversion. Thus, in a housing supply model I have been working on for some time, if levels of overall quality are specified, for any given quality level new construction permits achievement of that level at a lower total cost than can be attained by converting an existing unit to the given level from some different starting level. The discrepancy between the two in total costs is greater the greater the required change through conversion from starting to target quality level.

These fundamental features may depreciate in terms of rental earning ability, indeed may even be totally written off in an accounting sense, and yet may continue to exert technical constraints on conversion because they *physically* remain. Not economic relevance but physical relevance is the basis of this influence. Explicit demolition costs are needed fully to undo the constraints, and demolition services should represent a genuine component of the production function.

Groups 3, 4, and 5 exert decreasing constraints on "coversions" in a broad sense of deliberate quality changes in existing units, with 5 alterable almost without constraint. But while these groups of characteristics can be more easily varied, they are also less important components of the housing package from the point of view of the user; and considerable alteration in these components increasingly strains basic complementarities with the more fundamental aspects of the housing package. Thus, increasing the frequency of redecorating does less and less to enhance living in a tiny apartment with abysmal plumbing. Even various combinations of changes in these types of components should have decreasing enhancement effect on user quality as the latter diverges increasingly from conventional balance with the more long-lived features of the housing unit.

Thus, conversion seems to involve a technology of decreasing returns to scale, whatever combination of inputs is involved (and whether or not new construction involves constant returns to scale). The more basic components affect user welfare strongly but are increasingly expensive in real resource costs. Demolition is required to liberate some aspects of the technical opportunities, but demolition requires a heavy use of resources, and this must be included as a genuine cost of the process. The less structurally intrinsic components are easier to vary in different combinations, but they are likely to have progressively less effect on user welfare when attached to unchanged basic features of the housing unit, and thus increasingly large package additions must be made to obtain equal impact on quality—a possibly more pronounced situation of decreasing returns to scale than for more basic conversions.

It is not clear what groups of components are included in "quality capital" as employed in the paper. The selection of a 15 percent depreciation rate in the original version (now reduced to 10 percent after serious questioning) plus oral discussion at the conference suggest that categories 4 and 5 and some shorter-lived items of 3 are intended. This seriously restricts the scope of the analysis, since it omits what many researchers in the field would consider the most important aspects of conversion. Property owners are not likely to attempt more than modest changes in quality by resort to these components alone. Larger quality changes are very likely to involve the more basic components as well. Yet, for the reasons given above, the criticism against a technology of constant returns to scale holds even for this reduced menu of conversions.

The above emphasis on technical constraints and complementarities has a broader significance than merely to suggest that constant returns are inappropriate. It implies that long-run outcomes are *much more* influenced by past and present supply decisions than the authors allow. (In the model the constant low cost of production in the long run wipes out all influence of the past after an extremely modest transition period.)

Given a present stock of housing with specific character, as demand changes to create new market opportunities, the newly attractive quality levels can be obtained at lower total cost through new construction rather than by converting existing units. (Such conversions have rising average cost functions.) But some of these latter might nonetheless outcompete the new units because the decision to convert is based on conversion plus opportunity costs, not total costs, and this sum is often much lower than total costs. (Net revenue at the original quality level, which would be foregone by conversion, comprises the opportunity cost.) Technical constraints on the *particular* units presently existing with help determine where such conversion can successfully compete with new construction and thus help determine the character of the overall response, even though new-construction technology in principle dominates conversion in the long run.

The long run, indeed, in this view, does not totally differ in character from a succession of short-run transitions, unlike in the Ingram-Oron model. Existing units do not disappear in any long run: they are maintained or converted, and so they continue to exist *in every period*, imposing their influence on the overall supply posture. Short-run sequences *are* the long run. Throughout this process, the character of existing stocks in each period is both a reflection of past supply decisions and an important influence on future ones.

Temporal sequences resulting from policy and other changes impinging on the system are an important part of the study. Its sharp cleavage between short-run transitions and long-run equilibriums, one of the presumed fruits of its distinctions among different types of housing input, is in fact based on an overly simple conceptualization. The difficulty stems from the authors' relative neglect of the market aggregation level—with that variety of competitive relationship whose absence we noted early in these remarks.

One final remark should be made about the production function.

A distinction should be made between the technology involved in raising quality and the technology involved in lowering it. This is especially important if quality capital is meant to include elements of the basic structure of the housing unit, with the result that, e.g., changes in the "scale" of the unit are envisaged. Raising quality is typically accomplished by positive investment of resources: a form of construction. Lowering quality can, however, be accomplished by either a comparable form of investment, i.e., by using resources to provide less space in more units, or by allowing the condition or operating services to decline, i.e., by refraining from spending resources. These are likely to involve different cost characteristics and require different gestation periods—an asymmetry between upward and some downward conversions.

ESTIMATION OF THE ELASTICITY OF SUBSTITUTION AND THE DISTRIBUTION FACTOR

The use of annual average rent per room as a measure of structural quality is unsatisfactory. It confounds structural quality with the balance of market forces. Neighborhoods and other aspects of housing units differ and influence average rent. These are not controlled for in the authors' procedure.

The original use of the consumer price index to represent the price of operating inputs was questionable because the latter comprise specific expenditure items and types of labor services that do not move dependently with the index over the business cycle. In the present version of the study, the CPI is supplemented by the fuel and utilities index, and this is an improvement. The problem of proper representation is still not solved, but the present procedure probably gives a more tolerable approximation.

"Guesstimates" for the relative elasticity of substitution for high-rise and low-rise structures may be inappropriate. The authors give 0.5 for low-rise and 0.6 for high-rise structures because of their belief "that a large 'plant' offers more possibilities for substitution than a small 'plant'." In fact, the reverse may be true. A high-rise structure is more complex than a low rise, with many tightly complementary linkages among structural components. Architectural constraints are probably more formidable for high-rise than for low-rise structures, permitting less substitution among components *once the structure is already built* (the authors' belief probably holds for the planning stage). The guesstimates used in the study may err both in absolute and comparative terms. This is important because in the simulations performed much depends on the elasticity of substitution.

In the original version of the study a depreciation rate of 15 percent per year was chosen for quality capital. That seemed much too high if quality capital covered significant aspects of the housing unit. The criterion for depreciation in this use is not marketability (or risk) of the unit but the exercise of constraints in conversions. The authors have now lowered it to 10 percent per year. This is certainly in the right direction. Moreover, if quality capital *is* restricted mostly to appliances and other nonintrinsic installations, as the conference discussion suggested, 10 percent may be appropriate. But, as I suggested above, this would considerably limit the scope and interest of the study. A more inclusive category, to make possible significant conversion possibilities, would call for a still lower depreciation rate.

PRICE EXPECTATIONS AND AGGREGATE GESTATION PERIODS

The analytical model proceeds on the assumption that each supplier (owner) has perfect knowledge of the relation between rent levels and quality levels over at least a planning interval of four or five years.

This appears to neglect some important aspects of rents as market phenomena. For example, housing supply typically has a long gestation period. A producer, whether of new or converted units, will often not know what other similar supply activities are "in the works" at any time. This can affect price—notably through triggering uninformed supply behavior. Secondly, it seems to omit the market effects of types of endogenous supply behavior competitive with the type of conversion focused on, namely, new construction and structural conversion. Changes in these latter supply modes should affect price; hence, when known or anticipated by quality converters, they should influence the behavior of the latter. If supply responses through other modes had short gestation periods, each converter could easily perceive the market price effects, and the assumed correct predictions of these would be apt. But gestation periods for the other modes are also lengthy—some lengthier than for this mode. So the same uninformedness holds here too.

Another issue, in addition to the prediction problem created by long gestation periods, is the aggregate competitiveness across supply modes. The proposed aggregate response of the supply mode in question will influence the aggregate response of the supply modes competitive with it and thus change market opportunities. Unless these two-way intermodal relationships are comprehended in the model in an explicitly dynamic setting, it is difficult to interpret the meaning of the assumption of accurate individual rent-quality predictions over the planning period.

FUNDING AND INTEREST RATES

The model assumes an unlimited amount of funds can be borrowed at a given fixed interest rate. This neglects the possibility of a (smoothly) rising cost of capital as a function of the level of new construction and conversions and thus partially endogenous. Alternatively, it neglects the possibility of credit rationing.

OVERALL EVALUATION

This study represents a useful inquiry into some of the theoretical and empirical issues involved in modeling housing supply. Many important issues have been excluded—as must be the case in all finite research. Unfortunately, however, some of these exclusions bias the results concerning what is *included*. The treatment of some of the empirical issues is defective in a way that shows how inherently difficult the area is to work in.

Comments on Chapter Eight

Marion Steele

This rigorous study by Ingram and Oron is of major importance because of the way it treats heterogeneity in housing. Its treatment is unique among housing models because, on the supply side, the production functions for different characteristics of housing are allowed to differ, and on the demand side, different characteristics of the housing bundle are entered as separate arguments in the utility function. This treatment, and only this treatment, makes it possible to focus on a question of crucial concern for public policy: What bundle of housing characteristics would a household consume after receiving a housing allowance?

To emphasize the importance of this question, let us pose the following: Would voters support a housing allowance if recipients used it merely to purchase better-located housing? If in fact voters would support an allowance only if it were used to increase the quality and size of dwellings, the simulation results suggest great difficulty for any allowance program. For these results show the interaction of demand and supply resulting in a tiny decrease, or no decrease at all, in the amount of the lowest-quality housing. Is this arresting result to be taken seriously? Quite seriously, I believe, but there are some problems in the analysis.

One problem is the incomplete specification of the characteristics of the housing stock. Ingram and Oron distinguish four: structure type, structure quality, neighborhood quality, and accessibility. To be complete, the specification should include another characteristic: dwelling unit size. As the concepts are currently defined, neither structure type nor structure quality encompasses this characteristic.

On the one hand, structure capital refers just to the foundation and shell. There is nothing explicitly disallowing the possibility of a given shell containing, say, three large units instead of four smaller ones; and in the simulation experiments the authors use two structure types which differ in number of dwelling units but not in dwelling unit size. On the other hand, structure quality does not encompass dwelling size. We infer this from the high depreciation rate (10 percent) assumed for quality capital, and from the characterization of increments in quality capital as maintenance. Furthermore, in their empirical estimation, the authors take rent per room to represent quality; this allows quality to reflect the size of rooms, but not their number. In my view, dwelling unit size should be explicitly included as a separate characteristic, rather than merged into either the structure type or structure quality concepts. There is substantial evidence that the demand parameters for these three aspects of housing differ greatly.[1]

A further problem in the authors' treatment of heterogeneity is their lack of complete carryover from the analytical section to the simulations. While structure quality is endogenously determined in the simulations, structure type is not. In addition, in the simulations, as in the analysis, neighborhood quality is exogenous, and of course, dwelling unit size is omitted. Thus, in the simulations we have two polar extremes of supply elasticity: the supply of structure type—and the neighborhood—is perfectly inelastic, while, because of the nature of the assumed production function, the supply of structure quality is perfectly elastic. Ceteris paribus, then, the increase in structure quality resulting from a housing allowance is biased upward, and the change in structure type (and dwelling unit size) is biased downward. In view of this, the actual simulation result—an absence of any change in the number of units of the worst quality level in the less desirable neighborhood (Table 8-9, middle section, rows one and two)—is indeed remarkable.

We suspect that if two kinds of changes were made, the results would be much more favorable to a housing allowance. First, the authors' demand equations assume that (1) the strength of preference for neighborhood quality relative to structure quality is precisely the same for low-income as for high-income households (Table 8-4) and (2) the elasticity of the probability of a household's choosing a particular quality level *declines* as the quality level declines (Equation (8-27)). The Bailey (1966) hypothesis of segregation suggests that assumption (1) is inappropriate and should be changed to make low-income households prefer neighborhood quality relatively less strongly. This, plus a change in assumption (2) to a constant elasticity, would substantially increase the structure quality demand of households in the allowance-receiving groups. And as the authors comment, simulation results for the quantity of quality are certainly sensitive to changes in the demand parameters (Table 8-4 and 8-7).

The second kind of change I suspect would make a substantial difference to the results would be the introduction, as suggested above, of dwelling size as a separate characteristic. Some of the housing allowance used to purchase neighborhood quality would be diverted to increase the number of rooms. Since I suspect that the number of rooms, especially in low-rise structures, is relatively elastic in supply, the simulation result might be a substantial reduction in the number of units with few rooms. Voters would be inclined to accept an allowance program, I believe, if it resulted in more privacy (less crowding) as well as greater structure quality.

These comments point up the importance of the specification of an "additions" function; this would be required where dwelling unit size is taken to refer to square feet of space rather than number of rooms. This problem is, of course, closely associated with the knotty problem of specifying a function for cost of conversion to a different structure type. No such function is given, but perhaps the problem would become more tractable if space and number of rooms were explicitly part of the model.

Finally, I would like to see the supply side of the model modified to accommodate the effects of income and property taxes. These do not properly belong under the heading of "fixed costs" (Equation (8-3)). Often, appraisal practice makes property tax a function of total capital (i.e., here, K_t), so taxes rise with increments in quality capital. This increases the price of quality capital relative to the price of operating inputs, and also increases the price of quality.

NOTE TO COMMENT ON CHAPTER EIGHT

1. See David (1962) and note that to a large extent the owner-tenant split is a proxy for a structure-type split. Also see Straszheim (1975, tables 4.5-4.7) but note that the latter assumes that elasticities do not change with income.

REFERENCES

Bailey, Martin. 1966. "Effects of Race and Other Demographic Factors on the Value of Single Family Homes." *Land Economics*, May.

David, Martin. 1962. *Family Composition and Consumption*. Amsterdam: North-Holland.

Straszheim, Mahlon, R. 1975. *An Econometric Analysis of the Urban Housing Market*. New York: National Bureau of Economic Research.

Part IV

Invited Student Papers

Chapter Nine

Housing Discrimination and Job Search

Susan C. Nelson

INTRODUCTION

The effect of housing discrimination on the employment opportunities of urban blacks has been the subject of much debate since John Kain's influential article in 1968. Kain's conclusion that the elimination of housing segregation would produce a substantial number of additional jobs for blacks has been challenged on several grounds: on his methodology, by the observation that there still is an adequate supply of jobs in the inner cities despite decentralization, and by the assertion that other factors, such as the strength of local aggregate demand and employment discrimination, seem more important.[1]

Distinguishing the empirical effects of the various issues involved is a complex process. By simplifying and abstracting from considerations that are empirically problematical but theoretically unimportant (such as the extent of employment discrimination), however, the model of job search in a spatial context presented here examines the ways that constraints on blacks' residential mobility might affect their employment situation. I do not try to determine whether or not housing discrimination exists; that has been frequently and extensively examined elsewhere.[2] Rather, if blacks who initially live in the inner city are victims of housing discrimination, the model predicts, not surprisingly, that their average wage is lower in central-city jobs and higher in suburban areas than it would be in the absence of a locational constraint. In addition, their employment will be more concentrated near the center of the city. The impact of housing discrimination on the duration of unemployment, however, cannot be determined.

The analysis proceeds as follows: The urban setting is described. A model of random, sequential job search is applied to two job hunters, a black and a white, who begin searching from residences in the center of the city. It is assumed that housing discrimination prevents the black from changing his residential location. By using the concept of stochastic dominance, implications may be drawn on the impact of housing discrimination on black employment opportunities. These conclusions are modified when a less extreme and more realistic version of discrimination is assumed.

THE CITY

The setting for the model is a circular city[3] much like that described in Mills (1972). The following assumptions are made: (1) There are two main sectors—production-employment and housing—which compete for land in the city and determine locational patterns there. (2) Some housing and some employment occur in all areas of the city. All parcels of land the same distance from the center contain the same economic activities. (3) Land in the very center of the city is valued most highly because of agglomeration economies or proximity to transportation facilities. (4) If production functions permit substitution between inputs, then because proximity to the CBD has value, land rents as a function of distance from the CBD decline at a decreasing rate (for proof, see Mills 1972, Chap. 5). The ratio of capital and labor to land will be highest in the CBD, thereby economizing on the scarce resource of central land; hence, employment density $[D(k)]$ will also decline with k, the number of miles from the CBD: $D'(k) < 0$.[4]

An equilibrium distribution of housing services occurs when no household can increase its utility by moving. It is assumed that households have no preference for either city or suburban living per se. Then, since employment density decreases with distance from the CBD, a given quantity of housing services can command a higher price if it is nearer, rather than farther from, the CBD. People will pay more for a location that requires lower transportation costs. This reinforces the pattern of land rents decreasing with distance from the center of the city, and implies that housing prices $[P(k)]$ also will be lower at more distant locations: $P'(k) < 0$.

Let the quantity of housing services (H) demanded be a function of permanent income, price, and tastes. A person with a given permanent income and employed at any distance k_1 from the CBD, such that $k_1 \leqslant k_2$, will find his utility is maximized (i.e., he lives at an equilibrium location) if he resides at a distance k_2 from the CBD, where moving further out would increase transportation costs more than it would save on housing expenditures, and moving further in would increase housing costs more than it would lower commuting costs.[5] If the transportation function is linear of the form $T = m + t$ u, where u is the straight line distance between home and work, the equilibrium location occurs where $P'(k)_2 H(k_2) = -t$. If by chance a person's employment is situated farther from the CBD than k_2, he would choose to live at or as near as possible to his work, since the optimal amount of commuting for him is zero.

THE SEARCH

In this setting, two workers, B and W, living in the center of the city at $k = 0$ begin looking for work in occupation Z. Both employment and vacancies occur as fixed proportions of total employment at all locations in the city. Employment in Z/total employment = a; total vacancies/total employment = c. Thus the density of openings in this job category equals $\alpha D(k)$, where $\alpha = a\,c$. B and W are identical in all respects except race: they possess the same amount and quality of human capital and the same preferences, face the same employment opportunities at the same wages (no employment discrimination exists), have access to the same employment information systems, share the same commuting and search cost functions, and have the same permanent income. B experiences discrimination in the housing market, however, while W does not. In this section, discrimination takes an extreme form: B is unable to move from his[6] initial location while W is free to locate his residence in an optimal relation to any job he accepts.[7] Another, more realistic form of discrimination is assumed: the costs to B associated with moving from the CBD are high but noninfinite.

In the first instance, any nominal wage offer Y at a distance k_1 will be worth more to W than to B in utility terms if a noncentral residence is optimal, because of the declining housing price function. The difference in the value of $Y(k_1)$ to B and W can be approximated by comparing the "real wages" that this implies for each worker, where the real wage equals the wage from the employer minus housing expenditures, transportation costs, and moving expenses (if relevant) for the worker's residential location if he accepts the offer.

$$y_b(k_1) = Y(k_1) - P(0)H + T(k_1 - 0) \qquad (9\text{-}1a)$$

$$y_w(k_1) = Y(k_1) - \min[P(0)H + T(k_1 - 0); P(k_1)H + M^*; \quad (9\text{-}1b)$$

$$P(k_2)H + T(k_2 - k_1) + M^*]$$

where

y_b and y_w = real wages of B and W, respectively, for an offer of Y at k_1;

$T(k_i - k_j)$ = commuting costs, which are some function of the difference between the distances indicated within the parentheses;

H = quantity of housing demanded at $P(0)$;

M^* = moving costs discounted over the expected length of employment; if M = total moving costs incurred in period 0, M^* is defined by:

$$M = \sum_{i=1}^{n+1} \frac{M^*}{(1 + p)^i}$$

where p is the discount factor; and n, the expected number of periods of employment;

0 = initial residential distance from the CBD;

k_1 = distance of employment from the CBD;

k_2 = equilibrium residential distance from the CBD for jobs at $k_1 \leqslant k_2$, where $T' = -P'(k_2)H$.

So that these real wages will represent at least monotonic transformations of levels of utility for B and W, W's housing consumption is held equal to B's. Otherwise, if housing demand were quite price-elastic, W's housing expenditures might exceed B's (in spite of the lower price facing W) causing y_w to be less than y_b even though W's utility could be the higher. Analyzing W's behavior with the implicit assumption of a price elasticity of zero results in a lower bound to the amount by which W's utility exceeds B's.

The costs of moving include the costs of finding a new home, any psychological costs, and the actual expenses of packing, hiring a van, etc. M^* is taken as a constant, although costs probably do increase to some extent with distance moved even within the metropolitan area.

The decision whether or not to move, given employment at k_1, is made by comparing the costs of living at the initial location with the costs at k_1 and k_2. Thus W will choose to move if:

$$P(0)H + T(k_1 - 0) > \min [P(k_1)H + M^*; P(k_2)H + T(k_2 - k_1) + M^*]$$

$$(9\text{-}2a)$$

The circle of radius $\overline{k}_1$ such that at $\overline{k}_1$,

$$P(0)H + T(\overline{k}_1 - 0) = \min [P(\overline{k}_1)H + M^*; P(k_2)H + T(k_2 - \overline{k}_1) + M^*]$$

$$(9\text{-}2b)$$

forms the boundary between the region in which employment could be located and the worker would not benefit from moving either to k_1 or k_2 ($k_1 \leqslant \overline{k}_1$ in the no-move region) and the area for which moving would be beneficial ($k_1 > \overline{k}_1$ for the move region). If the no-move area is small, the worker will be considered very mobile. As can be seen from Equation (9-2b), the tendency to move depends on three factors. Ceteris paribus, if transportation costs are high, the worker is more apt to move, and $\overline{k}_1$ will be small. If the housing price function is very steep (i.e., the gradient is large), moving will be beneficial more often than if the gradient is small. And clearly the lower M^*, the smaller is the worker's no-move region. In this context, housing discrimination could be viewed as raising B's costs of moving so high that nowhere in the metropolitan area would the benefits of moving exceed the costs.

Assume that nominal wage offers in occupation Z at each k_1 ($0 \leqslant k_1 \leqslant k^*$), where k^* equals the distance from the CBD to the edge of the city, are distributed according to the set of non-single-valued functions $[Y|k_1]D$. Such distributions can persist if, for example, the cost of maintaining vacancies is higher for some firms than for others; then the former would offer higher wages to raise the probability of filling their openings more quickly. B and W are aware of these densities and hence of the distribution of real wages each faces in the city: $f(y_b)$ and $g(y_w)$, with $F(y_b)$ and $G(y_w)$ the respective cumulative distributions. Since the real value to B of any nominal wage offer is less than or equal to the value to W, it may be said that $g(y_w)$ is larger than $f(y_b)$ in the sense of first-degree stochastic dominance (FSD) as defined in Hadar and Russell (1969, p. 27):

$$G(y_w) \leqslant F(y_b) \qquad (9\text{-}3)$$

for all y in the interval $[0, L]$, where L is the maximum possible wage offer. $g(y_w)$ may be considered to strictly dominate $f(y_b)$ if (9-3) holds and if for some y in $[0,L]$, $G(y_w) < F(y_b)$. This will occur if for employment located at some k_1 within the boundary of the metropolitan area the inequality in Equation (9-2) holds and if it is optimal for W to move outside the center of the city. Strict FSD also implies strict second-degree stochastic dominance (SSD), which is defined as:

$$\int_q^L G(y)dy < \int_q^L F(y)dy \qquad (9\text{-}4)$$

for all lower bounds q in the interval $[0, L]$ (from Hadar and Russell 1969). The domination of the distribution of real wage opportunities facing W over that available to B will be used in determining the relation between B's and W's expected wages.

Job search occurs as a random sample drawn from $f(y_b)$ and $g(y_w)$; one draw is allotted per period, as if each worker went to the employment service and was given one randomly selected firm to check each day.[8] The worker must decide whether to accept or reject the offer in the same period in which it is made. (If no offer is made, the search can be considered as having found a nominal wage of zero.) It has been shown (McCall 1970, Nelson 1970, and Kohn and Shavell 1974) that the optimal strategy, the one that maximizes the present value of expected wealth, is to reject if the discounted expected benefits of searching outweigh the costs of another search, and to accept if the reverse is true. This produces a critical value called the acceptance wage, or reservation wage: if the offer exceeds the acceptance wage, accept it; if not, reject and search again (see among others, McCall 1970, Rothschild 1973, and Mortensen 1970).

This can be represented as:

$$S = \sum_{i=1}^{n+1} \frac{\int_{\overline{y}_b}^L (y_b - \overline{y}_b)f(y_b)dy_b}{(1+p)^i} = \sum_{i=1}^{n+1} \frac{\int_{\overline{y}_w}^L (y_w - \overline{y}_w)g(y_w)dy_w}{(1+p)^i} \qquad (9\text{-}5)$$

$\overline{y}_b$ = real acceptance wage for B;
$\overline{y}_w$ = real acceptance wage for W;
n = expected number of periods of employment;
p = discount factor; and
S = cost of the next search.

Simplifying (9-5), we obtain at the limit, as n approaches infinity,

$$S = \frac{1}{p} \int_{y_b}^{L} (y_b - \overline{y}_b) f(y_b) dy_b = \frac{1}{p} \int_{y_w}^{L} (y_w - \overline{y}_w) g(y_w) dy_w \qquad (9\text{-}6)$$

Search costs include such factors as out-of-pocket costs of transportation to the job site; time costs of the trip and the interview, valued at the minimum wage or whatever other value the worker places on his leisure[9]; costs of information on potential vacancies; and the psychological costs of any disutility the worker experiences in searching such as discomfort in a job interview or uncertainty about whether or not an offer will be forthcoming. For simplicity the costs of one search, S, will be assumed to be the same for B and W and to be constant in all periods and over all job locations. Clearly, more plausible assumptions would be that search costs increase with the distance between the job and the initial residential location and with the length of time the worker has been unemployed.[10] Realistically, S also is higher for B than for W because, for example, the informal information systems accessible to W are superior to those available to B, since W is more likely to have friends and relatives who are employed and whose employment is more dispersed throughout the city.

Given the structure and assumptions outlined above, any differences in the search process undertaken by B compared to W would be attributable only to discrimination in the housing market, preventing B from changing his residential location.

Proposition A

If $f(y_b)$ is strictly dominated by $g(y_w)$, B's real acceptance wage must be less than W's: $\overline{y}_b < \overline{y}_w$.

$$\int_{\overline{y}_b}^{L} y_b f(y_b) dy_b - y_b F(y_b) \Big|_{\overline{y}_b}^{L} = \int_{\overline{y}_w}^{L} y_w g(y_w) dy_w - y_w G(y_w) \Big|_{\overline{y}_w}^{L}$$

$$(9\text{-}7)$$

Simplifying and integrating by parts:

$$y_b F(y_b) \Big|_{\overline{y}_b}^{L} - \int_{\overline{y}_b}^{L} F(y_b) dy_b - \overline{y}_b [1 - F(\overline{y}_b)] = y_w G(y_w) \Big|_{\overline{y}_w}^{L}$$

$$- \int_{\overline{y}_w}^{L} G(y_w) dy_w - \overline{y}_w [1 - G(\overline{y}_w)] \qquad (9\text{-}8)$$

$$\overline{y}_b + \int_{y_b}^{L} F(y_b)dy_b = \overline{y}_w + \int_{y_w}^{L} G(y_w)dy_w \qquad (9\text{-}9)$$

If $\overline{y}_w \leqslant \overline{y}_b$, (9-9) becomes:

$$\overline{y}_b + \int_{y_b}^{L} F(y_b)dy_b = \overline{y}_w + \int_{y_w}^{\overline{y}_b} G(y_w)dy_w + \int_{y_b}^{L} G(y_w)dy_w \qquad (9\text{-}10)$$

Since $[\overline{y}_b - \overline{y}_w] = \int_{y_w}^{\overline{y}_b} dy_w$, (9-6) is equivalent to:

$$\int_{y_b}^{L} F(y_b)dy_b - \int_{y_b}^{L} G(y_w)dy_w + \int_{y_w}^{\overline{y}_b} [1 - G(y_w)]\,dy_w = 0 \qquad (9\text{-}11)$$

But since by assumption $g(y_w)$ strictly dominates $f(y_b)$,

$$\int_{y_b}^{L} F(y_b)dy_b - \int_{y_b}^{L} G(y_w)dy_w > 0$$

and if $\overline{y}_b \geqslant \overline{y}_w$, $\int_{y_w}^{\overline{y}_b} [1 - G(y_w)]dy_w > 0$. Hence, the equality in

(9-11) cannot hold if $\overline{y}_b \geqslant \overline{y}_w$.
    If, on the other hand, $\overline{y}_w > \overline{y}_b$, (9-9) becomes:

$$\overline{y}_b + \int_{y_b}^{\overline{y}_w} F(y_b)dy_b + \int_{y_w}^{L} F(y_b)dy_b = \overline{y}_w + \int_{y_w}^{L} G(y_w)dy_w \qquad (9\text{-}12)$$

and

$$\int_{y_w}^{L} F(y_b)dy_b - \int_{y_w}^{L} G(y_w)dy_w - \int_{y_b}^{\overline{y}_w} [1 - F(y_b)]\,dy_b = 0 \qquad (9\text{-}13)$$

Again, since $g(y_w)$ dominates $f(y_b)$, the first term in (9-13) is positive and $\int_{y_b}^{\overline{y}_w} [1 - F(y_b)] dy_b$ is nonnegative; so the equality can hold. Thus, the assumption that the distribution of effective wages for B is strictly dominated by the distribution for W implies that W's effective acceptance wage will exceed B's.

Proposition B

Depending on moving costs for W, in some range of k_1, $(0 \leqslant k_1 < k_i)$ B's nominal acceptance wage will be less than W's, and for k_1 greater than k_i within the city, the opposite will be true.

Proof: Let $\overline{k}$ be the distance at which moving becomes beneficial for W. Let B's and W's nominal acceptance wages for employment at any k_1 be defined, respectively, as:

$$\overline{Y}_b(k_1) = \overline{y}_b + P(0)H + T(k_1 - 0) \tag{9-14a}$$

$$\overline{Y}_w(k_1) = \overline{y}_w + \min[P(0)H + T(k_1 - 0); P(k_1)H + M^*; \tag{9-14b}$$

$$P(k_2)H + T(k_2 - k_1) + M^*]$$

These represent the minimum wages that must be offered B and W, such that they will not expect another search to make them better off than if they accepted the current offer.

$$0 \leqslant k_1 \leqslant \overline{k}_1: \overline{Y}_w(k_1) - \overline{Y}_b(k_1) = \overline{y}_w - \overline{y}_b > 0$$

In this region B and W incur the same housing and commuting costs. Since throughout the city W's real acceptance wage exceeds B's, here too will W's nominal asking wage be higher than B's by the amount that their real acceptance wages differ: $\overline{Y}_w(k_1 \mid k_1 \leqslant \overline{k}_1) - \overline{Y}_b(k_1 \mid k_1 \leqslant \overline{k}_1) = \overline{y}_w - \overline{y}_b$.

$$\overline{k}_1 < k_1 < k_i: \overline{y}_w - \overline{y}_b > Y_w(k) - Y_b(k)$$

Defining k_i as that distance at which $\overline{Y}_b(k_1) = \overline{Y}_w(k_1)$; $\overline{Y}_w(k_1)$ still exceeds $\overline{Y}_b(k_1)$ but by less than $(\overline{y}_w - \overline{y}_b)$.

$$k_i < k_1 < k^*: \overline{Y}_w(k_1) < \overline{Y}_b(k_1)$$

B's nominal acceptance wage is greater than W's, meaning that B will reject offers that W accepts (if $k_i < k^*$).

An example of the pattern described above is shown in Figure 9-1.[11] It implies that the average wage for employment near the center of the city (specifically, within a radius of k_i) will be lower for blacks than for whites. The opposite would be true at jobs beyond k_i—blacks who are employed there would expect to be paid more than their white coworkers.

Superficially, this pattern might suggest that central-city firms discriminate against blacks, while suburban firms act in their favor. However, this result has been produced by explicitly excluding employment discrimination; the outcome is due only to the constraint housing discrimination puts on blacks' residential location.

Proposition C

Housing discrimination has an indeterminate impact on the length of unemployment, or duration of search, of B relative to W. Only if the real wage distribution were more precisely specified could any comparisons be made.

Proof: Since the probability that the next offer made will be acceptable to B is $[1 - F(\overline{y}_b)]$ and to W is $[1 - G(\overline{y}_w)]$, the relative size of $F(\overline{y}_b)$ and $G(\overline{y}_w)$ would indicate whether B had been unemployed on average longer than W, or the opposite. Unfortunately, both $F(\overline{y}_b) > G(\overline{y}_w)$ and the reverse are consistent with the model. In terms of Figure 9-2, point C must be to the left of A, but

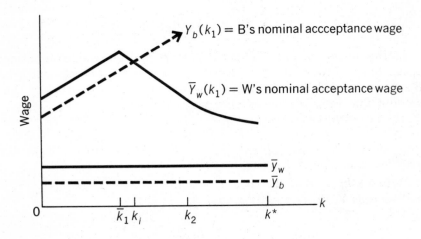

k = number of miles from CBD.

Figure 9-1.

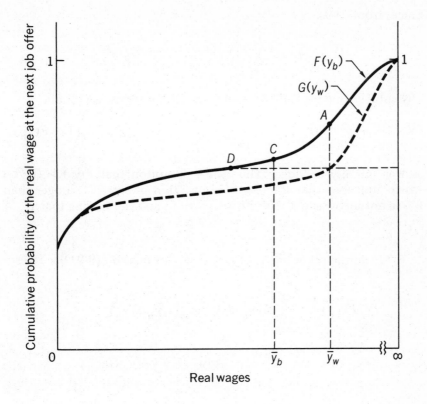

Figure 9-2.

it can be either to the right or left of point D. Here, $F(\overline{y}_b) > G(\overline{y}_w)$, but the opposite is also possible.

(a) If housing discrimination in this model causes B to search longer than W, $F(\overline{y}_b) > G(\overline{y}_w)$ and $Pr(b) = [1 - F(\overline{y}_b)] < [1 - G(\overline{y}_w)] = Pr(w)$; so $\overline{y}_b[1 - F(\overline{y}_b)] < \overline{y}_w[1 - G(\overline{y}_w)]$. Equation (9-9) may be rewritten as:

$$y_b F(y_b) \Big|_{\overline{y}_b}^{L} - \int_{\overline{y}_b}^{L} F(y_b) dy_b < y_w G(y_w) \Big|_{\overline{y}_w}^{L} - \int_{\overline{y}_w}^{L} G(y_w) dy_w$$

(9-15)

or,

$$\overline{y}_b F(\overline{y}_b) + \int_{\overline{y}_b}^{L} F(y_b) dy_b > \overline{y}_w G(\overline{y}_w) + \int_{\overline{y}_w}^{L} G(y_w) dy_w$$

Since, from (9-9),

$$(\bar{y}_w - \bar{y}_b) = \int_{y_b}^{L} F(y_b)dy_b - \int_{y_w}^{L} G(y_w)dy_w$$

by substituting into (9-15), then rearranging terms, we obtain

$$\bar{y}_b F(\bar{y}_b) - \bar{y}_w G(\bar{y}_w) > \bar{y}_b - \bar{y}_w ; \bar{y}_w [1 - G(\bar{y}_w)] > \bar{y}_b [1 - F(\bar{y}_b)]$$

as was initially assumed. Thus the assumption that $F(\bar{y}_b) > G(\bar{y}_w)$ which indicates that B's expected duration of search is longer than W's is not inconsistent with Equation (9-9) and the finding that $\bar{y}_w > \bar{y}_b$.

(b) If on the other hand, $F(\bar{y}) < G(\bar{y}_w)$, Equation (9-9) becomes:

$$y_b F(y_b)\Big|_{y_b}^{L} - \int_{y_b}^{L} F(y_b)dy_b - \bar{y}_b + \bar{y}_b F(\bar{y}_b)$$

$$= y_w G(y_w)\Big|_{y_w}^{L} - \int_{y_w}^{L} G(y_w)dy_w - \bar{y}_w + \bar{y}_w G(\bar{y}_w)$$

$$-\bar{y}_b F(\bar{y}_b) - \int_{y_b}^{L} F(y_b)dy_b - \bar{y}_b > -\bar{y}_w G(\bar{y}_w)$$

$$-\int_{y_w}^{L} G(y_w)dy_w - \bar{y}_w$$

Multiplying through by -1 and subtracting

$$\bar{y}_b + \int_{y_b}^{L} F(y_b)dy_b = \bar{y}_w + \int_{y_w}^{L} G(y_w)dy_w$$

from both sides leads to the conclusion that $\bar{y}_b F(\bar{y}_b) < \bar{y}_w G(\bar{y}_w)$, which is simply a restatement of the initial assumption.

The condition that $g(y_w)$ dominates $f(y_b)$ and the resultant implication that $\bar{y}_b < \bar{y}_w$ clearly are insufficient for determining whether $F(\bar{y}_b)$ is greater or less than $G(\bar{y}_w)$. Thus, housing discrimination appears to have no general predictable effect on the relative length of search undertaken by B compared to W.

Proposition D

Unless W is totally immobile residentially, B's employment will be more centralized than W's.

Proof:

Case I. For any location of employment, W always benefits from moving out of the center of the city.

Regardless of where he works, W will choose to move from the center of the city, either to k_2, or to k_1 if k_1 is greater than k_2. Since his real acceptance wage is independent of the location of employment, the value to him of a given nominal wage rises continually with distance from the CBD, and so his nominal acceptance wage falls with distance. Because the reverse is true for B (for a given nominal wage, CBD jobs are worth the most to him) and his asking wage rises with distance, the relative probability of B's becoming employed at any location compared to W's probability is a decreasing function of distance from the CBD, regardless of the distribution of wage offers by firms. Thus, housing discrimination, which prevents B from moving, causes B's employment to be more concentrated near the center of the city than it would otherwise be.

Since the amount by which W's real acceptance wage exceeds B's is unknown, no comparison of their nominal asking wages averaged for the whole city can be made.

Case II. W never chooses to move, regardless of the location of employment.

In this instance the real opportunities available are identical for both workers, and any housing discrimination that B experiences is irrelevant, since he, like W, would not choose to leave the central city even if he could. The nominal acceptance wages of both types of workers will rise with distance from the CBD. Their actual employment distributions depend on the distribution of wage offers, but B will have the same probability as W of accepting a job at any location.

Case III. For some locations of potential employment, W will move.

Again, because the real opportunities available to W are superior to those facing B, the former's real acceptance wage will exceed the latter's: $\overline{y}_w > \overline{y}_b$. For employment in the center of the city and in the rest of W's no-move zone, the housing and transportation costs would be the same to both workers. Consequently, W's nominal acceptance wage will exceed B's for any job in W's no-move region: $\overline{Y}_w(k_1) > \overline{Y}_b(k_1)$ for all k_1 less than k_i. Thus W is less apt than B to become employed in this area, but if W does accept a job there, his nominal wage will on the average be higher than B's at the same location.

On the other hand, in W's move area, his probability of accepting employment is greater than B's (unless marginal transportation costs are very small[12]). Thus B's employment will be more centralized than W's, but B's expected wage for working in the central city would be less than W's, while W's average wage near the edge of the city would be higher than B's there. The residential mobility of W determines the size of this no-move area and, thus, whether the distribution of B's and W's employment is quite different or only slightly so. The greater the number of firms for which W would find moving beneficial, the more centralized will B's employment be relative to W's.

From comparing B's employment and expected wage distributions over distance with W's under various conditions of mobility, it is clear that unless W is as immobile without discrimination as B is with it, the extreme form of discrimination considered here makes B's employment more centralized and lowers his average nominal wage near the CBD as well as reducing his real wage everywhere, but raises his nominal wage farther out in the city. No conclusion can be reached, however, on his expected nominal wage relative to W's over the whole city without specifying the model more precisely.

MODIFIED FORM OF HOUSING DISCRIMINATION

Clearly, the assumption that housing discrimination totally prevents blacks from moving out of the center city is not true: some blacks do live in suburban areas, although their representation is much lower than their income alone would warrant (Census 1973); and, more relevant for the model under consideration, some blacks move from the central ghetto to the suburban ring. Hence, a more reasonable assumption about the form housing discrimination takes would be then that blacks can move to suburban areas but that the move is much more costly for them than for whites.[13] The additional costs could result from the difficulties and unpleasantness of dealing with white realtors; the refusal of some whites to sell or rent to blacks, forcing them to visit more housing units before finding an acceptable one; or an uncertain reception by white neighbors. Thus, housing discrimination could impose high but noninfinite costs on blacks who move out of the inner city: $M_w < M_b < \infty$.

In this case, B calculates his optimal residential location in the same way that W does. If a job is located beyond $\overline{k}_1^b$ (the distance at which B is indifferent between staying in the center city and moving), he will move either to k_2 or to k_1, whichever is greater. $\overline{k}_1^b$ occurs where:

$$P(0)H + T(k_1^{-b}) = \min[P(k_2)H + T(k_2 - k_1^{-b}) + M_b^*; P(k_1^{-b})H + M_b^*]$$

If $\overline{k}_1^b \leqslant k_2$, B's optimal residential location for any job for which he chooses to move will be the same as W's. It does not matter that M_b exceeds M_w, since moving costs that are independent of distance moved, as assumed here, do not enter the calculation of k_2. Only for jobs located between $\overline{k}_1^b$ and $\overline{k}_1^w$ will B and W have different residential locations: W will choose to leave the central city while B will not.

This fact results in some differences between the search processes undertaken by B and W. Since the same nominal wage offers are available to both workers, the real value of any offer to W will always be equal to or greater than the value for B. At all locations beyond $\overline{k}_1^b$, the real wage for W will exceed B's. Again the distribution of real wage opportunities available to W, i.e., $g(y_w)$, will dominate those facing B, i.e., $f(y_b)$. Therefore, as was shown in Proposition A, $\overline{y}_w > \overline{y}_b$.

The nominal acceptance wage for W will again exceed $\overline{Y}_b$, at least to $\overline{k}_1^w$, by $(\overline{y}_w - \overline{y}_b)$. Between $\overline{k}_1^w$ and $\overline{k}_1^b$, $\overline{Y}_w(k_1)$ is decreasing and $\overline{Y}_b(k_1)$ increasing. Beyond k_1^b:

$$\overline{Y}_w(k) - \overline{Y}_b(k) - [(\overline{y}_w - \overline{y}_b) + (M_w^* - M_b^*)] \qquad (9\text{-}16)$$

Since the first term is positive and the second negative, the sign of $[\overline{Y}_w(k) - \overline{Y}_b(k)]$ can only be determined if the terms of Equation (9-16) are known more precisely. Intuitively, if M_b is quite large, the situation is similar to the case originally examined, where discrimination prevented B from moving at all and caused $\overline{Y}_b(k)$ generally to exceed $\overline{Y}_w(k)$ at points beyond $\overline{k}_1^w$. Thus it seems probable that $|M_w^* - M_b^*|$ exceeds $(\overline{y}_w - \overline{y}_b)$, and $[\overline{Y}_w(k) - \overline{Y}_b(k)]$ is negative beyond $\overline{k}_1^b$ (as is shown in Figure 9-3), but this cannot be proved as a general rule.

As with the extreme version of housing discrimination, the relative duration of search for B and W in this instance remains indeter-

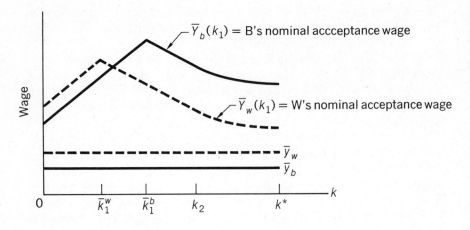

k = number of miles from CBD.

Figure 9-3.

minate. However, if it were true that $\overline{Y}_b < \overline{Y}_w$ for all k_1 (as seems unlikely), then B would clearly expect to find an acceptable job more quickly than W. If $\overline{Y}_w < \overline{Y}_b$ for some k_1, the answer would again depend on the specific distributions.

One definite conclusion, though, may be drawn concerning the relative concentration of employment. Around the center of the city, where $\overline{Y}_w(k) > \overline{Y}_b(k)$, blacks have a higher probability of receiving an acceptable offer than whites. Not only will blacks' employment be more centralized, but their average wage (at least within the circle of radius $\overline{k}_1^w$) will be lower than the average for whites working in the same area, again even in the absence of any racial discrimination in the labor market.

SUMMARY

The framework outlined here is an attempt to describe one mechanism through which racial discrimination in the housing market could affect the employment situation of blacks by constraining their residential location. The conclusions are not surprising. Simply because the type of discrimination postulated here limits residential mobility, it induces blacks to follow a different job search pattern than they would in the absence of housing discrimination. As would have been expected, housing discrimination lowers the real income of blacks from what would have prevailed in the absence of constrained residential location. This is true even in the suburbs, where discrimination perhaps raises their average wage. It forces blacks to take lower wages in the central city besides possibly concentrating their employment there.

This is only part of the story, though. A general equilibrium analysis would include the response of firms, such as adjustments through factor substitution and plant relocation, to the effects of housing discrimination on the labor market behavior of blacks. The land and housing price-distance functions would also be expected to shift. As long as $P(k)$ had a negative but increasing slope, the conclusions in this study would remain valid. It might become possible, however, to draw broader implications such as the effects on white workers, firms, relative housing prices, and the level and efficiency of production.

NOTES TO CHAPTER NINE

1. Criticism on methodology comes from Saks-Offner (1971) and Masters (1974); on central-city labor demand, from Noll (1970), Fremon (1970), and Lewis (1969); on aggregate demand conditions from Mooney (1969); and on employment discrimination, from Harrison (1974).

2. See von Furstenberg et al. (1974, pt. 2) for a good summary of the literature.

3. "City" as used here is synonymous with SMSA (Standard Metropolitan Statistical Area) or metropolitan or urbanized area concepts, not simply the region legally known as a city. "Center of the city" means the central business district (CBD), and central city or center city and suburbs are used loosely to refer to areas near the center and near the edge of the city, respectively.

4. If wages vary systematically with distance, rents and employment density may not decline with distance. It is necessary to make the additional assumption that either the value of a central location is large enough, or the capital-labor ratio at all distances is high enough for variations in the land rental bill to overshadow variations in the wage bill.

5. At k_2, ∂ (transportation costs)$/\partial k = -\partial$ (housing costs)$/\partial k$.

6. All workers will be referred to as males to simplify the references, although the analysis is applicable to a work force of both sexes.

7. B could be allowed to move within a specified area around the CBD defined as the ghetto, but this would only produce the same results with a more complex analysis.

8. It would be preferable to allow a worker to search first those potential jobs that would afford him the highest utility—for B, CBD jobs, then those next to the CBD, etc.; and for W, jobs at the edge of the city. Salop's model (1973) includes a similar optimal search order, in which the firms with the highest expected wage offers are searched first. However, the costs in terms of complexity seem to outweigh the benefits of more realism.

9. A more desirable though more complicated measure of opportunity cost would be the current wage offer, as in Salop (1973), since this more accurately reflects the income foregone if the worker searches again.

10. If search costs are allowed to increase with the length of search, the acceptance wage will be lower the greater the duration of search. As the reservation wage drops, if it falls so low that the value of welfare payments or other non-labor-market activities exceeds it, the worker will leave the labor force and join the ranks of the discouraged workers.

11. There are two instances in which the pattern in Figure 9-1 does not hold: (1) If the parameters are such that at no employment location does W choose to move out of the center of the city, $P(0)H + T(k^* - 0) < P(k^*)H + M^*$ This is essentially the situation for B, whose "moving costs" effectively prohibit him from leaving the ghetto. This seems highly unlikely, given that a much greater fraction of workers employed in the ring of SMSAs live in the ring rather than living in the central city and commuting out.

(2) A less extreme version of this condition would be that only at a very distant k_1 would W decide to move, and that the falling $\overline{Y}_w(k_1)$ would not have intersected the rising $\overline{Y}_b(k_1)$ by k^* Since the difference between B's and W's searches arises from B's inability to move outside the ghetto and since the most likely state of the world includes frequent benefits for W from moving, these two extreme conditions will be ignored.

12. Very low marginal transportation costs could prevent B's nominal acceptance wage from ever equaling W's at any distance by causing $\overline{Y}_b(k_1)$ and $\overline{Y}_w(k_1)$ to be so flat that even at $k_1 > \overline{k}_1$, where $\partial \overline{Y}_b(k_1)/\partial k_1 > 0$ and $\partial \overline{Y}_w(k_1)/\partial k_1 < 0$, the two curves might never intersect at $k_1 \leqslant k^*$.

13. Price discrimination is another form which housing discrimination might take. Unfortunately, little could be concluded about its effect on black employment opportunities. The real acceptance wage for W would exceed that for B because of stochastic dominance. Beyond that, little else can even be considered probable: whether $\overline{Y}_b(k_1)$ is greater or less than $\overline{Y}_w(k_1)$ at any location is uncertain and, therefore, so are relative concentrations of employment by race. The comparative lengths of search are again totally indeterminate. Consequently, there seems to be little point to a more complete analysis of the effects of price discrimination.

REFERENCES

Census. 1973. U.S. Bureau of the Census. *Census of Population: 1970. Mobility for Metropolitan Areas.* Subject Reports, PC(2)-2C.

Fremon, Charlotte. *The Occupational Patterns in Urban Employment Change, 1965-1967.* Urban Institute, 1970.

Hadar, Josef, and William Russell. 1969. "Rules for Ordering Uncertain Prospects." *American Economic Review*, March.

Harrison, Bennett. 1974. "Discrimination in Space: Suburbanization and Black Unemployment in Cities." In von Furstenberg et al., eds. (1974).

Kain, John. 1968. "Housing Segregation, Negro Employment and Metropolitan Decentralization." *Quarterly Journal of Economics*, May.

Kohn, M., and S. Shavell. 1974. "The Theory of Search." *Journal of Economic Theory*, October.

Lewis, Wilfred. 1969. "Urban Growth and Suburbanization of Employment: Some New Data." Mimeographed. Washington, D.C.: Brookings.

Masters, Stanley. 1974. "A Note on John Kain's 'Housing Segregation, Negro Employment, and Metropolitan Decentralization'." *Quarterly Journal of Economics*, August.

McCall, J.J. 1970. "Economics of Information and Job Search." *Quarterly Journal of Economics*, February.

Mills, Edwin S. 1972. *Urban Economics*. Glenview, Ill.: Scott, Foresman.

Mooney, Joseph. 1969. "Housing Segregation, Negro Employment and Metropolitan Decentralization." *Quarterly Journal of Economics*, May.

Mortenson, Dale. 1970. "Job Search, the Duration of Unemployment, and the Phillips Curve." *American Economic Review*, December.

Nelson, Phillip. 1970. "Information and Consumer Behavior." *Journal of Political Economy*, March-April.

Noll, Roger. 1970. "Metropolitan Employment and Population Distribution and the Conditions of the Urban Poor." in John Crecine, ed., *Financing the Metropolis: Public Policy in Urban Economics*. Urban Affairs Annual Reviews 4. Beverly Hills, Calif.: Sage.

Rothschild, Michael. 1973. "Models of Market Organization with Imperfect Information: A Survey." *Journal of Political Economy*, November-December.

Saks, Daniel, and Paul Offner. 1971. "A Note on John Kain's 'Housing Segregation, Negro Employment and Metropolitan Decentralization'." *Quarterly Journal of Economics*, February.

Salop, S. 1973. "Non-Random Search and Unemployment." *Review of Economic Studies*, April.

von Furstenberg, George M. et al., eds. 1974. *Patterns of Racial Discrimination*. Volume I: *Housing*. Lexington, Mass.: Lexington Books.

Chapter Ten

Some Economic Effects of Residential Zoning in San Francisco

Marcy Elkind Avrin

INTRODUCTION

Zoning can be viewed as a political or legal constraint under which the urban property market must operate. Two possible purposes exist for the adoption of a zoning ordinance by a city. The first is based on the acceptance of the notion that external diseconomies associated with land use exert important influences on urban property values. Zoning restrictions in this case are instituted in an effort to eliminate those external diseconomies which the construction of "undesirable" property features might impose upon other properties in any given zoning district. Zoning seeks to minimize total external effects by separating land uses. The restrictions increase the efficiency of the urban property market to the extent that they cause the price of a parcel of land to equal its true marginal product without causing the prices of "equal" parcels of land to differ. Thus, for a zoning ordinance to increase the efficiency of the local property market, it should remove any existing externalities without artificially constraining the supply of land in any given use.

The second purpose of zoning involves fiscal considerations. A municipality has the incentive to restrict the use of land for purposes that would impose the greatest burden on the fiscal budget. Zoning is a useful means of doing so. If it is successful, it serves to decrease the efficiency of the urban property market

Note: I thank Richard Muth and Michael Boskin of Stanford University for their helpful comments during the preparation of this study.

by causing the price of land in the overly restrictive uses to be higher than is efficient.

Effect on Property Value

The possible ways by which zoning may affect property value are shown in Figures 10-1 through 10-4. Figures 10-1 and 10-2 represent the case in which zoning causes a general increase in property value. This situation would occur if zoning increased the desirability of property by promoting neighborhood stability and limiting density. In Figure 10-1, no externality-related border effects exist. Before zoning, the unit price of a property in use X is P_x; and the unit price

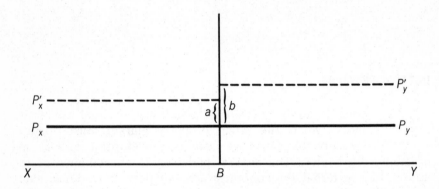

Figure 10-1.

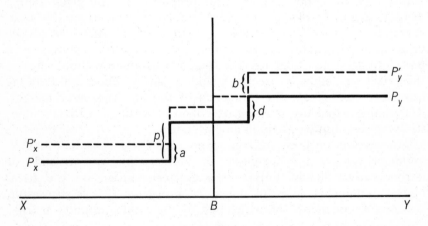

Figure 10-2.

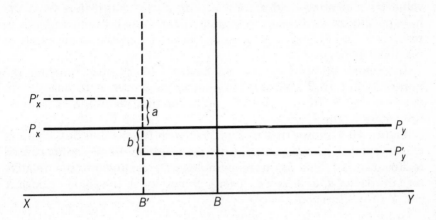

Figure 10-3.

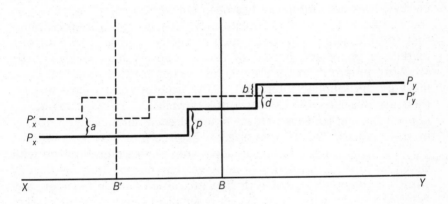

Figure 10-4.

of a property in use Y is P_y. After zoning, the combination of the stability and the limited density effect causes the price of X to increase by a to P'_x and the price of Y to increase by b to P'_y.

In Figure 10-2, border effects between X and Y types of properties exist and fragmented ownership of property is assumed. Before zoning, the price of interior X and Y properties are P_x and P_y, respectively. The price of a border X property is $P_x + p$ and that of a border Y property is $P_y - d$. Zoning increases the price of interior X and Y properties by a and b, respectively, to P'_x and P'_y, causing them to differ by an amount equal to $d + p + (b - a)$.

Figures 10-3 and 10-4 represent the case in which zoning affects value by allocating land among uses in a way that differs from the market allocation. Property designated for those uses but which is in restricted supply increases in price. The price of the other types of property declines.

In Figure 10-3, in which no border effect exists, moving the border from B to B' causes P_x to increase by a to P'_x and causes P_y to decrease by b to P'_y. The price differential between X and Y properties is, therefore, $a + b$.

Figure 10-4 shows that in a market with fragmented ownership in which border effects occur, the price effect of a zoning-caused reallocation of land is more complex. Depending on the relative magnitudes of a, b, p, and d, a general increase in the value of both X and Y properties could occur.

Complex Issue

Despite the possible detrimental effects on the urban property market, a zoning ordinance has been enacted in every major city in the United States except Houston. At first glance, it seems strange that the efficiency effects of such a widely used tool to control a market as important as that of urban property have received little scholarly inquiry.[1] There are several reasons for this situation. First, most of the scholars interested in the issue of zoning have focused their attention on the question of externalities: To what extent do nonconforming land uses create external economies or diseconomies in the market?[2] Those focusing on externalities have encountered great difficulty in developing an adequate research methodology with which to produce quantifiable answers. The market they are dealing with is so complex that it is difficult to design a study to isolate any external effects, which may be quite small in relation to the market as a whole.

Second, it is difficult to design a study of price effects in efficiency terms, using market price data and controlling for possible externalities, as long as the externalities issue itself is unresolved.

Finally, suitable data are unavailable. Property values are affected by so many variables that the potential data requirements of any conclusive study are enormous. These data requirements are difficult to meet because most of the available data on property values and characteristics are both inaccurate and confidential. Often, several sources must be consulted to obtain complete data on a given property.

In this study I attempt to determine whether zoning does in fact create inefficiencies in the urban residential property market. I attempt to determine whether zoning causes nonoptimal pricing by misallocating land among uses. In order to isolate this effect on price, I use both a time series and a cross-sectional approach. The time series analysis is based on repeat sales prices of given properties in each of four residential zoning categories in San Francisco. In the cross-sectional approach, zoning is included as a dummy variable in a regression which attempts to explain the variation in the sales price of individual properties. A major change in the residential zoning of San Francisco in 1960 allows both methods to be directly addressed to the zoning issue and makes it possible to avoid many of the complications encountered in previous studies.

The results are generally the same using either method, lending conviction to the conclusion that zoning in San Francisco creates inefficiencies in the urban residential property market by causing land to be allocated in a nonoptimal way among uses. I found no evidence that land use externalities exist.

DATA

The records of the San Francisco assessor's office on the sales of individual properties were used to obtain the price and year of "good" sales of a sample of properties between 1950 and 1973. A "good" sale is defined as one which reflects the true market value of the property.

Since time series were wanted, properties that were not sold at least twice during the period studied were excluded from the sample. Also excluded were properties that did not conform to the zoning ordinance or whose zoning had been changed since 1960. Finally, properties currently or previously located in redevelopment project areas, federally assisted code enforcement areas, or conservation areas were also excluded. Given the nature of these programs and their timing, they could cause price effects that would bias the results.

For the cross-sectional model, data on the various property characteristics included in the regression were obtained from the San Francisco assessor's office, the City Engineer, and the Census (1961). Appendix 10A contains a description of the sample in terms of these characteristics.

A property located on the same block or across the street from a less restrictive zone was defined to be in the neighborhood of that zone; information as to which properties were so located was obtained from detailed zoning block maps. The definition is based on the results of the few previous studies that have directly or indirectly dealt with the concept of neighborhood: Bailey (1966), Mieszkowski

(1972), Ridker and Henning (1967), Reuter (1974). The studies show that the concept as related to land use involves a relatively small area.

Zoning in San Francisco

The San Francisco data are particularly useful to a zoning study because of the unique situation which occurred in the history of residential zoning there. Until 1960 three types of zoning existed: commercial, industrial, and residential. Residential properties were divided into two districts. The First Residential district allowed only single-family, detached homes; the Second Residential district was unrestricted as to residential use. In 1960 a new zoning ordinance was adopted. The basis for its adoption was the belief that an increasing number of use-related external diseconomies were adversely affecting the value of certain properties in the Second Residential district. The purpose of the ordinance was to limit the spread of these externalities by restricting the density of any new development in individual areas. In doing so, it removed the threat supposedly felt by various property owners that new development would cause the quality of life in their neighborhoods to deteriorate. The new development owners feared involved the replacement of existing residences in their neighborhood with higher-density structures. This phenomenon was a common occurrence because by 1960 very little undeveloped land existed in the city.

From 1948 to 1958, the 1960 ordinance went through seven published drafts. In final form, it divided the Second Residential district into five new districts, their essential differences being in the restrictions on maximum density (San Francisco Department of City Planning 1972). The districts and their restrictions are as follows:

R1. one dwelling per lot or one dwelling per 3,000 square feet;
R2. one two-family dwelling per lot, or one dwelling per 3,000 square feet;
R3. one dwelling per 400 square feet;
R4. one dwelling per 200 square feet;
R5. one dwelling per 125 square feet.

Dissatisfaction with the R3 standard caused it to be changed in 1963 to 800 square feet per dwelling, because the 400-square-foot standard established in 1960 was not resulting in the type of neighborhood the planners had intended.

TIME SERIES ANALYSIS

The time series approach used allows any zoning-related change in the rate of increase of property value in each of the post-1960 zoning districts to be isolated. (The R5 district is not used because of the small number of properties zoned for that use.) Basically, it involves testing for any zoning-caused discontinuity in the trend of the price index, which is based on sales prices of properties in each group. These four separate yearly housing price indexes cover the years 1950-1973. Each index is based on observations of two sales prices of given properties whose zoning was changed from Second Residential to one of the post-1960 categories. If the zoning of a property does not change during the period between sales, the use of repeat sales data controls for the influence individual property characteristics have upon value. Thus, the price indexes are free from the effects of any externalities that were present at the time of both sales. In this regard, an externality is no different from any other property characteristic.

The indexes were constructed by using a regression method for combining price relatives. The method was chosen for several reasons. First, it was efficient because, in constructing the index number for a given year, information contained in future sales prices was used. Second, standard errors of the estimated index numbers could be computed, providing some basis on which to judge their reliability. Finally, the effects of certain property features on property values could be measured individually. In particular, the effect of zoning on properties located near less restrictive zones could be separated from the effect on those that were not.

The regression method is based on the following model developed by Bailey, Muth, Nourse (1963).

$$\text{Let: } R_{itt'} = (B_{t'}/B_t)U_{itt'} \text{ or}$$

$$r_{itt'} = -b_t + b_{t'} + u_{itt'}$$

$$(10\text{-}1)$$

where $R_{itt'}$ is the ratio of the final sales price in period t' to the initial sales price in period t for the ith pair of transactions with initial and final sales in these two periods; B_t and $B_{t'}$ are the true but unknown indexes for period t and t' respectively, with $t = 0, 1, \ldots, T-1$, and $t' = 1, \ldots, T$; and the lower-case letters stand for the logarithms of the variables denoted by the corresponding capital letters. Assume that the residuals in log form, $u_{itt'}$, have zero means and identical variances, σ^2, and are uncorrelated with each other.

Estimation of the unknown B's is then treated as a regression problem. Let x_t take the value -1 if period t is the period of initial sale, $+1$ if t is the period of final sale, and 0 otherwise, for each pair of transactions. The index is normalized by letting $B_0 = 1$ or $b_0 = 0$. Using these conventions, Equation (10-1) becomes:

$$r_{itt'} = \sum_{j=1}^{T} b_j x_j + u_{itt'} \tag{10-2}$$

or, in matrix notation: $r = xb + u$. In each zoning category the price index for year j is thus the antilog of b_j.

This model is modified in order to determine whether the rate of increase of the price of a property is influenced by its location on the border of a less restrictive residential zone. A significantly different behavior of the price trend of border properties in response to the zoning would indicate that the phenomenon of residential "use" externalities may in fact exist. Zoning does not protect border properties from future land use externalities as it does interior properties.

In order to analyze the border effect, Equation (10-2) is modified as follows:

$$r_{itt'} = \sum_{j=1}^{T} b_j x_j + a \sum_{j=1}^{T} czx_j + u_{itt'} \tag{10-3}$$

where $z = 1$ for j greater than or equal to 10 (= year 1960) and zero otherwise, and $c = 1$ for a border property and zero otherwise. Then the equation becomes

$$r_{itt'} = \sum_{j=1}^{T} b_j x_j + ac \sum_{j=10}^{T} x_j + u_{itt'} \tag{10-4}$$

where the summation of x_j is the number of final sales made after the change less the number of initial sales.

The separate effect of the border characteristic on property values is measured by the antilog of a. Including this term in the price index model eliminates any border effect from the estimated index numbers. It essentially restricts the analysis of the indexes to "interior" properties.

The trend of the price indexes is shown in Figure 10-5.[3] The estimates of the price indexes and border-property coefficients are presented in Appendix 10A. The logarithm of each index number and the standard error of each logarithm provide evidence on the accuracy of the individual index numbers.

Positive coefficients of the border term indicate that zoning does not increase property value by stopping the spread of mixed land uses. If it did so, the border properties would be expected to have a lower price than the interior ones, given that the zoning does not legally prevent the former from being in the neighborhood of a more dense residential land use.

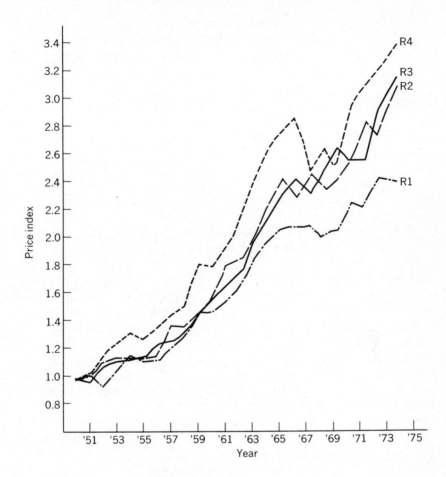

Figure 10-5. Price Trends.

Discontinuity Model

The following model is tested for each zoning category to determine when the assumed discontinuity or switch in the trend of the price index occurred:

Let

$Index_t$ = property value index in year t

CPI = purchasing power of the dollar (Census 1973)

T = time trend

Z = shift in trend due to zoning

A = effect of the 1966 property reassessment

u = normally distributed random error terms which have zero means, variances of σ^2, and are uncorrelated with each other.

Then

$$Index_t/CPI_t = a_0 + a_1 T + a_2 Z_t + a_3 Z_t T_t + a_4 A_t + u_t \qquad (10\text{-}5)$$

where

$t = -9, -8, \ldots, 0, 1, \ldots, 13$
$T_t = t$
$Z_t = 0$ for t less than S (defined below); 1 otherwise
$A_t = 0$ for t less than 6; 1 otherwise.

The regression was calculated eleven times for each zoning category, with $S = -5, -4, \ldots, 0, 1, \ldots, 5$. The discontinuity occurs in year S for which the regression has the smallest sum of squared residuals.[4]

The housing price index numbers in each zoning category are normalized by the purchasing power of the dollar in order to remove the influence of the general rate of inflation on the determination of the switching point. If this were not done, the fact that prices are generally increasing at an increasing rate would tend to cause the most likely switching point to be biased toward a later year. This normalization has a disadvantage, however, in that it constrains the increase in the value of a property to be directly proportional to the purchasing power of the dollar.

A study of the sum of squared residuals resulting from this model shows that, given the assumption that a switch in conditions occurred, the most likely year of its occurrence was 1963 for properties in the R1, R3, and R4 zoning districts and 1965 for those in R2 (Table 10-1). It is understandable that 1963 was the most likely year of the switch in all but one of the zoning districts. Until then, the ordinance, though approved, was expected to undergo a major change of unknown extent. Also, changes in market conditions are signaled to sellers by a lag, through their own sampling experience and the buildup of observable changed conditions in other sales. The fact that the switch does not occur in the year of the adoption of the ordinance may be due to this lag.

After determining the most likely year of the switch for each of the four zoning categories, I examined the validity of the original assumption—that a switch does in fact occur. A reliable determina-

Table 10-1. Sums of Squared Residuals for Test of Discontinuity in Price Indexes

	R1	R2	R3	R4
Equation (10-6): no switch	.31066	.3478	.3516	.6090
Equation (10-5): switch model				
1955	.30906	.3384	.3502	.6070
1956	.3058	.3359	.3469	.6078
1957	.2870	.3143	.3440	.5929
1958	.2569	.3151	.3271	.5568
1959	.2086	.2650	.2813	.4664
1960	.1946	.2167	.2426	.4577
1961	.1452	.1567	.1991	.3619
1962	.0961	.1493	.1406	.2451
1963	.0583	.1150	.0816	.1791
1964	.0605	.0927	.0893	.2177
1965	.0707	.0812	.1148	.2513

Note: Equations are defined in the accompanying text.

tion of whether a switch in fact occurs is difficult. In order to make a determination, the following model, which represents the situation that no switch in conditions occurs, was estimated:

$$Index_t/CPI_t = a_0 + a_1 T_t + a_2 A_t + u_t \qquad (10\text{-}6)$$

for $t = -9, -8, \ldots, 0, 1, \ldots, 13$.

If no switch occurs, the mean value of a_1 and a_2 will be different from 0. Ideally, an F test would be used to test the following: $H_0 =$ no switch occurs; $H_1 =$ a switch does occur. Let S_0 denote the sum of squares of deviations from the regression line estimated for the year of most likely switch (10-5) and S_1, the sum of squares of deviations from the regression line based on one situation (10-6). Then

$$(S_1 - S_0)/S_0 \times 17/2 \sim F_{2,17} \qquad (10\text{-}7)$$

This is not a conclusive test, because the dividing point between the two situations is not given exogenously but is presumably a maximum likelihood estimate based on actual observations.[5] Hence the variance ratio would tend to be larger than if the value of S were given exogenously. If the critical values of the F distribution with 2 and 17 degrees of freedom are used, the procedure will result in the rejection of the null hypothesis more frequently than would otherwise be the case because the determination of S from the data reduces the number of degrees of freedom for the denominator of the variance ratio and increases the number for the numerator.

Despite the problems with this test, it does provide strong evidence that a zoning-related switch occurred. This is seen in the pattern of the likelihood ratios calculated using the sum of squared residuals (SSR) of the models for various switching points. A study of the SSRs of the models with switching points before 1960 shows that a switch was unlikely in those years in all zoning categories. A switch was, however, likely to occur in 1963 and in all following years. The likelihood of a switch occurring after 1960 increases as the switching point becomes more recent until 1963 for R1, R3, and R4 districts and 1965 for the R2 district.

Given that a switch in conditions occurred, it would be difficult to determine whether the entire amount of the switch was due to zoning. If the switch was only partially due to zoning, the interpretation of the effects of zoning would be more accurately made in terms of the relative change in value among categories. The extent to which the differences in levels and in their rates of change vary among zoning categories is, in any case, the valid measure of the inefficiency caused by zoning.

Results

The degree of discontinuity in the change in the level of prices in the various zoning districts is seen in Table 10-2. The coefficients of Z and ZT represent the disruption in the trend of prices for each of the four zoning districts, R1, R2, R3, and R4. The results are presented for a discontinuity in 1963. The way in which this effect is interpreted depends on a key assumption, namely, that no other factors which influence the general price level of all housing occurred at the time of the zoning change. If this assumption can be made, then the entire price level effect can be attributed to zoning. The results, in view of this assumption, show that the effect, represented by the coefficient of Z, increases with the maximum density permitted by the zoning ordinance. Increases of 42 percent, 43 percent, 47 percent, and 58 percent are noted in the R1, R2, R3, and R4 zoning districts, respectively. In 1950 dollars these increases amount to $4,410, $5,940, $9,550, and $11,500. If this first assumption cannot be made, then the zoning effect may only be discussed in terms of the relative price effect of zoning among zoning districts. In relative terms, the price of R4 properties jumped 11 percent more than R3 property prices, which in turn jumped 4

Table 10-2. Price Effect of Zoning, 1963

Variable[a]	Zone R1			Zone R2			Zone R3			Zone R4		
	Coef.	SE	T	Coef.	SE	T	Coef.	SE	T	Coef.	SE	T
Constant	1.239	.023	52.0	1.338	.033	40.7	1.294	.028	46.7	1.52	.041	37.0
ZT	−0.065	.010	−6.67	−0.052	.014	−3.80	−0.055	.012	−4.76	−0.074	.017	−4.28
Z	0.424	.053	8.02	0.434	.074	5.84	0.470	.063	7.50	0.586	.093	6.31
T	0.039	.005	8.12	0.047	.007	7.02	0.0413	.006	7.35	0.061	.008	7.34
A	0.011	.061	0.182	−0.042	.086	−0.49	0.064	.072	0.885	−0.129	.107	−1.20
R^2	0.9451			0.9430			0.9606			0.9389		
DW	1.89			1.79			1.70			1.89		

aZT = rate effect; Z = price level effect; and A = reassessment effect.

percent more than R2 prices, which jumped 1 percent more than R1 prices.

In interpreting these changes, it is useful to recall some of the previous discussion. If zoning were imposed upon a prezoning market equilibrium with no border effects (Figure 10-1), it must affect prices in all zones by equal amounts if no divergence from optimality is to result. With a prezoning equilibrium under fragmented ownership and border effects (Figure 10-4), however, the results are different. By correcting the private market's overallocation of land to use X by shifting from B to B', the boundary separating X and Y use, the prices of all properties previously in X use could rise. Because of the positive boundary differential in X use, the rise in prices along the old boundary, B, will tend to be smaller than in the prezoning X interior area. Under the latter set of initial conditions, prices in both X and Y use might also increase because of the stabilizing effect zoning has on neighborhoods in general.

Since no border price effects were found in estimating the four zoning category price indexes, it is difficult to attribute the post-zoning price rise for all zoning categories to correction of market overallocation of land to denser uses. Rather, the price rise would have to be attributed to the stabilizing effects of zoning. The greater percent price increases for the denser zoning categories, however, are inconsistent with an optimal allocation of land among the different post-zoning categories. As argued above, optimal zoning would imply that prices would increase by equal amounts after zoning if the latter's only effect were to provide greater stability.

Evidence of this stability effect supports the theory that participants in the urban property market do not have homogeneous tastes. Prices of property in all districts increase because buyers are secure in their knowledge of the future of the neighborhoods into which they are purchasing. Since zoning affects properties that border on more dense districts no differently than those which do not, buyers who do not mind being near denser uses purchase border properties and those who receive negative benefit from this type of location purchase interior ones. In both cases, buyers are willing to pay for the knowledge that their neighborhood will not change in a way contrary to their taste.

Not only is the pattern of price increases found inconsistent with optimal zoning, it is inconsistent with the hypothesis that zoning eliminates the threat of externalities. The magnitude of the price increase is positively related to density. A reverse order in the magnitude of the increase among zoning categories would be expected if zoning served to remove the threat of externalities from the property market. It could be argued that zoning would, for example, increase the value of R1 properties more than R3 ones because single-family dwellings are more threatened by dense uses than are apartments. Also, given this effect, zoning could potentially increase the value of R1 properties to a greater degree because a stable neighborhood may be more important to homeowners than to apartment dwellers.

Most important, though, is the kind of restriction imposed by the San Francisco zoning ordinance. Since the less restricted zones can be employed for any more restrictive use, the rezoning produced little change in the R4 areas, restricting only R5 developments. After the zoning, a developer who owned an R4 property could still choose among several types of structure, and select the one that commanded the most value. If, for example, he could make more money building a single-family home than an apartment, he was free to do so. The restrictions were greatest in the R1 areas, where any higher-density development was forbidden. The owner of an R1 property could not take advantage of the market in the same way as an R4 owner. Therefore, if prevention of adverse future externalities were the only factor at work, the price effect of zoning would have been highest in the R1 areas and lowest in those zoned R4, rather than the reverse, which is in fact observed.

Prices might increase with allowable density not only because owners of high-density property could take advantage of the market, but also because of actual demand conditions for housing in the city. Demand for high-density structures is increasing faster than the demand for other types of dwellings. Thus, given that zoning is imposed largely according to the 1960 land use pattern, it is likely to allocate too little land to the denser uses and too much to the others. The shift in demand is seen in the rise in the proportion of all dwelling units that were in apartment buildings—from 28 percent in 1950 to 76 percent in 1960 (San Francisco Department of City Planning 1967). The shift is also noted in Table 10-2, where the coefficient of the time trend T is much smaller for R1 properties than for those in R4, indicating an aggregate change in demand away from single-family homes.

Table 10-2 also shows that the effect of the zoning change on the real rate of change of prices was negative in all zoning districts. The decrease in the rate was 7.4 percent in the R4 district, 6.5 percent in R1, 5.5 percent in R3, and 5.2 percent in R2. In relative terms, the rate of change of prices of R4 properties switches 0.9 percent more than those of R1 properties, which in turn switch 0.3 percent more than those of properties zoned R2. Both the absolute rate effects and these differentials are quite small in comparison with the differential zoning-caused shift in the real price level among districts.[6]

The rate effects in general are somewhat puzzling in that they are negative in sign. A positive effect was expected for R2, R3, and R4 because zoning, by allocating properties to nonoptimal uses, could potentially cause the supply of a given type of dwelling to meet a given demand at a higher price than would be dictated in the unconstrained market. For example, zoning may designate uses in such a way that the properties most likely to be converted to a given use in the free market are not zoned for that use. In doing so, zoning forces more expensive conversions, making the supply curve of dwellings of these types more price-inelastic. This situation occurs, for example, when a property which is a prime candidate for conversion to an apartment house is zoned for a single-family home.[7] Zoning does not cause conversions to R1 type of properties to be more costly, since it does not in any way limit the number of properties which can be converted to single-family homes.

Only the following ex-post explanation can be given for the negative effect. Home buyers and developers may have overestimated the positive impact zoning would have on the city. This overestimation would cause the initial price effect of the zoning ordinance to be too high. The decrease in the rate of increase of property values after the zoning would, therefore, serve to correct for this effect.

CROSS-SECTIONAL ANALYSIS

The economic effects of zoning were also studied by including the zoning category as a dummy variable in a regression which attempts to explain the variation in the sales price of individual properties. The unique zoning situation in San Francisco makes it possible to determine what the price of residential land would be in an "unzoned" equilibrium and, therefore, to measure the zoning-caused distortion.

Before 1960 all Second Residential properties were essentially "unzoned residential" in that they were unrestricted as to residential use. Depending on demand, a high-rise building or a single-family dwelling could be built on any of the properties. The value of each property was, therefore, determined by the property characteristics and supply and demand conditions in the entire residential property market. In an equilibrium situation, the variation in property value among Second Residential properties was due to the various property and neighborhood characteristics and was unaffected by residential zoning. After 1960, the variation in property value among these same properties was also influenced by the new zoning ordinance. The value of Second Residential properties before 1960 can, therefore, be used as a base from which to measure the actual amount of distortion, if any, caused by zoning. Property values of the Second Residential properties before the zoning change can be considered to be the values of "unzoned" residential properties. Given a pre-1960 property market equilibrium and no border effects, any difference in value between pre-1960 and post-1960 sales not related to time and to the various other property and neighborhood characteristics can be considered to be a distortion due to zoning.

The regression is a reduced form of the supply and demand equation for housing. It is postulated that the value of a house is an additive function of its lot, neighborhood, and structural characteristics. Value is expressed in constant 1950 dollars because the observations are sales of structures over a twenty-year period. Since a cross-sectional analysis implies an equilibrium market at any point in time, a deflator must be used in order to adjust for shifts in aggregate levels of demand over the years. An example of such a condition is a change in the average level of income of the general population. Thus:

$$P_i = a_0 + a_1 S_i + a_2 L_i + a_3 N_i + u_i \qquad (10\text{-}8)$$

where S_i, L_i, and N_i are vectors of characteristics of the ith structure, lot, and neighborhood, respectively, and a_1, a_2, and a_3 are vectors of unknown coefficients.

Dependent Variable
Given the purpose of the study, a dependent variable must be used which allows for an accurate estimate of the significance of the zoning dummies. Since the effect of zoning, along with most other property characteristics, is proportional to the total finished area of the improvement, and since previous studies have shown that the variance of the disturbance is related to the total finished area (Brown, n.d.), the dependent variable used is real sales price per square foot of total finished area. The use of this variable eliminates the problem of heteroscedasticity, which would bias the estimated variances of the estimated coefficients.

Real sales price per square foot of total finished area is also used to estimate the effect of various factors on property values in each zoning district separately. Comparing the correlations among districts is helpful in providing evidence as to the characteristics with which zoning interacts to create value. However, other than the externality interaction, the results of the main analyses in this study do not decompose this effect into its various components. By comparing the effects of the various characteristics among districts, questions such as the following can be answered: Is the relative price effect of zoning on a property with and without a view greater for an R4 zoning classification than for an R1 designation? This would be the case if a view is more important to the value of properties in the R4 district than in the R1 district, for example.

In order to produce results somewhat comparable to those of the time series analysis, the logarithm of the real sales price is also used as a dependent variable in an estimating equation.

Independent Variables

The combined sales prices of land and improvements were studied in order to determine whether zoning causes the value of equal parcels of land to differ among zoning categories. The price of the land is a function of the price of the improvement which is in turn a function of the supply and demand for that type of dwelling. In order to discover the extent to which zoning causes the prices of equal parcels of land to differ among zoning categories, the effect of the improvement on price must be removed. Therefore, six characteristics of the improvements are included in the regression: number of floors (*FLOOR*), number of rooms (*RMS*), number of units (*UNITS*), total finished area (*TFA*), basement (*BSMNT*), and age at time of sale (*SLAGE*). Furthermore, all characteristics of the lot and its surroundings whose effect on price could be falsely attributed to the zoning effect must be included in order to obtain unbiased results. The variables which must be accounted for meet two criteria: they influence property values and they occur to different extents in each of the various zoning categories.[8] Eight of these types of variables have been included. The descriptions in Appendix 10A show that they occur to different extents in each of the various zoning categories.

Assumptions were made as to the proper forms of the independent variables. The logarithmic form was used for distance to the CBD, total finished area, lot frontage, and lot depth. It is hypothesized that they affect price per square foot of total finished area in a way that increases with their magnitude, but at a decreasing rate. The results of using other forms of these variables show that their form does not affect the conclusions about the effect of zoning.

Because of the limited purpose of this study, independent variables representing various quality-quantity relationships were not included in the equations. Zoning is believed to interact with total finished area. The interaction term, however, drops out when price per square foot of total finished area is used as the dependent variable.

Results

The estimates of the hedonic indexes are presented in Table 10-3. Since the time series results indicate that 1963 was the year of greatest zoning impact, estimates are also presented using 1963 as the year of the zoning change. The differences between these results and those for 1960 are not significant.

The magnitude of the price effect of zoning is indicated by the deviation between the price per square foot of total finished area in each of the various zoning districts and the price per square foot of unzoned land. The results show these differences to be $2.40 for R1 properties, $3.20 for R2 properties, $3.60 for R3 properties, and $4.40 for R4 properties. These results are expressed in 1950 prices. Since the mean sales price is $11.90 per square foot, the figures indicate that the zoning effect is considerable.

This model, given that the error terms are homoscedastic, also provides evidence concerning the significance of the other independent variables in explaining the variation in property value. Of the variables tested, number of floors, basement, corner location, and view all added significantly to value. Lot frontage and lot depth added significantly to property value per square foot of total finished area in a way which increased with magnitude at a decreasing rate. Property age at time of sale, total finished area, and distance to the CBD all detracted from value per square foot of total finished area in a way which increased with magnitude at a decreasing rate. The effect of the percent nonwhite on the block is inversely proportional to magnitude. The coefficients of *COMX* and *RESX* are positive, indicating that the value of properties that border on commercial or denser residential districts is not adversely affected compared with interior properties in a given district.

The results of the semilogarithmic model show that the real prices of properties zoned R1 are 21 percent higher than those which are unzoned. The prices of properties zoned R2, R3, and R4 are 32 percent, 36 percent, and 44 percent higher, respectively. These estimates are significant at the 0.005 level.

Table 10-4 presents the results of the linear model estimated for each zoning district separately. They show that zoning interacts with certain property characteristics to create value. This means that the change in value which zoning causes is directly dependent on the characteristics of the properties in the various districts. Any charac-

Table 10-3. Cross-sectional Results

	Dependent Variable: Price per Sq. Ft. of Total Finished Area (thous. dollars)				Log (price) 1960	
Independent	1960		1963			
Variables[a]	*Coef.*	*SE*	*Coef.*	*SE*	*Coef.*	*SE*
Z1	.0024	.0006	.0023	.0005	0.2101	.0474
Z2	.0032	.0006	.0033	.0006	0.3178	.0477
Z3	.0036	.0006	.0035	.0006	0.3641	.0465
Z4	.0044	.0006	.0042	.0006	0.4371	.0468
RESX	.0006	.0003	.0004	.0003*	0.0395	.0264*
COMX	.0000	.0000	.0002	.0004*	0.0032	.0303*
YR	.0001	.0000	.0001	.0000	0.0121	.0030
FLOOR	.0010	.0004	.0008	.0004	0.0647	.0306
BSMNT	.0009	.0003	.0007	.0003	0.0756	.0232
RMS	.0000*	.0000*	.0000	.0000*	0.0021	.0054*
UNITS	.0000*	.0000*	.0001	.0002*	0.0167	.0131*
CORN	.0011	.0005	.0012	.0005	0.1181	.0420
GRADE	.0000*	.0002	.0002	.8809*	−0.0080	.0188*
VIEW	.0012	.0004	.0013	.0004	0.0898	.0346
SLAGE	−.0000	.0000	−.0000	.0000	−0.0077	.0006
LFTA	−.0070	.0006	−.0068	.0006	0.4408	.0460
IRREG	−.0005*	.0008	−.0004	−.5118*	−0.0536	.0643*
LDIST	−.0023	.0006	−.0025	.0006	−0.0905	.0472
NW60	−.0000	.0000	−.0001	.0000	−0.0056	.0007
LFRONT	.0034	.0007	.0035	.0007	0.2462	.0580
LDEPTH	.0015	.0005	.0015	.0005	0.0813	.0416
Constant	.0515	.0045	.0505	.0045	−1.2118	.3662
R^2	.5489		.5472		0.7312	
No. of observations	727		727		727	

*Not significant at .05 level of confidence.

[a]Variables: Z1, Z2, Z3, Z4 = R1, R2, R3, R4 zoning districts, respectively. *RESX* = residential border; *COMX* = commercial border; *YR* = year of sale; *FLOOR* = number of floors; *BSMNT* = basement; *RMS* = number of rooms; *UNITS* = number of units; *CORN* = corner; *GRADE* = grade; *SLAGE* = log of age at time of sale; *LTFA* = log of total finished area; *IRREG* = irregular lot; *LDIST* = log of distance to the CBD; *NW60* = percent of nonwhites on block in 1960; *LFRONT* = log of lot frontage; *LDEPTH* = log of lot depth. The terms *COMX* and *RESX* indicate whether a given property borders on a commercial district or on a higher density residential district. I included them in order to restrict the analysis to properties which are interior to a given zoning district.

Table 10-4. Cross-sectional Results by Zoning District

Independent Variables[a]	Dependent Variable: Price per Square Foot of Total Finished Area (thous. dollars)							
	R1		R2		R3		R4	
	Coef.	SE	Coef.	SE	Coef.	SE	Coef.	SE
RESX	−.0003	.0005	.0018	.0009	.0012	.0011	.0009	.0015
COMX	.0018	.0008	−.0003	.0013	−.0007	.0009	.0000	.0011
YR	−.0000	.0000	.0001	.0001	.0002	.0001	.0002	.0001
FLOOR	.0007	.0009	.0006	.0009	.0019	.0012	.0016	.0010
BSMNT	.0004	.0004	.0022	.0009	.0024	.0009	.0007	.0010
RMS	.0002	.0002	.0009	.0003	.0002	.0002	.0002	.0001
UNITS	−.0017	.0012	−.0008	.0009	.0006	.0004	−.0000	.0004
CORN	.0004	.0008	.0004	.0017	.0013	.0014	.0015	.0015
GRADE	.0003	.0003	.0000	.0006	.0004	.0008	.0002	.0009
VIEW	.0014	.0008	−.0002	.0012	−.0007	.0010	.0034	.0014
SLAGE	−.0000	.0000	−.0000	.0000	−.0001	.0000	−.0001	.0000
LFTA	−.0055	.0008	−.0128	.0020	−.0106	.0018	−.0110	.0016
IRREG	.0005	.0010	.0025	.0027	b	b	−.0022	.0020
LDIST	−.0007	.0010	−.0026	.0026	−.0015	.0014	−.0084	.0024
NW60	−.0000	.0000	−.0001	.0000	−.0000	.0000	−.0000	.0000
LFRONT	.0053	.0013	.0073	.0026	.0004	.0027	.0057	.0017
LDEPTH	.0019	.0011	.0053	.0014	.0009	.0016	.0040	.0013
Constant	.0312	.0075	.0597	.0213	.0910	.0156	.0819	.0114
R^2	.4764		.5363		.5944		.5689	
No. of observations	204		103		117		139	

[a]For identification of variables, see Table 10-3, footnote a.
[b]No such lots in sample.

teristic whose coefficients differ among districts interacts with zoning to create value. Several interesting results may be noted. First, *VIEW* adds $3.50 per square foot to the value of an R4 property but does not significantly affect the value of properties in the other districts. Second, the age of a building detracts more from the value of R4 and R3 properties than from those zoned R2 and R1. Third, distance to the CBD appears to have an important influence on R4 properties only. Finally, lot frontage has a significant effect on all properties except those in the R3 district and is greatest for those zoned R2. Lot depth is also most important in R2 properties; a one-foot increase in depth causes the value of an R2 lot to increase approximately $2.30 more per square foot of finished area than an R4 lot.

CONCLUSION

In this study a strong case is made for the proposition that residential zoning in San Francisco affects values in the urban residential property market to different degrees which are determined by the zoning classification. The results of both the time series and cross-sectional studies indicate that, by providing stable neighborhoods and by limiting the growth of the city in general, zoning affects the demand for residential property, causing the value of all properties to increase. Its effect on the relative supply of properties among uses causes differential levels of increase in property values in the various zoning districts. The magnitude of the effect increases with allowed density; the value of R4 properties, on which high-rise buildings are permitted, is affected most. This finding is inconsistent with optimality in the property market.

The results of the cross-sectional estimation for each of the zoning districts separately shows that zoning interacts with certain property characteristics to create value. The evidence shows that the change in value which zoning causes is directly dependent on the characteristics of the properties in each district.

No evidence is provided that boundary externalities exist in the urban residential property market. The indication is that zoning does not cause the value of properties near zones of commercial or denser residential use either to decrease or to increase less than that of interior properties in a given district. Furthermore, the pattern of price increases found among zoning categories is inconsistent with the hypothesis that zoning eliminates the threat of externalities. These findings indicate that land use externalities do not exist, but the point is not conclusively proved.

APPENDIX 10A

Table 10A-1.   Characteristics of Sample Properties

	R1	R2	R3	R4
Average 1950 sales price (000 dollars)	11.7	13.8	20.3	19.8
Average total finished area in square feet (TFA)	1261	1888	2812	4123
Average lot frontage in feet (FRONT)	26.8	27.0	27.4	30.1

Table 10A-1 (cont.)

Average lot depth in feet (*DEPTH*)	95.0	100.4	97.9	98.4
Average number of floors (*FLOOR*)	1.1	1.6	1.9	2.3
Average number of units (*UNITS*)	1.1	1.5	2.4	4.1
Average age (*AGE*)	39.4	57.9	62.5	66.5
Average percent nonwhite on the block in 1960 (*NW60*)	10.3	5.9	14.0	15.5
Number of properties with a view	14	23	28	26
Percent of properties with a view (*VIEW*)	5.4	18.1	19.3	13.0
Number of corner properties	47	29	38	54
Percent of properties with corner location (*CORN*)	8.3	5.9	7.9	11.8
Average peak-hour auto travel time to CBD in 1969 in minutes (*DIST*)	17.9	16.9	13.9	11.9
Percent of properties which border on commercial zone (*COMX*)	3.4	8.5	23.0	23.8
Percent of properties which border on zones of higher (denser) residential use (*RESX*)	28.5	40.1	17.3	10.0

Table 10A-2. Price Index of *R*1 and *R*2 Properties (figures in parentheses are standard errors of logs)

	R1 Properties			R2 Properties		
Year	*Index*	*Ln Index*	*N*[a]	*Index*	*Ln Index*	*N*[a]
1950	1.000	0.000	42	1.000	0.000	30
1951	1.030	0.0296 (−0.0425)	32	1.028	0.0279 (0.0651)	28
1952	0.9574	−0.0434 (0.0448)	29	1.122	0.1153 (0.0612)	32
1953	1.073	0.0706 (0.0378)	51	1.150	0.1400 (0.0598)	33
1954	1.174	0.1606 (0.0372)	52	1.161	0.1497 (0.0626)	27
1955	1.136	0.1281 (0.0355)	61	1.153	0.1430 (0.0565)	41
1956	1.140	0.1312 (0.0415)	36	1.162	0.1504 (0.0574)	44
1957	1.234	0.2107 (0.0392)	48	1.381	0.3231 (0.0578)	35
1958	1.310	0.2702 (0.0401)	43	1.359	0.3072 (0.0530)	58
1959	1.486	0.3962 (0.0364)	69	1.494	0.4015 (0.0598)	43

Table 10A-2 (cont.)

Year	R1 Properties			R2 Properties		
	Index	*Ln Index*	N^a	*Index*	*Ln Index*	N^a
1960	1.496	0.4029 (0.0385)	52	1.604	0.4727 (0.0608)	43
1961	1.586	0.4614 (0.0388)	52	1.817	0.5974 (0.0605)	49
1962	1.697	0.5293 (0.0386)	60	1.877	0.6302 (0.0591)	58
1963	1.879	0.6308 (0.0364)	83	2.015	0.7007 (0.0591)	57
1964	1.996	0.6912 (0.0377)	67	2.263	0.8170 (0.0562)	90
1965	2.082	0.7335 (0.0388)	61	2.422	0.8850 (0.0598)	53
1966	2.099	0.7418 (0.0450)	29	2.298	0.8324 (0.0667)	31
1967	2.095	0.7396 (0.0422)	42	2.452	0.8970 (0.0714)	25
1968	2.016	0.7011 (0.0430)	37	2.360	0.8591 (0.0659)	36
1969	2.058	0.7222 (0.0415)	40	2.435	0.8901 (0.0680)	29
1970	2.256	0.8139 (0.0453)	29	2.610	0.9598 (0.0693)	29
1971	2.214	0.7952 (0.0400)	52	2.840	1.046 (0.0634)	44
1972	2.420	0.8841 (0.0397)	57	2.729	1.005 (0.0654)	38
1973	2.404	0.8775 (0.0401)	47	3.089	1.128 (0.0641)	39
Border	1.08	0.0767 (0.0298)	–	0.9600	−0.0413 (0.0443)	–
Total			585			496
R^2			.4512			.2446
DW			1.842			1.859

aNumber of initial and final sales.

Table 10A-3. Price Indexes of *R*3 and *R*4 Properties (figures in parentheses are standard errors of logs)

Year	R3 Properties			R4 Properties		
	Index	Ln Index	N[a]	Index	Ln Index	N[a]
1950	1.000	0.000	32	1.000	0.000	31
1951	0.9974	−0.0025 (0.0564)	29	1.025	0.0251 (0.0688)	28
1952	1.095	0.0907 (0.0537)	32	1.160	0.1485 (0.0587)	37
1953	1.132	0.1240 (0.0464)	52	1.281	0.2475 (0.0664)	37
1954	1.144	0.1349 (0.0501)	41	1.310	0.2702 (0.0643)	33
1955	1.161	0.1493 (0.0505)	32	1.286	0.2516 (0.0650)	35
1956	1.255	0.2269 (0.0492)	37	1.363	0.3096 (0.0635)	38
1957	1.299	0.2615 (0.0537)	34	1.459	0.3777 (0.0643)	46
1958	1.342	0.2942 (0.0481)	50	1.519	0.4182 (0.0616)	53
1959	1.481	0.3930 (0.0475)	62	1.826	0.6024 (0.0655)	44
1960	1.589	0.4634 (0.0477)	62	1.812	0.5948 (0.0684)	39
1961	1.667	0.5166 (0.0492)	58	1.935	0.6600 (0.0618)	60
1962	1.781	0.5772 (0.0484)	66	2.162	0.7712 (0.0612)	64
1963	2.023	0.7048 (0.0486)	65	2.478	0.9074 (0.0616)	66
1964	2.189	0.7836 (0.0480)	67	2.633	0.9681 (0.0677)	42
1965	2.325	0.8436 (0.0496)	57	2.754	1.013 (0.0643)	52
1966	2.426	0.8865 (0.0519)	44	2.855	1.049 (0.0768)	22
1967	2.323	0.8430 (0.0520)	44	2.455	0.8984 (0.0834)	18
1968	2.489	0.9121 (0.0557)	29	2.630	0.9668 (0.0720)	31
1969	2.645	0.9726 (0.0564)	31	2.493	0.9135 (0.0714)	29

Table 10A-3 (cont.)

	R3 Properties			R4 Properties		
Year	Index	Ln Index	N^a	Index	Ln Index	N^a
1970	2.571	0.9443 (0.0625)	21	2.941	1.079 (0.0735)	24
1971	2.545	0.9342 (0.0555)	28	3.121	1.138 (0.0724)	27
1972	2.915	1.070 (0.0488)	57	3.199	1.163 (0.0699)	35
1973	3.107	1.134 (0.0590)	26	3.374	1.216 (0.0710)	33
Border	1.06	0.0594 (0.0436)	–	1.01	0.0075 (0.0825)	–
Total			525			462
R^2			.4408			.2461
DW			1.824			1.813

aNumber of initial and final sales.

NOTES TO CHAPTER TEN

1. Recent work on the subject has been done by Siegan (1972), Plosser (1972), and Sagalyn and Sternlieb (1973).

2. The major works in this area are by Crecine, Davis, Jackson (1967), Rueter (1974), Mieszkowski (1972), and Bailey (1966).

3. The erratic behavior around the year 1966 has a logical explanation in that a major reassessment of all residential property in San Francisco occurred in that year. This reassessment was mandated by California Assembly Bill 80, passed in July 1966, which required each county assessor to assess all taxable property at 25 percent of his estimate of the full cash value. A study of the capitalization of this reassessment indicates that it began in January 1966 (Smith 1971).

4. The likelihood that a discontinuity occurs in year S is inversely proportional to the sum of squared residuals in the regression for year S is seen in the following: The logarithm of the maximum likelihood for a given value of T is: $L(S) = T \log \sqrt{2} - T \log \hat{\sigma} - (T/2)$, where T = total number of observations (Quandt 1958).

5. Quandt (1960) suggests that the difficulty could be avoided by not using a maximum likelihood estimate for S but instead, arbitrarily deciding upon S such that $S = T/2$ if T is even and $S = (T + 1)/2$ or $(T-1)/2$ if T is odd (where T is the total number of observations). Although this procedure eliminates one difficulty, it creates another in that either of the situations is likely to be contaminated with observations from the other. This will impair the power of the test.

6. The coefficient of the assessment term is not significant, perhaps because the model is not formulated properly to estimate a true value for the capitalization of the increased tax. The effect of any factor which would cause demand to increase in the years after the assessment or which would cause property values to increase for any other reason is included in this coefficient.

7. The fact that most apartments in the city are built on sites which were formerly occupied by single-family homes indicates that this elasticity effect may have occurred (San Francisco Department of City Planning 1967). Some of the properties zoned R1 may have been the least costly sites for R2 and R3 properties. In prohibiting such conversion, the zoning ordinance could easily have caused the supply of R2 and R3 types of structures to become more price-inelastic.

8. Since the study deals with a very specific issue, the number of variables which must be included in the analysis is reduced. In the study, I attempt to determine how much of the variation in property value is due to the zoning misallocation of land among uses through zoning. Because of this, the effects of all the determinants of demand on price are included in the measure of the zoning effect. A general shortage of all land is measured by the constant. A differential shortage of land among zones means that zoning is misallocating supply and, therefore, the measure of this shortage is part of the zoning effect.

Also, it is not necessary to include the effect of certain property characteristics which are randomly distributed among zoning categories but which interact differently with the different categories to affect price. The purpose of this study is to determine the total effect of zoning, including the effect of all interactions of which it is composed.

REFERENCES

Bailey, Martin J. 1959. "Note on the Economics of Residential Zoning and Urban Renewal." *Land Economics*, August.

_____. 1966. "Effects of Race and of Other Demographic Factors on the Value of Single-Family Homes." *Land Economics*, May.

Bailey, Martin J.; Richard F. Muth; and Hugh O. Nourse. 1963. "A Regression Method for Real Estate Price Index Construction." *American Statistical Association Journal*, August.

Brown, Sam Lovett. n.d. "Price Variation in New Houses, 1959-1961." Manuscript only. U.S. Bureau of the Census.

Crecine, John P.; Otto A. Davis; and John E. Jackson. 1967. "Urban Property Markets: Some Empirical Results and Their Implications for Municipal Zoning." *Journal of Law and Economics*, October.

de Leeuw, Frank. 1971. "The Demand for Housing: A Review of Cross-Section Evidence." *Review of Economics and Statistics*, February.

Mieszkowski, Peter. 1972. "Notes on the Economic Effects of Land-Use Regulation." Paper prepared for the Congress of the International Institute of Public Finance. New York. Mimeographed.

Plosser, Charles. 1972. "A Study in the Effects of Residential Zoning Restrictions on Land Value." Urban Economics Report 78. University of Chicago, Graduate School of Business. June.

Quandt, Richard E. 1958. "The Estimation of the Parameters of a Linear Regression System Obeying Two Separate Regimes." *Journal of the American Statistical Association*, December.

_____. 1960. "Tests of the Hypothesis that a Linear Regression System Obeys Two Separate Regimes." *Journal of the American Statistical Association*, June.

Ridker, R.G., and J.A. Henning. 1967. "The Determinants of Residential Property Values with Special Reference to Air Pollution." *Review of Economic Statistics*, May.

Rueter, Frederick H. 1974. "Externalities in Urban Property Markets: An Empirical Test of the Zoning Ordinance of Pittsburgh." *Journal of Law and Economics*, March.

Sagalyn, Lynne B., and George Sternlieb. 1973. *Zoning and Housing Costs.* New Jersey: Rutgers University Center for Urban Policy Research.

San Francisco Department of City Planning. 1967. *Changes in the San Francisco Housing Inventory 1960-1966.* San Francisco: San Francisco Department of City Planning, September.

_____. 1972. "City Planning Code." *San Francisco Municipal Code.* San Francisco Board of Supervisors.

Siegan, Bernard H. 1972. *Land Use Without Zoning.* Lexington, Mass.: Heath.

Smith, R. Stafford. 1971. "Property Tax Capitalization in San Francisco." *National Tax Journal*, February.

Census. 1961. U.S. Bureau of the Census. *U.S. Census of Housing: 1960.* Vol. III. *City Blocks.* Series HC(3), No. 67.

_____. 1973. *Statistical Abstract of the United States: 1973.*

Comments on Chapters Nine and Ten

Eugene Smolensky

I am a discussant in an anomalous position, since I (along with Ingram) selected the studies by Nelson and Avrin as the best in our competition. They were the best of a good lot and I must and will say what they contribute. I will also offer some criticisms, but, of course, since I obviously think highly of them, those criticisms will be far from stinging.

It has been maintained that zoning is not required for the efficient allocation of land among alternative uses and that in practice the purpose of zoning is to allocate land inefficiently so as to maximize the narrow benefit-cost calculus of the city's initial residents. Proof of the former proposition lies mostly in the polemical descriptions of Houston by Siegan.[1] Proof of the second proposition has been the findings that zoning conversions in particular cities have resulted in large changes in land values. Both sorts of evidence have serious deficiencies, and it is therefore important to have this evidence by Avrin, confirming one of the propositions and rejecting the other. Needless to say, however, Avrin's study will not, indeed cannot be, the last word on the subject.

I am particularly concerned with what might be labeled the counterfactual to Avrin's time series analysis, which is, I think, that in an unconstrained market, over a decade or so, prices of land in different uses would rise proportionately. This is an assertion not only that the market is in equilibrium at the outset, as she notes, but in equilibrium over the whole of the period. Now we know that over decades, using Census data, density gradients not only rose and fell at their intercepts, but that their slopes changed, even before zoning was finally sanctioned by the Supreme Court in 1926. The increasing and then decreasing slopes of density gradients, which theory suggests must follow from shifting rent gradients, suggest the obvious: that a whole lot of factors including the high cost of demolition will retard equilibrium in housing markets over long periods. Failure to standardize for these factors raises questions about both of Avrin's conclusions, especially since her cross-sectional data suggest that the zoning categories are correlated with density and, hence, with rent gradients (peak-hour auto travel time to the CBD rises monotonically from R4 to R1). A plausible question, for example, is: Did anticipations of BART (Bay Area Rapid Transit) have the effect of stretching out the city while increasing densities at nearly every distance, with the growth in R1 occurring at the extensive margin where conversion would be cheapest?

Now of course Avrin can say she only claimed the zoning was nonoptimal and not that markets could do better, but that would be a copout, I think.

I turn now to Nelson's study. To John Kain's credit, in two instances he has gone beyond the usual issue in the literature on discrimination in housing (do blacks pay more?) to important subsidiary hypotheses. One, the issue here, is whether discrimination against blacks, particularly nonprice discrimination, adversely affects employment and the nominal wages of blacks relative to whites. Kain's approach was empirical, and Nelson's theoretical supplement is both welcome and required. What is most surprising to me about Nelson's study is how little she can adduce from her bold simplifications.

On the basis of her model, Nelson cannot say anything definitive about either unemployment or nominal wages. She can show that real wages will be lower for blacks in her model, but I suspect that even this result is not very robust. Application of her model to the data will have to deal with the fact that black housing, while more concentrated near the CBD than white housing, nevertheless generally moves out toward and into the suburbs in a broadly triangular wedge. The powerful simplification of the Muthian circular city which underlies much of the work of Mills and his students is I think a poor abstraction for studying both race and income distribution. It may nevertheless be possible to save the Kain hypothesis, reformulated in real terms as Nelson has cleverly transformed it, by appeal to the higher transport costs confronting blacks because of segregation and because of the radial nature of the public transport net (a fact indeed relied upon by Kain), but even here I wonder if the Kain conjecture would survive the demand-side adjustments hinted at by Nelson at the end of her study.

In short, whether Nelson intended to do so or not, Kain's judgment that segregation in housing leads to higher unemployment and lower nominal wages has been seriously undermined.

NOTE TO COMMENTS ON CHAPTERS NINE AND TEN

1. Bernard Siegan, *Land Use Without Zoning* (Lexington, Mass.: Heath, 1972).

Comments on Chapters Nine and Ten

Stephen P. Coelen and
William J. Carroll

Many of the contributors to this volume suggest in their studies that exogenous environmental change in the economic system finds its way into the housing market. Measurement of the impact of that change on the housing market provides useful information on the nature of the change; and, in particular cases, this information may be all that we have for evaluation of alternative public policies. The majority of the studies deal with the need to develop general equilibrium models for interpretation and measurement of the property value reaction (the terms "property" and "housing" are used synonymously). This ability is required if we are to discern from the morass of all the conflicting effects of simultaneous determinants of property values the rather minute effect of a single incremental change. Only then can cross-sectional modeling (which has the data simplicity of dealing with only a single point in time) be satisfactory. Most of the studies dealing with general equilibrium do, in fact, utilize the cross-sectional methodology as a basis for empirical technique.

Avrin's study is different from the others' since she also uses time series data to measure the effects of an environmental change—the extension of zoning in San Francisco. This dual use of time series and cross section is potentially valuable because the techniques yield seemingly similar information but use different data sets, so that the robustness of estimation is improved.

Note: We are indebted to the Army Corps of Engineers under contract DACW31-75-C-0018 for funding the research underlying these comments.

However, in using the techniques, concern should then be given to the compatibility and interpretation of the estimates.

Because we are inclined to discount the absolute effects of zoning that Avrin calculates, owing to her heroic assumption that no macro factors influenced the general price level of all housing contemporaneously with the impact of the zoning, consider her time-series-based conclusions on the relative effects of zoning: that the price of R4 properties jumped 11 percent more than that of R3; R3 properties, 4 percent more than R2; and R2, 1 percent more than R1. Conflicting with this is information from the logarithmic form of Avrin's cross-sectional results: "... the real prices of properties zoned R1 are 21 percent higher than those which are unzoned" and that "the prices of properties zoned R2, R3, and R4 are 32 percent, 36 percent, and 44 percent higher, respectively."

Let the unzoned property values be R0 and the values of properties in zoned areas be R1, R2, R3, and R4. Avrin's cross-sectional results imply that R1 = 1.21 R0; R2 = 1.32 R0; R3 = 1.36 R0; R4 = 1.44 R0. From this we can conclude that R4 = 1.0588 R3; R3 = 1.0303 R2; R2 = 1.0909 R1, which is at variance with the time series results. The time series and cross-sectional models present the following relative price changes:

	Time Series	Cross Section
R4:R3	11%	5.88%
R3:R2	4	3.03
R2:R1	1	9.09

The margin of estimation variance provided by the standard errors associated with the two techniques is not large enough to explain such discrepancies. This leads us to a general evaluation and interpretation of the relationship between such time series and cross-sectional measures.

Envision a tripartite city in which one part is not currently zoned and has never been zoned, one part has been zoned for a long time, and one part was previously unzoned but has recently been zoned. Assume a single zoning classification, and denote the never-zoned area as J, the always-zoned area as K, and the recently zoned area as I. The latter has experienced a change in environmental conditions of the type outlined at the beginning of Avrin's study. The time period t_0 is unambiguously before and T_0 unambiguously after anticipation of and adjustment to the zoning of area I. In other words, t_0 can be taken as the last period of long-run equilibrium before the zoning and T_0, as the first period of long-run equilibrium after zoning. While zoned and unzoned properties are highly substitutable, consider them to be in different markets, since Avrin concludes that zoned properties may be viewed quite differently; i.e., buyers of such property "... are secure in their knowledge of the future of the neighborhoods into which they are purchasing." Properties in area I are assumed initially (t_0) to make up part of the market of homogeneous properties lacking zoning. This market also includes all the properties in area J. As area I becomes zoned, properties in I move from the unzoned market (i.e., the J market) and by period T_0 are homogeneous units in the K market. Assuming reasonable competition in the J and K markets, housing prices in these markets (denoted by subscripts) are equalized in the respective periods so that

$$_I P_{t_0} = {_J P_{t_0}} \text{ and } _I P_{T_0} = {_K P_{T_0}} \tag{10B-1}$$

These prices indicate a measure of the total hedonic value of attributes associated with respective property types. In this simple case an equilibrium adjustment is assumed in markets for products that differ only by the flow of benefits associated with zoning. Hence, two hedonic values (H) can be calculated for such benefits in equilibrium periods t_0 and T_0:

$$H_{t_0} = {_K P_{t_0}} - {_J P_{t_0}} = {_K P_{t_0}} - {_I P_{t_0}} \tag{10B-2}$$

and

$$H_{T_0} = {_K P_{T_0}} - {_J P_{T_0}} = {_I P_{T_0}} - {_J P_{T_0}} \tag{10B-3}$$

The ambiguity inherent in the existence of two measures arises because the hedonic, cross-sectional measures can be constructed at many points in time.

The time series (TS) measurement of the effect of zoning on properties in area I is defined as

$$TS = {_I P_{T_0}} - {_I P_{t_0}} = {_K P_{T_0}} - {_J P_{t_0}} \tag{10B-4}$$

No ambiguity exists in this definition.

When the relationships developed in (10B-1) through (10B-4) are used, it is clear that the measures may not be identical. Adding and subtracting equal quantities on the right-hand side of (10B-4), we obtain

$$TS = {}_KP_{T_0} - ({}_JP_{T_0} - {}_JP_{T_0}) - {}_JP_{t_0} + ({}_KP_{t_0} - {}_KP_{t_0})$$

and substituting from Equations (10B-2) and (10B-3):

$$TS = H_{T_0} + {}_JP_{T_0} + H_{t_0} - {}_KP_{t_0}$$

hence $TS = H_{T_0}$ if and only if $H_{t_0} = {}_KP_{t_0} - {}_JP_{T_0}$. This can occur only if there is no price reaction in the unzoned area arising from the zoning of area I (i.e., ${}_JP_{T_0} = {}_JP_{t_0}$). Similarly, $TS = H_{t_0}$ if and only if $H_{T_0} = {}_KP_{T_0}$ which would require no reaction of the K properties to the zoning of area I, so that ${}_KP_{t_0} = {}_KP_{T_0}$.

For any sizable zoning program impact the conditions ${}_KP_{t_0} = {}_KP_{T_0}$ and ${}_JP_{t_0} = {}_JP_{T_0}$ would not be expected to hold because of the market reactions of transferring I-area properties out of the J market and into the K market.

These notions may be extended into a structural model capable of empirical estimation. The demand relations are written as functions of all relevant commodity prices:

$$_JQ_t^D = f_J({}_JP_t, {}_KP_t, {}_XP_0) \tag{10B-5}$$

and

$$_KQ_t^D = f_K({}_KP_t, {}_JP_t, {}_XP_0) \tag{10B-6}$$

where ${}_KQ_t^D$ and ${}_JQ_t^D$ are the demand quantities in the zoned and unzoned markets respectively and ${}_XP_0$ is the price of some composite good. The long-run supply curves are written simply as functions of the prices in respective housing markets and an exogenous price of building materials:

$$_JQ_t^S + {}_IQ_0 - {}_IQ_t = g_J({}_JP_t, {}_yP_0) \tag{10B-7}$$

$$_KQ_t^S + \mu_I Q_t = g_K({}_KP_t, {}_yP_0) \tag{10B-8}$$

where ${}_KQ_t^S$ and ${}_JQ_t^S$ are the quantities of properties in the K and J areas supplied to the K and J markets respectively; ${}_IQ_0$ is the initial fixed quantity of property in area I supplied to the J market; ${}_IQ_t$ represents the additional properties in the K market which had each been subdivided, on average, into μ_I properties from the original ${}_IQ_0$

properties, and $_yP_0$ is the price of a composite building supply good. Subdivision by a factor such as μ is usually the consequence of zoning change. The short-run supply functions need not be defined to locate the initial and final (postzoning) equilibriums, since these are meant as long-run equilibriums. However, the short-run functions are used implicitly, for example, by the inclusion of the terms $(-_IQ_t)$ and $(+\mu_I Q_t)$ in Equations (10B-7) and (10B-8), respectively. The model is completed by adding the equilibrium equations:

$$_JQ_t^D = {}_JQ_t^S + {}_IQ_0 - {}_IQ_t \tag{10B-9}$$

and

$$_KQ_t^D = {}_KQ_t^S + \mu_I Q_t \tag{10B-10}$$

Application of the model prior to any of the given set of properties in area I before implementation of zoning is carried out by simply assuming $_IQ_t = 0$. With the introduction of zoning in area I, $_IQ_t$ is greater than zero, entering exogenously into the simultaneous equation system, (10B-5) through (10B-10), to reflect the number of properties coming under zoning specifications.

From such a model it is easy, at least conceptually, to derive the reduced forms for the endogenous variables $_JQ_t = {}_JQ_t^S + {}_IQ_0 - {}_IQ_t - {}_JQ_t^D$, $_KQ_t = {}_KQ_t^S + \mu_I Q_t = {}_KQ_t^D$, $_KP_t$, and $_JP_t$. The reduced forms then yield the important derivatives, d_JQ_t/d_IQ_t, d_KQ_t/d_IQ_t, d_KP_t/d_IQ_t, and d_JP_t/d_IQ_t, which can be used to construct the measures specified in (10B-1) through (10B-4) above:

$$H_{t_0} = {}_KP_{t_0} - {}_JP_{t_0}$$

$$H_{t_0} = {}_KP_{t_0} - {}_JP_{T_0} = H_{t_0} + \frac{d_KP_t}{d_IQ_t} - \frac{d_JP_t}{d_IQ_t}\, {}_IQ_t$$

and

$$TS = {}_KP_{T_0} - {}_JP_{t_0} = {}_KP_{t_0} + \frac{d_KP_t}{d_IQ_t}\, {}_IQ_t - {}_JP_{t_0}$$

$$= H_{t_0} + \frac{d_KP_t}{d_IQ_t}\, {}_IQ_t$$

The preceding has demonstrated the conceptual differences both between cross-sectional and time series estimates and between inter-temporal cross-sectional estimates. In the framework of implement-ing a simultaneous equation methodology (Equations (10B-5) to (10B-10)), there is no a priori expectation about possible interrela-tionships except on a case-by-case basis, where the forces operating in affected markets may be evaluated to yield expectations about such relationships.

In this note we have focused on the difference in time series and cross-sectional methods and their associated empirical estimates, including the difference in the cross-sectional measures that can be obtained from different temporal applications of the hedonic method. We are left with the problem of interpreting these various measures and of knowing which to select to provide the right kind of information. The solution can be developed from the old debate found in the papers of Ridker and Henning (1967), Freeman (1971), and Edel (1971) over Ridker and Henning's erroneous generalization that their cross-sectional regression coefficient for pollution (on housing values) multiplied by the number of affected properties gives an expected response to pollution abatement in the housing market. These arguments suggest that cross-sectional work is partial equilib-rium modeling and cannot be used to obtain general equilibrium results of the market reaction to more than a marginal change of some environmental variable—in Avrin's case, zoning.

There are really two kinds of environmental change that are troublesome—changing the environment more than marginally at a single observation (property, census tract, etc.) and changing the environment marginally but at more than one marginal observation. It is a solution of the second difficulty that is sought by the majority of contributors to this volume, with their concentration on general equilibrium models of residential location. Edel's comment (1971, pp. 10-11), too, suggesting that Ridker and Henning's erroneous calculations provide accurate welfare information, is applicable to the second problem. From that debate, without proof, we offer the following suggestions:

1. For the case of a marginal change in the environment at a marginal observation, the cross-sectional measure correctly states both the appropriate welfare standard of willingness to pay for the environmental change as it is capitalized into the land (property) market and the actual land value reaction that would be observed to result from the change.

2. For the case of a marginal change in the environment, at more properties than just the marginal property, as would be the case for zoning under certain conditions, the cross-sectional results correctly states the average willingness to pay but is unlikely to forecast

accurately the actual land value change. This is related to open city-closed city models of Polinsky and Shavel (1975) and the suggestions of Edel (1971).

3. For the case of a more than marginal change in the environment confined to a marginal property, the cross-sectional result is likely to measure correctly neither the land value reaction nor the welfare change because of less than perfectly elastic demands for most environmental commodities. However, joint use of cross-sectional measures taken before and after the environmental change may give information that averaged together approximates the average marginal willingness to pay over the relevant range of environmental conditions. This average multiplied by the number of units of change may approximate the changes in property market values.

4. For nonmarginal changes both of observations (properties) and of environmental conditions, or in Avrin's case, a set of institutional constraints throughout a market area, the cross-sectional measures are likely only to approximate the welfare measures and not the actual market changes, and then only by multiplying the average of the two temporal cross-sectional results by the number of units affected by the change in environmental conditions.

While the cross-sectional measures under all four conditions yield very useful information, it is clear that they fall short most when asked to give full information in cases of simultaneous changes at many properties. It is then that they fail to give information on expected actual market changes. It is especially in these cases that time series measures are most powerful. The time series method directly evaluates the impact of actual environmental changes already implemented in the economic world and therefore the method compares pre- and postevent prices to determine the market reaction. The shortcoming of the time series approach as a method is its ability to accomplish only this result, failing (except in the case of marginal changes) to measure any welfare standards.

Our conclusion is to urge much greater care in the application of the methods of time series and cross-sectional analysis to housing market data. The measures will always bear some relation to each other but need not convey the same information. Without the application of both, full information on environmental impacts will not be recovered.

REFERENCES

Edel, M. 1971. "Land Values and the Costs of Urban Congestion: Measurement and Distribution." Paper presented at "Man and His Environment." A symposium on the political economy of the environment. Paris, France, July.

Freeman, A.M., III. 1971. "Air Pollution and Property Values: A Methodological Comment." *Review of Economics and Statistics*, November.

Polinsky, A.M., and S. Shavell. 1975. "Air Pollution and Property Value Debate." *Review of Economics and Statistics*, February.

Ridker, R.G., and J.A. Henning. 1967. "The Determinants of Residential Property Values with Special Reference to Air Pollution." *Review of Economics and Statistics*, May.

Index